Reprints of Economic Classics

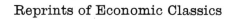

ECONOMY OF THE LABOURING CLASSES

ECONOMY

OF THE

LABOURING CLASSES

BY

WILLIAM LUCAS SARGANT

[1857]

REPRINTS OF ECONOMIC CLASSICS

AUGUSTUS M. KELLEY · PUBLISHERS
NEW YORK 1968

First Edition, 1857

(London: Simpkin, Marshall & Company, 1857)

Reprinted 1968 by
AUGUSTUS M. KELLEY · PUBLISHERS
New York New York 10010

Library of Congress Catalogue Card Number
68-20177

PRINTED IN THE UNITED STATES OF AMERICA
by SENTRY PRESS, NEW YORK, N. Y. 10019

ECONOMY OF THE LABOURING CLASSES.

ECONOMY

OF

THE LABOURING CLASSES.

BY WILLIAM LUCAS SARGANT,

AUTHOR OF

" THE SCIENCE OF SOCIAL OPULENCE."

LONDON:

SIMPKIN, MARSHALL, AND CO.

1857.

CONTENTS.

CHAPTER VI.

CHAPTER VII.

CHAPTER VIII.

CHAPTER IX.

CHAPTER X.

CHAPTER XI.

CHAPTER XII.

CHAPTER XIII.

CHAPTER XIV.

CHAPTER XV.

CHAPTER XVI.

CHAPTER XVII.

CHAPTER XVIII.

APPENDIX.

NOTE ON CHAPTER XII.

NOTE ON CHAPTER XIII.

INTRODUCTION.

In the following volume, I have brought together a great number of facts relating to the condition and habits of the labouring classes in Great Britain and on the Continent. I have availed myself to a considerable extent of M. Le Play's recent French work, *Les Ouvriers Européens.* Before proceeding to publication I thought it right to acquaint the author with my intention. M. Le Play replied, that in writing his elaborate and laborious work, he had no view to pecuniary advantage: but that he had recently conferred gratuitously on another person, the right of publishing a second edition; and that the intention was to bring it out in several languages, and in English amongst the number. He therefore requested that I would not make use of his work in such a way as to interfere with the rights conferred on the new publisher: that I would not quote the words of the original, so as to supersede the necessity of referring to the proposed edition. I have endeavoured carefully to meet the wishes here expressed: I have retrenched from my original manuscript several quotations which would have added to the interest of my work, but the use of which might possibly have been open to objection. I have mentioned several of M. Le Play's Cases as illustrations of the different régimes; and I should have been glad to give an abridgement of those cases. But though this would not have been an infringement of M. Le Play's request not to use the words of the original, it would have tended to diminish the desire of resorting to the new edition. As the case stands, I hope I have done nothing calculated to satiate the curiosity of my readers; but that what I have written will stimulate them to seek a fuller acquaintance with the *Etudes*.

M. Le Play's long work is a very admirable one; and in its laborious collection of facts, and its cautious induction, is strikingly opposed to that swarm of wild theories which, from the Abbé Sièyes to M. Emile de Girardin, have misled and disgraced public opinion in Paris. Men of high distinction have acknowledged the author's merits, and have united with him to form the *Société Internationale des études pratiques d'Economie Sociale*: an institution that proposes to collect facts relating to the working classes throughout the world. The names of M. Villermé as President, and of M. M. Dumas, Gasparin, Michel Chevalier, Geoffroy St. Hilaire, as Members of the Committee, are proofs of the importance attached to the Society. It is gratifying to see the great thinkers of France devoting themselves to sober observations on social economy, and abandoning those unfounded and outrageous speculations which have hitherto led them greatly astray.

Edgbaston, Birmingham, 1857.

AUTHORS REFERRED TO.

I HAVE referred in this work, to authors many of whom have attained to the honour of several editions. I therefore give a list of the editions I have made use of. I hope I may not appear guilty of ostentation in furnishing these particulars. In reading books in which reference has been made to previous authors, without mention of title, or of the page from which the quotation is given, I have often been disposed to complain of the indifference, or indolence, of the writer who has neglected to furnish these particulars.

CENSUS of 1851, CHESHIRE's Results of, 1854.

DE TOCQUEVILLE's France before the Revolution: English translation, 1856.

EDEN, SIR F. M. On the Poor, original edition.

ENGLISHWOMAN IN AMERICA, same.

ENGLISHWOMAN IN RUSSIA, same.

HEAD, SIR F. B. Pampas, edition 1826.

HUTTON, Life of, edition 1817.

      ,,   Court of Requests, original edition.

      ,,   History of Birmingham, edition 1819.

JACOB's REPORT on Trade in Foreign Corn, 2nd. edition, octavo, 1826.

JACOB's Travels in Germany, &c., quarto, 1820.

LAING's Norway, 1851.

LE PLAY's Ouvriers Européens, original edition.

M'CULLOCH's Adam Smith, 1839.

MALTHUS, Population, 1826.

　　　,,　　Principles of Political Economy, 1820.

PRICE, DR., Doctrine of Annuities, &c., 1779.

　　　,,　　Observations on Reversionary Payments, &c., 1783.

REGISTRAR GENERAL: there are two editions, the ordinary blue book, and an octavo for the use of the registrars. When I refer to the octavo, I say so in each case.

TOOKE on Prices, the original edition.

YOUNG, ARTHUR, on Ireland, 2nd. edition, octavo, 1780.

　　　,,　　　　France, 2nd. edition, quarto, 1794.

　　　,,　　　　Annals of Agriculture, 45 vols., original edition.

CHAPTER I.

In the following work I am greatly indebted to the information afforded by the *Etudes* of M. Le Play. With regard to the facts that have relation to English workmen, I have made far more use of English authors; but with regard to the facts that have relation to foreign workmen I rely principally upon M. Le Play. The *Etudes* constitute an elaborate work, published in 1855. The author is Head Engineer of Mines, and Professor of Metallurgy in the Government School of Mines in Paris. M. Le Play, in the performance of his duties, has visited various countries of Europe, and in the course of twenty years has stayed in Norway, Sweden, Russia, Turkey, Germany, Switzerland, Spain, England. His occupations brought him much in contact with miners and other persons employed in working metals: he was led to observations as to their mode of life, their habits, their means of living, their relation to their masters. The results being recorded, M. Le Play naturally extended his enquiries to other classes of workmen, and especially those of France.

M. Le Play has given his observations to the world, under the sanction of the Emperor Napoleon, in a form more attractive to the student than to the ordinary reader. The one folio volume contains as much matter as many ordinary octavos; and is crowded with facts and figures which are repulsive to one who reads for amusement, but are of high

importance to those who are bent on a thorough acquaintance with the subject treated of. I have gone through the
work, pen in hand, with a view to arrange under different
heads all the results of M. Le Play's observations. I was
not fully aware of the great value of his book at first: but
when I afterwards renewed my acquaintance with other
authors, Malthus, Arthur Young, &c., with the intention of
comparing their labours with his, I felt the inferiority of
theirs both as to fulness and precision.

Malthus read very widely and carefully in order to illustrate and enforce his principles: he went over ancient and
modern history, books of travels in every continent, and
volumes and pamphlets on economical and political science.
He also travelled into several European countries with the
express object of obtaining information. Arthur Young
personally explored several countries very carefully, and
having looked at every thing with the eye of a practical
farmer, recorded his observations with great precision. But
neither Malthus nor Arthur Young penetrated far below the
surface. Malthus had no means of visiting the log house of
the Norwegian peasant, or of the Russian serf. Arthur
Young saw the outside of the French cabin, and shuddered
at the rags and dirt of the peasant: but he did not get
much beyond this. M. Le Play's proceedings were of a
very different character. On visiting a place, he fixed on a
particular family, and made very minute enquiries as to the
age of the different members, the nature of the engagement
between the man and his employer, the rate of wages if
there were any, the entire gains derived from the principal
and subsidiary occupations, the kind of food, clothes, and
shelter, the means of education, the supply and expense of

medical attendance, the degree of religious fervour, the age
at which marriage was contracted, the diversions, the manners, the prevalence of foresight or improvidence, the
assistance rendered by the Government or by individuals,
as to every thing in short which distinguishes the condition
of different labourers, or which marks their advancement in
civilisation.

But while M. Le Play has furnished us with statements
on all the points I have mentioned, he directs our attention
especially to the physical condition of the labourer. The
leading idea of the book seems to me to be this : that while
Europe has made great advances in wealth and civilisation,
the condition of the working classes has not improved in
the same proportion ; and further, that the new era has been
particularly unfavourable to the weak in body or mind, and
has perhaps placed them in a worse position than the one
they occupied in former times. There is here something
like an echo of the complaint frequently made, that while
the rich have become richer, the poor have become poorer.
M. Le Play shows a very amiable sympathy with the indigent and the distressed.

In order to give a more exact notion of the book, I will
take a particular example of a workman whose circumstances are detailed. I will take one of the few English
cases : and while this will give us some familiarity with our
author, it will enable us to test his accuracy by comparing
his statements with what we ourselves know. It is generally supposed that when a Frenchman attempts to delineate
any thing English, he is extremely apt to fall into awkward
blunders. If we should find this to be the case in the
present instance, we need not on that account condemn the

whole work: but if we should happily find, on the contrary,
that the representations of the English workmen have a
great appearance of truth, and are free from any striking
distortions, we shall be disposed to place confidence in the
statements made as to other countries.

Of the thirty-six cases given, only four are English ones:
viz., those of a London cutler, of a Sheffield cutler, of a
Sheffield carpenter, and of a Derbyshire iron melter. I will
take that of the Sheffield cutler as representing a much
larger class than the others.

In the first place, a description is given of the situation
and characteristics of the town. We are told that Sheffield
is placed in the midst of one of the richest and most extensive coal-fields in this kingdom: that the soil and climate of
Yorkshire are well adapted for the growth of the corn and
the rearing of the cattle required for the subsistence of the
town population: and that canals and railroads give easy
access to other parts of the kingdom, and especially to Hull,
the port by which are brought in the Swedish steel-iron
from Stockholm and Gottenborg. Sheffield, it seems, in
the middle of the 17th century, at the time of the Common-
wealth, was only a village, but is now the seat of the
greatest manufacture in the world, of steel, of steel goods, and
especially of cutlery. The superiority of Sheffield is owing
partly to its situation, but mostly to the intelligence and
activity of its population. It possesses a considerable number
of factories, but the greater part of the work is performed
in separate workshops. One circumstance strikes M. Le
Play as peculiar, though it is familiar enough to many of
us: the mechanics do not labour at their own houses, as
they generally do under the same circumstances on the

Continent, but they hire a shop into which a shaft of a neighbouring steam-engine is carried, and they pay a weekly rent both for the shop and for the use of the steam-power. The same arrangement is found occasionally on the Continent, as, for example, at Solingen, the Prussian rival of Sheffield, and also in Paris. The capitalists who employ these men are more like merchants than manufacturers. The men work sometimes for one master and sometimes for another, but the better class of masters give permanent employment to a certain number of workmen. In Sheffield, as in other English manufacturing towns, the workmen have recourse to mutual associations as a protection from various contingencies, and many classes of them have adopted an organisation peculiar to themselves to prevent the consequences of a cessation, or of a deficiency, of employment.

Such are the preliminary remarks in the case I am explaining, but I have given only an epitome of what is said. It must be remembered that I am citing this case very much with the intention of testing the accuracy and trustworthiness of our author; and I think that thus far we may be well satisfied as to the correctness of the statements, even if we are not familiar with the town of Sheffield. There are some portraits, of which we say at once, without knowing the original, that the likeness must be a good one.

Under the second head we find that the workman in question is thirty-eight years old, and that his wife is of the same age : that they married at twenty-one : that they have had eight children, of whom five only are living : that these are all girls, and that the eldest, aged 16, supports herself as a sempstress.

We find next that the husband is Irish, and that the wife is English, that the one is a Roman Catholic, the other a Protestant, but that both are quite negligent of religious observances : that both of them are mild and of good morals : less addicted than most English workmen to hearty eating, and very temperate as to drinking : like other English workmen, improvident, living up to their income, but quite resigned to privations caused by slackness of trade, and without envy towards the richer classes.

The neighbourhood is salubrious ; the man though of a feeble form has good health, but the woman and the children are delicate. The man secures medicine and attendance for himself by paying sixpence a week to a club. The wife and children have to pay a medical man when they are ill, and in the wife's last illness, eighteen medical visits, including medicine, cost 27s. to 28s., or 1s. 6d. a visit

The Sheffield workmen, we are further told, are of two classes : the unskilled labourer at day wages, and the skilled mechanic who has learned his trade by a longer or shorter apprenticeship, and who is paid by the piece.

This concludes five preliminary notices, and I repeat that the picture so far has every appearance of being a correct likeness. We now come to a detailed statement of the property possessed by the family. First as to fixed property : so far from the man having acquired any, he owed his landlord at the end of 1849 the sum of £11., which, however, two years afterwards was reduced to £9. 10s. His other possessions, not including clothes and furniture, are set down as worth about £5. or £6. ; and consist principally of tools. The man, therefore, has little to depend on for maintenance, except the wages he may earn. His trade is that of mounting, i. e. of putting handles on knives. He employs his leisure in cultivating a garden round his house. The wife employs herself in managing the house, in looking after a pig and a few fowls, and in making and selling ginger beer. Three of the five children attend school regularly: one of them is too young for school, and the eldest supports herself by sewing. It is observed that the cultivation of a garden is quite unusual among the Sheffield workmen, who are generally ignorant of any means of occupation except their own trade. The man before us is an Irishman, and has therefore an hereditary taste for the soil.

The food of the family consists principally of wheaten bread, butcher's meat, pork, potatoes, tea, coffee, sugar, and beer, taken at four meals every day: with the addition in the winter of some porter, and in the summer of what M. Le Play amusingly describes as two gaseous refreshing drinks called pop and treacle beer; water, however, being the principal drink.

The house is situated in the suburbs, and the rent is 3s. 6d. a week. The workshop is in the town and costs 3s. 3d. a week.

The clothes and furniture are kept with moderate neatness, and are estimated as worth about £21. I cannot say that I place the same reliance on the figures in this and the other estimates, that I place in the facts stated before. The description of the house, of the food, of the pop and treacle beer, have accuracy on the face of them : but a correct estimate of the value of clothes and furniture would be difficult for an Englishman and is impossible for a foreigner. Happily, such an inaccuracy does not much affect the general truth of the picture: it is not a matter of much

importance whether these clothes and furniture are worth
£21., as we are told, or whether they are worth £15. or
£30.   I should add that each article of furniture is set
down with the exactness of an appraiser, and that the prices
affixed seem moderate enough.   We have a bed with cur-
tains £1.; two other beds 10s. each; three pair of spare
sheets at 3s. the pair; a clock with weights 6s.   The whole
of the clothes worn by the man the wife and the five
children are set down at £7. 10s.   One can scarcely suspect
these prices of much exaggeration.

Another section of this report gives an account of the
recreations enjoyed by the family.   The man seldom goes
from home, and indulges very little in drinking, but he
spends about £2. a year in keeping pigeons and canary-
birds.   He gives his family an unusually good dinner on
Christmas Day, and takes them to the fairs that are held
twice a year.   Here again I must confess that M. Le Play
has given us a portrait that has the appearance of an excellent likeness; except, perhaps, that we may suspect our
Irish workman of having used a little blarney in the account
of his decided moderation in drinking.

We have now some statements of a more general character.   The increase of the manufactures of Sheffield causes
a demand for more hands than are supplied by the natural
augmentation of population; and there is consequently an
influx from other parts of Yorkshire and of the rest of
England, as well as from Ireland.   This immigration into
Sheffield, and into other centres of manufacturing industry,
tends to raise the condition of country labourers.   These,
however, on first entering a town are obliged to rest satisfied with employments that require mere bodily strength:

and in Sheffield especially, the trades' unions exclude them from manufactures, but admit their children. The father of the man before us came from Ireland and brought up his sons in Sheffield, and articled this one to a knife mounter. At twenty years old the man began to work on his own account, with tools of his own. At twenty-one he married. Unfortunately, he and his wife, having no disposition to save, and always spending the whole of their gains, have not the means of buying materials for extending the business, nor even of taking an apprentice. If they could do the latter, they would probably add six shillings a week to their income: but with their improvident habits they would be unable to maintain an apprentice in times when work was wanting. However, when trade is good the man does employ a boy, from whose work there arises a profit of three shillings or four shillings a week. On the whole there is no cause but improvidence that prevents this family from rising in the social scale; most of the large traders of Sheffield having sprung from the same rank.

The Sheffield mechanics generally, we are told, have the same want of providence. But they have constantly been in search of an organization calculated to mitigate the ill results that ensue in times when trade is bad. Many of the trades conceive themselves to have accomplished this object by means of their Unions, of which the fundamental laws are three: 1st, severe restrictions on the introduction of new hands; 2nd, an invariable scale of wages; 3rd, pensions to men out of work, from a fund raised by the contributions of those who have employment. The masters submit to these arrangements, exhibiting in this matter a spirit of conciliation, which is one of the characteristics of England: and

under this organization, strengthened by the Continental
events of 1848, says M. Le Play, the unionists passed
through the long depression of trade that prevailed from
1847 to 1849, without failing in their engagements. I will
not enumerate the advantages stated as following from these
combinations. I will merely add that in M. Le Play's
opinion, the Unions have held their ground only because
the men have evinced decided moderation in their demands.
This is rather too favourable an account, I think, of the
well known associations of Sheffield. It exhibits the bright
side of the picture. Most Englishmen know that there is
also a very dark side. I am myself no enemy to trades'
unions and combinations amongst workmen; but I share
with others a detestation of illegal violence and bloodshed.
Unfortunately, the Sheffield mechanics have been dishonor-
ably distinguished by a resort to violence and bloodshed in
carrying out their purposes.

The workman in question does not belong to any Union,
the one established in his branch of trade having been
broken up. The only provision that he makes against misfortune is his contribution to a sick-club as mentioned
before. When trade is bad therefore, the family has to
submit to many privations.

We now come to two accounts given in much detail: first,
an account of the annual gains of the family: second, of its
annual expenditure.

Under the head of the annual gains we have first, the
income derived from fixed property, which in this case is
nothing. It may seem needless to introduce this item, but
the reason of introducing it is, that one form of accounts is
used in the various cases given, and of which this is one.

In comparing different cases it is very convenient to find the same form of account used for all, and to see at once that while the charcoal burner of the Alps has no property of any kind that yields him an income, and the Sheffield cutler has no fixed property that yields him an income, the silver caster of Schemnitz has a house and orchard worth £40., and that yields him an income of several pounds a year, besides moveable property of some value. We have secondly, the moveable property that gives an income; and this consists principally of tools, with a small addition for the few domestic animals kept. The whole value is put down at about £5.: the annual income at about six shillings. This is one of the estimates to which I have already alluded as not appearing to me to have any great value. It is difficult to say what part of a workman's gains is derived from his tools, and what part is derived from his industry in using them. I have known cases in which a man destitute of tools has been obliged for that reason to work under another man at a considerable reduction of wages; so that for the want of £2. or £3. the wages have been reduced by several shillings a week. The possession of £3. would here add £5. or £10. to the annual income; and it would scarcely be correct to set down the annual income from these tools so low as a few shillings a year, while they really yield many pounds a year.

The second head of the annual receipts of the family consists of the assistance rendered to them by other people: it includes two items; the sewing done for the family by relations, without any charge, and which is supposed to be worth about £1. 6s. a year; and the remission of interest by the landlord on the arrears of rent, those arrears amount-

ing to nearly £10., and the interest calculated at five per
cent. being therefore nearly ten shillings a year. As to this
last item a doubt may arise; the rent of small houses is
commonly in arrear, and for this reason a house is charged
at a higher rate than it would be charged at if the payments
were regularly made. The rent, therefore, may be held to
include the interest on arrears.

But there is another account here that to many persons
would seem of a still more doubtful kind. M. Le Play has
divided his " Budget of Receipts" into two parallel columns :
in one of these columns he gives the source from which the
receipts are derived ; and in the other the amount of them.
In the case of the silver caster of Schemnitz a house is
placed in the left hand column, and the receipt from the
house in the right hand one. In the case before us the
tools and the domestic animals are placed on the left hand
and the income on the right. But the assistance rendered
by other people, the saving and the remission of interest,
are placed in the right hand column, together with the
income derived from tools ; and there would naturally occur
a gap in the left hand column, since there is nothing equivalent to a house or to tools with which to occupy the space.
M. Le Play, however, has been trained to the precision of a
French official, and has devised a mode of giving an apparent
completeness to his tables. He regards all income as an
annuity, the value of which may be calculated. A man has
a government annuity of £10. for life : such an annuity has
a saleable value, and may be worth £50. or £150. according
to the age of the annuitant. So a man who receives an
average assistance of £1. 6s. a year, though he cannot sell
it, yet has that which is to him of as much value as a prin-

cipal of a good many pounds. M. Le Play puts this principal down at £15. 10s. The mode of calculation is not given, nor is it of much importance, since what we are concerned with is the income the workman receives, and not the number of years' purchase at which the income should be valued.

We now come to the man's wages, which are put down at about three shillings a day : but as the work is done by the piece this is only an approximation : however, three shillings a day would very probably be the earnings of such a workman as this one. The number of days' work is estimated at 300 in the year. After deducting the Sundays, we should have only thirteen days left unemployed in consequence either of idleness or of want of work ; and this could hardly be correct. When trade is good, indeed, the man may earn eighteen shillings a week all the year round, except at Christmas and other holidays : but on the average of years, good and bad included, I can scarcely believe that he would earn so much as this.

To these wages have to be added the gains obtained by the occasional employment of a boy, those from the pig and fowls, and from a few other trifling sources. The entire receipts of the year are thus brought up to £63. 10s., or upwards of twenty-four shillings a week : but on the average of years, and taking into consideration that some of the smaller items would not be generally regarded as constituting a part of the receipts, I should think that twenty or twenty-one shillings a week would be nearer the real receipts. This does not include the gains of the eldest daughter, aged 16, who is regarded as maintaining herself.

All these accounts have the peculiarity I have already pointed out : that in the left hand column every item of receipt is capitalised. The entire receipts of £63. 10s. are estimated as equal to a principal of £858. If this statement means any thing, I suppose it must be that the workman before us, with an annual income of £63. 10s., is as well off as another person who cannot work, but who has a principal of £860. If the workman should happen to die early, his family might dispute the accuracy of this calculation.

But though I differ thus far as to the form of one particular item in the accounts, and though I think further that the annual gains have been rather overstated, yet, on the whole, the " Budget of Receipts" seems to me to be singularly accurate. My confidence in the author is greatly confirmed by it.

The next account is the " Budget of Expenses," and is far more simple than the " Budget of Receipts." The food costs as follows :—Meat £10., wheaten bread £8., potatoes and other vegetables £5., tea, coffee, and sugar £4., besides many articles of smaller amount. The beer and other fermented liquors, including the refreshing gaseous drinks called pop and treacle beer, are set down as only £1. for the year : but as our Irish workman is not even a professed teetotaller, I cannot help suspecting that an amiable desire of standing well with M. Le Play has somewhat extenuated this article.

House rent, coal, and candles cost nearly £11. a year, or 4s. 3d. a week, of which the rent is about three shillings a week ; and this includes the garden as well as the house.

One remark has occurred to me as bearing forcibly on this question. I have read with some care the elaborate, though rather disorderly, volumes of Sir F. M. Eden, detailing the state of the English poor at the end of the last century. In that work occur many detailed accounts of the economy of labouring families. One peculiarity pervades most of these statements ; the income generally falls far short of the expenditure. Not, as it appears, that these families were constantly accumulating an increasing debt ; but that they liked to represent their incomes as low as possible, and their expenditure as high as possible. Workmen have always a tendency to understate their gains, fearing an attempt at reduction by their masters. M. Le Play has always contrived to surmount this difficulty, if it occurred to him : his accounts always represent an equality between the receipts and the expenses. Sir F. M. Eden, however, depended upon an agent whom he dispatched to different parts of the country : M. Le Play was his own agent.

I need not pursue these detailed accounts any further. My object at present is principally to test the accuracy of M. Le Play's observations, at the same time that I incidentally explain the mode he has adopted. The result of my enquiry into this example is to give me great confidence in the correctness of the work. Since there is so little in this case to excite any suspicion of inaccuracy, I am bound to believe the statements made in other cases where I am less able to judge for myself. If M. Le Play has contrived to be exact in England, a country where a Frenchman generally errs grievously, we may fairly presume exactness in his pictures of other countries, in many of which a

Frenchman is more nearly at home, and in none of which is he more a foreigner than in England.

It must not be supposed that this work consists only of cases: it contains some preliminary matter, and many inferences from the observations recorded. But the thirty-six cases, of one of which I have given the substance, form the staple, and they distinguish it from other writings on similar topics. There may be different opinions as to the value of the inferences, but there can scarcely be different opinions as to the value of the multitude of facts brought forward, if only we can believe that they are worthy of credit.

CHAPTER II.

I WILL now enter on some considerations of a more general character, and such as are suggested by this work.

We are apt to regard the working classes as those who live on wages paid them by an employer; and we are so familiar with this organisation of master and servant, that we overlook the fact that a large proportion of the labourers of the world have no employer or master. Indeed it has been broadly stated that in England alone is such an organisation general, and that in the world at large a majority of labourers have no employers. We need not go far to find one example, since in Ireland, before the famine ten years ago, the peasants commonly maintained themselves by the cultivation of a plot of potato ground, for which they paid a rent, with no employer or capitalist between themselves and their landlords. I have no wish to raise any question here as to the advantages of the one or the other arrangement. If the Irish were the only example of independent labourers, there would be a strong presumption against such an organisation as that under which they lived. But if we go to the United States, we find the settler in the woods felling his own trees and ploughing his land, with his own hands; and the arrangement of farmer and agricultural servant is by no means that ordinary thing which it is here. The same is true of Canada and other western colonies. In Australia,

a gentleman buys land, and sheep, and cows, but he must to
a great extent tend his stock himself, and his wife is unfortunate if she has emigrated without the power and the will
to milk and churn.

Even in old countries we find numerous examples like
that of Ireland, though not with results equally disastrous.
It is notorious that in France there exist very numerous
landed estates so small, as to make it impossible for the
owner who cultivates one of them, to employ any labourer
beyond his own family. What is less known, though equally
true, is, that a large number of these little properties
existed before the Revolution of 1789, and especially in
the Southern provinces. In Germany, again, there are a
great number of similar farms tilled by the owner and his
family. In Russia the land is cultivated on principles quite
different from those which prevail among us ; the labourers
being generally serfs attached to the estate, who are paid for
their work by the allocation of land for their own use, and
who do not receive wages either in money or in kind.
Indeed we are told that in some European dialects the very
word wages is unknown.

M. Le Play's work gives several examples of these different organisations, which vary so much from what we have
been accustomed to see. He carries his readers to the
eastern side of the Ural Mountains and to Southern Russia ;
he takes them among the charcoal burners in the Alpine
forests ; among the Calvinists of Geneva ; among the cutlers
of Solingen ; and the cobalt miners of Sweden. In some
instances the arrangements for the remuneration of the
labourer are very different from those which predominate
among ourselves.

Four modes of existence seem to demand our attention. First, the patriarchal, which is well known as prevailing among the Arabs : I will cite one example of it from this work. Secondly, the mode in which the labourer is permanently dependent upon his employer, and looks to his employer for maintenance at all times, even in sickness and old age. This state of things is found where slavery exists : the superannuated negro is safe in reckoning on the possession of a cabin and on such food and clothing as are necessary to support his life. The same relation exists in a modified form between the serf and his master. But it is seldom found in England, or in other countries where individual liberty has made much progress.

The care that the master thus takes of his subordinate may be called patronage, and it implies a corresponding dependence and submission on the part of the labourer. No man can be expected to be at the expense of rearing the children of his workmen, unless he is secure of their services when they are fit for work : and no man can be expected, except as an act of charity, to maintain a worn out workman, unless the workman has earned the claim by the devotion of his previous life to his master's service. This relation of master and servant, then, may be called the mode of patronage.

The third mode is that of Communism. I do not propose here to discuss the question so much agitated in France during the last ten years : I allude only to such Communism as really has existed, and still continues in a modified form in Spain. I will cite, in its proper place, the very interesting case of the last of the rural Communes of France.

The last mode is that which exists among ourselves. In England and Scotland, and, to a considerable extent, in Ireland also since the famine, the labourer works for a master. He is paid either according to the number of days that he works, or according to the quantity of work he performs : he is either a journeyman or a task worker. In towns, the employer frequently knows nothing of the private life of the workman : a manufacturer would be often puzzled if he were required to state the place of abode of any one of a hundred workmen, or to distinguish between the married and unmarried men, or between those who had families and those who had none. The mechanics exist in the eyes of the master very much as living machines, and would be divided by the master into skilful or unskilful, steady or the reverse, civil or rough mannered : but as to their domestic conduct, their religious sentiments, their diversions, the master knows nothing. No doubt there are many exceptions, but this is the rule. In sickness and old age, as in times when trade fails, the mechanic must depend on his previous savings, or on the sick-club he has himself supported, or, it may be, on the aid of the parish.

This absence of assistance on the part of an employer, towards workmen in sickness or old age or want of work, gives rise to many declamations on the part of benevolent persons, who see that, in respect to mere material existence, the superannuated or sick slave is in a better position than the superannuated or sick mechanic. Such writers hold it no satisfactory answer, when they are told, that the mechanic has enjoyed his liberty through life, and that he might have made a provision against the contingency under which he is suffering. They say that it is no kindness to give either a child, or a man, a degree of liberty that he is unfit to enjoy; and that an old age of destitution is ill compensated by youth spent in riot, and middle age spent in improvidence.

However, if we were to take the opinion of the persons most interested, I conceive that we should not find them desirous of surrendering their freedom. By many, no doubt, that freedom is abused, and it is lamentable to see men of any class, high or low, apparently reckless, careless, fearless, of what is past, present, or to come. But in order to restrain some madmen shall we put chains on those who are sane? Shall we say to the decent farm-labourer, or to the industrious, sober, mechanic, many of your brethren abuse their freedom; they live for the day, and fail to bestow a single glance on the future: therefore we will tie all you farm-labourers to the land and turn you from free men into serfs; while as to you mechanics, you shall be bound for life to masters who shall engage to maintain you at all times, and shall be at liberty to make what profit they can out of you, after supplying you with the necessaries of life?

We must all feel, of course, that such a remedy as this would be impossible: but if it were possible we should most of us feel that it is utterly undesirable. Just as the most beneficial government is that which interferes the least with the individual action of all its subjects, so the most beneficial organisation of labour is that which interferes the least with the individual action of workmen. A nation, indeed, is sometimes unfit for a free government, and a labouring class is sometimes unfit to be left to that degree of individual action which is found beneficial among ourselves.

The peculiarity of this organisation, then, that prevails among ourselves, is, that every labourer is left at liberty to choose his own place of residence, his own trade, his own employer. Instead of being fixed for life to an estate, or bound for life to a master, he is left to his own free will to choose for himself. But at the same time he ceases to have a claim on any capitalist for maintenance in sickness and old age: he must make provision for himself. The employer of labour in losing a bounden servant, acquires the liberty of choosing for himself whom he shall employ and how long he will employ him. Every individual, whether master or servant, makes his own election, according to his own unrestricted will and pleasure. In the patriarchal state of society the family predominates over the individual: in the mode of patronage the master and slave, or the seigneur and serf, are bound together by ties not easily broken. In the state of Communism, birth, custom, and law, determine a man's habitation and vocation. But in the mode which we are now considering, the individual man is left to shape his own course, and to work out for himself a position. This mode may properly be called Individualism.

These, then, are the four organisations we have to consider: the patriarchal, that of patronage, that of communism, and that of individualism.

In order to explain these more fully, I will refer to several cases given by M. Le Play. Each case shall illustrate one of the four modes in question.

The first I will refer to is also the first in M. Le Play's book. The man described is a shepherd living on the Eastern, or Asiatic, slope of the Ural Mountains. The man is one of a half migratory tribe of people, who seem much attached to their indolent mode of life, and who enjoy an abundance of the means of living. Among these Bachkir herdsmen, the patriarchal home generally contains the sons of the head of the house with their wives and children. The particulars of this case given by M. Le Play are very interesting. As an illustration of the second mode of existence I will refer to the Bulgarian forgeman in Central Turkey.* The man is a Christian, and lives under the domination of a Turkish master. The excellent relation that exists between them is highly instructive.

For the particulars of this case I must refer to M. Le Play's work, as I fear I should exceed the bounds of propriety if I were to furnish them. The case will be found well worth perusal. I delight in the picture of a Christian mechanic living at ease under a wealthy Turkish employer; treated by him with justice when he is at work, and with kindness when he is in want; able to discharge the debt which binds him to the Moslem, but so well content with his lot that he prefers to employ his treasure in adorning his wife, or improving his means of living. We are carried back as we read, to times when coal mines were rare and steam engines were unknown; when men looked to the forest for fuel and to the clouds for their motive power.

But as we read we feel that these things are of the past. If the question presents itself to us, can this state of society recur? we feel disposed to parody the saying of Canning; "repeal the Union? restore the Heptarchy!" With our fully peopled country, with our large manufacturing towns, with our restless mechanics, with our sense of personal inde-

* Le Play, 104.

pendence, we may just as easily restore the Ethelreds and Egberts as go back to the condition I have been describing. Such a condition would be impossible if it were desirable, and would be fatal to our greatness if it were possible.

But if we instinctively dismiss, as visionary, the notion of imitating this primitive organisation, we should be wrong in jumping at the conclusion that that organisation is under all circumstances to be condemned. It may be that arrangements which it would be fatal for us to adopt, are well fitted to other states of society.

It has been mentioned by Riehl, I believe, in his work on Germany, that it is necessary in an early state of society, for the master to have some hold on his servant. Nor is Riehl by any means original in this observation. It has occurred to many that where there exists an abundance of unoccupied fertile land, there is great danger that a community should become too scattered. Every man desires to be a master and none are willing to be servants. With land at my disposal why should I till the farm of another?

The same notion has been strongly expressed by Gibbon Wakefield in his " England and America." Mr. Wakefield insists on this opinion so strongly and in such unmeasured terms, that he goes far to countenance the continuance of negro slavery in the Southern States. It is true that where there exists an abundance of unoccupied land, it is necessary to enact laws against vagrancy, and may be even necessary to prohibit labourers generally from leaving the lands on which they are born. But absolute unconditional slavery goes far beyond this : it almost destroys all the legal rights of 'a slave; it renders insecure all family ties by putting the persons of the slaves practically at the command of the master, to use them or sell them; it gives to the white man an authority that very few persons can exercise without being themselves corrupted. But on the other hand there is on the part of the northern abolitionists something of fanaticism and of intolerance with which I cannot sympathise. Too many of them cannot see that to set some millions of negroes absolutely free, with liberty to wander wherever their fancy may lead them, in a country where land is to be had almost for the asking, and in a southern climate in which little labour is needful to procure such means of living as the slaves have hitherto enjoyed;—they cannot see that such a proceeding would be as fatal to the civilisation and ultimate well being of the negro race, as it would be to the present greatness of the United States. If it were possible, but I fear it is not, for the Americans to regard this subject without prejudice on the part of the Abolitionists, or irritation on the part of the Southerners, means might be found, no doubt, gradually but surely to erase this plague spot from the Republic, and thus to remove from the American the ridicule that attaches to him when he boasts of the freedom of his country.

Those who are desirous of promoting such a consummation would do well to study the organisation of labour in the East: to observe by what means it has come to pass that workmen and employers of different races and of hostile creeds have settled down into relations of peace and good will; how the cultivator is prohibited from deserting his seigneur, while the seigneur, by the exercise of justice and benevolence, makes the yoke so light as to be unfelt. The Christian planter may learn a humiliating lesson from the Moslem landlord.

We can see that some dependence on the part of the labourer, and of corresponding patronage on the part of the employer, are generally necessary in new countries. Without these, the abundance of fertile land leads to such a dispersion of the population as is a great obstacle to progress. Where every man gets land very easily and chooses it where he likes, each family may be far distant from every other. Association and co-operation are impossible : roads cannot be made : a household must supply itself with every thing it wants. To concentrate the population it is highly desirable to throw difficulties in the way of getting possession of new land. This is partially accomplished in our Colonies by the mode adopted of surveying and selling the unoccupied territory. In former times it was accomplished by the rougher modes, first of enslaving the labourer, afterwards of tying him to the land, while conferring on him legal rights and comparative freedom. Happily, all such restraints are unnecessary in old countries like our own.

Those who delight in drawing black sketches of the present state and future prospects of our working classes, and who insist mainly on the fact that there is no unoccupied land to resort to, should remember this fact : that it is very difficult for the working classes to be altogether free so long as the land of a country is part of it unoccupied : and that though, during the very short time that has elapsed since convict slavery has ceased, all our colonists are free, yet that in America, the boasted land of liberty, the uncultivated ground still presents the obstacle which hinders several millions of human beings from enjoying the ordinary rights of men.

This relation, then, of patronage on the one side and
dependence on the other, naturally arises in a country only
partially occupied, and is modified as the land is better
peopled. When the owner of land finds that he has no
difficulty in procuring labourers, he will cease to insist on
his right to retain his born thralls on his estate. He may
at first sell them the privilege of migration, as happens in
Russia at present, where the mechanic or trader in Moscow
or St. Petersburg, pays the *abrok* every year to his lord.
When a country is fully peopled as ours is, a landowner, far
from wishing to retain labourers on his farms against their
will, contrives rather to find means of diminishing the population : he pulls down cottages, discourages early marriages,
and promotes emigration. This relation of dependence and
patronage altogether ceases. The labourer is left to find
work where he pleases : the landlord assumes the right of
choosing his tenants, and the farmer assumes the right of
selecting what labourers he pleases. The employer of
labourers ceases to be their patron. He may still exhibit
kindness to them, may in many instances assist them when
sick, and relieve them when in distress. But such assistance
is casual and precarious, and is not given as a matter of
course and as a part of the payment due in consideration
of labour formerly rendered. It is true that in English
country parishes the poor law has prevented the entire
destruction of this kind of patronage. The landlord and
the farmer know that if a labourer is left by his master to
fall into distress, resort will be had to the workhouse, and
thus the poor rate will be increased. The consequence is
that the rate of wages in such parishes has some reference
to the needs of the labourer : it is felt that to give less than

a man can exist upon is no gain. Thus when the price of
bread is very high country wages frequently rise. This
check does not exist in the towns, and wages are determined
on principles more purely commercial. In my own experience for many years, I have found the wages of an
unskilled labourer to be fifteen shillings a week; and
whether the quartern loaf has been fivepence or tenpence, I
have not observed any rise or fall as to this common rate.
However kindly disposed a master may be, he cannot pay
much more than his neighbours if he means to carry on his
business with a profit. If the workman were a dependent
who could not leave him, he might pay more at one time
and less at another; but the independence of the workman
makes this patronage impossible.

I have found in practice the great difficulty that arises in
establishing any thing that approaches to this relation, now
it does not exist in our habits. Having been frequently
annoyed with strikes, I made an agreement with an entire
set of men that I would always pay them at the same rate
whatever might be the state of trade. I was to give one
shilling at all times for a given quantity of work. As there
were times when this was above the market rate, and as I
feared that when the market rate was higher than one
shilling the men might leave me, I bound the men to work
for me during a year or two years. This implied an obligation on my part to find them work at all times. The
arrangement went on satisfactorily several years; but at
last, an unusual demand arising, I voluntarily advanced my
wages from one shilling to one shilling and threepence. I
did this, not from any motive of philanthrophy, but as a
matter of prudence, fearing that my men would be discon-

tented at being paid a good deal below the current rate, and
knowing from experience how annoying is any appeal to the
law. My men, however, were not satisfied, but grumbled to
each other at being prevented from reaping the full advantage of the higher wages prevailing. They applied to an
experienced attorney and showed him a copy of the agreement : and when he asked them what plea they could offer
in order to cancel it, they told him that I had voluntarily
advanced their wages by one-fourth, and they fancied this to
be a fatal infraction on my part. Happily they had applied
to a man who was prepared to give them good advice.
" Go back to your work and don't let your master know
that you have been to me on this fool's errand. If he
should learn the fact you will be lucky if he does not
reduce you to the one shilling again ; and if he should do
so not all the attorneys in the world can save you from
working out your agreement at that rate."

In comparing this régime of Patronage with the Individualism that prevails among ourselves, I should be glad if
I could find facts decisive of the question, which régime
most promotes the happiness of the labourers. We are
told* that the Russian serfs are contented with their lot.
They are well fed no doubt, and well housed and smartly
dressed : but these results generally follow moderate industry where the population is thinly scattered over the
land. The serfs are much addicted to chanting their
national airs, and on Sundays and holidays, dressed in their
smart clothes, they sing before their cottages or before the
mansion of the seigneur. The *Englishwoman in Russia*
says that these airs are generally plaintive, being set in

* Le Play, 77—1.

a minor key. But whatever the airs may be, we cannot forget that negro slaves sing and dance when their work is done, and none more gay than they. But this live-liness is the result of a mercurial temperament throwing off its troubles and snatching an hour's enjoyment when it offers.

I do not mean to deny that the Russian serfs are happy : I only assert that the habit of singing and dancing in the intervals of work, proves nothing beyond the fact that those who thus amuse themselves have a certain elasticity of tem-perament.

I think that the régime of patronage is perfectly com-patible with the happiness of the dependents. The most extraordinary example that I know is that of Paraguay under the Jesuits. The natives were under the most entire subjection, and eat, drank, worked, prayed, and laughed, just as they were told. Their physical condition was excellent, and the only thing to be desired, I believe, was that the people had been less of pupils and more of men. In Canada, as I have been told by a very intelligent witness, a similar state of things, though in a milder form, existed among the French population. The Roman Catholic Priests were the directors of every family, and well did they use their power. But the curse of childishness was upon the people : they did not think for themselves ; they had little fortitude and less active resolution : they multiplied on the land handed down from their fathers, and shuddered at the thought of migration ; and thus, from excess of numbers, as it is said, they have fallen into comparative poverty and distress. There is no safety for man but in self-reliance : the passive happiness which results from favourable circum-stances is transitory and uncertain.

In no country is there more of this patronage and dependence than in Russia, and I think it likely that the serfs
are a happy race of people. The Russian landowners are, I
believe, kindhearted. We have testimony to this effect on
the part of the anonymous *Englishwoman in Russia;* and as
her remarks are generally much tainted with bitterness, we
may trust her praise the more. She speaks of acts of charity
and benevolence highly honourable to them ;* of their being
generally a goodhearted people.† She mentions an anecdote
shewing extraordinary attachment to the owner of an estate
on the part of the serfs; who having heard that the seigneur,
Count B—, on attaining his majority, had found his property
burdened with debt, subscribed among themselves no less
than £45,000 and offered this large sum as a present.‡ She
says in another place that the Russian seigneurs are hospit-
able, humane to their serfs, kindhearted and temperate,
though neither refined nor well informed.§ If all these
praises had come from the pen of an habitual eulogist I
should have thought little of them : but when I find them in
the same work which denounces the nobility as indelicate,
frivolous, devoid of truth, overrun with government spies of
every grade from the lowest to the highest rank, I am
inclined to think that the eulogium is worthy of attention.

No doubt, many hardships are suffered by the serfs at the
hands of hard and irritable superiors, and this very book
gives some instances. One of them is that of a seigneur
who had ill used his dependents to such an extent that they
determined on revenging themselves. They easily accomplished their resolution by entering his bed room at night

* p. 32.   † p. 68.   ‡ p. 145.   § p. 172.

and putting him and his wife to death.   But the singularity
of the case is that the seigneur slept with his window open,
in a room on the ground floor, and was thus exposed to the
attack.   There must be a general mildness of manners where
a master will thus trust his life to his dependents.   We hear
very different accounts of the mode of sleeping of the
Southerners in the United States.   A Charleston slave
owner would not rest securely without doors and windows
barred, and revolver and bowie knife at his side.

Yet, however contented and happy the Russians may be,
it is certain that a similar régime led to very different consequences in France before the revolution of 1789.   There the
noblesse had great privileges, and had the legal power of
exacting endless services or commutations from the peasants.
These inferiors, no doubt, ought to have received protection
and assistance in return, but such claims were miserably
neglected.   The great landowners generally resided in Paris,
and regarded it as banishment if the king ordered them to
go and live on their estates.   The greater part of the land
was held on the Métayer system, the landlord finding not
only land but even tools and cattle, and the peasant, a mere
ill paid servant, dividing the produce of the farm with his
lord.   That the peasants were intolerably wretched seems
proved by their readiness to seize the revolutionary period as
a means of revenging themselves, and by the brutality with
which they treated their oppressors.   The same régime,
then, that perhaps secures the well being of the Russian
peasants, was consistent with great misery in the case of the
French peasants : and it would be absurd to pronounce in
favour of a system which fails in one instance and succeeds
in another.

One explanation offers itself as to the difference between these two countries: the population of Russia is by no means large in proportion to the means of subsistence ; while the population of France appears to have been far too great. Arthur Young, after carefully inspecting most parts of France, about the time of the revolution, declared himself convinced that the population was too numerous by five or six millions,* and that if that immense superfluity were removed the country would be richer and stronger. As Young had rather a dashing way of writing, and was addicted to the use of round numbers, we might have been disposed to make a heavy deduction from his estimate, but that we have learnt from Ireland in the last ten years, that a country may sometimes spare a fifth of its population without loss and even with advantage. At any rate, the picture drawn by Young of the French peasantry, of their scanty food, their miserable cabins,† their women and girls in some places harder worked than horses,‡ and without shoes or stockings,§ while even the men might be seen at plough, barefooted, their want of employment and consequent idleness, may convince us that a great reduction of numbers would have been a blessing. If, then, we compare Russia of the present day with France of last century, we may conjecture that the happiness of the Russian serf is owing to the mildnesss of his superiors, and the thinness of the population, rather than to the peculiar system under which he lives. I may add that the government of the Czar appears far more ready to repress any excesses on the part of landowners, than the French king was formerly. Occasion-

* A. Young's France, 1. 414 & 482. † Ib. 1. 448. ‡ Ib. 1. 450. § Ib.

ally, even the French noblesse was called to account for its
misdeeds; and we have an interesting example of this in the
Grands Jours d'Auvergne, of which an account appeared a
few years back. But the Russian serfs seem to have quite
a habit of appealing to the provincial governors and through
them to the Czar. The *Englishwoman* gives us several
examples of these appeals. Nicholas, also, we are told, set
the example of liberating the serfs, by giving freedom to all
those on the Crown lands. Perhaps, therefore, it is not any
peculiar system, but the administration of the system, which
gives so much well being to the peasantry.

It cannot be disputed that many disadvantages attach to
this régime of patronage. Under it there is little room for
growth, whether of individual excellence or of national
greatness. Men are so much bound down by the fetters of
the system that it is difficult for them to advance beyond
the point which their fathers reached. We are apt to say
that this stationary condition of mind arises rather from
political than from social causes; but it would seem that it
is impossible to have what we should think a good political
system, unless by first reconstructing society. So long as
the people are utterly dependent on the seigneurs, they
cannot take an independent part in governing the country.
Not merely are the materials wanting for a democracy such
as that of the United States; they are wanting for a limited
monarchy such as ours, and even for an elective monarchy
founded on universal suffrage as in France. If any change
in the form of government took place, it must give greater
power to the aristocracy, and this probably would only rivet
the closer, the fetters which now bind the people. Let there
be an advance in the social condition of the middle and

lower classes, and political amelioration may then be hoped for. It is the system of patronage and dependence that stunts the moral and intellectual growth of all classes, which jealously shuts out knowledge, which fills the land with spies, and which represses, at whatever cost, all political movement not proceeding from the throne.

This régime is also, I conceive, unfavourable to the greatness of the country. It seems to me clear that the resources of a nation depend principally, not on the extent of its territory, not even on the extent of its population, but on the productiveness of its soil. A country as extensive as China, if ill peopled, has little command of means to make itself respected. If we can conceive China itself, with its prodigious population, yet so ill cultivated that there was barely food enough to supply the wants of its own cultivators, we may pronounce that it could have little influence in the affairs of its neighbours. But where as among ourselves every tiller of the soil raises three times as much food as his family consumes, there the resources of the nation are great. Now the system we are speaking of makes a productive agriculture impossible. Under that system farms are not held as they are among us, the tenant paying a fixed rent and getting all the produce he can. In France formerly some of the land belonged to small proprietors who themselves cultivated it; and these farmers, having the strongest motives for the exercise of skill and industry, got good crops. But the greater part of the kingdom was divided into large properties, and cultivated on the metayer system. This was not the case every where, but perhaps a sixth or seventh part was let for money rents. The tenant of a metairie paid to the landlord a certain portion of each

year's produce, just as formerly a tithe was paid to the
Church. The landlord, however, took a much larger share
than a tithe: in Champagne frequently a third, but elsewhere generally a half. This landlord's share was not
purely a rent. The farmers were so poor, and perhaps so
much afraid of exhibiting the little stock they possessed,
that the landlord had to find the necessary capital; not
merely permanent improvements and buildings, but sometimes also cattle and implements. A. Young* says " The
landlord commonly finds half the cattle and half the seed;
and the metayer, labour, implements and taxes; but in
some districts the landlord bears a share of these. . . .
Near Aguillon on the Rhone, the metayers furnish half the
cattle. Near Falaise, in Normandy, I found metayers where
they should least of all be looked for, on the farms which
gentlemen keep in their own hands; the consequence, then,
is, that every gentleman's farm must be precisely the worst
cultivated of all the neighbourhood. . . . At Nangis,
in the Isle of France, I met with an agreement for the landlord to furnish live stock, implements, harness and taxes;
the metayer found labour and his own capitation tax:—the
landlord repaired the house and gates, the metayer the
windows:—the landlord provided seed the first year, the
metayer the last: in the intervening years they supply half
and half. Produce sold for money divided. Butter and
cheese used in the metayer's family to any amount, compounded for at five shillings a cow. In the Bourbonnois the
landlord finds all sorts of live stock, yet the metayer sells,
buys, and charges at his will; the steward keeping an

* 1. 403.

account of these mutations, for the landlord has half the product of sales, and pays half the purchases. The tenant carts the landlord's half of the corn to the barn of the château, and comes again to take the straw. The consequences of this absurd system are striking : land which in England would let at about ten shillings, pays about two shillings and sixpence for both land and live stock."

It is worth noticing that while the owners of land thus lost the greater part of the incomes they might have got from a free and substantial tenantry, and while the nation lost the resources it would have derived from an increased productiveness, the tenants themselves were poor and discontented. It appears* that it was these men who were the plunderers and burners during the revolution.

I have no reason to think that the land is let in Russia on terms so complex and absurd as those I have quoted. We are told that, commonly, a serf has a plot of ground sufficient for the maintenance of his family. This is not the metayer system but that of the Corvée. Le Play says† that in the south and east where land is plentiful, the Corvée is general, and that the peasants give half their time to their seigneurs, and that this amounts, deducting holidays, to 125 days in the year. This Corvée is, no doubt, an improvement on the metairie, but yet it is not to be compared in efficacy to the letting of land at a fixed rent.

And these, or similar, systems of cultivation seem essential to the existence of the régime of patronage : for if the farmers held their land on the term of payment of a fixed rent, finding all the stock themselves, and, therefore, being

* A. Young, 2. 154.   † 67. 1 and 58. 1.

men of capital, their dependence on the landlords would cease. It is true that there might be individual instances of capitalist farmers continuing serfs, just as many rich Russian traders are serfs and pay the *abrok*. But such a state of things could not be common. If the farmers generally were substantial tenants they would soon cease to be serfs.

One of the worst features in the régime of patronage is that it is only temporary, unless we suppose that the world should cease to advance and should relapse into the sluggish state of the middle ages. But we cannot believe this as to Russia, where the Crown is constantly urging forward the emancipation of the serfs. Nor can I willingly believe this of the United States, where the slavery of several millions of people exhibits patronage and dependence in their most unfavourable colours. After all, the question is very much one of the growth of population. We see in the Bulgarian case, out of which these remarks have sprung, that serfdom may become almost a name: that the tenant, though tied to the land, does not feel his chain, because he could not better himself by breaking it. Now, if the Russian population should increase so fast as to press on the means of subsistence, so far from the seigneurs desiring to retain their serfs, they will be disposed to assist them in emigrating to other countries. So in the United States: if we can overleap in imagination the long period that must elapse before the fertile land is all occupied, we may conceive a state of things in which a slave will be a torment and not a profitable possession. But, in the mean time, both these great countries are haunted with perpetual fear of change. In the States this question of slavery poisons every political question : the Northerns are oppressed with disgust and shame when they hear the echo of the driver's whip: the Southerners tremble at one time in anticipation of a servile war, at another at threats of a legal emancipation. In the one case they dread assassination, torture, female dishonour; in the other case ruin for themselves and their children. In Russia, too, we are told that fears are entertained of bloody revolutions. If such things should happen they will not spring, I conceive, from those serfs whose condition we are considering, but rather from the large class of personal dependents, whose condition is more at the mercy of a capricious master. Yet, if we are to credit the favourable accounts we receive of the kindness of the Russian seigneurs, there cannot be much danger of a rising of any sort. We, however, who have passed beyond this state of patronage, have reason to rejoice in our emancipation.

Another disadvantage that attends this system, is, that dependents are exposed to the danger of living under a harsh superior. It is very well to say that among ourselves a wife may have a coarse or cruel husband; a child may have a selfish unfeeling father; an apprentice may be tied to a negligent brutal master, and that in most of these cases the connection is indissoluble. Unfortunately, the Russian serf has the risk of all these miserable contingencies, and has the risk besides of a superior who is selfish, tyrannical, dissolute, a spendthrift, or a gambler. The *Englishwoman* mentions the case of a Polish lady in Russia, who contracted some considerable card debts that she was unable to discharge. Necessity sharpened her invention. She had several girls in her household who possessed beautiful heads of hair: the lady cut off these coiffures and sold them: with the proceeds she paid her debts of honour. But to have the hair cropped

is, in Russia, a degrading punishment, and would subject
these poor girls to the jeers of their acquaintance. It is
observed that the small proprietors are commonly more
exacting than the owners of large estates, except in the case
of absentee landlords, when the estate is very often entrusted
to a German steward, who has little sympathy with the serfs.
It is a great misfortune to an English tenant to have a harsh,
grasping, landlord, but at the worst the tenant can leave his
farm.

If any persons are possessed with such a fanatical love of
authority and submission, as to desire to restore among ourselves a régime of patronage, they will do well to observe the
difference of manners and feelings in one country and
another. The *Englishwoman* tells us that she was on one
occasion staying in the country with a Russian lady of
amiable and polished manners. Our informant being one
day out of doors, witnessed, unknown to the actors, a strange
scene. The hostess was walking, with an inflamed countenance, behind a young serf, her gardener; and as she walked
she struck him repeatedly on the back with her clenched fist,
while he was humbly begging her to pardon him. The
young man, no doubt, was glad to compound for his fault, by
so harmless a punishment; but the want of dignity on the
part of the mistress is shocking to our decorous manners.
On another occasion an additional footman, brought up from
the country, was guilty of many gaucheries, and was
threatened with punishment for his next offence. Soon
afterwards he threw a dish of gravy over his master, and
when we expect to find that he is flogged for his presumption, he is told to go and stand in the corner of the
room during the rest of dinner. I admire this childish

simplicity, but I feel that the great difference in our own manners would alone make it impossible to imitate such a system.

At the same time I must confess that the case of the Bulgarian manufacturer suggests to us in England the question whether we do all that we ought. There is a notion pretty generally entertained by English manufacturers, that they have little to do with their men except during the hours of work. One manufacturer, it is said, buys of another; he deals with him regularly every month, or every week : such a connection does not give the buyer any right to interfere with the domestic concerns of the seller; and it would be thought very impertinent if the buyer were to tender advice to the seller as to his conduct, or as to the management of his children. In the same way a manufacturer employs a workman regularly for years : he sees him at his work every day : the man gives his labour in return for money, just as the seller gives goods in return for money. What right has the manufacturer to interfere in the private arrangements of the workman, more than he has to interfere in the private arrangements of the manufacturer who sells to him ?

I should not have thought it necessary to state this opinion, had I not found that it has possession of gentlemen towards whom I feel the highest respect; nor, perhaps, unless I felt that my own conduct had been influenced by it. It is evident, however, that the case of two manufacturers is not the same as that of master and workman. The two manufacturers are presumed to be equal : the master and workman are presumed to be unequal in edu-

cation, in providence, in wealth. An employer has generally more influence over his workpeople than he has
elsewhere.

When a factory is situated in the country, unless the
master assist in furnishing medical attendance, education,
provident institutions, religious instruction, it is probable
that the working classes will be destitute of all these. We
can hardly doubt that in such a situation it is one of
the duties of property to render assistance. But in towns
the case is not so plain. Mechanics there live in a very
scattered way, some of them near to their work, but many
of them at considerable distances from it. Some of them
for the sake of having a garden, or from early associations,
live quite in the country two or three miles away : others
will be found in the outskirts of the town : and even those
who live in the town have often half a mile or more to walk.
If, then, a large manufacturer establishes a school on his
premises, it will be conveniently available only for the children of the moderate number who live close at hand. If it
should be required that the children should come from the
more distant homes, that necessity will be felt as a hardship.
Similar difficulties occur in towns, as to other acts of patronage on the part of employers.

There is another obstacle which might not be thought of
by any but a practical man. Serious causes of irritation
often arise between masters and men. I have mentioned
before what happened to myself, when I attempted to prevent a recurrence of strikes, by giving an uniform rate of
wages. When the men tried to cancel their agreements
with me, on the plea that I had already violated the agree-

ments by voluntarily raising the rate of wages, they did what seemed to me a very ungracious act. I had just cause for irritation. I know that these men are just towards each other, and so far honest towards me that they would not take a straw from me. Yet if one of my equals had treated me in such a way I should scarcely have said of him that he was one of " the noblest works of God." I know that workmen have two codes of morality, one among themselves, and another between themselves and their employers. This duplex code is no doubt wrong. But it is needless for us to complain of it so long as in many respects we also have a double code. Adam Smith said that if a man professed to have scruples of conscience about smuggling, he deserved to lie under the suspicion of unusual hypocrisy. Eighty years have improved our national morals : yet a man who smuggled a box of cigars or a cask of brandy, would not be shunned in society. The distinction carelessly drawn by the lower classes is of the same description. These men sympathise with each other and feel that it is a shame to rob each other : they feel little sympathy with their master, just as he feels little sympathy with the government; and thus the mechanic does not feel it a shame to wrong his master, nor does the master feel it a shame to wrong the government.

It may be thought that where a master exercises much patronage, the relation between him and his men will be so far changed that the causes for irritation will cease. I do not doubt that those causes will be lessened, but I cannot hope that they will come to an end. A few years ago an example occurred fitted to illustrate this. In a manufactory with which I am intimately acquainted, a great deal of money, as well as trouble, was expended in promoting the well-being of the men : among other things many thousand pounds were expended in building schools. A surgeon was engaged, and every man had the benefit of his attendance, but was required to pay a penny a week for this advantage. The workmen were hired for a term of years at a fixed rate of wages. During the currency of these engagements trade became very good, and mechanics so much in demand that if these men had been at liberty they could have obtained higher wages than those they were earning. A sense of right would have told them that since the masters always fulfilled their engagements to the men, they had a right to expect a similar honesty in return. But mechanics have not yet risen to the height of such an argument : they no more scruple to break an agreement with masters than masters in many cases scruple to evade payment of a part of their income tax. The men in question had no pretext of necessity since they were in the receipt of high wages ; £2. to £3. a week. But the most affluent mechanic feels little sympathy as to money matters, with a master who lives in comparative splendour, with a mansion and servants, carriages and horses : and as to a simple sense of duty, I fear the want of it is not confined to any class. In the present case the workmen endeavoured to escape from their bond, and had the audacity to plead that the masters had broken the agreement, by stopping the penny a week for medical attendance. Happily, such a plea is no more sanctioned by the law of England than it is by conscience.

Indeed our law favors agreements between masters and men. It will not, to be sure, allow a man to sell himself into slavery : it will not support a one-sided agreement, by which a man binds himself to work for a particular master, while no corresponding provision is made on the other side. Till within a few years it has always been held that a master must undertake to find full work during the period of the agreement, and that in default of such a provision the agreement was void. By a late decision of Lord Campbell, however, on an appeal from Petty Sessions, it has been ruled that it is sufficient if a master finds at all times a reasonable amount of employment. Under any circumstances, the failure of a master to provide the stipulated employment does not cancel the agreement, but only gives the workman an appeal to a magistrate to order the payment of wages. It is to the credit of workmen that such appeals are rare : that when they see trade bad and a master doing his best to employ his men, they very seldom insist on their right to full employment and full wages. It ought also to be remembered that when in a good state of trade they wish unfairly to break their engagements, they are often instigated to do so, either by rival masters, or by unscrupulous agents.

The cases I have mentioned may, perhaps, serve to convince some persons, that even where a good deal of patronage is exercised by masters, cases of irritation will still arise between them and their men. The masters, seeing the worst side of their men's characters, frequently form a poor opinion of them, and forget that there may be many virtues exhibited at home ; that the men may be tender husbands and kind fathers ; may be self-denying and cheerful in adversity, though in a state of prosperity they are grasping, improvident, and open to just imputations of ingratitude. Now, we must not expect that manufacturers, any more than other men, should practice a great amount of reflection. Most of us, in actual affairs, are guided by what has the appearance more of instinct than reason, though in truth we are guided by reason, but not by a train of reasoning. Many very successful men say that they feel themselves incapable of close application to anything like elaborate argumentation : that in embarking on a new speculation, in deciding to give credit to one buyer and to refuse it to another, and even on the bench, in committing one prisoner and acquitting another, in sentencing one petty offender to twenty-one days' and a second to six months' imprisonment, they are guided by their first impression, which they generally find more trustworthy than an opinion formed by reflection. Such men, in arguing with you, seek to convince you of their own accuracy, and by no means propose to correct their own opinions. Now, this being the ordinary character of men of business, and therefore of manufacturers, it cannot be a matter of surprise that the notion they form of their workmen is an unfavourable one ; since they judge by what is on the surface, and do not, by reflection, penetrate any deeper. And, it may well be doubted whether any great amount of patronage can be beneficially exerted under such circumstances. The workmen who seem to the master to be the best men, because they are regular at their work and respectful in their manner, may really be avaricious, selfish, hard hearted, and servilely minded : while others who are restless and irregular, may be kind hearted and well intentioned. If schools and provident societies can be organised independently of a master's influence, perhaps they are more likely to attain their ends and to become permanent.

I do not say this in order to relieve manufacturers from the responsibility of promoting such institutions. It is incumbent on them, as on every one else, to promote them: and it is even more incumbent on them than others, both because they gain their incomes directly from the labour of workmen, and also because their constant association with workmen ought to cause a strong interest in their welfare.

CHAPTER III.

I now come to the third of the four modes of existence that I have mentioned : the first being the patriarchal, the second that of patronage, and the third that of communism. As in the two first instances, I begin with one of the cases given by M. Le Play.* The man here described is a founder in some French iron-works, situated in the Nivernais. The man himself is a journeyman, but his place of living leads our author to an interesting description of a rural commune which is lately extinct.

There is nothing very remarkable in the mode of existence of this man. He rather belongs to the régime of patronage ; for though he is at liberty to leave his employment when he pleases, yet he remains permanently attached to the works. And the proprietor feels himself bound to retain his old servants, and to assist them when employment is scarce. It seems, however, that in these small manufactories, where iron is made with wood for fuel, there is not the same uncertainty in the demand which is found in the extensive works where coal is used. Probably, most of the iron produced is used in the neighbourhood, and from the high price of French iron it is certain that little of it can be exported. This kind of demand is naturally more uniform than the speculative demand arising from foreign mercantile houses. There is a tendency, however, to a diminution of this excel-

---

* Page 242.

lent relation between master and workman. We have here again an example of the transitory character of patronage at the present day.

M. Le Play's investigation of this case was made in 1842, and writing at that date, he seizes the opportunity of mentioning the disorganisation that had taken place in the ancient communities of peasants. Up to a recent period, these had preserved in all their integrity, under circumstances honourable to the old French régime, the practice of agricultural associations, which were formerly very common and which still exist elsewhere. The last community of this sort in France, was that of Saint-Benin-des-Bois, and was well known as the Communauté des Jault : it had been established more than 500 years. In 1842 this community still existed, but " this last remnant of the genius of other ages was constantly threatened with ruin on the one hand by the destructive interference of the new civil laws, by the developement of the spirit of individualism, and by the weakening of the religious character among the latter generations : on the other hand by the legitimate love of independence which is the principal power of modern societies."

" It is remarked that these new tendencies coincide with the weakening, if not with the destruction, of paternal authority : this evil having reached such a point that it is almost impossible for a tenant or a metayer to keep many of his children to help him in his work. The practice of employing strangers on wages was formerly uncommon, but seems likely to become the rule in occupations of this kind. The principle of communism, then, is disappearing in this country, even in the domestic circle."

M. Le Play gives a very interesting account of the community I have mentioned, but I must refer for the particulars to the original work.* The narrative of the Communauté des Jault, has to me the interest of a romance, with the additional advantage of possessing the truth of history. This was the last of the ancient rural communities of France. In reading of it, I am pleased with the antiquity it exhibits, and with the glimpse it affords us of a state of manners lately existing in the very heart of Europe, but utterly different from any thing to which we are accustomed.

To the Frenchman, this community has an interest very different from any thing that we feel: it furnishes to him a model of a state of society, towards which the desires of a multitude of enthusiasts, and even the faint hopes of some able men, have been directed. But Socialism and Communism have so few advocates among ourselves, that we do not feel this additional interest in the case. Looking at it coolly, and without that polemical spirit which in France circumstances have rendered almost inevitable, I feel that this Jault Community presents no example for our imitation. It is inconceivable that, in the present day, men should submit to the laws neccessary for the success of such an institution. An almost despotic power was conferred on the chief. He had the unlimited command of the purse of the Community: he distributed the periodical produce, at his own pleasure, to the different families: he assigned to each family the work it was required to execute. In the performance of every one of these delicate functions, to

---

* Page 247.

how many suspicions of egotism, of partiality, of nepotism, must the chief have been exposed. I can understand a Scottish clan submitting to the decrees of its chief as to the responses of an oracle; devoting itself to his service, waiting upon his nod. But a Highland chief had the prestige of birth, he was the lineal descendant of a race of heroes, whose origin was lost in the mountain mists: the deeds of his forefathers formed the burden of the poet's song. The Highland chief himself was a man of comparative education and wealth, among followers, ignorant, poor, and in time of peace, wretched. But in the Community we are considering, the master was placed in circumstances the reverse of all these. His descent was exactly that of every one around him: he was brought up among themselves, with no better education, and no more pretensions to wealth than they had. His monarchy was an elective one, the weakest of all monarchies. One would have thought that the first day of his administration would have been the last: that every member would have been discontented at the task imposed upon himself, and at the share of produce conferred on himself. So far from wondering that the Community has become extinct, I am astonished to find that it could exist during 500 years. No doubt, at the time of its commencement, individualism was impossible: every man was compelled to attach himself to a superior of some sort, in order to save himself from becoming a prey to the oppressor. The Jault preferred a Community to a seigneur, as a superior. In the present day, when every man may shape his own course in safety, such dependence on a superior is unnecessary; and the external pressure being withdrawn, it is inconceivable that such institutions should

arise and prosper. A spirit of passive obedience is inconsistent with the practice and teaching of the century; and
this spirit, impressed on particular races by tradition,
has passed away from France as it has from our own
country. It is a futile pursuit to attempt to revive it,
and therefore are Communities such as this become impossible.

This picture, then, of a Community that is extinct, is
rather curious than instructive. But we have in M. Le
Play's third case an existence of temporary communism
that, if less interesting, is more available as an example.

In Russia, as in many other countries, regular migrations
of labourers take place from one part of the country to
another. We have ourselves an illustration of this practice
in the Irish reapers, great numbers of whom formerly came
over here every year, leaving their families at home. The
practice of migration, however, seems to be carried to a
greater extent in Russia. We are told* that a great part of
the labourers of the towns are of this migratory class.
These men inhabit the towns for longer periods than those
during which the Irish reapers remain here, but they retain
their affection for their native place, and carefully save
money to enable them to settle there in the end. The
peculiar organisation, too, of Russian society, naturally
recals these men into the country. M. Le Play remarks,
as a consequence of this state of things, that the towns
exhibit no signs of that immense multitude of persons
without any settled means of living, which is seen in other
countries.

* M. Le Play, 76. ix.

The working classes in Russia do not live like ours, each family separately ; but they herd together on the patriarchal system, several families of the same blood inhabiting one house, and possessing their property in common. Every one, therefore, from the time of birth, is constantly surrounded by a numerous tribe of relatives. When a labourer determines to migrate to a town in search of fortune, being unused to a state of isolation, he naturally seeks to supply a substitute for the association to which he is accustomed. This he finds in what bears the name of an *artèle*.

M. Le Play gives a full account* of a man who, as a member of one of these artèles, goes once a year to St. Petersburg, to labour as a porter, returning to spend each winter at home. The emigrants work together, eat, drink, and live in common, and throwing their earnings together, divide the surplus at the end of the season.

Besides this association in the towns where the emigrants work, another artèle is formed among them in their native village, as soon as they determine to quit it. This arrangement is made with a view to facilitate the journey. We have an account† given of one that took place at a village two hundred miles from Moscow.

The examples of Communism that I have hitherto given, are interesting, but are not of general application. There is another kind of common rights found in many European countries and to a very wide extent. In England a century ago, the quantity of common land was very large, and it was only when our wars with Napoleon greatly raised the price of wheat, that inclosures proceeded with rapidity. When

---

* Le Play 76. 2.   † Ib. 76. 2.

A. Young wrote his travels in France, in 1789, these English inclosures were being made slowly.

Young was a decided enemy to common lands. He was a practical farmer, and filled with zeal for an improved agriculture; and, therefore, he could not endure the sight of good land yielding poor crops. He speaks* of " fields burthened with detestable common rights :" of † " the open arable fields of Picardy, &c. . . . cursed with all the mischievous circumstances known in similar cases in England, such as rights of common pasturage, commencing on given days, when under corn and throughout the fallow year." Elsewhere ‡ he says " Immense tracts in all the provinces of the kingdom (of France) and on almost all the principal rivers, are commons ; consequently cursed with rights absolutely subversive of all ideas of good husbandry."

It is worth while to enquire how far Young was correct in these views. That he was correct in regarding common rights as an obstacle to agricultural improvements, there can be no doubt. Every one agrees with him that the produce obtained from land subject to these rights, is very far less than the produce obtained from the same land after it is divided among individuals. If the numerous inclosure acts of the present century had not been passed, the periodical produce of this country would have been far less than it is. By this change the power of our little island to support population is become far greater than it was before. The advantage is at least as important as if the boundaries of the island had been enlarged by means of land rescued

---

* Young's France, 1. 360.   † Ib. 399.   ‡ Ib. 383.

from the sea. To the extent of the change, the greatness of the nation has been increased.

But the extent of production is not the only thing of importance: it is not generally the first thing. A productive agriculture is commonly of greater moment than any thing else. If the whole population is engaged in raising the first necessaries of life for themselves, not having even a surplus of these for exportation, none remain for other pursuits, none even for soldiers and sailors. A people so situated cannot be great, though it may perhaps be happy and contented. But a productive agriculture, by means of which one family can raise enough raw produce for three families, causes a very large *disposable* population; and a moderately large country possessing such an agriculture will have great influence and consideration in the world. Now there is every reason for believing that the inclosures in England caused a great improvement in the productiveness of the lands inclosed, and thus contributed to the greatness of this nation.

But a country may be great without being happy, and an addition to its greatness may perhaps not always add to its happiness. The produce of a people may multiply, the productiveness may increase, yet the distribution may be so unfortunate as not to secure a well fed, well supported, population. Now, A. Young tells us,* on the subject of inclosures, "under the new government (1789) which is establishing in France, I have great doubts whether any progress can ever be made in this great and leading step to all useful improvements in agriculture: as far as the present

---

* Young, France, 1, 400.

constitution can be understood, it is the will of the *people*
that is to govern; and I know of no country where the
people are not against inclosures. The Tiers Etat and
Clergy of Metz expressly demand that the edict of inclosure
shall be revoked: that of Troyes, and Nismes, and Anjou,
make the same request; another, that the right of commonage in forests shall be granted to the neighbouring
parishes. The nobility of Cambray declare that commons
ought not to be broken up. Nay, some of the *cahiers* go
so far as to say, that the commons which have already been
divided ought to be thrown open again."

A. Young, residing as a farmer in the country parts of
England, had seen inclosures made; and indeed he speaks in
the preceding page of "Commissioners" and of "the
Herculean labour, as the French would esteem it, of making
a fair division, without appeal." We may therefore take his
word for it, that inclosures were in his day unpopular in
England as well as in France.

Now, I by no means wish to assert that inclosures are
injurious: I should be most unwillingly convinced that they
are so: it would be with a heavy heart that I should have
taken part in preventing measures directly tending to raise
the greatness of England. But I see at the same time that
there is another side to the question: that the interests
of the individual commoners may have been different from
those of the nation, considered as a nation. A man born
with a common-right may have found that in practice he
could live in a manner that satisfied him. But he may have
felt certain that if the common lands were divided, and
he took his portion, he would sink at last into indigence.
No doubt, the land assigned to him was worth far more,

in consequence of the division, because it might be broken up and cultivated at the will of the owner: and the change would give it a large saleable value. But the freeman might feel that with the habits he had formed, such property would soon pass out of his hands. Under the practice of commonage he could continue to keep a cow or two, and had foresight enough to provide for replacing one of these if it accidentally died: but with a piece of valuable land at his disposal, borrowing would soon take place. The money so obtained being once spent could never be recovered.

This facility of borrowing on land, and this tendency to borrow upon it, explain what may perplex the readers of M. Le Play; I mean his constant denunciations of the practice of usury. The legion of small proprietors in France, most of them suffer under this scourge. They are in the situation of the Irish gentlemen: the land is not their own: they are nominally the proprietors, and they slave and sweat in their efforts to repay their loans, or at least to meet the interest due, but generally they slave and sweat in vain.

I can understand, therefore, that in this and other ways, the first effects of an enclosure would be injurious to the population of a parish. It would require the springing up of another generation before the advantages would be felt. It is clear, however, that rights of common would not make a neighbourhood prosperous. A. Young * says, "You must visit the great farms in Beauce, Picardy, part of Normandy, and Artois, and there you will find no more population than what is regularly employed and regularly

* A. Young's France, 1. 484.

paid; and if in such districts you should, contrary to this rule, meet with much distress, it is twenty to one but that it is in a parish which has some commons that tempt the poor to have cattle—to have property—and in consequence, misery. When you are engaged in this political tour, finish it by seeing England, and I will show you a set of peasants well clothed, well nourished, tolerably drunken from super-fluity, well lodged, and at their ease; and yet amongst them, not one in a thousand has either land or cattle." I quote this passage to show that in A. Young's travels he had found peasants with common rights living in a state of misery. I do not agree with him that the possession of land and cattle was the cause of the misery: nor indeed was this Young's deliberate opinion; but he had a dashing way of settling matters which often made him inconsistent with himself. His powers of correct observation were most valuable, but his habit of reflection was not of a high order.

This opinion, that common rights do not necessarily secure the well-being of the labouring classes is confirmed by M. Le Play. He gives us * an example to justify his opinion. He exhibits to us a very unpleasant state of society in the commune in question.

M. Le Play goes on to say that the custom of *vaine pâture* greatly interferes with the success of the district. Altogether, this is a very unsatisfactory sketch of the effects produced in France by a communal organisation. And this is a serious matter, because the quantity of common land in France is very large. It is estimated † at the

---

* Le Play, 241. 1 and 2.   † Ib. 235, 1.

present day, at about 2,800,000 hectares of fallows and peat soils used for pasture, 1,700,000 hectares of wood, and 200,000 hectares of arable land, meadows, and various other property; making a total of something like ten million English acres. The value is supposed to be seventy million sterling.

The custom of vaine pâture, mentioned above, deserves explanation. M. Le Play says, " vaine pâture is the custom which authorises proprietor farmers to feed their domestic animals by allowing them to graze on adjoining properties belonging to other persons. Sometimes this right is confined to poor persons making use of the lands of the rich. This case, which is still very common in France, has more or less the character of a kindness granted by tolerance. At other times, on the contrary, the right is exercised among little proprietors of the same condition, and in circumstances more or less easy, who share to about the same extent in the advantages or evils of the custom. This latter is the case to which peculiarly apply the French laws that regulate the custom of vaine pâture."

This extract is sufficient to give us some idea of what is meant by *vaine pâture*, and of the circumstances which have caused its retention. It is obvious that its retention is principally owing to the great subdivision of the French land, under the provisions of the law of inheritance, by which property at the death of the possessor is divided among the children, instead of being left to the disposition of the testator, as among ourselves. This is not the place to discuss the propriety of that law; but however favour-able we may be to subdivision, or opposed to the privileges of eldest sons, we shall all agree that the French practice is very defective. 'If every child ought to take an equal share of his father's property, he ought to take it in such a way as not to injure his neighbours, and not to ruin the agriculture of his country. A perverse heir ought not to have the power of insisting on his right to an actual share of every plot of ground left by his father. A man dies leaving three children and three plots of ground, all of equal value. Let each child take one of these plots, and let all draw lots for the first choice. No! says one of the co-heirs, I do not like this risk : I cannot bear to think that hereafter I may find my lot to be of less value than those of my brothers; nor do I wish that either of them should make the same discovery as to his. Let us avoid all ill feeling, by splitting each of the three plots into three equal parts, and by each of us taking one of them. This suspicious, litigious spirit, seems to be the cause of the incredible extent to which the subdivision of French land has proceeded.

It may seem wonderful that it should have advanced so much, but it is quite a mistake to suppose that it commenced after the revolution of 1789. The truth is that in many parts of France, and especially in the South, property descended equally to all the children before the Revolution, just as it does now. Every reader of A. Young is aware of this fact. For example, Young says,* writing just at the beginning of the Revolution, "The small properties of the peasants are found every where, to a degree we have no idea of in England; they are found in every part of the kingdom, even in those provinces where other tenures

* A. Young, France, 1. 402.

prevail; but in Quercy, Languedoc, the whole district of the Pyrenées, Béarn, Gascoigne, in part of Guienne, Alsace, Flanders, and Lorraine, they abound to a greater degree than common. In Flanders, Alsace, on the Garonne, and in Béarn, I found many in comfortable circumstances, such as might rather be called small farmers than cottagers; and in Bas Bretagne many are reputed rich: but in general they are poor and miserable, much arising from the minute division of their little farms among all the children. In Lorraine and the part of Champagne that joins it, they are quite wretched. I have, more than once, seen division carried on to such excess, that a single fruit tree, standing in about ten perch of ground, has constituted a farm, and the local situation of a family decided by the possession."

This subdivision of the soil, long continued as it has been, may account for the wide spread custom of vaine pâture. And an unfortunate result this is, according to our notions. We cannot conceive how a man should devote all his heart to his labour, when his property is subject to be overrun by others in this way. It is certain, however, that notwithstanding this discouragement, these small properties, and other small properties in France, are cultivated most industriously: were this the place for it I could adduce irresistible evidence of the fact.

At the same time, whatever may be the tendency of small properties, the tendency of Communism must, we should think, be towards carelessness of the interests of the Commune: we can hardly believe that a man will so zealously promote the well being of his village, as he will promote that of his family.　We find in Young * an example of great waste committed by a Commune.　He says, "A considerable portion of their mountains (the French Pyrenées) is underwood, and a much larger has been; for the destruction of them making every day is not credible to those who have not viewed them.　Passed frequently through several woods near Bagneres de Luchon, in which the woodmen were at work, riving and cutting beech staves for casks; I was shocked to see the destruction they made, which could not have been more wasteful or lavish if they had been in the midst of an American forest.　Large and beautiful beeches are cut off, three, four, and five feet high, and those noble stumps left to rot; whole trees which on trial would not rive well, left for years, and now rotting untouched; and in working those we saw nothing but clean cuts taken, three or four feet perhaps in fifty, and the rest left on the ground in the same confusion in which it fell.　The destruction is so general in this noble forest of Lartigues that it is almost destroyed; there is no young growth for succession; and in ten or twelve years it will be a bare mountain, with a few miserable shrubs browsed by goats and other cattle.　In some tracts which I passed at a few leagues distance, towards the walks of the Spanish flocks, there are some forests destroyed in such a shameful manner, that to a person from a country where wood is of any value, must appear incredible."

" These woods are commons belonging to the Communities of the parishes, upon which every inhabitant assumes the

* A. Young, France, 2. 106.

right, and practises the rage of depredation. So careless of the interests of posterity, or rather so inflamed against every idea but that of the present moment, that in the general opinion there will be an undoubted scarcity in thirty years amidst what have been, and yet are in some districts, very noble forests."

It is not to be supposed, however, that such abuses as to forests are inseparable from a communal organization. A. Young in another place* tells us, "The mountains belong, as in the French Pyrenées, to the parishes; each inhabitant has a right to cut what wood he pleases for fuel and repairs, in the woods assigned for that purpose; others are let by lease at public auction, for the benefit of the parish, the trees to be cut being marked; and in general the police of their woods is better than on the French side; when woods are cut they are preserved for the next growth."

It appears, then, that community of property does not necessarily lead to waste, though it would seem to tend in that direction : we can hardly believe that if the woods in the French Pyrenées had been private property, there would have taken place such waste as Young describes.

It may be thought that another evil tendency must exist in these communities : that every one born a member having a right to share the privileges, the ordinary restraints on the increase of population would be thus withdrawn. Why should a young man refrain from marriage, when he is secure of such a maintenance as that to which he has been accustomed ? But it must be remembered that the common

* A. Young, France, 2. 306.

rights we are now speaking of, are not like those which prevail in Russia, where several families of married brothers
live together, and each member has a claim to a share of the
whole gains of the household; and that they are not like
those of the ancient Community of the Jault, where an
organisation similar to the Russian, existed on a larger scale
and as to a more distant kindred. The Communes we are
now speaking of leave every man to provide for his own
family as to most of the means of living, and only furnish
him with partial assistance: in some cases merely with a
run for his cattle, or with wood for fuel and for building; in
a third case * with help in distress, with education for the
children and with medical assistance.

It is believed † that, so far from population being increased by these means, a curb is actually put on premature
marriages. Mr. Mill has a notion that the time may come
when a man who marries and has a family without the
means of supporting it, will be regarded as a public enemy.
Such a proceeding is now looked upon as imprudent and
somewhat discreditable. But as knowledge becomes more
diffused, Mr. Mill thinks, people will see that such a man is
the enemy not only of himself and his family, but of all
other candidates for employment and maintenance. Now
whatever may be the case hereafter in the world at large, I
can well understand that in every commune this feeling may
exist, and that there may be in this way a strong tendency
to prevent an undue increase of numbers. It often happens
in human institutions, that the immediate and obvious
tendency is counteracted, and more than counteracted, by

* Le Play, 187. 2.   † Ib.

another recondite tendency developed unexpectedly. An institution for the relief of distress has an obvious tendency at first to do that which it professes; but if it is carelessly organised it causes improvidence, and brings into existence more distress than it relieves. We are told that the Cornwallis settlement of land in India, which appeared calculated to relieve the occupiers from oppression, has, in fact, exposed the poor Hindoos to greater sufferings than those it removed. Mr. Malthus at all times denounced the poor laws as parents of evil; and when he first wrote, he maintained that the poor laws tended, among other things, to an undue increase of population, by making every man secure of a maintenance for his family. In his later editions, however, he withdrew this particular charge, having found that this tendency was counteracted by other provisions of the law. The case seems to be the same in these Communes, which when they are well constituted appear to restrain and not to promote, an undue augmentation of population.

On the whole, I should suppose that the Communal system as it actually existed in France, was formerly beneficial to the labouring classes. I have already remarked that in the days of less civilisation than the present, individualism was impossible: that every labourer must have a dependence on some one else. Either he must have been a client of some great landowner, or he must have been a member of a Commune. If he had tried to go alone, he would have been the prey of the first spoiler. Were we to draw a comparison between patronage and communism, we should see that each system had its advantages. An enlightened patron might do much to promote the progress of his dependents, whereas a Community is remarkably conser-

vative of evil as well as good. We have seen that inclosures
are generally unpopular, and are forced upon the people by
a higher power: and though in some places primary instruction is given at the expense of the Communes, education is
very often repulsed by the rural labourers as tending to
raise the sons above their parents, and thus to weaken the
essential quality of filial reverence. A Commune may,
therefore, be expected to remain in a stationary state, or
to advance very slowly, while a society depending on an
enlightened patron, will make much more rapid progress.
Communism is, like aristocracy, eminently conservative,
while patronage, like absolute monarchy, is as uncertain as
is the character of the ruling patron.

But at no time must we expect to find either of these
systems sufficient in itself to secure the happiness of the
people. Much must depend on surrounding circumstances,
and more on the character of the people themselves, this
character being principally the result of preceding circumstances. If the population has been pushed beyond the
means of subsistence, no form of administration can ward
off indigence and misery.

We have seen an example in which prudence, sobriety,
industry, were insufficient to make a community prosperous,
although the population was not large, nor, apparently,
increasing. But in this case there was the pernicious
custom, carried to excess, of so splitting up the land that
each man had to cultivate a number of little gardens, instead
of one compact farm. This peculiarity is not the result of
Communism, but of individualism, carried in that direction
to excess. Communism brings a partial remedy, such as it
is, in the form of *vaine pâture*, roughly removing the evil so
far as pasturing the flocks is concerned.

We find another example* in old Castille, of a community of which many of the members are in poor circumstances. Here also the soil is generally divided into very small properties, while the Commune possesses a great extent of wood and pasturage. The people here, however, are said to be improvident, idle, and very much prejudiced against innovations. On the other hand they retain the personal dignity of the Spaniard, with habits of sobriety. In this case Communism has failed to preserve the people from the natural consequences of idleness, prejudice, and want of foresight.

It is worthy of notice that Communes prevail very much in Spain ; and this fact is quite in harmony with what we have always heard, as to the amount of local self-government which prevails in the Peninsula, and which has been handed down from the middle ages. In a political point of view, this Communism is of the highest importance, as offering a barrier against the abuse of the royal power, and against the extension into Spain of the French system of bureaucracy.

Then again, though this kind of partial communism, that does not supersede private property, but is subsidiary to it, though this communism does not secure well being to the people, yet it is not by any means inconsistent with well being. We have seen that no man could be more opposed to common rights than was Arthur Young : that he speaks of " land cursed with common rights," and regards those rights as " detestable." Yet in one place he confesses that, as it appeared to him, these very rights promoted the prosperity of the people.

* Le Play, 176.

Young extended his enquiries into Italy and Spain, and
gives much curious information about parts of both those
countries. In Catalonia,* he found immense quantities
of mountain and other waste land. Travelling 340 miles
through the province, he estimated that not one acre in
a hundred was under cultivation. "When this fact is
connected with the reputation which the province has, of
being, next to Valentia, the best cultivated, and without
exception, the most industrious in Spain, conclusions very
unfavourable to the state and policy of that monarchy, must
necessarily be drawn by every reader." He says that "the
poverty of the people in the interior country is striking:
their towns old, ill built, dirty, and wretched; the people
ill dressed, and generally deficient in the wealth best adapted
to such a country, cattle. In the higher Pyrenées this is
not so much the case; they have cattle, and are *in every
respect in a better condition,* owing to the plenty which
great commons give in a country of good pasturage, and
where wood is in profusion. Even Young, notwithstanding
his strong prepossession, could see that in this particular
case the common rights were attended with well being of
the people: nay, he even attributes the well being to the
great commons. At the same time, he gives the Catalans
credit for great industry. He says, "We could in no
part of Catalonia, condemn the people for want of industry;
on the contrary, they seem very well to merit the character
they have gained: the activity which is seen through all
the towns upon the coast, and they are very numerous and
very populous, can hardly be greater in a country submitted
to numerous festival days by its religion. . . . . Even

* A. Young's France, 2, 317.

in the interior country we saw everywhere signs of much industry . . . . the height to which they climb the mountains in order to find a spot tolerably level, for cultivation, shows that their minds and bodies are ready for laborious exertions whenever there is a prospect of enjoying the reward." The case then, seems to stand thus: the Catalans are an industrious people: in the towns and some parts of the country they are poor, ill clothed, ill fed: in other parts where extensive common rights prevail they are in a tolerably good condition: not that they are more industrious, but that they have a better supply of pasturage and of wood. I do not conclude that these common rights are the cause of the better condition: I only conclude that common rights are perfectly consistent with a good condition of the commoners.

Among other parts of Italy, A. Young visited Tuscany, and he notes the reforms introduced into that Dukedom.* The sovereign at that time was Leopold, whom Young most justly praises as a truly enlightened prince. Leopold, says Young, abolished tithes, established a perfectly free trade in corn, extinguished the national debt that had existed from the time of the republic, and besides many other changes, abolished all rights of commonage throughout his dominions, and gave universal powers of inclosure. It is added in a note that "By the general regulations for the district of Florence, of May 23rd, 1774, it is ordered that all the landed property of the communities, kept in administration or let, shall be sold, or let on long lease." It appears to us, who are accustomed to proceed with great caution

* A. Young's France, 2. 254.

in all political changes, that such sweeping alterations as these, made by the mere fiat of an absolute sovereign, savour too much of revolutions. But the latter half of the last century was a time of changes, and it would have been happy for the world if no revolution had been more sweeping than the Tuscan one, and if every ruler had possessed half the enlightenment and half the real benevolence of Leopold. If he had lived a century later, he would probably have conducted his reforms with more consideration for the vested interests of individuals.

As to the issue of these changes, we have always been told that Tuscany is one of the most flourishing and contented of the States of Italy. Young mentions that the immediate result of the reforms was highly satisfactory. "The effects of such an enlightened system of government have been great : general assertions will not describe them so satisfactorily to a reader as particular instances. Signor Pauletti, who has been curé of the parish of Villamagna forty three years, assured me that the forty farms of which it consists have risen in value full 2,000 scudi each in that time, which is about cent. per cent. on their former value ; this improvement has been chiefly wrought of late years, and especially in the last ten." It is perfectly possible that this improvement in the value of landed property was general, and that the reforms introduced did greatly increase the productive powers of the population.

I shall conclude my remarks under this head, by referring to M. Le Play* for an account of an iron work conducted on communistic principles. "In the centre of the Alpine

* Le Play, 133.

chain, just as in Carinthia, forest property is often very much divided: charcoal prepared by labourers similar to what are described elsewhere, is consumed in iron works of two distinct kinds."

" The works of the first kind, placed under conditions mentioned before, belong to great proprietors and to companies, who arrange with the owners of the forests the price of charcoal, with an understanding, however, among each other, such as to avoid an undue competition."

" The works of the second kind belong to small proprietors of forests, who conduct them on a principle of community, in order to secure a regular demand for their charcoal. These communities of peasant manufacturers, are similar to those that are found in Sweden, and were formerly very numerous in the chain of the Alps. There are still to be seen in the Upper Bergamasque valleys a certain number of high furnaces worked on this principle."

M. Le Play goes on to say, that the communities of iron founders of this province, consist of small farming proprietors: and he mentions one of these furnaces which is the property of fifteen persons, in different proportions; each shareholder having the right of using the furnace during a week at a time.

The whole account is well worth reading, and is to me very interesting. I cannot help sharing the regret implied in the remarks, as to the probable extinction of these long established institutions. But the law of progress seems always to infer also a law of destruction. Every railroad constructed, much as it benefits the world at large, throws out of employment, and perhaps devotes to destruction, hundreds, or thousands, of carriers and coachmen and stable

boys. To them it is no consolation that the world is the
richer.for the change: their part of the world, they themselves, their families, their friends, are reduced from
competency to want. It is the same throughout nature:
life is maintained by destroying life. The gentle Hindoo
who shudders at the notion of feeding on blood, finds himself destroying myriads of insects in every draught of water
that he takes. There is no reason, however, because evil
cannot be avoided, that we should not try to reduce that
evil to the smallest compass, and on the benevolent desire
to do this is founded our extreme tenderness in England
for vested interests. I cannot feel surprise that the same
desire in the rulers of other countries, leads them to
procrastinate in the introduction of the principles of free-
trade. They may naturally pause before doing what tends
to disturb arrangements handed down for centuries. I am
myself persuaded that free trade is destined ultimately to
be the rule everywhere, and that it ought to be such; but
I am by no means sure of the desirability of carrying it
out at once, without any regard to the interests that would
be disturbed by such a sudden and momentous change.
As regards these Alpine furnaces, it is to be hoped that
they will be superseded in other ways, without serious
injury to the owners. It would seem that the principal
advantage of the manufacture, is the outlet given to the
wood grown. The iron is regarded as timber in a concentrated form, since every ton of iron requires many cart
loads of trees to make it. Destroy the sale of the iron,
and the forests become almost valueless. But it is possible
that the changes taking place, all over the world, in the
means of transport, may confer on these woods another

value. It is true that a railroad cannot be carried up the steeps of the mountains, but if one should be brought to the foot of them, means might be found, as elsewhere, of carrying the trees down. As civilization and population advance, less land is applied to the growth of wood, while more wood is every day wanted. However interesting then, these Alpine furnaces are, as relics of a time that is passing away, it is to be hoped that they will be superseded, just as it is to be hoped that the laborious hand mills of the East will be superseded by water or steam mills; and as it is to be hoped that hand labour of every sort will be more and more superseded by machinery, and by inanimate propelling powers.

I here conclude my remarks upon Communism. The régime is one that prevailed greatly in former days, and still has much sway in France but still more in Spain. In England it may almost be said to have passed away. It appears every where to have receded as civilisation has advanced; and though it may offer some resources to the indigent and improvident, which are wanting under the régime of Individualism, yet it is so much opposed to progress, to the development of individual energy, and to the advance of national greatness, that I cannot wish it restored.

I say nothing here of the efforts that have been made in France to introduce communism as a new social régime: not such communism as prevails in the country parts of France and Spain, where each man has his little property and looks to his common rights merely as subsidiary; but a communism more resembling that of the Jault, though on a more extended scale; under which all men shall live in societies like those of the early Christians, with all things in common. These schemes are less interesting to us than to our French allies, because they can hardly be said to have any root among us. Godwin is scarcely read; Owen's New Lanark is not heard of; other and inferior projectors have disappeared. It has not been our ill fate, to have wild adventurers thrown by a strange chance to the head of affairs, with power to apply the national purse to the carrying their grotesque schemes into execution: Buckingham Palace has not been the abode of the head of the Communists, nor have the royal equipages been applied to the conveyance of his sacred person. The various schemes, however, that have succeeded each other in France, would form an amusing and instructive subject even for us; and we might probably learn from them important lessons, as to the evils that attach to the régime that actually prevails among us, and as to the value of various correctives which have in this country been applied.

CHAPTER IV.

I HAVE now arrived at the fourth and last mode of existence of workmen; that of Individualism; in which men neither strengthen their weakness by living in common with other married members of the family, under the government of a patriarch, nor live in a state of dependence on a superior, receiving patronage in return, nor depend wholly, or in part, on common rights, for their maintenance. Among ourselves every one is free to go where he chooses, to live in a village or in a town, to follow what vocation he pleases, to be a farm labourer or a mechanic, to work at any trade and in any place, to marry when he likes, and to bequeath his property in any way he sees fit, leaving his family, if he so wills it, to beggary, and enriching strangers with his lands and moveables. Such is the system of Individualism, where every thing, almost, is left to the will of the individual, where no man has a legal claim for assistance from a patron, and only in a few instances even from his kindred.

Before I say any thing more as to the peculiarities of this régime, or as to its excellencies and disadvantages, I will, as in the other cases, give an example from M. Le Play. I might have referred to the case already given as a test of our author's accuracy, I mean that of the Sheffield cutler, but I take this opportunity of noticing a different example taken from Paris, as being one that is interesting in itself and that shows M. Le Play's studies in a new light.

The case I select is* the last of the thirty-six given by M.
Le Play, and is that of a rag-picker in Paris in the year
1851. It is interesting to me as showing by what steps
downwards a man may fall into this humiliating occupation,
as well as what degree of degradation is necessarily implied
by it.

The rag-picker in question " lived in a street little frequented, though broad and clean, running between the
Panthéon and the *Val-de-Grâce*, on the verge of the *faubourg
St. Marceau*. A short time before, he lived in the middle
of this *faubourg*, the narrow and dirty streets of which are
the usual abode of rag-pickers. The new habitation was
chosen partly from motives of health, partly from a wish to
be near the dealers who buy his goods once in three or four
days. Rag-pickers find a difficulty in obtaining houses any
where out of certain neighbourhoods, the offensive character
of their trade making them unpopular. This family forms
an exception, in consequence, principally, of unusual neatness and cleanliness. The family besides rises, in point
of morals, above the ordinary run of Parisian workmen,
whether the resident or the migratory ones."

A full account is then given of the different members of
this family ; of the husband, wife, and daughter ; of their
ages, habits, means of living ; of the history of the husband
and of his disposition and sentiments. The history of the
man reads, perhaps, something like a romance, though it has
no incidents that are at all surprising, and nothing out of
the ordinary career of persons left to shift for themselves
and possessed with a spirit of adventure. The incidents are,

* Le Play, 272.

of course, derived from the man himself, but as they are not
such as tend to his glorification I see no reason to doubt
their accuracy. Some years ago I had the opportunity of
testing the correctness of an account given by a working
man of his own history. The *Morning Chronicle* at that
time was collecting a series of such narratives : one of the
collectors, a gentleman of literary eminence, was introduced
to me ; he read me a history of the life of a workman whom
I knew, and I was rather surprised to find how little there
was to find fault with.

After having read M. Le Play's work I met with an
account of a meeting of the rag-pickers in Paris. It was
given in the *Daily News* of about September, 1856, and
is interesting when taken in connection with the above
account.

" The rag-gatherers *(chiffonniers)* of Paris have long
possessed a mutual benefit society, and they recently
demanded and obtained permission from the police to hold
a meeting for the purpose of examining its accounts and
revising its statutes. The meeting was held a few days
ago at a public-house bearing the sign of the Vieux Drapeau,
in the Quartier Saint Marcel. Forty-eight delegates, nomi-
nated by the whole of the rag-gathering fraternity, were
present, and each of them on entering deposited 20c., which
were disbursed in paying for the room and for sundry bottles
of *vin ordinaire*. The senior delegates were *pro tem.* called
to the chair, which was half of a cask turned bottom upwards,
and six delegates who knew how to read, and five who knew
how to write were proposed as candidates for the posts of
president and secretary. An election of these two digni-
taries having been made, the senior resigned his seat to the

elected president. Taking possession of the cask, the latter embraced the senior, and then delivered a speech, in which, after expatiating on the honesty of the rag-gatherers as a body—proved, he said, by their always giving up anything of value they might happen to find, and by their rarely figuring before the tribunals for robberies or other offences—he gave an account of the operations of the benefit society since the last meeting, and pathetically exhorted his 'dear brethren' to be friendly to each other, and united. The secretary then read, one by one, the statutes of the society, which are fifty-two in number, and asked if any delegate had any alteration to propose in them. Only two were subjected to discussion; the 17th, which provides for the "fraternal division" amongst the rag-gatherers of particular districts of the heaps of rubbish and filth that may be deposited in them; and the 52nd, relative to the contribution to be paid per month to the society, and the amount to be allowed to sick members. The first mentioned article, after due debate, was modified to the effect that not only should the heaps aforesaid be reserved to the rag-gatherers of the districts, but that on no account should one rag-gatherer presume to encroach on the heap of another; and the second was, on account of the present dearness of food modified so as to make the monthly contributions of members 50c., instead of 25c., and the daily allowance to the sick 60c., instead of 30c. The statutes having been formally approved of, a resolution adopted in previous meetings, declaring that the oldest member of the rag-gathering fraternity, one S—, aged 85, called 'the General,' should for the rest of his life be freed from any monthly payments to the society, but should enjoy all its advantages,

that he should besides be allowed 250 grammes of tobacco
a month, should have a seat of honour at all meetings and
banquets, and should at the latter be entertained gratis,
was passed unanimously with loud applause. The treasurer
was then called on to produce his accounts and cash. The
accounts having been examined, were declared correct, and
the balance in hand, which consisted of 77f. 95c., and was
deposited in an earthern pot, was counted, and was also
found exact. The delegates then removed to a public-house,
called the Pot Tricolor, at the Barrière de Fontainbleau,
where a banquet was provided for them. This place has
always been the grand rendezvous of the rag-gathering
fraternity, and formerly it was divided in three parts—one
called the " Chamber of Peers," for the élite of the calling;
that is, those who possessed a good basket, a good lantern,
and a *crochet* with the handle ornamented in copper; the
second, called the " Chamber of Deputies," for those who
possessed such things of an inferior quality, or in a dilapidated state; and the third, which was called the " Saloon
of the True Prolétaires," for the "lower orders," who had
neither basket, nor lantern, nor *crochet*, and who, consequently were obliged to pick up rags with their fingers, and
carry them in bags. But on the present occasion it was
determined that, in accordance with the progress of democratic ideas of late years, and as a mark of friendly feeling,
all distinctions of rank should be broken down, and that the
aristocracy, middle class, and lower orders of the profession
should meet at the same table. The chairman, on taking
the chair, proposed that henceforth this determination should
be vigorously adhered to as a fundamental rule of the rag-
gathering community, and his proposition was adopted with

acclamations. The guests then proceeded to attack the good things provided for them. The dish of honour was a gigantic olla podrida; the wine was ordinaire, and was contained in a high earthen jug called the "Petit Père," which was constantly being replenished from a cask called the "Mauricaud;" and the dessert was composed of the strong cheese Girarmè, of radishes, and of a petit verre of a horrible sort of brandy. The banquet was very gay, and at the dessert several toasts were drunk—one of them to "the press," which, said the president, enlightened the world, and, by its large consumption of paper, caused rag-gatherers to live. A collection made for the poor closed the banquet: it amounted to 9fr. 75c. At former gatherings the utensils of the table were chained to it, but on this occasion they were left free. The guests, however, were required to deposit the value of them, and when they gave them up on leaving the deposit was restored."

Such is the account given by the *Daily News*. Of its authenticity I have no means of judging, especially as no reference is given to any French authority. If the account be a correct one, the ordinary rag-picker is very inferior to the individual described by M. Le Play. The incident of formerly chaining the dinner equipage to the table, and that of now requiring a deposit of its value, seem to indicate no extraordinary confidence in the honesty of the fraternity. But there is here nothing inconsistent with M. Le Play, since he expressly warns his readers that the habits and manners he describes are not those of a class but of an individual.

The example I have selected from M. Le Play seems to me well fitted to illustrate the régime of Individualism, as distinguished from the three other régimes. Under the patriarchal system, a man may migrate from home, but he commonly regards his native place as the one to settling in which his hopes are directed : he toils and saves that he may return and die among his relatives. Under the system of patronage, as it exists among the slaves and their masters in the United States, and among the serfs and their seigneurs in Russia, a man does not necessarily labour for his master or on the estate of his seigneur. He may obtain permission to seek another master on condition of paying a capitation tax : but in the end he retraces his steps to his native home, and in return for his tax, looks to his master or his seigneur for assistance in distress and in old age. Among the Communes also, men migrate and often spend their early days elsewhere, but commonly with the expectation of saving a little property, and of claiming their birthright to a share of the common privileges. The case we have been considering is different from all these. The man was successively domestic servant, soldier in his native country, soldier in Algeria, printer, rag-picker, printer again, soldier a third time, deserter, and finally rag-picker. No family of married brothers awaited his return home, no seigneur demanded a capitation-tax and offered patronage, in his native place, no common rights were open to his claim : he wandered over the earth at his pleasure, free from control but devoid of sympathy. Such is Individualism.

There is no danger of our supposing that this régime necessarily leads men to such a course of life as this : we who live under the régime, know by experience that the results of it vary as do the characters of men. But lest a false impression should remain on our minds, I will cite

another case from an entirely different source. The name
of William Hutton is little known out of the neighbourhood
of Birmingham, where he flourished and died ; though a
notice some years back in a popular periodical introduced
him to an increased circle of readers. Hutton's life gives
as favourable a view of what individualism can accomplish,
as the case of the rag-picker gives an unfavourable one.
It shows how a man sprung from the lower class of the
people, half starved in his boyhood, illiterate, and during his
youth possessed with a distaste to instruction, struggling
during many long years with the narrowest circumstances,
in danger at one time of being thrust out of a parish
lest he should become chargeable to the poor rate ; may
at last by industry, energy, and frugality, acquire a competency, and finally attain to affluence, to a leading
position among his fellow citizens, and even to a highly
respectable reputation as a literary man.

Hutton's life was written by * himself but published by
his daughter. He was born in Derby in 1723, and was little
favoured by nature as to appearance ; for his mother, as he
tells us, said, that " he was the largest child she ever had,
but so very ordinary (a softer word for ugly), she was afraid
she should never love him." He adds that " whatever were
her parental affections then, he had no cause to complain
during the nine years of her life." His father at this time
must have occupied a decent position, as he was chosen
constable. But besides his gross misconduct which afterwards plunged his family into misery, he seems to have been
chargeable with a great want of parental affection ; for

* Life of William Hutton, 2nd edition, 1817.

Hutton says of his youngest brother, that his father, as he believes, never gave him a kiss in his life, " and I have the same inducement to believe he never gave me one, till I was twenty-three years of age, nor should I have been favoured with that, though the favourite son, had he been sober, but we all know liquor inspires the man."

At four years old Hutton was sent for a time to reside with an uncle and some aunts, his father's means being at the time very narrow. These people looked on him as an interloper, and taunted him with his ugliness : one of the aunts took him one day to a tavern where she got drunk, and he records his childish wonder at her constant falls on her way home. After a time he penetrated the mystery.

On his return to his father's house, he appears to have been decently dressed, as he speaks of his best suit, a cocked hat, and a walking stick. He was sent to school to " Mr. Thomas Meat, of harsh memory, who often took occasion to beat my head against the wall, holding it by the hair, but never could beat any learning into it : I hated all books but those of pictures." When he reached the age of seven years, after several abortive schemes for employing him, he was sent to the silk mill. But " it was found upon trial that nature had not given me length sufficient to reach the engine ; for out of 300 persons employed in the mill, I was by far the least and the youngest. It is happy for man that invention supplies the place of want. . . . A pair of high pattens were fabricated and tied fast about my feet to make them steady companions. They were clumsy companions which I dragged about one year, and with pleasure delivered up. I had now to rise at five every morning during seven years ; submit to the cane whenever convenient to the master; be the constant companion of the most rude and vulgar of the human race, never taught by nature, nor ever wishing to be taught. A lad, let his mind be in what state it would, must be as impudent as they, or be hunted down. I could not consider this place in any other light but that of a complete bear-garden."

It appears, however, that the boy was treated with a good deal of consideration. He was a favourite of two of the clerks and of many of the children; he was found playing at push-pin in church whither he had been enticed to go, but he was ridiculed, not punished: his hat blew off into the river, the mill owner replaced it for him with one having a silver tassel. At home he stole all his mother's stock of apples, but instead of punishing him she concealed his fault. But on another occasion when he imprudently replied to his mother's just reproaches, she secured him a chastisement, which according to the notions of punishment that then prevailed was none too severe.

In the year 1733, when Hutton was in his tenth year, occurred the great calamity of his life, the death of his mother. The Chinese are said to have a proverb, that the three greatest misfortunes which can happen to a man, are the loss, in boyhood, of his father, in middle age, of his wife, in old age, of his son. Those who have unhappily experienced these misfortunes know how true is the adage. They have felt in their own persons how ill the place of a father is supplied, even by the most sensible and affectionate mother: how the waywardness of youth wants its due control; how little the inexperience of the mother can supply the worldly knowledge which is communicated by a father, unconsciously, and without effort: how a young man, abandoned to his own crude notions and visionary expectations, either makes shipwreck of his life and dies disgraced, or at the best falls into errors, and incurs obligations, which it requires the devotion of a long term of years to redeem. But in Hutton's case the blow was of a different kind: he lost his mother. Probably to him this was a greater misfortune than the loss of his other parent. The mother seems to have been sensible and affectionate, as well as able to exercise a wholesome influence over her husband. But a father who never kissed even a favorite child, unless when maudlin in his liquor, could not be expected to exert an useful control over his family. Had he died, his widow would have been pinched, but the children might have maintained themselves and her, at any rate with such assistance as in England can always be obtained by the deserving.

A few days after the mother's death, the father determined on giving up housekeeping: he sold the furniture, spent the money, and took lodgings for himself and three children with a widow who had four of her own. "My mother gone, my father at the alehouse, and I among strangers, my life was forlorn. I was almost without a home, nearly without clothes, and experienced a scanty cupboard. At one time I fasted from breakfast one day till noon the next, and even then dined upon only flour and water boiled into an hasty-pudding. I was also afflicted with the chin-cough and biles." The father "spent all he could get in liquor."

In 1735 the summer being very dry, the water was insufficient to keep the mill regularly going, and this gave the boys some holidays. The following year, "Richard Porter, my master, had made a wound in my back with his cane. It grew worse. In a succeeding punishment, the point of his cane struck the wound, which brought it into such a state that a mortification was apprehended. My father was advised to bathe me in Keddleston water. A cure was effected and I yet carry the scar." However indignant we may feel at such brutality, we cannot much wonder that in times when a schoolmaster punished a little boy by dashing his head against the wall, a manufacturer should use his cane with indiscriminating harshness; and that in the case of a boy in a bad state of health, the above frightful consequences should follow. The use of the stick, though it has not quite disappeared from among us, flourishes only in the East.

When Hutton was in his thirteenth year, he exhibited some signs of the talent that afterwards distinguished him: he paid a visit of three days to Nottingham, and on his return gave such a description of his journey " as could not be expected from his age. Every auditor looked up to him, and he took the lead in conversation." As he approached fourteen, it was necessary to fix on a permanent trade: the father refused his consent both to wool-combing, his own trade, and to stocking-making, his brother's trade; but at last consented to the latter. Hutton left the silk mill, after cutting his initials on a rail: fifty-three years afterwards, and again eighteen years after that, the old man visited the scene of his early labours. Even the long period of half a century had failed to erase from his mind the memory of his sufferings. " Many hundreds had quitted the place during my stay, but not one with regret; a place

most curious and pleasing to the eye, but which gave me
a seven years' heart-ache. No friendships are formed there
but such as the parties are willing to break."

In his fifteenth year Hutton removed to Nottingham, to
remain thirteen years. He went to live with his uncle,
whom he describes as generous, friendly, and seriously religious, but linked to a wife who was hypocritical and
niggardly, and who ruled her husband. He complains that
the terms agreed upon were too hard, as he was required
to earn 5s. 10d. a week, with the understanding that if he
fell short or exceeded this sum, the loss or profit was to
be his own. Out of this supposed fund of his own he was
to find his clothes. The stocking trade must have yielded
better wages then than it does now, comparing it with
other trades, if a boy of fourteen could fairly be required
to earn 5s. 10d. a week on the average. The result was
that during the first year he earned less than the stipulated
sum. The following year he got into the " fine frame,"
and was expected to earn 6s. 9d., and from the difficulty
of surpassing this, found himself badly dressed. " Youth
is the time to dress; the time in which it is not only
excusable but laudable. I envied every new coat: I had
the wish to earn one but not the power." His complaint in
this respect seems justified by more than wounded vanity :
for the first quarter of 1740 was unusually cold, so cold
that people complained of finding their breath frozen on the
sheet at night; yet Hutton at the beginning of the frost,
which was the severest part, wore a thin waistcoat without
a lining, and no coat. A boy who was earning five shillings
to six shillings a week, when wages were much lower, and
living much cheaper than at present, had a right to warm

clothing. No wonder the apprentices were dissatisfied. Of
the two who were in the house when Hutton first went,
"the lesser ran away and was heard of no more; and the
greater was sold, and ruined his master." (I suppose,
transferred for a consideration to another master whom he
ruined.) Another staid from Monday till Saturday. A
fourth came from Derby, ran away, returned, and finally
enlisted. Hutton is not much given to praise, and therefore I wonder he calls his uncle a generous and friendly
man, unless we are to suppose that the penurious treatment
of the apprentices is to be ascribed to the aunt. He says
of her, "I was to be grudged every meal I tasted. My
aunt kept a constant eye upon the food and the feeder.
This curb galled my mouth to that degree that to this day
I do not eat at another's table without fear. And afterwards, under the head of 1740, "The frost, followed by
an untoward summer, brought on a rise of provisions. It
was considered by the mistress as almost a sin to eat."

Matters now went on more smoothly: a "genteel suit of
clothes" was obtained: "I was rising into notice: a foundation was laid for a brighter day, when an unhappy quarrel
between my uncle and me, upon a mere trifle, caused me
to run away, blasted my views, sunk me in the dust, and
placed me in a degraded point of view, from which I did not
recover for five years." The account given of this piece
of folly is too long to be transcribed, but it is well worthy of
study by all who have any interest in apprentices: by
masters, who may learn the unjustifiable absurdity of violent
conduct: by magistrates, who may see how a boy of talent,
spirit, and general good conduct, may be hastily driven into
absconding. From my limited experience I should say that

in my own neighbourhood, masters are sometimes guilty of aggravated assaults on their apprentices, but that magistrates are generally very unwilling to punish an apprentice for neglect, unless the youth has been summoned before them repeatedly.

The race week was the occasion of the quarrel. Some time was lost, and in the last day, a deficiency of an hour, followed by a foolish question on the part of the uncle, and a truthful, but perhaps impertinent answer, led to a beating so severe and long continued that the whole neighbourhood was disturbed. The youth was nearly eighteen years old, made some pretentions to dress, and was more hurt in mind even than in body. " How should I face those whom I had often laughed at and whipped with the rod of satire ?" His fellow apprentice had often proposed that they should run away together, but Hutton declares that he was restrained by an unwillingness to cause a loss to his uncle. If the other apprentice had gone with him the loss would have been double : he therefore went alone. He packed up his moveables in a bag, took 2s., which I am sorry to say were not his own, and left the town. The first day he arrived at Derby, and narrowly missed being seen by his father. The second day he reached Burton, having travelled twenty eight miles and spent nothing. " I was an economist from my cradle and the character never forsook me." At Lichfield he was robbed of his bags containing his best clothes, but this did not disturb his resolution to see Nottingham no more. He wandered to Walsall, Birmingham, Coventry, Nuneaton, Hinckley ; and was everywhere met with the same observation that he was a runaway apprentice. At the last of these places a Derby man persuaded him to return home, and he reached Derby about a week after he first ran away, and then returned to his work at Nottingham. It appears that years elapsed before he recovered his self respect, and five years before he could again afford to dress decently.

Hutton was always active, and at this time was more bent on amusing himself than on raising a fund by over-work : he attended meetings for the practice of athletic exercises, and obtained a bell-harp on which he taught himself to play. He also constructed a dulcimer, the box being made out of an old trunk once the property of Thomas Parker, the first Earl of Macclesfield. He showed in this instance both the mechanical aptitude and the perseverance, which afterwards enabled him to rise from the ranks of the *stockingers*. He had no tools but the hammer-key and plyers used in his trade, a pocket knife, and a fork with one remaining prong. He sold his musical instrument for sixteen shillings and bought a coat.

In 1744 Hutton was of age, and he thought with anxiety that " he had hitherto been under the care of others, but now must attend to the compass himself, and steer the vessel." His prospects were not bright. " I had served two seven years, to two trades, neither of which I could subsist upon. During this servitude I had earned about £7. over-work, which with a debt I had contracted to my uncle, of thirty shillings, had frugally furnished me with apparel."

It appears that he had before this time got rid of his boyish aversion to books. " My uncle took notice of me. I attended him in his walks and his visits ; had some knowledge of history, and could speak tolerably well. The rebellion broke out, which produced sufficient matter for inquiry and conversation." He was now living as a journey-man with his uncle, and wanted to have a frame on his own account, but his aunt's malignant influence prevented this. The following year he borrowed £10. from his brother-in-law, and bought a frame of his own.

Hutton owed his subsequent rise in life, indirectly, to his fondness for books, and partly to his poverty which pre-vented him from buying books in the ordinary way. To gratify his taste he bought works of small value in worn-out bindings. " I learnt to patch, procured paste, varnish, &c., and brought them into tolerable order; erected shelves, and arranged them in the best manner I was able. If I purchased shabby books, it is no wonder that I dealt with a shabby bookseller who kept his working apparatus in his shop. It is no wonder, too, if by repeated visits I became acquainted with this shabby bookseller, and often saw him at work; but it is a wonder and a fact, that I never saw him perform one act but I could perform it myself, so strong was the desire to attain the art. I made no secret of my pro-gress, and the bookseller rather encouraged me, and that for two reasons: I bought such rubbish as no one else would; and he had often an opportunity of selling me a cast-off tool for a shilling, not worth a penny. As I was below every degree of opposition, a rivalship was out of the ques-tion. The first book I bound was a very small one, Shaks-peare's Venus and Adonis. I showed it to the bookseller. He seemed surprised. I could see jealousy in his eye. However he recovered in a moment, and observed that though he had sold me the books and tools *remarkably cheap*, he could not think of giving so much for them again. He had no doubt but I should break."

" He offered me a worn-down press for two shillings, which no man could use, and which was laid by for the fire. I considered the nature of its construction, bought it, and paid the two shillings. I then asked him to favour me with a hammer and a pin, which he brought with half a conquering smile and half a sneer. I drove out the garter-pin, which being galled prevented the press from working, and turned another square, which perfectly cured the press. He said, in anger, ' If I had known you should not have had it.' However I could see he consoled himself with the idea that all must return in the end. This proved for forty-two years my best binding press."

Soon after this the uncle died, and Hutton felt his loss severely, having been really attached to him. Trade was very bad, and his frame being his own the hosiers would not employ him, because they had barely employment for their own frames. It appears a great hardship that a man should be set aside because he has a little property of his own. But on the other hand, I presume, when trade was good the owner of a frame earned far more than the hirer of one. A man who chooses to be a master must inevitably take the risks that attach to the position. I have seen a similar hardship in my own town. A mechanic when trade is good, runs into debt with his master, while his comrade, an equally good workman, keeps out of debt. When trade falls off and only one of the two men can be employed, the master keeps the debtor that he may work out the sum owing. The provident man is discharged to sink or swim as he may. I cannot praise the wisdom or the justice of the proceeding. During this year, Hutton tried his pen for the first time: he produced some trifles in rhyme which were never published: he speaks modestly of them, and, no doubt, justly. He seems often to have had wishes for marriage, and records, pleasantly enough, attentions paid him by various women. However, he had a true Malthusian determination not to burden himself with a family that he could not support. If the world generally, possessed half as much self control, indigence would soon cease.

Hutton was now in his twenty-sixth year, engaged in a trade that yielded poor wages, and such as would not allow him to settle in life. " I had observed such severe penury among the married stockingers, that the thoughts of a wife were horrid, unless I had been in a situation to support one." He naturally, therefore, was desirous of turning to account the knowledge of bookbinding that he had picked up. He occasionally got a book to bind from an acquaintance, but in order to set up in the trade, better tools and materials were wanting. His sister obtained three guineas for him, sewed them up in his shirt collar to save them from thieves, and with eleven shillings in his pocket he set out to walk to London. He walked fifty one miles the first day, in spite of blistered feet, and spent fivepence: the third day he reached London. He was fond of seeing "curiosities," but he spent only one penny in this way, for a sight of Bedlam. His provincial notions caused him some astonishment at St. Stephen's. " As I had always applied deification to great men, I was surprised to see a hawker cram her twopenny pamphlet into a member's face: and that he, instead of caning her, took not the least notice." It would seem that the use of the stick to support authority had declined in London, but still prevailed elsewhere. He had travelled 125 miles to London, spent three days there, was

on foot the whole time staring at the public buildings, and
started to walk home again with four shillings in his pocket.
He fell lame, shed some tears, as was his habit in common
with Homer's heroes and Frenchmen, determined to bear
his pain, and on the ninth day reached home, having spent
10s. 8d. Adding the loss of six days work, this was as cheap
travelling as if third class railway trains had commenced
running. It beats M. Le Play's migratory Russians.

After consultation with his attached sister, Hutton determined on settling at Birmingham, but as a preparatory step
opened a shop on market days at Southwell. The following
year he removed to Birmingham; he was still so poor that
he had no great coat to protect him from the rain. He
made a start with a degree of success that satisfied him.
He found he could live on five shillings a week, and at the
end of a year had saved £20. Apparently, he must have
earned about thirteen shillings a week: it is rather singular
that he should have done so ill at Nottingham; if as an
apprentice boy of fourteen to fifteen years old he gained
five shillings to six shillings a week, surely he might have
gained fifteen shillings to eighteen shillings a week as a
man. One difficulty now occurred. Birmingham, indeed,
was not a corporate town, and therefore there was no book-
binders' guild to prevent the approach of a stranger: but
the overseers of the poor regarded every new comer with
jealousy, and had the power to remove him. During two
years he was threatened with the exercise of this authority.
With many misgivings, in his second year, he took a house
at the annual rent of £8. He soon enjoyed the pleasure
of " frequently amusing myself with marshalling in battalion
fifty bright guineas, a sight I had not been accustomed

to." At thirty-two years old he married, and married very happily.

Hutton had now ceased to be a workman : he belonged to the middle classes of society, had a few hundred pounds of capital, and had laid the foundation of a fortune. He was, therefore, removed from that class with which this book is concerned. I will only add that he continued to be a thriving man, became a paper dealer, lost many hundred pounds by a mill-speculation, purchased a good deal of land, became overseer, was appointed one of the Commissioners of the Court of Requests for the recovery of small debts, continued for twenty years the most influential of those Commissioners, wrote several books such as Histories of Derby and of Birmingham, and a History of the Court where he presided, begat sons and daughters, and dying, at a very advanced age, left his property to descendants of his own name who still flourish in the town of his adoption. The great incident of his later life arose out of the riots of 1791. He was a Dissenter and obnoxious to some of the Church-and-King rioters : they burnt him out ; and though he ultimately recovered a great part of his pecuniary loss, he was so disgusted with this treatment that he refused to take any more part in the affairs of the town.

This example may well be put as a set off against M. Le Play's rag-picker, to show what Individualism can accomplish. At one time no prospects could be more discouraging: Hutton in early life was steeped in poverty to the very lips. A half-starved child in a mill, punished with dangerous severity, an apprentice shivering in the frost without a coat, a runaway wandering over the country, not free from a charge of felony, a stockinger without employment, a self-taught bookbinder narrowly escaping removal by the over-seers as a probable pauper, he seems to have experienced most of the mortifications to which indigence is exposed. Afterwards he enjoyed success, wealth, power, literary success. It is said that his own struggles did not make him very sympathetic with others in distress, if, at least, his sympathy is to be estimated by his readiness to render assistance. He knew how hard it is to get money, and he valued money accordingly. Perhaps it would be fairer to say that that which was a praiseworthy frugality when he was earning thirteen shillings a week, became parsimony in the capitalist and landowner; and that the laudable habit of thirty years' continuance was too strongly formed to be broken.

This life of Hutton discloses to us the great difficulties that a working man frequently has to contend with. Cases like this are of daily occurrence, and it would be well if there were no worse cases. Hutton's father seems to have been a man of sense, and desirous of putting his children forward in life. He was reluctant to put this son to stocking weaving: it was his poverty rather than his will that consented. But this poverty was the result of his own improvidence and intemperance, these bad habits having altogether gained the mastery after the death of his wife. Thus was Hutton taught a trade by which, as it seems, he could make but a very scanty living. I have always heard that the stockingers are miserably paid, and I am rather pleased to be told that this was the case formerly. I am glad to find that their present depressed state has been handed down from former days and is not of modern growth. The cause of this wretched condition I suspect to be the habit of taking a number of apprentices. The uncle appears to have had three of them regularly, and if all had served out their articles and adopted the business, this one man would have added three workmen to the trade every seven or eight years. If he continued this practice during thirty years he would have brought twelve men into the trade. This calculation is hypothetical, and many deductions have to be made to reduce it to practice: but there is quite enough left to make it probable that this was the cause why the men were so badly paid. Let the enemies of combinations say what they please, I should think such workmen fully justified in combining together to limit the number of apprentices, if they could see a chance of obtaining success in their attempt.

If any one is desirous of having another example of the struggles of a working man, I would advise him to read once more the life of Dr. Franklin, who from beginnings not quite so mean as Hutton's, rose to an eminence infinitely higher: a man who "snatched the thunderbolt from heaven and the sceptre from tyrants." * Franklin was many years a contemporary of Hutton, having been born seventeen years earlier. He was fortunate in possessing an excellent father, a man of sense and good conduct. He was to a great degree self taught, having been taken from school at ten years old, the age at which boys are now generally put under the care of a master. He was afterwards apprenticed to his brother who was a printer; but he took an unfair advantage of a legal difficulty, stole away, and contrived to

---

* Eripuit cælo fulmen, sceptrumque tyrannis.—*French Epitaph.*

get to New York and thence to Philadelphia. This ill conduct he mentions as one of the errors of his life. Another error was his conduct to the young woman he ultimately married. He came to London, and though he was engaged to her, never wrote to her, but treated her with entire neglect: the results being that she married another man who deserted her, and that Franklin afterwards married her without any certainty that the former husband was dead. A third error that he frankly records was of a pecuniary character, and in the eye of the law was of a far graver cast: a friend authorised him to receive a sum of money; he received it, but instead of remitting, spent it. This was going rather near to the commission of embezzlement, but in after years the money was repaid.

Such was the commencement of the life of a great, and really good man; and to make the prospect less promising, he became a dabbler in metaphysics of a bad kind. "I was scarce fifteen, when after doubting by turns several points as I found them disputed in the different books I read, I began to doubt the Revelation itself. Some books against deism fell into my hands; they were said to be the substance of the sermons which had been preached at Boyle's lectures. It happened that they wrought an effect on me quite contrary to what was intended by them. For the arguments of the Deists which were quoted to be refuted, appeared to me much stronger than the refutations. My arguments perverted some others, particularly Collins and Ralph: but each of these having wronged me greatly without the least compunction, and recollecting Keith's conduct towards me, (who was another freethinker), and my own towards Vernon

and Miss Read, which at times gave me great trouble : I began
to suspect that this doctrine, though it might be true, was
not very useful." Under the former impressions he had
published a pamphlet with a motto from Pope, " Whatever
is, is right," &c. ; " and which from the attributes of God,
his infinite wisdom, goodness, and power, concluded that
nothing could possibly be wrong in the world : and that
vice and virtue were empty distinctions, no such things
existing." Afterwards he wrote a pamphlet on the other
side of the question, but " The great uncertainty I found
in metaphysical reasonings disgusted me, and I quitted
that kind of reading and study for others more satisfactory."

Such was the unpropitious commencement of the great
philosopher, politician, patriot, and legislator ; of a man destined to earn a reputation as wide as the world, and second
only to that of the immortal Washington. Many persons
witnessing his early career, acquainted with the dangerous
tenets he had adopted as to the indifference of vice and
virtue, and reading by this light the errors and vices of
which he was guilty, would have thought him more likely
to prove a felon than a patriot, destined rather to spend
his latter days as a convict, than as an honoured envoy of
his country in Paris.

The humiliating incidents of Franklin's early life, seem
to me the most valuable part of his autobiography ; a part
which should be studied by fathers, by schoolmasters, by
employers, by magistrates. We may learn from it what
we require to be reminded of at every turn, that we should
not judge of any man by a single action, or even by two

or three actions. Burns, a man sorely tempted, sings that though we may pretty well judge what a man has done, we know not what he has resisted. We of the middle classes, gently nurtured, provided with every thing we really want, carefully trained for the vocation to which we are destined, yet neither flattered by menials nor pampered with indulgences, can scarcely estimate the temptations to which other classes are exposed. We are far too exacting towards our sons, our dependents, and those charged before us with petty offences. Yet we must be aware that in our own class, offences are committed, and especially by the young whose moral habits " are still in the gristle," and have not hardened into the strength of manhood. I have myself known several instances of boys of my own standing who have been found out in petty thefts, not such as robbing an orchard out of bravado, but petty thefts of a mean kind : yet these boys have turned out men of high principle and unquestioned honour. I have sometimes deeply regretted to hear that a boy has been expelled from a large school for such a fault. Far better, in my opinion, for a first offence of such a kind, to almost abstain from punishment, to treat it as too grave a matter for ordinary discipline, to caution the offender solemnly, and then, if a second offence occurs, to expel him.

Neither masters nor fathers should expect so much as they do. In reading the life of Niebuhr the historian, I was painfully struck with the horror he expressed at the mere notion that his son could be guilty of any grave wrong. Such a morbid fear tends to cause the evil dreaded, because it leads to withholding a boy from ordinary temptations, and thus fails to develop the mental muscle which alone can be a permanent protection. In dealing with the working classes the same leading idea should be present. They are always exposed to far greater temptations than are offered to us: let us overlook, or slightly punish, first offences, or, strictly speaking, an offence on the first conviction.

CHAPTER V.

HAVING given these cases to illustrate Individualism as distinguished from other social systems, it is natural to enquire what are the advantages and disadvantages that attach to it. The great and striking advantage is, that it gives room for a freer development of man. If we were all of us mere animals, with no desires for any thing better than the pleasures of the body, if we were distinguished from the lower races only by this, that while they are governed by instinct we are governed by reason, they and ourselves being equally bent on animal gratifications and equally incapable of any thing higher, if our boasted reason were good for nothing but to enable us the better to eat and drink and warm ourselves, and to enjoy all the other agrecable sensations of which our frames are capable, it might be a question whether what we call advances in civilisation would not really be a misfortune. It might be contended that races in a more backward state than ours, being more secure than ourselves of freedom from want, are really in a better state than ourselves. I do not by any means give my assent to such a proposition even as this, though I can understand how it may be believed. But if we regard man as something far higher than a mere animal, if we feel within ourselves emotions before which our bodily pleasures fade into insignificance, if we experience mental gratifications such as lead us to contemn our outward sensations by comparison, if the most worldly of us are conscious of aspirations after something more noble than the epicurean enjoyments of the day, we shall then pronounce the most worthy of our esteem that social system which tends in the highest degree to develop these higher functions of our nature. Judged by this test it can hardly be doubtful that Individualism is the régime we should prefer. We can scarcely believe that the thinking being, the moral agent, can grow to perfection where he is subject to the absolute control of a chief, who has power to dictate to him the hours he shall labour, the work he shall perform, the amusements he shall enjoy: so drilled to obedience, how can a man's powers be called forth ? It is by thought and consequent action, by resistance to temptation, by a struggle with difficulties, that, in the highest sense, a man is made. Under the control of Communism the prosperous Hutton, a useful citizen and an example of successful energy to his neighbours, would have been all his life a dull tiller of the soil, or at best the head of a household of such tillers of the soil. In countries where society is so constituted, slow is the advance, stagnant and dull is the little world of men. If we turn to Patronage, is the slave better situated ; is the serf even better situated ? Bowing to the nod of a master or a seigneur, worshipping a created man as the arbiter of his destiny, there is no room for the growth of his understanding or of his heart.

But putting aside this question as to the higher destinies of man, and regarding him only in a material light, as a creature whose first business is to secure the means of existence in such plenty as to make life a blessing, is it true, as M. Le Play alleges, that if Individualism raises many men to a higher elevation, it leaves others to sink lower than they would sink under other circumstances? No doubt it is true that it is a dangerous thing to emancipate men suddenly from control to which they have long been accustomed. A boy carefully brought up by his parents at home, kept from the knowledge of evil, watched day and night with tender solicitude, turns out at the mess table or the university the wildest spirit in his circle. The negroes at the Cape, in many instances, we are told, set suddenly free by our Emancipation Act, refused to work any more than was necessary to keep themselves in existence and to obtain a supply of liquor; gave themselves up to drunkenness and debauchery; and found a lot probably far more wretched than the one they had escaped from. But these are solitary instances. The evils are caused by the suddenness of the change. To appreciate freedom men must be trained to it: they must learn gradually to resist temptation when left to themselves. Now, taking the case where men are born to perfect freedom of action, as in the Western States of Europe, is it true that there is more misery, more indigence, than in countries like Russia, where family communism and patronage are both in full vigour? We have not the means of answering this question by a reference to facts. If we were at liberty to send a royal commission, or a parliamentary committee, into Russia, (a mode of enquiry that has M. Le Play's warm approval as to our own kingdom), the examination of competent witnesses would probably disclose miseries which at present are unnoticed, but which would excite our indignation. It was formerly supposed that Scotland, with a very informal poor law, was blessed with a better administration of the indigent than we could boast of securing with a world of machinery and at a frightful expense. Some influential persons found reason to doubt the efficiency of the Scotch administration of charity : a parliamentary enquiry took place : the result covered the self-satisfied boasters with confusion. It was found that the system which had prevailed was cheap, or more properly speaking parsimonious ; for a thing is not in the best sense cheap unless it is also good. The system cost little, but it did its work badly. The widow and the orphan, the aged and the cripple, lived or died as it might happen : if they died they were buried out of the way ; if they lived they were unheard, and perhaps felt no particular sense of injustice, since they were treated as all so situated were treated. I say nothing of pauper lunatics, because in our own country, with all our expense, the treatment of those unhappy beings has not long been such as would bear the light. Now if we could go to Russia with the means of analysis that we took with us to Scotland, we might perhaps find things going on there such as to make us hesitate, before saying, that the squalid misery of our great towns is worse than any thing in Russia. If we brought out the inmates of Russian log-houses and examined them, we might find, as we found in Scotland, unsuspected and heart-rending distress.

To make the comparison complete, many other points would have to be noticed. Especially we should have to consider the effect of a failure of a harvest. A dearth may happen any where ; in many countries famines are perfectly possible. Harvests will vary from year to year, and in some regions, we are told, they occasionally fail almost altogether ; and a very important feature in any régime is its power of

warding off such a misfortune, or of mitigating its consequences. In England deaths from immediate starvation are
very rare, even in those worst parts of our large towns which
are so justly denounced. There must be years, I suspect, in
Russia when thousands are unable to obtain food to keep
them alive. According to law, as promulgated by the Czar,
every landowner is bound to keep in his granaries corn
enough for a year's consumption : but the *Englishwoman
in Russia* tells us that during the Irish famine, when prices
went up very high in consequence of the efforts of our
government to import food, the Russian seigneurs were
induced by the unusual rates to empty their granaries and
so to leave their serfs to the risk of starvation. Dependence
on a patron must always be precarious, since the character
of the patron is uncertain : a good and experienced man to
day may be succeeded by a young man, a spendthrift or
gambler, to morrow.

Besides, the influence of the seigneur may be used for
evil. It appears that in the military recruiting which is
constantly going on, a certain number of men is required
from an estate, and it is left to the seigneur to determine
who shall go. If a serf behaves ill, it is a common thing to
threaten that unless he amends he shall be sent as a soldier.
This may generally be a useful means of coercion, and may
serve to stimulate the idle, and to curb the refractory : it
may, however, be grossly abused, and become the means of
obtaining from serfs concessions that no free man would grant.
The absence of a brother may be convenient to a licentious
lord or to his deputy.

This patronage is, on a small scale, and in a modified degree, what absolute power is. We see the abuse of the

latter in such works as the pyramids, which are imagined to have cost myriads of human lives, and of which the huge blocks may be regarded as cemented with human blood: we see it too, in such cases as the building of St. Petersburg, which is believed to have been effected at a sacrifice of a hundred thousand men, dead of cold, and toil, and fever. If Individualism allows its hundreds or thousands to perish by the fault of themselves or of their husbands and fathers, the system of patronage and dependence sacrifices millions to gratify the whims of superiors.

M. Le Play refers the growth of Individualism principally to two circumstances, the invention of the steam engine, and the adoption of coal instead of wood as manufacturing fuel. Under the old construction of society, manufactures were to a considerable extent carried on in towns, but these were limited by the organisation of trades into guilds. A man could not work as a carpenter or a smith, unless he had been regularly initiated by serving as an apprentice, and by shewing afterwards that he could work in such a way as not to disgrace his trade. The various rich companies of London, the Goldsmiths, the Merchant Tailors, and a score of others, are remnants of these arrangements. In some parts of the Continent they still exist in full vigour; and a man cannot be employed in Vienna, for example, without having served as an apprentice; then, having made the tour of the country he works as a journeyman, and finally, if he can raise funds, he buys a mastership, of which the number is limited. Some persons have thought this organisation advantageous as setting a natural limit to population in this direction; but it is far from true that such arrangements preserve a manufacturing population in a good condition. A man, after all, can only be safe when he is the master of his own destiny, and when training has made him equal to the task.

However, whatsoever might be the advantages of this system, it is pretty clear that the two circumstances I have referred to were quite enough to break it up, independently of the tendency of the age to throw off all restraints. The great inventions in the iron trade, of smelting with coke instead of charcoal, and of using rollers instead of tilt hammers, by wonderfully reducing the cost gave an impetus to the trade that has extended the manufacture a hundred fold. This has caused a concentration of a vast population in the coal districts. The invention of the steam engine greatly promoted this concentration. Before the time of Watt, water furnished the only available motive force, since windmills were not found of sufficient power, or uniformity, for any thing like general manufacturing purposes. Even water has the disadvantages of being greatly diminished by the droughts of summer, and, in cold countries, of being frozen into stillness during many winter months : it can only be depended on during spring and autumn, whereas steam is equally available at all times. Streams are still used to turn mills, the steam engines being generally an addition to the motive force of the world, and not a substitute for the water-power already appropriated. We find from M. Le Play that the town of Solingen in Rhenish Prussia, is the most important place on the Continent for the manufacture of cutlery, being superior to our Sheffield as to the commoner articles, in which a low price rather than excellence is required. The mills at Solingen continue to depend upon water for their power : as a consequence of this the workmen have been much scattered over the country round, so as to take advantage of the falls of the streams. Of late years there has been a tendency to a concentration of the forgers and other workmen in the town itself, though the grinders must of necessity remain on the banks of the streams. If steam engines were introduced into the town, the grinders, like the other men, would have to leave the country. Thus, the use of coal for smelting iron, and the adoption of steam as mill power, have collected the workmen formerly scattered among the forests for fuel, and on the courses of streams for water power, and have concentrated them near the coal fields.

New districts of population have thus grown up, and have superseded the old seats of industry, or have thrown them, by comparison, into the shade. These new masses of people, springing into existence just at the time when the doctrines of *laisser-faire* were spreading among the reading classes, and when a jealousy of government interference was felt by the majority, received but little attention from any one; were left to their own devices; and were allowed in many neighbourhoods to fall into an uncultivated, semi-barbarous, condition, disgraceful to the world. It may be a matter to rejoice in, that guilds and organised trades, were not introduced into Staffordshire and Lancashire, that any man who could learn to work at a furnace or at a pair of rolls, should be at liberty to do so; but it is a matter of deep regret and shame, that the morals, and even the physical condition, of the people, were left to hap-hazard.

M. Le Play looks with pain at the concentration of population in the coal districts of the world, and casts a regretful glance at the manufactures of former days, dispersed among the hills and forests, and up and down the river courses. The cessation of manufactures during the heats of summer, he regards as a means of recruiting the health and spirits of the mechanics, by setting them at liberty to help the farmers in their reaping. The cessation during the winter furnishes the opportunity of carrying the heavy goods to market in sledges, and gives time to the mechanics to repair their houses, furniture, and clothes. This primitive organisation, which makes men half mechanics, half agriculturists, has to M. Le Play a much greater charm than he finds in the manufacturing districts, where men toil from childhood till death at one unvarying employment. He feels that though the division of labours makes industry more productive, it is unfavourable to the development of happiness : that a man who spends all his days in front of a furnace is inferior to him who varies his employment by reaping in the summer, and by domestic occupations in the winter : that a man who all the day and every day is cutting out, or nailing together, boxes, is inferior to him who executes every variety of carpenter's labour, besides being his own gardener, smith, and tailor. This notion is something like that of Adam Smith, who thought that, comparing town and country labourers, the mechanic must be inferior to the farm labourer in intelligence, because the mechanic is constantly repeating one simple process, while the farm labourer is a ploughman to day, a sower to morrow, and on a third day goes to market or turns his hand to hedging and ditching. That Adam Smith was mistaken is tolerably evident to every one who is familiar with these two kinds of labourers. Town mechanics have plenty of faults, but want of intelligence is not among the number : they are far more quick witted than country labourers. The concentration of population, the collision of minds, the better opportunities of education, the higher wages which enable mechanics to meet together more in public houses, all tend to sharpen the wit whatever other consequences may follow.

Concentration of population, then, has its advantages. Indeed, a certain degree of concentration is so necessary to progress in civilisation, that the means of securing it in the early stages of society have been made a matter of grave discussion. Mr. Gibbon Wakefield, in his *England and America*, has expressed himself very strongly as to this necessity, and has used phrases which may almost seem to convey a defence of slavery on this very ground, as being under some circumstances the only means of accomplishing the concentration required. At the same time there is, of course, a limit to this as to every other principle. Concentration of population, like most other things, may be in excess.

I sympathise with M. Le Play in his approval of a population which unites in the same individual the character of mechanic and country labourer, if only such an union can be formed without serious detriment to the efficiency of work. It is often a wonder to me how mechanics spend the many days in the year which they cannot employ in their trades. In small towns many of them have gardens, either around their houses, or detached from them at a short distance. But as manufacturing towns grow, these arrangements become impossible for most men. I myself have seen hundreds of acres of small gardens of this sort converted into ground for building, to the great vexation of the previous occupants. The tending these small plots occupied many an idle day which now hangs heavily, and kept thousands of men out of taverns. The time may come when, by means of railroads, mechanics may again have the country put within their reach, when they may have the opportunity given them of passing and repassing a few miles every day, so as to have a house with a garden, and even with land enough to keep a cow. Such an opportunity would, I believe, much tend to raise the character, as well as to improve the health of the town population.

But whatever may be the advantages of a concentration of population up to a certain point, or its evils when it is in excess, it seems pretty clear that, as M. Le Play states, it is this concentration around the coal fields that has almost extinguished the old régime of manufactures which were placed, like the works in the Alps, to be near the forest fuel; and that this concentration has helped to put an end to the old trades and guilds of corporate towns. Thus have the invention of the steam engine, and the application of coal to the manufacture of iron, been the means of greatly promoting the extension of Individualism.

But there is one instance in which, as it seems to me, such an extension has taken place from causes of an entirely different character. If there be any country in which manufactures have made little progress, it is Ireland: the linen manufacture is the only considerable one that is spoken of as flourishing. We never hear of any Irish iron, and the common fuel of the people is peat. Yet Ireland certainly changed very much during the last century as to the organisation of labour, and the change that took place was from a régime of Patronage to one of Individualism. I must, however, qualify my assertion here thus far, that some iron was made in Ireland during the last century, though on a very small scale.

The best authority that I am acquainted with as to the state of Ireland in the last century, is Arthur Young, from whom I have already quoted pretty largely as to the condition of France. Young's Tour in Ireland took place before the one in France, and in introducing this latter he refers to his former book, quoting a conversation with a friend to account for the small sale of his Irish book. I quite agree with the respondent that the form of that book was well contrived to prevent people from reading it : that it contains much valuable information, but is arranged in such a way as to make it about as well adapted for ordinary perusal, as Johnson's Dictionary or the Penny Cyclopædia. Young took his Tour in Ireland in the years 1776 to 1778. I give some extracts, by means of which the reader will see how different was the condition then from what it was half a century later.

But I will first quote a passage cited by Hume in his Essay on Taxes, from Sir William Temple. Speaking of Ireland, Temple says " when by the largeness and plenty of the soil, and scarcity of the people, all things necessary to life are so cheap, that an industrious man by two days' labour may gain enough to feed him the rest of the week ; which I take to be a very plain ground of the laziness attributed to the people, for men naturally prefer ease before labour."

Young says * " The food of the people being potatoes is a circumstance not of less importance: for when the common

* A Young's Ireland, 2. 198.

food of the poor is so dear as to be an object of attentive economy, the children will want that plenty which is essential to rearing them; the article of *milk, so general in the Irish cabins,* is a matter of the first consequence in rearing infants."

Again :* " But in Ireland the cabin is not an object of a moment's consideration : to *possess a cow* and a pig is an earlier aim."   The remainder of this passage, however, shews that if their food was then superior to what it was afterwards, yet their condition in another respect was at that time as low as it could well be.   "The cabin begins with a hovel erected with two days' labour, and the young couple pass not their youth in celibacy for want of a nest to produce their young in."   As to clothes, I forget who was the author of a well known jest; though I think it was Foote, and the *mot* is certainly of a hundred years : the jester said that he had formerly wondered what the English beggars did with their cast off rags, but on visiting Ireland he understood what became of them.

Young in another place,† says under the head of " The labouring poor," " respecting the number of cows, it generally appeared that by far the greater part (of the Irish peasantry) have one or more."

Elsewhere, ‡ discussing the cottar system, the advantages of which he perceives, he says, " Generally speaking, the Irish poor have a fair bellyful of potatoes, and they have milk the greater part of the year."   And § " If any one doubts the comparative plenty which attends the board of a poor native of England and Ireland, let him attend to their meals; the sparingness with which our labourer eats his bread and cheese is well known: mark the Irishman's potato bowl placed on the floor, the whole family on their hams around it, devouring a quantity almost incredible: the beggar seating himself to it with a hearty welcome, the pig taking his share as readily as the wife, the cocks, hens, turkies, geese, the cur, the cat, and perhaps the cow—and all partaking of the same dish. No man can often have been a witness of it without being convinced of the plenty, and I will add the cheerfulness that attends it."

The following is on the state of improvement.* " To judge of Ireland by the conversation one sometimes hears in England, it would be supposed that one-half of it was covered with bogs, and the other with mountains, filled with Irish ready to fly at the sight of a civilised being. There are people who will smile when they hear that in proportion to the size of the two countries, Ireland is more cultivated than England, having much less waste land of all sorts." This was written eighty years ago, when, in spite of Young's constant diatribes in his books, inclosing went on languidly in England, and before the continued high price of wheat and other produce had caused the rage for English inclosure acts which prevailed during the first part of the French war.

Elsewhere, Young states the productiveness of Irish farming as very inferior to that of English, though he pronounces the Irish soil as decidedly the better. For example.† " And to this extreme bad management of adopting the exploded practice of a century ago instead of

* 2. 72.   † 2. 92.

turnips and clover, it is owing that Ireland, with a soil acre for acre much better than England, has its products inferior." He says that probably there were not many more bogs remaining, than were wanted for the supply of fuel.

Again,* Young complains of the prevalence of cattle, and of the neglect of tillage among the farmers. " But keeping cattle of every sort is a business so much more adapted to the laziness of the farmer, that it is no wonder the tillage is so bad. It is every where left to the cottars, or to the very poorest of the farmers." When Young praises the soil as being superior to our own, he says nothing of the climate. Now in this respect, no doubt, Ireland, from its proximity to the Atlantic, is less adapted than England for ripening grain. The constant rain is favourable to grass but very disadvantageous to wheat, and, as I have been told, cattle have of late years proved to be the more profitable produce. Young, I believe, had no intention of censuring the farmers for not growing green crops with a view to stall feeding their cattle, for as far as I know, he was not very friendly to innovations in the routine of a farm, except in cases where the proper rotation of crops had not been already adopted, and stall feeding was scarcely talked of eighty years ago.

At the time of Young's visit, the cottar system still prevailed to a considerable extent, and the relation of master and servant, with payment of wages, was not predominant as it was then, and still is, in England. We are told † " But it is necessary here to explain the common cottar system of labour in Ireland, which much resembles that of Scotland

* 2. 92.　　　　† 2. 108.

till very lately, and which was probably the same all over
Europe before arts and commerce changed the face of it. If
there are cabins on a farm, they are the residence of the
cottars ; if there are none, the farmer marks out the potato
gardens, and the labourers who apply to him on his hiring
the land raise their own cabins on such spots : in some
places the farmer builds ; in others he only assists them
with the roof, &c. : a verbal compact is then made, that the
new cottar shall have his potato garden at such a rent, and
one or two cows kept him at the price of the neighbourhood, he finding the cows. He then works with the farmer
at the rate of the place, usually 6½d. a day, a tally being
kept, half by each party, and a notch cut for every day's
labour : at the end of six months or a year they reckon and
the balance is paid. The cottar works for himself as his
potatoes require."

£.   s.   d.

" The rates of 1 13 10 (for potato ground), and

1 11   3 (for keep of a cow),

Total   ...   3   5   1

appear to be very reasonable : if two cows are kept, the
total is only £4. 16s. 4d., from which it is evident, as far
merely as this charge goes, there is no oppression upon
them which can ever amount to starving. In particular
instances, where there is much inhumanity in the greater
tenants, they are made to pay too high a rent for their
gardens ; and though the price at which their cows are
supported may not appear high, yet they may be so poorly
kept as to make it very unreasonable. I believe, from what
I saw, that such instances are not uncommon."

This cottar system was not universal in Young's time. "There are a great many cabins, usually by the road side, or in the ditch, which have no potato gardens at all. Ireland being free from the curse of English poor laws, the people move about the country and settle where they will. . . . These people are not kept by any body as cottars, but are taken at busy seasons by the day or week and are paid in money; consequently having no potato garden, they are necessitated every year to hire a spot of some neighbouring farmer. . . . . The cabins in little towns are in the same situation."

But as to the cottar system we find,* "Relative to the cottar system wherever it is found, it may be observed that the recompence for labour is *the means of living.* In England these are dispensed in money, but in Ireland in land or commodities. In the former country paying the poor with anything but money has been found so oppressive, that various and repeated statutes have been made to prohibit it." After stating some advantages and disadvantages of the Irish mode as actually practised, Young goes on to say that "an Irishman loves whisky as well as an Englishman does strong beer; but he cannot go to the whisky house on the Saturday night, and drink out the week's support of himself, his wife and his children, not uncommon in the alehouse of the Englishman."

We see from these quotations what the cottar system in Ireland was, and that though it was not universal, or anything like it, it prevailed generally in the country parts. We see also what was the general condition of the peasantry

* 2. 112.

in the years 1776 to 1778. We find as a rule, an abundance of potatoes and a good supply of milk : the same miserable cabins that are seen at present ; and for anything that appears to the contrary, the same disgraceful rags of clothes. But if we compare this state of things with that which has obtained since, we must confess that the condition of the poor during the interval greatly deteriorated. The ordinary peasant then was a cottar : he was possessed of a little property ; besides the pig he had a cow or perhaps two cows. He had sufficient ground allotted to him, at a moderate rent, to enable him to provide his family with an ample supply of potatoes ; and his one or two cows which were kept for him at a fair charge, furnished him with milk. How many peasants, fifty years later, had two cows or even one ? How many had an abundance, or even a necessary supply of potatoes ? If Young's visit had been made in one year only, we might have suspected that the season had happened to be an unusually plentiful one ; but as the tour was continued during three years, this explanation can hardly be given. Even then, the fact remains that the peasants were commonly possessed of one or two cows. I am not arguing here, that the state of the Irish was better than that of the English, or better than that of any other nation : if I were making such a comparison, great allowance would require to be made for the visitation of famine ; and it appears from a late report of the Census Commissioners, that famine has in all periods been a frequent scourge of Ireland. But I am comparing the Irish of last century with the same people in our time, and we have a too painful recollection that within these ten years a famine of the most horrible kind returned again, and in spite of all we could do, laid Ireland utterly prostrate. That country then has always had its seasons of want, and in respect to its ordinary condition deteriorated greatly during the period from 1776 to 1846.

Now in the earlier part of this period, as we have seen, the cottar system prevailed, and this system was one of patronage and dependence. Compared with labourers working for wages only, the Irish cottar relied much more on his superior: since the English labourer having agreed for a certain rate per week, spent his money as he pleased, besides that he received a definite price in the coin of the realm; while the Irish landlord might oppress and ruin his cottar by starving his cows and in many other ways. Young draws a distressing picture of the abuses of authority that he found. They are less to be wondered at when we remember that the dominant caste was of English extraction, and that the peasantry was a conquered race, alien in blood, language, and religion.

"Before * I conclude this article, I must observe that happiness depends not merely upon payment of labour, clothes, or food; the subordination of the lower classes, degenerating into oppression, is not to be overlooked. The poor in all countries and under all governments, are both paid and fed, yet is there an infinite difference between them. This enquiry will by no means turn out so favourable as the preceding articles. It must be very apparent to every traveller through that country, that the labouring poor are treated with harshness. . . . . . The age has improved so much in humanity, that even

* 2. 126.

the poor Irish have experienced its influence, and are every day treated better and better; but still the remnant of the old manners, the abominable distinction of religion, united with the oppressive conduct of the little country gentlemen, or rather vermin of the kingdom, who never were out of it, altogether bear still very heavy on the poor people, and subject them to situations more mortifying than we ever behold in England. The landlord of an Irish estate inhabited by Roman Catholics, is a sort of despot who yields obedience in whatever concerns the poor to no law but that of his own will." . . . .

" A * landlord in Ireland can scarcely invent an order which a servant labourer or cottar dares to refuse to execute. Nothing satisfies him but an unlimited submission. Disrespect or any thing tending towards sauciness he may punish with his cane or his horsewhip with the most perfect security : a poor man would have his bones broke if he offers to lift his hand in his own defence. Knocking down is spoken of in the country in a manner that makes an Englishman stare. Landlords of consequence have assured me that many of their cottars would think themselves honoured by having their wives or daughters sent for to the bed of their master; a mark of slavery that proves the oppression under which such people must live. Nay, I have heard anecdotes of the lives of people being made free with, without any apprehension of the justice of a jury. But let it not be imagined that this is common; formerly it happened every day, but law gains ground. It must

* 2. 127.

strike the most careless traveller to see whole strings of
cars whipt into a ditch by a gentleman's footman to make
way for his carriage." . . . . " The execution of
the laws lies very much in the hands of Justices of the
Peace, many of whom are drawn from the most illiberal
class in the kingdom. If a poor man lodges a complaint against a gentleman, or any animal that chooses
to call itself a gentleman, and the Justice issues out a
summons for his appearance, it is a fixed affront, and he
will infallibly be *called out.* . . . . The colours
of this picture are not charged. To assert that all
these cases are common, would be an exaggeration; but
to say that an unfeeling landlord will do all this with
impunity, is to keep strictly to truth."

To these long quotations of passages that interested
me greatly when I first read them many years ago, I
will add, that Malthus * speaks of the Cottar System
as aiding the use of the potato in causing the singularly
rapid increase of the Irish population. I cannot myself
see the ground of this opinion. He elsewhere † says,
" In Norway and Sweden, particularly the former, where
the agricultural labourer either lives in the farmer's family,
or has a portion of land assigned to him in lieu of
wages, he is in general pretty well fed, although there
is but little demand for labour and considerable competition for such employment." The Irish cottar system
much resembled the houseman system of Norway: and,
as it seems to me, both systems tend to prevent an
undue increase of population. If by the interference of

---

* Principles of Pol. Ec. pa. 260.   † Ib. pa. 368 (note.)

the better classes a stop had been put to the construction
of hovels by the wayside, if farmers and proprietors had
countenanced no labourers but the cottars, the working people
would probably have acted as the Norwegians do : they would
have remained unmarried until they could get a situation
as cottar. This delay would have prevented the undue
multiplication of families. If the English poor laws had
existed in Ireland, the overseers would have had the power
of removing those squatters, on the ground that they
would become chargeable to the parish. We have seen
in the life of Hutton that this power was well known,
and that Hutton himself narrowly escaped being removed
from Birmingham, thrifty as he was, and though he
offered to become a ratepayer.

We see now that the working classes of Ireland formerly lived to a great extent under a régime of patronage
and dependence. We know that this state of things
was changed, though at what time the change took place
and when it was complete, I am not aware. During
all the discussions on Ireland in my time, I do not
remember to have heard any thing about cottars, nor any
thing about the possession by the peasants of a cow.
Abundance of potatoes has usually been as rare as cottar-
ship and cow-keeping : the ordinary state of the peasant
has been one of dearth, varied only by alternations of
famine and pestilence.

In the course of half a century, then, the régime of
patronage died out in Ireland, and that of Individualism
succeeded. Every one was left to do as he pleased, to go
where he pleased, and to lie down and die undisturbed and
unregarded when food was not to be had. But it cannot

be said in this case that the change was caused by a concentration of population around the coal fields, or by the substitution of steam engines for water mills. There can be little doubt that it arose from the excessive increase of population. As the able-bodied labourers multiplied, they bid against each other for work: the landowners found it less troublesome to employ those who were not cottars: the increasing poverty of the workmen favoured this change, by making it difficult to obtain a cow: and at last the cottar system ceased. Thus the peasant was no longer dependent upon a patron for a cow's grass and potato ground, and he worked for wages whenever any one would accept his services; but unfortunately the habit of cultivating a plot of ground for the support of a family, had taken root, and the peasant, unrestrained by overseer or landlord, married, spent a couple of days in constructing a hovel, obtained an odd corner of soil, lived on the produce, and brought up a family to ever increasing poverty. The Individualism of Ireland has been the result, not of steam engines and coal fields, but of the consistent carrying out of the eulogised maxim of *laissez-faire*. England, says Arthur Young, is cursed with a poor law. Under that law a labourer is not allowed to take up his abode in a parish where he has no employment, to be himself half starved, and to bring into the world a family destined to fill the workhouse. Ireland was free from this so called curse, and the advocates of the *let alone* system have little reason to rejoice in the results. Happily this English curse of the poor law has now been fairly introduced into Ireland, and we may hope that, aided by the wholesome changes that have succeeded the awful famine of ten years ago, the evils caused by former neglect may be removed. But the whole world may learn a lesson : it may see that Individualism, however excellent in itself, requires a people fit for its reception. Let those who clamour for the immediate and unconditional emancipation of slaves throughout the world, consider this ; and satisfy themselves whether it would be a wiser thing to give economical freedom to a race brought up in social dependence, than it would be to give political freedom and representative institutions, to a people like the Hindoos who have always been the prey of the strongest hand.

CHAPTER VI.

We see, then, how Individualism may arise, and to what consequences it may lead when it is left altogether to itself. It is worth while to enquire how it has acted in England, and by what circumstances it has been modified. There was a time when in this country, as in the rest of Europe, people had not the entire liberty of action which they now enjoy ; there was even a time when the working classes were serfs, not to say slaves. I am not about to recapitulate the statements of distinguished writers as to the way in which that state of things was abolished : I only propose to enquire what are the peculiar arrangements by which, in passing from a system of restrictions to one of economical freedom, we have avoided many of those evils which attach themselves to this new condition, and under which other nations, as Ireland for example, have suffered.

First, let us see what are some of the advantages obtained under other industrial organisations. We have already noticed what they are under the patriarchal régime. In times and places where men are indisposed to work hard, it is a matter of the highest importance that their labour should be rendered as efficient as possible, and that the household expenses should be reduced to the lowest point. Both these requirements seem to be accomplished by the patriarchal system. The household commonly consists, in Russia, of an elderly man and several sons, all of them, perhaps, married, and possessed of families. If each able bodied man in this little community were at liberty to do what work he pleased, nothing but confusion could ensue: but the chief appoints to every one his task. If, again, instead of living in this one household, each married son had a hut of his own, and earned his living independently, there would be an entire absence of co-operation, and particularly of that kind of co-operation called division of labours. Among ourselves the capitalist takes the place of the patriarch: the hired servant is substituted for the adult son. The inequality of rank and property supplies the means of a different and more efficient organisation.

The patriarchal régime must have its advantages in respect to frugality of living. Among the less civilised nations, women are required to do far more work out of doors than is exacted from them in more advanced societies. In a household consisting of several families, the young wives may take it by turns to arrange the house, prepare the meals, and watch the children, leaving the other wives at liberty to go to their occupations out of doors. In short, this régime secures a good deal of co-operation and consequent efficiency of labour, that could hardly be obtained in any other way, in the state of civilisation in which we find the régime prevailing.

Besides this, there exist in the system, the means of repressing ill conduct and of helping the weak and distressed. In all countries, and in every place, some of the strong will tyrannize over the weak. It is revolting to recollect how much brutality comes to light through the medium of the English police courts: how masters are found abusing their apprentices, and husbands maltreating their wives. I am unwilling to think so ill of civilisation as to suppose that it causes these horrors: no doubt they exist also in half civilised countries. But in a patriarchal household a wife must find much protection from extreme violence, in the sympathy of the other members. It may not be thought wrong in such communities, for a husband to administer moderate chastisement for sauciness or disobedience; and a nut stick as thick as the little finger, which is popularly supposed to be the legal instrument of a husband's anger here, may there be regarded as too gentle a means of correction. But a wife in danger of injury to life or limb, must certainly find amongst her relatives, close at hand, that protection which in an isolated habitation she would be deprived of.

Then as to the large class of the weak in body, the imbecile in mind, the thoughtless, the recklessly improvident, individualism leaves them to the practice, and to the consequences, of folly or imbecility. The patriarchal system seems to provide for such persons. The strong minded, and the vigorous in body, toil, not for themselves alone, but rather for the household to which they belong. The physical and mental powers which with us are applied to the advantage of the individual, are there applied to the advantage of the little community. We have seen how, even in the temporary associations, the artèles of the great towns, the members share alike in the gains of the body, though there must often be great inequality in the quantity of labour contributed by different men: much more must this principle easily prevail in households consisting of near relatives, with an hereditary or elected chief. I do not imagine that in such a state of society there exists more benevolence, kindness, disinterestedness, self abnegation, than exists where individualism prevails. But a sense of interest has at first moulded communities into this form, and custom long continued renders the form permanent.

We have seen also, what are the benefits arising to the lower classes from the system of patronage on the part of the superior, and of a corresponding dependence on the part of the labourer. The system is in its fullest vigour where slavery prevails. There, the infant is the property of the master, and interest incites him to have it fed, clothed, and tended in such a way as to develop all the powers of its body: the child and youth have the same powerful claim on the master: and up to manhood slaves may probably on the average be better taken care of than freemen of the working classes. Even in after life, the master has a strong interest in keeping his slaves in good working order; and this can only be accomplished by feeding them well and giving them a sufficiency of clothes and shelter. When a slave has arrived at old age and is become too decrepit to work, the master has no direct interest in supporting him. But few old men are incapable of doing something, and even if they are so, the simplest principles of humanity dictate that the master who has benefited by the manhood of the slave, should maintain him when he is no longer able to earn his living. Grievous as are the complaints made as to the proceedings of slave owners, I am not aware that they are charged with neglect of infancy or of old age. Particular cases of such neglect might be found, and many particular cases: but before we propose to condemn a community for the faults of exceptional members, let us purge our own nation from the taint of similar offences.

There exists also in slavery, and even in serfdom, a considerable abatement of the evils arising from improvidence on the part of the working classes. Among free labourers, go where you will, you find improvidence generally prevailing : nothing is brought out by M. Le Play's studies more strongly than this fact. In the east and in the west, in the temperate zone and in the tropics, as all authors agree, the labourer scarcely looks forward beyond the day. He marries without any secure prospect of a maintenance ; he spends the whole of his gains when he first marries, without reflecting that in a few years he may have half a dozen additional mouths to fill; he makes no provision against old age and infirmity, and only some faint provision even against sickness. Now a slave cannot be improvident, because to him providence is impossible. He depends on his master : he knows that if he is sick he will be fed and doctored ; that when he is old he will be decently maintained: he marries with the cheerful consent of his master, who regards children as a valuable property : and the greater the number of mouths to be fed, the more the maintenance that is willingly supplied him.

Even under serfdom the same is true. A Russian nobleman cannot now sell his serfs from the land they inherit : he may sell the land with the serfs upon it : he can prevent the serfs from leaving his estate, and can compel them to cultivate the soil. His property is valuable very much according to the number of serfs he possesses, and therefore he has a strong interest in having them well treated and in securing their physical well being. Under these restraints, a serf may be guilty of some improvidence and recklessness, yet he is not sufficiently his own master to do this with impunity. If any serf behaves in such a way as to be a scandal to his neighbourhood, the seigneur selects him as a suitable man for a soldier, as well fitted to be food for powder. He is marched off, and his village sees him no more.

I do not mean to defend either slavery or serfdom. I presume that in early stages of society both states successively are inevitable, and that without them, a concentration of population, and a systematic cultivation of the earth, would have been nearly impossible. But I am not ignorant of the frightful evils that slavery brings in its train: the brutality and insolence on one side, the cringing servility on the other; the unavowed polygamy; the licentiousness of youth; the dislike to labour on the part of the predominant class. While, however, I see and deplore these, I have thought it right to inquire what compensation exists in the system, what good qualities it possesses, and how among freemen we find substitutes for those good qualities.

As to communism we have found that it also carries with it some advantages. The communism which has actually prevailed of late years to any extent, is only of a partial kind: men have small properties, and the means of living are eked out by certain common rights of pasturage, or of cutting fuel, or of both. The case of the Jault commune, which is now extinct, was but a remnant of former days, and was, after all, only a slight extension of that patriarchal system, or family communism, which still prevails in Russia.

That kind of partial communism which consists in a right on the part of every family to pasturage, or fuel, has its advantages. One of the greatest of these is that it cannot become the subject of bargains: a man cannot borrow money on his share of common land, as he can on land that belongs to himself separately. His right is not alienable as private property is. But it is found that among small proprietors of land, one of the great misfortunes is, the facility with which they can borrow: and though they need not use or abuse this facility, yet it is no new observation that, often the sight of means to do ill deeds makes deeds ill done. Another advantage is, that a man having a right of pasturage without any charge, feels desirous of exercising his right, and is unwilling to throw it away for the benefit of others. This leads the commoners to possess cattle and sheep, and causes prudence and frugality as means of obtaining them. It is true, as we have seen, that A. Young thought lightly of the possession of this kind of property by working people, and declared that common rights, cattle, and misery were usually found together; and that our ordinary labourers were better off than members of communes elsewhere. There may, however, have been other circumstances which Young omitted to consider. It may be said also, that the Irish in Young's time frequently had cattle, and that yet their state was not so good, taking clothes and houses into account, as the state of our own labourers. The mere possession of this kind of property, then, is not so efficacious as we might have expected. On the other hand, it seems that whatever may have been the state of the Irish peasant when compared with the state of the English labourer, the state of the Irish peasant formerly, when he possessed cattle, was far superior to that of the same peasant at a later date when he possessed no cattle. Though the cow did not lift the Irishman into a condition better than that of his English brother, it lifted him into a condition far better than that he has himself since occupied. On the whole it cannot be doubted that it is an excellent thing for a peasantry to contract the habit of possessing property : it induces self-respect and independence, it restrains premature marriages, it promotes providence and frugality. The partial communism I have been speaking of, so far as it causes the working classes to possess more property than they otherwise would, must be beneficial; though it is possible that the disadvantages that attend the practice of common rights, may more than outweigh the benefits, and particularly in an advanced state of civilization.

Such then, are some of the benefits derived from these régimes which are found to precede that of Individualism. By the introduction of this latter, society certainly loses some of the advantages enumerated, and I intend to enquire how far this is the case. Even if the loss were entire and unmitigated, it might happen that the benefits arising from Individualism were so many and so great, as to more than counterbalance the deprivation: but it will be easy to shew that in many instances the loss of a particular benefit is supplied in another way. For example, under the system of patronage in its broadest extent, the owner of a slave is bound to maintain him in his old age: among ourselves an employer leaves every man to himself to make provision for his future wants: but it was found long ago that if this principle were fully carried out, and if old people were abandoned to suffer the consequences of their previous improvidence, many would have to pine in distressing indigence, and some would die of want. The Government at this point steps in, and by means of the poor laws, makes arrangements to prevent consequences so deplorable. The place of the private patron is supplied by the workhouse authorities. In most countries this system of state relief does not exist, but it is to some extent supplied by private charity, which is often carefully organised, as we have seen in the case of the rag picker of Paris.

However, before I carry out the enquiry what substitutes Individualism provides for the benefits obtained by other régimes, I propose to attempt an estimate of the actual state of the labouring classes in different countries, as to the means of living. I am aware that the knowledge I possess is insufficient to make such an estimate of any very high value; yet my course of reading, and especially that which I have adapted since I became acquainted with M. Le Play's labours, has furnished me with some information that I am desirous of communicating.

CHAPTER VII.

THE first point that naturally engages our attention is the rate of wages paid in different countries; though as in many parts of the world wages are almost unknown, this test of condition is an imperfect one. We have also to remember that the wages in money are only of importance as a measure of the commodities the workman can command; and that the difference of prices of wheat, clothing, and other necessaries, in one place and another, renders money wages an imperfect standard of well being.

I will take the case of Russia first. In that country, the custom of paying wages seems hardly to exist except in the towns. In the rural districts, the peasants work for their seigneur, and are paid in a way that prevailed formerly in other countries, but which has almost ceased among more civilised nations. In France, before the revolution, the practice was known under the name of Corvée. The peasant has a portion of ground assigned to him, of sufficient extent to enable him to support his family by cultivating it. He gives a nominal half of his time to the cultivation of his seigneur's estate, and the other half to the cultivation of his little farm.* We may regard this arrangement in two lights: we may say that the peasant, instead of paying a money rent

* Le Play, 67. 1.

for his farm, gives half of his time as a rent: or we may say that the seigneur hires his peasant half the year, and instead of paying him money wages, allots him a portion of land. In the towns, however, wages must of course be paid; and the ordinary rate in Russia seems to vary from 10d. to 1s. 8d. a day, i.e. five shillings to ten shillings a week. Out of this, the labourers have to pay the *abrok*, or capitation fee to their seigneur, unless in the rare cases where the labourers are free. M. Le Play tells us that this payment of the *abrok* is made willingly, because the emigrant peasant generally returns in the end to his native village; while the payment keeps up his connection with it, and entitles him, on his return home, to share whatever advantages the seigneur dispenses to his serfs.

In Norway, we find * men connected with the Cobalt mining, getting 1s. 4d. to 1s. 8d. a day, besides several privileges of some importance. Mr. Laing, † an excellent authority from his residence in the country, says that the wages of a common labourer in Norway are 4½d. a day with victuals, and those of a carpenter ninepence. He also mentions the wages of a neat handy maid servant as thirty shillings to forty shillings a year; and those of a house-keeper as £4. to £5. a year.

In Vienna, a joiner ‡ earns, working by the piece, about thirteen shillings a week, but the individual mentioned as earning this sum seems to have been rather of a helpless sort. His wife was at one time a domestic servant, and up to eighteen years old received £2. 12s. a year, but coming

---

* Le Play, 103. 1.   † Laing, edit. 1851, pa. 71.   ‡ Le Play, 122. 1.

to Vienna she got £7. 10s., and afterwards £10. a year.
Subsequently she adopted a trade, by working at which she
earned nearly two shillings a day. I am rather surprised to
find these wages so high.

Solingen in Rhenish Prussia, the great rival of our
Sheffield, has had an increasing trade, and the labourers
are said therefore to be well off. M. Le Play tells us that
a particular man * at piece work gets two shillings a day.
The grinders, he tells us, make high wages, but he does not
say how much. He adds that they are intemperate, and
that other workmen with moderate wages are better conducted. The grinders whom I have known in England have
generally earned high wages, but I am not disposed to think
that they were more intemperate than other mechanics : I
have known several who were quite of the highest class of
working men. I have been told by an English manufacturer that in Solingen the grinders work in a way that
shows much carelessness of life : that they stand in positions
such as to expose them to be struck by a stone when it
breaks, instead of being protected by a massive block of
wood and heavy chains as among us ; and that they grind
on dry stones, whereas among ourselves all heavy grinding
is done with wet stones to prevent dust. The Solingen
grinders, if the facts are so, must be subject to many
accidents and to frequent disease of the lungs, and therefore may well be reckless and intemperate, as men who live
from day to day.

It is generally thought that high wages produce intemperance. They always give the power to be intemperate

* Le Play, 153. 1.

where the disposition exists, and there will therefore be
more intemperance when times are good than when they are
bad. But many mechanics who regularly get high wages
are very steady and temperate, while others, in the same
circumstances, are mere sensualists. The worst men I have
known among those who uniformly earn high wages, are the
Staffordshire mill and forge men: they are coarse and
illiterate, without any tastes beyond a love of bodily pleasures; and high wages are to them perhaps a misfortune.

We find in A. Young some valuable notices of the rate
of wages in France about 1789. His general impression
was that the French labouring poor were very wretched.*
He states the average wages † at 9½d. a day, and those of
masons and carpenters at 1s. 3d. a day. He believed the
average wages of English labourers at that time to be
nearly 1s. 5d. a day. On the other hand the price of bread
in France was only 1d. a lb., whereas the price of bread
in England was 1¾d. a lb. This comparison, however,
is between the common French bread and the good
English bread. Young after stating these facts remained of opinion ‡ that our labourers were in the far
better condition. He says § that mechanics in France
in 1789 earned 1s. 1d. a day, and women 7½d. a day.
M. Le Play gives a case of a farm labourer in France
of the present day, and makes his income from all sources
to amount to about nine shillings a week, but the
wages about 9d. a day. Though I give these statements
of A. Young's as I find them, I much suspect their
accuracy. In saying that the English rate was 1s. 5d.

---

* Young's France, 1. 453. 454. † Ib. 1. 446. ‡ Ib. 1. 447. § Ib. 1. 565.

a day, he may mean the average rate, and that is got at with great difficulty. The usual, or ordinary farming rate in England in 1792 or 93, does not appear to have exceeded seven shillings a week, with some addition for the summer months. But wages were rising from 1789 to 92. So far our labourers were not so well off by 1s. 6d. a week, as Young represents. On the other hand, he overstates the price of bread, which in the early part of the last century was 1¼d. a lb., and about 1789 was 1½d. a lb., in the neighbourhood of London.* This makes a difference of 1d. a loaf compared with Young's statement: and this compensates for a large part of the over estimate of wages.

The rate of wages in Ireland is tolerably notorious, as having been before the famine of ten years ago, about sixpence a day generally, but double that in the north. At present, we are told, the rate is much higher, and I trust it will continue to be so.

As to England formerly, a good deal has been written, and Mr. M'Culloch gives us a table in his valuable Commercial Dictionary.† It consists of the wages paid at Greenwich Hospital. I extract a few items :—

	Carpenters.		Bricklayers.		Plumbers.	
	s.	d.	s.	d.	s.	d.
1730	2	6 per day	2	6 per day	3	0 per day
1750	2	8 „	2	6 „	2	6 „
1810	5	8 „	5	2 „	5	9 „
1835	5	5 „	4	9 „	5	5 „

* M. C. Com. Dict. ed. 1840. 953.   † Ib. 952.

These are taken from extensive tables that contain prices of commodities principally, and Mr. M'Culloch says of them " The following table of the prices of the various commodities, and of the wages paid to different descriptions of tradesmen, at Greenwich Hospital, for the last one hundred years, is the most complete of the sort that has been published; and is one of the few that are founded upon data, the accuracy of which cannot be questioned. Unfortunately it applies only to a small part of the country."

I do not mean to question the perfect accuracy of these tables: I have no doubt that the prices there set down were those actually paid. As regards the commodities it may be presumed that the prices indicate pretty nearly the market value at the time they were bought. Neither as to the wages do I mean to doubt that the rate recorded is the one actually paid; but I think it far from certain that it indicates the rate prevailing even in the neighbourhood of Greenwich. I am not aware what has been the system on which prices of repairs have been fixed, but whatever may have been nominally the system, it is certain that in the course of a hundred years there will have been great variations in the practice, and that at times there will have been carelessness and favouritism on the part of the authorities. Even in private families there is a considerable degree of indifference as to the rate of wages charged by occasional workmen, and if bills were inspected it would be found that for a given amount of labour one family pays half as much again as another. The workman will always take care that he gets enough for his work, but the employer does not as regularly take care that he secures enough work for the money. When prices fluctuate as they did during the French war, the workman will generally take advantage of the opportunity to raise his charge very soon, but will show less alacrity in reducing his charge. Thus we see that in the early part of last century a carpenter and a bricklayer, at Greenwich, were paid 2s. 6d. a day, that their prices rose during the war to 5s. 2d. and 5s. 8d., but that down to 1835 they had only fallen to 5s. 5d. and 4s. 9d.

It would be far more satisfactory if we could get the wages paid at different periods in a manufactory. A trader has the same motive for reducing wages that a workman has for raising them. The master who at home has little anxiety to save sixpence a day in the charge of an occasional gardener or of a carpenter, will take some pains, and will even submit to the annoyance of a strike, to prevent a rise of wages, or to accomplish a reduction. When a manufacturer finds himself undersold, and in imminent danger of losing his business, he must resort to measures for lowering the cost of his goods; but all the savings he could effect by paring down the wages at home, would not amount to any sum he cares about. For this reason, the wages paid by manufacturers are a far better guide to the value of labour than are the wages paid by families, or by public bodies.

Working people employed directly by consumers get better paid on the average than those employed by manufacturers or by shopkeepers : no lady would think of paying a sempstress so low as a shopkeeper pays. It may seem for this reason to be our duty to give employment as far as we can to workpeople directly, without the intervention of a middleman. In some cases this is a duty. But very often

a sempstress employed by a shopkeeper is not at liberty
to work for private families, and if she should do so she
would lose her regular employment. If she gets less for
a day's work than she would get in a private family, she
has the advantage of constancy of work, and this is even
of more importance than a higher rate: better earn ten
shillings every week than one pound for a week occasionally
with intervals of idleness and starvation.

I have found various notices of the rate of wages scattered
through the works of several authors. A. Young in the
same place * in which he gives the French rates, says that
the English farm labourer at that time got on an average
about 1s. 5d. a day, but the English mechanic 1s. 8d., and
women ninepence. A. Young was himself a farmer, he was
probably a worse authority for towns than for the country,
besides that in the towns labourers being often paid by
the piece, and their earnings varying very much, it is difficult
to obtain an average rate. Young speaks of great luxury
among our mechanics, and states that no such luxury was
found in the same class in France. According to my notion
of the meaning of words, it would have been more correct
to say superfluity instead of luxury: mechanics, when
compared with ordinary farm labourers, certainly enjoy many
means of living that are beyond the mere necessaries of life.
M. Le Play, accustomed to catalogue the moveables of
labourers of every sort, notices that a good deal which is
superfluous, is commonly found in town habitations.

Young in his Irish tour † says that among the linen
manufacturers, weavers of fine cloth earned 1s. 5d. a day,

---

* Young's France, 1, 565.   † Young's Ireland, 2, 297.

weavers of coarse cloth 1s. 0½d. a day, and spinners 3¼d. a day. These wages, as he says, were double and treble the gains of ordinary labourers : but then, as we have seen before, the husbandry labourers maintained themselves to a great extent by means of the potato ground and the cow.

In the life of Hutton which I have noticed at some length before, it appears that he was put apprentice to his uncle, a stocking weaver, and that at fifteen years old* he was expected to earn for his master 5s. 10d. a week, and that the following year, being put to finer work, he was expected to earn 6s. 6d. a week. It was stipulated that he should find his own clothes out of what he gained by over work, not reckoned in any particular week, but in the aggregate. He complains that the bargain was a cruelly hard one. At first sight we should say, that if a boy of fifteen could earn 5s. 10d., and a boy of sixteen, 6s. 6d., a man's wages must have been a good deal more than Young mentions as mechanics' earnings thirty years later. But there are some trades, requiring little bodily strength, in which the nimble fingers of a lad will travel over the ground at least as fast as a man's. The penury in which, as Hutton tells us, the married stockingers lived, shews that the rate of wages was very poor. Hutton's uncle and master, worked on his own account, with looms of his own, and his gains were probably derived principally from his apprentices, of whom he had three, and sometimes even five.

Hutton in another work gives us a glance, here and there, into the income of Birmingham workmen a hundred years ago. It seems that the custom existed then as now, of

* Hutton's Life, 95.

having apprentices who lived with their parents, and received stipulated wages, which increased with the boy's age. We are told * that these wages varied from 3s. 6d. to 8s. This is far less than what Hutton himself was expected to earn for his uncle master at Nottingham: but the person who paid an apprentice 3s. 6d. might expect him to do work worth twice the money, and would certainly not take him with a promise to teach a trade unless with some expectation of profit.

We hear also, † that the wages of a common labourer were 8s., and this agrees pretty nearly with Young's account, ‡ already quoted, which makes such labourers earn on the average 7s. 6d. to 8s. 6d. a week.

Mechanics' wages, we find § were very various, being in some instances as low as 10s., and in others as high as 42s. a week. I can readily believe that this serious difference existed.

At another page ‖ of the same book, we meet with a wheelwright who charges only at the rate of 1s. 2d. a day for his work.

Money wages in towns have certainly risen greatly since those days. An ordinary unskilled labourer in Birmingham will not take the most common situation with the intention of keeping it, under 15s. a week. Mechanics' earnings are as various as they were in Hutton's time, and they, of course, fluctuated with the state of trade. Within my own experience, a mechanic getting 16s. to 17s. a week looks upon himself as a martyr: at 20s. to 21s. he grumbles a

---

* Hutton's Court of Requests, 158.   † Ib. 190.   § Ib. 190.

‡ Young's France, 1, 446.   ‖ Ib. 269.

little; and at 30s. feels himself in clover. I speak here
of men with a moderate degree of skill. In some manufactories that have a reputation for excellence to support,
the masters object to pay by the piece, on account of
preventing the men from slighting their work. I believe
that 30s. a week would be commonly given under these
circumstances, with additional payment for everything
beyond ten hours' work in the day. Any man possessed
of unusual skill as a caster, or turner, or tool maker, or in
many other branches, gets a great deal more. Many also
add to their earnings by employing boys under them, some
of the boys being apprenticed to these mechanics.

With regard to agricultural wages I have no special
information. Every one knows that there is a considerable
variation, comparing different parts of the country : that
they have been as low as seven shillings in Dorsetshire, while
they were as high as twelve shillings in Lincolnshire : and
that the free trade and the gold discoveries have had a
decided tendency to raise the rates. In the country parts
of Warwickshire I have found within a few years that twelve
shillings a week were reckoned high wages, and such as
would be given only to a first-rate hand. The farmers round
Birmingham, I understand, give two shillings a day, and in
some parishes even 2s. 6d. The labourers prefer this rate
in their native village to two shillings or three shillings a
week more in the town. It must appear strange to an
American, who thinks little of a migration from New England to the other side of the Appalachian mountains, that a
peasant should vegetate on seven shillings a week in Dorsetshire, when by a journey to the other side of our little
island he would find himself in a district where twelve shil-

lings a week are commonly paid. But we know that the emigrant into a new county would be looked at coldly. The farmers would be very glad of him in the autumn to help them with the harvest, and the more so since the famine has diminished the supply of Irish reapers. But at other times the employers would give the preference to the men of their own parish, and under fear of an increased poor rate would hesitate to encourage the settlement of an unnecessary family. Besides, the landowners and their agents, from the same fear, would refuse to supply a stranger with a cottage, or with land as a site for a cottage. There are no such obstacles to a migration into towns, and a great many labourers do find their way to manufacturing districts. Formerly, as we have seen in Hutton's life, the overseers had a power of interfering, and of removing any one likely to become chargeable to the parish, but that practice has passed away. The American, then, may well wonder that wages should continue so low any where as 1s. 2d. a day, when a man by changing his residence to a town might double his earnings. The fact of this apathy is certainly a proof of a stagnant state of mind, a half civilised disposition to take things as they are, a slothful inclination to refuse any present hardship in hope of future advantage. I was recently told by a manufacturer in Staffordshire that he accidentally engaged a countryman as a wagoner, and that finding him an useful man he gave him the prevailing rate of wages, although the man asked at first considerably less. The poor fellow thought himself in an eldorado, in spite of the smoke that surrounded him. He asked leave to go and see his friends, and when he told them what he was getting, displaying perhaps some purchases

that seemed to them of an extravagantly costly nature,
several of them followed him into the manufacturing district, and, as a result, the country parish was so denuded of
labourers that the farmers had to raise their wages to save
themselves from being inconveniently deserted. It is to be
hoped that the spread of intelligence, and of railways, will
cause an equalisation of wages through the kingdom, or
rather that the wages of the south will be brought up to
those of the north.

Malthus * in his work on population quotes A. Young
as desiring that a labourer should have secured to him a
peck of wheat as a day's wages : Young reckons that a
family of six persons consumes forty eight bushels of wheat
a year, and that as a peck a day would amount to seventy
bushels for forty seven weeks, besides five harvest weeks,
there would at this rate remain a considerable overplus for
rent, clothes, and other things. In the next page, Malthus
says that he thinks a peck of wheat not by any means
excessive wages. On this principle wages would be
thus : —

	s. d.			s. d.	
When wheat is at 32	0 the quarter, wages would be	6	0 a week.
"	34 8	"	"	6 6	"
"	37 4	"	"	7 0	"
"	40 0	"	"	7 6	"
"	48 0	"	"	9 0	"
"	56 0	"	"	10 6	"
"	64 0	"	"	12 0	"

Now, both Young and Hutton agree that common labour
in England about eighty years ago was paid for at 7s. 6d.

* Population, 2. 493.

to 8s. a week: and at that time, therefore, wheat should have been at about forty shillings to make the working man well off. The actual price from 1746 to 1765 was about thirty six shillings a quarter, but these dates are rather too early for us. The actual price from 1756 to 1775 was about forty five shillings. Wages therefore, should have been one shilling a week higher to make the labouring man at his ease.

At the present time two shillings a day are called good wages in the country, and we ought to find the price of wheat at sixty-four shillings. The actual price for the last six years has been about 53s. 6d, and for the six years previously about the same. During the last twelve years, therefore, the price has been about 53s. 6d. : and it follows that at 1s. 8d. a day, or 10s. a week, the labourer would have been well off, while a man earning twelve shillings a week would have a considerable superfluity. For men living in towns there is an additional expense in house rent, but if we allow two shillings a week for that, a man earning fifteen shillings would be as well off as one in the country who earned thirteen shillings. Bread is nearly as cheap as in the country, whatever wheat may be. Clothes, furniture, and superfluities are certainly far cheaper in towns.

But there is a manifest inaccuracy in this mode of calculating wages. It would be quite correct if working people bought nothing but bread, or if the prices of other commodities varied exactly with those of bread. But when wheat rises, clothes do not rise at once, nor even for a long time. It certainly is true that a permanent rise of food causes at last a rise of wages, and therefore, a tendency to rise in the prices of manufactures : but in modern days this tendency has been counteracted by improved modes of manufacturing, and by reductions in the cost of the raw material. Thus, while in the last hundred years, food and wages have both risen greatly, manufactured goods of the highest importance have fallen.

Young supposes a man to earn seventy bushels of wheat in forty seven weeks: in the five weeks of harvest he may earn much more than common, but we may suppose this excess to be equal to what he loses by sickness or occasional idleness. The man, therefore, will earn about seventy eight bushels a year, and a family of six persons, consuming forty eight bushels would have an overplus of thirty bushels for rent, clothes, &c. Now, formerly, this thirty bushels would be worth only 4s. 6d. a bushel, or about £7.: at present the thirty bushels are worth as much as 6s. 8d. the bushel, or £10. The thirty bushels are worth now, £3. more than formerly; and supposing rent, clothes, &c. to cost no more than formerly, the labourer with a peck of wheat a day would be £3. a year richer than he was when wheat was at thirty-eight shillings the quarter.

One other matter seems to have turned in favour of the labourer. Young speaks * of the price of bread in England as 1¾d. the pound: wheat is now at about the same price as when Young's Tour in France took place, reckoning an average of ten or twelve years in each instance. But bread is not on an average so high as Young speaks of. The quartern loaf, as sold by the large bakers I am acquainted with, weighs fully 4¼ lb. When wheat is at forty shillings, the quartern loaf is sold at about fivepence, though the

* Young's France, 1. 447.

quality of the wheat sold in the markets varies considerably, and prevents the price of bread from following exactly the average price of wheat. I have said that the average price of wheat during the last twelve years has been about 53s. 6d., and the price of the quartern loaf will be found to have been about 6¼d. But at 1¾d. a lb., the price of the quartern loaf should have been nearly 7¼d. This would give an advantage of one penny a loaf, or about one shilling a week to a family of six persons. But, as I have already said, Young appears to have been inaccurate in his statement, and the difference is not so great as it would seem.

It is quite probable, according to our experience, that the price of bread should have fallen as compared with the price of wheat. Bread is a manufacture, of which wheat is the raw material : but manufactures generally have fallen greatly during the last seventy years : bread, therefore, so far as it is a manufacture may be expected to have fallen ; or, what is the same thing, the cost of manufacturing bread from wheat may be expected to have fallen.

On the whole there seems no reason to suppose that English wages have fallen during the last hundred years. That money wages have risen indeed, is certain ; and there seem good grounds for believing that the working classes have greater command of the means of living than they had a century ago.

The consideration of the subject of wages does not, to any great extent, furnish the means of comparing ourselves with other nations, because in a great part of the world, as I have already noticed, the organisation of country labour is not founded on the practice of employing workmen at a fixed rate per day, or by the task.

CHAPTER VIII.

NEXT to the wages earned, the kind and quantity of food consumed by workmen, is the matter of highest importance. M. Le Play is well qualified by his varied experience to give us much valuable information on this branch of the subject.

He tells us * that in Europe the different kinds of grain must be placed in the first rank as food : and that when by positive necessity men are obliged to have recourse to a frugal diet, grain becomes so predominant as to swallow up two-thirds of the income available for food, and even a half of the entire income of a family. When, however, there is an improvement in ease and well-being, a larger proportion of income is devoted to other food, especially to fatty substances, to meat, and to fermented liquors : so that in some cases the cost of grain does not amount to an eighth or even to a twelfth of the entire expenditure of a family. We are referred for proof of these facts to particular examples among the thirty-six cases by which the volume is illustrated.

M. Le Play hesitates what word to employ to express with sufficient generality, that which, I think, we understand by grain : he desires to include rice and maize, as well as wheat, barley, oats, &c. He fixes on *blé*, as the best

* Le Play, 31. 2. 19.

word for his purpose.   But referring to the definition of
this word in the *Dictionnaire de l' Académie,* he is led to
make a remark worthy of the attention of untravelled
persons : that many nations are altogether ignorant of the
use of bread; so that even in Europe the greater part of
grain is prepared, not as bread, but in various other forms,
by baking and boiling.

He remarks,* that races of men exhibit an obstinate
attachment to their hereditary modes of preparing grain ;
and this to such an extent, as to furnish a means of detecting
a community of origin between different tribes, as well as
a means of estimating the degree of progress in civilisation.
In Africa and Asia, grain continues to be frequently ground
or otherwise prepared, in every house, instead of being
ground by windmills or water-power.   It appears that the
introduction of such improved mills into Algeria has greatly
strengthened the French ascendency, and by liberating
the women from the severe labour they formerly groaned
under, has paved the way for other European customs.   A
similar advantage accrued to the Russians in their intercourse with the migratory tribes of Asia.

M. Le Play's travels have not led him among any people
that consumes rice as a principal article of diet, and therefore, in none of his thirty-six cases is there any illustration
of the use of that food.   He remarks that it may perhaps
have a considerable advantage in the speed with which it is
cooked.   He does not, however, mention two important
facts connected with it.   The first is, that rice is of very
uncertain productiveness.   It is grown in hot climates, and

* Le Play, 32. 1.

is dependent on abundant moisture for success : in favourable, or even ordinary, seasons, it is capable of maintaining a great population by its two crops a year; but if the periodical rain fails, the rice plant languishes, the harvest is gone, and the miserable population has no resource but to lie down and die. The famines of rice-fed India have been too horrible to think upon. It is possible to mitigate the evil by means of artificial irrigation, but in the absence of such precautions, rice must be regarded as a very precarious and dangerous food. I am happy to find that in Hindostan, the East India Company is really doing something very considerable in this important matter. I am informed by Major Eyre, (the distinguished author, as Lieutenant Vincent Eyre, of some notes on the humiliating Cabul disaster, in which he was a prisoner and wounded,) that the great Ganges canal is a work of far more importance than any of the boasted water communications constructed by the Moguls of old. This canal is, together with its branches, not much short of a thousand miles in length, and has cost three millions sterling: it is in truth a new channel of the Ganges, and it is expected that it will fertilise the whole of the Douab, which is now comparatively a desert. It seems that the Bramins looked very suspiciously at this interference with the sacred river, but that finding it hopeless to struggle against their self-willed masters, the English, they adopted and consecrated the new river. It is only just to Lord Auckland to remember that the canal was projected and determined on under his administration. If such works as these became general in India, famines would be reduced to dearths, and the objection to rice as a principal food would be so far diminished.

A. Young gives an interesting account of the arrangements made for the irrigation of Lombardy. The necessity
of the case has led to an organisation exhibiting great
ingenuity.* " The power of effecting the great works
in irrigation which are visible over this whole country
(Piémont) depends very much on the law, which supposes
the right and property of all rivers to be vested in the king;
consequently all canals taken from them are bought of him;
and this ensures another regulation, which is the power of
carrying the water when bought, at the pleasure of those
who buy it, where they think fit. They cannot, however, cut
across any man's ground, without paying him for the land
and the damage; but the law does this by regulations
known to every one, and no individual is allowed a negative
upon a measure which is for the general good. The pur-
chasers of water from the king, are usually considerable
land owners, or communities that have lands wanting water;
and it is of no consequence at what distance these lands
may be from the river, whence the water is taken, as they
have a right to conduct it where they choose, provided
they do not cut through a garden or a pleasure ground."
. . . . The water is sold † " per hour, per week, and
even half an hour, and down to a quarter. The common
price of an hour per week for ever is 1,500 livres."

This irrigation is not used for rice alone, but for clover
and all sorts of crops; it must however be especially important to rice, which is very dependent on moisture,
and a failure in which, when it is the main food of a
district, is a more serious misfortune than the failure of

* Young's France, 2. 167.   † Ib. 168.

green crops. Will the time ever arrive when our noble
dominions in India are watered with the same exactness as
is described above ? When this is the case, the objections
to rice as the staple food of Hindostan will be greatly
mitigated. The absolute power which the English possess,
backed by their irresistible military organization, seems to
place in their hands the means of redeeming India from
that liability to famine which has hitherto distinguished
that country.

But there is another objection to rice as an article of
large consumption : I mean the unwholesome nature of its
cultivation. It has been said, that at the best of times
a rice ground is a marsh, and in the worst season a swamp.
How should we like our country covered with meadows
constantly exhaling miasmata fatal to health ? Let any one
who is familiar with a fenny country answer the question.
Take Romney marsh as a very favourable example. It has
been drained by deep ditches cut in every direction, and is
converted into fine pasture ground, on which thousands
upon thousands of sheep are fattened for the London
market. The land is so excellent that it lets as pasture
at the high rate of £4. an acre, and has let at similar
rates for nearly a century.* Yet so unwholesome is the
neighbourhood, that few even of the better classes, with
all the advantages of abundant food, clothing, and shelter,
are fortunate enough to escape the ague. How much
worse would it be if the whole expanse down to Ten-
terden Steeple were periodically overflowed with fresh
water !

* Young's Annals of Agriculture, xi. 278.

On this interesting topic, I again quote A. Young.[*]
" Passing the Sessa, which exhibits a bed of five times as
much gravel as water, in three or four miles the quantity
of rice is considerable : the stubble is green and in wet
mud.; the sheaves thin." . . . . " The rice-grounds
receive but one ploughing, which is given in the middle
of March, and the seed sown at the end of the same month,
in water to the seedman's knees, which is left on the ground
till the beginning of June, when the crop is weeded by hand,
by women half-naked, with their petticoats tucked to their
waists wading in the water ; and they make so droll a figure,
that parties in pleasantry, at that season, view the rice-
grounds. When the weeding is finished, the water is drawn
off for eight days ; and it is again drawn off when the
ear begins to form, till formed ; after which, it is let in
again till the rice is nearly ripe." . . . .

I fear that in England the pleasantry of going to see
these poor weeders, even in the warmth of June, would be
thought an amusement of a very bad sort. I do not wonder
at the concluding paragraph. " In the great road there is
a stone at five miles from Milan, nearer than which it is
prohibited to sow rice." We need not regret that the
coldness of our climate prevents us from growing this
detestable crop, though it appears to be a very profitable
one in a pecuniary point of view. " Of the produce of the
rice-grounds in the Veronese, they reckon one third for
expenses, one third for water, and one third profit."

As M. Le Play is ignorant of the objections that attach
to rice for a principal food, so he is ignorant of the objec-

* Young's France, 2, 237.

tions that attach to a similar use of the potato. Nor indeed
is he happy in his statements respecting this tubercle. He
speaks of it as having scarcely been introduced into common
use in Europe until the present century ; a statement he
would not have made if he had been at all acquainted
with the history of Ireland, or even with so much of it
as I have already quoted for another purpose from A.
Young. It appears that a hundred years ago, the potato
was the main support of the Irish, just as bread was of
the English, though indeed, at that time the Irish enjoyed,
what they have since lost, a good supply of milk as an
addition. If M. Le Play's remark had been confined to
continental Europe it might probably have been correct.

M. Le Play is certainly right when he says that con-
flicting opinions have been entertained as to the results of
the extended culture of potatoes. "Some eminent physiologists regard as an error of *hygiene,* and a sort of public
calamity, the substitution of the potato for grain, when it
is adopted in a considerable proportion by people ill furnished besides with animal food. The observation seems to
indicate, in truth, that this substitution implies a diminution
of muscular power and of physical energy. No workman
whose food has the potato for its principal base, can get
through the work performed by the Bergamasque smith who
feeds principally on maize." Another error here occurs in
the statement that "no where, however, does the potato
appear to have altogether superseded grain." Let the Irish
for a century past determine whether this is true.

But though M. Le Play is aware of the difference of
opinion that exists as to the potato, he does not seem aware
of several grounds of difference. Physiologists, I conceive,

are tolerably well agreed in pronouncing the potato a wholesome food, and perhaps the only solid one that contains
all the elements necessary to life and health. Even Adam
Smith observed that it must be a tolerably good diet, since
the Irish chairmen, and other labourers, on migrating to
England had every appearance of health. True, it might
be objected to Smith that at that time the Irish children
had the advantage of milk from the cow, another article
of food peculiarly favorable to health even when taken alone.
The late famine confirmed the favorable opinion of the
wholesomeness of the potato, the want of it in the workhouses and other establishments having led to scurvy and
other diseases. The Registrar General tells us that judging
from the facts observed on a wide scale, the potato is, at
present, an essential article of food; and that the disease
of scurvy, which had almost been forgotten, reappeared
in 1847, after the potato crop had failed.* We find in a
subsequent report,† that " the potato cannot be replaced
by bread, beans, or peas, alone, and that in its absence,
an extra allowance of fruit, green vegetables, or herbs, is
required. Scurvy, in consequence of the neglect of this
precaution, prevailed extensively in the spring of the year
1847, after the first great destruction of the potato crop."
If there is little difference of opinion as to the excellence
of the potato so far, neither is there much difference as to
its nutritive power; all agreeing that though potato eaters
may have good health, they cannot have any great muscular
vigour, and are quite incapable of getting through much
heavy labour.

* Reg. Gen. 8vo. 9, 34, and 13, Q. Return, 5.   † Ib. 16, Q. R. 3.

For people, then, not required to perform hard work, the potato is a tolerably good food, better indeed, than wheaten bread taken alone, or than any form of oats taken alone, or even than meat taken alone. A man who lived solely on wheaten bread, or on oats, or on animal food, and who also took but moderate exercise, would have a poor chance of health; whereas a man who has abundance of good potatoes may enjoy excellent health so long as he works but moderately.

The real objections to the use of the potato as a principal article of food, are of quite a different character, and seem to me unanswerable. Indeed the Irish famine of ten years ago is a commentary on the arguments, such as no Englishman will hastily forget. Hundreds of thousands of people struck down by simple unmitigated starvation, produce an impression not easily effaced. But the objections were felt long before, and are well put together by Mr. M'Culloch in a note * on his edition of Adam Smith.

The first objection is this: "potatoes being the cheapest species of food hitherto cultivated in Europe, and the Irish labourers being wholly dependent upon them, their wages are regulated by the lowest standard. Whenever, therefore, the potato crop happens to be deficient, they are left without resource." . . . . "It may be said, perhaps, that had potatoes not been introduced, corn of some sort would have been the lowest species of food; and that had its supply happened to fail, the population would have been as destitute as they are at present when potatoes are deficient." If it were worth while to pursue this argument

* M'Culloch's A. Smith, 1839. Note v.

any further, I should point out that the important question is, what effect is produced upon a people now, and under the actual circumstances of the world, by the adoption of the potato. This root has come into general cultivation in many places, and it may be interesting to speculative minds to enquire whether the world has benefited by it: but what the statesman and philanthropist really want to know, is, whether at the present day it is desirable for the working classes to throw aside wheat, and oats, and rye, and adopt potatoes instead. Looked at in this light, the objection here made is, I think, a sound one. If the potato fails, the wages of the potato eater are insufficient to enable him to pay for maize or oats: if the wheat crop should fail in any particular province, and the supply from other parts should be impossible, the wages of the wheat eater would be sufficient to enable him to pay for maize or oats. To say, as is sometimes said, that the wheat eater in such a case would resort to potatoes, seems fallacious, because it supposes an available stock of potatoes, without pointing out where it exists. The stock of maize is easily found in many parts of Europe and in a large portion of the United States.

But the supposition that wheat should ever fail in a particular province, to the extent that actually occurs in the case of potatoes, is altogether arbitrary, and unfounded in fact. The variation in price from year to year is a partial test of this fact, though the price varies also from other causes. Mr. M'Culloch says that potatoes are six times as dear in one year as they are in another, and this estimate was formed before the late famine. Now it is certainly true that wheat varies considerably, and to such an extent as to

cause great suffering to the lowest classes: yet the price
does not vary any thing like the price of potatoes. The
quartern loaf furnishes a better criterion than the measure
of wheat, both as leaving no doubt about quality, and as
being the thing which is really consumed. Now in the
last twenty years I have scarcely known the quartern loaf
sold under fivepence or above one shilling; and except
during the Irish famine, when the kind interference of
England artificially raised the price of wheat to such a
degree as most seriously to pinch our own population, the
quartern loaf has seldom risen much above tenpence. The
usual range may be said to be from fivepence to tenpence.
Probably the ordinary variation of potatoes may be as three
or four to one. But we may estimate the difference of
these variations by supposing that the quartern loaf rose
under an ordinary state of dearth, to 1s. 3d. or 1s. 8d., and
continued at that height for months together. Great as
is the suffering when it rises to tenpence, what would it
be at that higher rate?

The reasons why potatoes should vary in price more
than wheat, are quite obvious. No fact is better known
than this: that in countries not possessing easy communication with their neighbours, one province may be enjoying
abundance of bread while another is in the agonies of
want. It is the facility of transporting grain from one
country to another, that saves Europe from the repetition
of the famines of ages ago. But however excellent may
be the means of communication, it is never a cheap operation to carry potatoes to any considerable distance, both
because of the large quantity required compared with the
moderate bulk of grain, and also because of the damage

done in carrying a comparatively soft and tender commodity. Each province of Ireland and of every other potato eating country, must depend principally on its own neighbourhood for a supply; and it is only when the scarcity becomes very pressing that distant places can be resorted to.

There is another reason equally powerful. Wheat keeps well from year to year, and a crop of good quality is kept to some extent for two, three, or even five years*: whereas potatoes cannot be kept from one year to another. Even towards the close of the agricultural year, I have heard complaints in an English gaol with which I am acquainted, that there is a deterioration in the quality of the potatoes, and to such an extent as seriously to injure the health of the prisoners: if the same crop, even to the limited extent to which potatoes are used in this case, were kept till a second year, very serious consequences would probably follow. In the case of wheat, a good crop is held over to some extent to supply any deficiency of future years, but in the case of potatoes the crop is consumed within the year, and any deficiency cannot be supplied by the excess of former seasons.

We cannot wonder, therefore, that the price should vary as three, four, or even six to one, when we remember the alleged uncertainty of produce, the great cost and damage of conveying from a distance, and the impossibility of storing a surplus from one season to another. These seem to me strong grounds for regretting that any people should adopt the potato as a principal article of subsistence.

* Tooke, Prices 4, 415 note; and Jacob, Corn, 27.

It is singular that the use of this food should have prevailed in Ireland so much sooner than in other places. M. Le Play, as I have already said, states erroneously, that nowhere is it used exclusively. A. Young speaks of it * as being in his time "an article which ninety nine hundredths of the human species will not touch." Again, † speaking of a place in Lorraine he says, that "there are more potatoes than I have seen any where in France; twelve acres were at once under the eye." And on the next page, "These minutes show that it is in very few of the French provinces where this useful root is commonly found; in all the other parts of the kingdom, on inquiring for them, I was told that the people would not touch them: experiments have been made in many places, by gentlemen, with a view to introduce them for the poor, but no efforts could do it."

These observations refer to a period seventy years ago. It appeared, however, that at that time the culture was increasing in France. M. Le Play notices ‡ as a singularity that in Old Castille now, potatoes are not generally grown. He also says that in Britanny § the quantity grown is increasing. In Norway, as Mr. Laing tells us, they are very much used for the purpose of distilling brandy from them.

If there exists a considerable diversity of opinion on the subject of rice and potatoes, so does there exist also a considerable diversity as to butcher's meat. Among the middle classes of society, among the traders, and lawyers,

* Young's France, 1. 363. † Ib. 2, 77.

‡ Le Play, 176, 1. § Ib. 230, 1.

and other professional men, there is too great an exertion
of the brain, with too little exercise of the muscular powers.
The result is generally a want of vigorous health. This
is one cause of the success of the various quackeries of
the day, and this leads also to the making of various
experiments on diet by many men, who seek merely their
own ease, and not a reputation for invention. I have had
several friends who have tried the effect of abstaining from
meat : in only one instance that I remember has the practice
been continued, and in all the others I have been told
that a want of vigour and of power of work was soon felt.
The one who continued to abstain permanently was a
French gentleman, long settled in England, and of a florid
countenance with a full habit of body. I think it is stated
that the eminent Adam Fergusson who died in old age,
some forty years back, took no meat during many years :
but that he was driven to this course by determination of
blood to the head. There are cases, no doubt, where such
abstinence is the best curative treatment. On the other
hand there are persons who require a generous diet to
keep them in health, and even in life, and if such persons
should be induced to join the sect of vegetarians, the
consequences would soon probably be fatal.

It seems to be acknowledged that vegetables furnish the
same elements of fuel and of fibrine that are obtained from
flesh : but it is clear that we obtain a far larger quantity
of nutriment by eating a certain weight of meat than by
eating the same weight of vegetables. If a man leads a
quiet life, he may find time to swallow a sufficient quantity
of bread, or even of potatoes, to supply the muscular waste
that takes place. But if a man has to task his bodily powers

to the utmost, he must take his food in the concentrated form of flesh, qualifying it of course with a mixture of vegetables. Let the vegetarians go among the navvies, and try if those brawny fellows can get through their herculean tasks on a diet without meat: let them go to the trainers, and see if these people can turn out a prize-fighter, or a pedestrian, on such a regimen. I have read of a man who was trained on gin as his drink, but I never heard of one who was brought up to his task on vegetables.

I have no doubt that many of ourselves take a great deal more meat than does us good: men of robust, full habit, not taking any severe exercise, but contenting themselves with a daily walk of three to four miles, or a daily ride of twice that distance, should use meat rather as a condiment, a seasoning to other dishes, than as as a main article of diet. It is an innocent experiment for a healthy person to give up meat for a time : it is a dangerous one to live on nothing but meat for a time ; and I have known serious damage result from it. The greater part of the Irish have lived on vegetable food for a long time past, and we have seen that in the last century, when they added milk to their potatoes, they were pronounced by Adam Smith and Arthur Young, to be a healthy race. But we are told that the fur hunters of North America, who in their travels necessarily subsist on flesh and nothing else, suffer much from this diet, in spite of the severe toil they undergo.

The unwholesomeness of a meat diet is strongly confirmed* by a fact, the knowledge of which we owe to our invaluable

---

* Reg. Gen. octavo, 14. xxi.

registers of mortality, together with the complete census of our population and their trades. It has long been known that certain occupations shortened the lives of those who followed them. It is natural that tailors should suffer from their want of exercise, bakers from the stove heat in which they live, grinders from the dust they inhale, innkeepers from the quantity of liquor they swallow. But it comes out that to this list must be added the butchers. It has been suggested that the shortness of these men's lives may be owing to the putrefying offal that surrounds them, but it is more likely to be owing principally to the excess of meat they swallow. It has long been remarked that butchers commonly, have florid complexions : this peculiarity cannot be the result of impure exhalations. I have even seen it offered, as a proof that butchers and their families are not great meat eaters, that their notion of a dainty is not a joint of beef, but fish or poultry. I should regard this as a proof that they are satiated with their daily meals of flesh, and that they do use it habitually.

The most remarkable example I know of a people subsisting almost entirely upon animal food, is that of the Gauchos, described by Sir Francis Head. Most persons are familiar with the lively account of Captain Head's travels of thirty years back. He found the descendants of the Europeans living on the vast plains, or Pampas, in a condition not more than half civilized ; too idle to cultivate the ground, and surrounded by vast herds of cattle and horses. Sir Francis, then a young captain in the Royal Engineers, and a man of great ability in his profession (as I am assured by one of ·his brother officers, himself a most competent judge,) threw himself among these wild people, and found himself scampering along the wilderness with any guide, young or old, that came first to hand. His food was tough beef, and his drink was water, and he found no temptation to eat or drink more than was good for him. With this primitive fare he rode from post to post, and after all the hindrances caused by having to catch fresh horses from the plains, he contrived to cover eighty, one hundred, or one hundred and twenty miles a day; and this for many days in succession. Arrived at his journey's end for the day, he masticated his tough beef and threw himself on the ground with his saddle for a pillow. Even Sir Walter Scott's Highlander, who indignantly kicked away a snowball that his effeminate son had adopted as a pillow, would scarcely have grudged our captain his saddle for his head. The meat diet does not seem to have produced any bad effects, nor was it likely to do so, at any rate for a considerable time, being worked off by a ride all day long on rough half-broken horses, with the aid of pure air to stimulate digestion.

In conversation on this topic of the necessity of meat to support great bodily exertion, I have heard it remarked, that in some parts of the world men are found possessed of great muscular power, and who nevertheless are quite without meat as a diet. The porters of Constantinople have been instanced. We know from Eastern Tales that the Turks eat meat when they can get it, *kabob*, or roast meat, being one of the dishes with which we are familiar as being sold in the cooks' shops of Stamboul. But it may be that the porters are too poor a race to be able to indulge in this dish. Accepting the alleged fact as true, there is nothing inconsistent with the opinion I hold, as I will show.

A similar objection is made by a comparison of our town and country population. The well paid mechanic eats meat daily, and he is generally slight made, with narrow shoulders, and slouching gait, and ill-developed muscles: the plough-man, with a more uncouth appearance, has a broad pair of shoulders and brawny arms, though he gets nothing more nutritious than bread and cheese, and thinks himself for-tunate if he secures some roast beef once a year for his Christmas dinner.

But I reply to both these instances, that there is a con-fusion of ideas, if it is supposed that they disprove the importance of meat as an article of diet. I make no doubt that muscular power may be developed on vegetable food. This development depends on the exercise of the muscles at least as much as on the nutriment taken. Coop a boy up in a cell, give him no exercise, and feed him as you will, he will grow up with a flabby condition of flesh and devoid of muscular power. Put another boy in country air, feed him on potatoes and milk, give him a little hard work to do every day, and his limbs will grow and become strong. All persons familiar with calisthenic exercises or gymnastics, know how fast the strength of the arm increases with gradual and judicious exercise.

Now a country labourer is brought up from boyhood, to employments that bring his muscles into severe action: at one time he stoops to weed, at another he rubs down a horse much taller than himself, or helps to load a cart high above his head. The mechanic performs over and over again a few simple operations; with his work generally in one position. The farm labourer, commonly paid by the day, gets through no great quantity of work, but that work is of a severe kind: the mechanic, paid by the piece, is on the stretch all day long, but performs no operation that brings the muscles much into play. The advantage of meat to a mechanic, is not that it enlarges and strengthens his muscles to a degree for which he has no need, but that it supplies him with nutriment in a concentrated form, and requiring little time for digestion, and that it therefore enables him to work with activity a greater number of hours, and to get through a greater quantity of work than would be possible with a vegetable diet. I am speaking here of that class of mechanics to which the objection in question has reference: there are other classes, such as blacksmiths, and all the numerous people employed in forges and rolling mills, who not only get through a great deal of work, but whose muscular development is very great. The constant waste that takes place in the frames of such workmen would be very imperfectly supplied by any amount of vegetable food.

A mechanic of this latter kind, with whom I am well acquainted, went to Belgium, and after a few years' absence returned home. He worked in a village near Liége, and he told me that besides the annoyances of ignorance of the language and of dislike to the drinks of the country, he was greatly inconvenienced by the want of a daily supply of meat. He had to arrange with a butcher to send each day from Liége, as meat was not to be got in the village. He spoke with some contempt of the vegetarian natives, who on a Sunday indulged in a mouthful of meat just to give a flavour to other food. But he evidently despised them the most for the small quantity of work they performed. I went into some particulars with him, and though I did

not find his statement altogether correct, in alleging that
the Belgian's work for a day was only half of an Englishman's, I did come to the conclusion that the Belgian got
through only two thirds as much as an Englishman.

It is not certain that the difference of diet accounts for
the whole variation in the quantity of work. We know
that an Englishman is on the average a considerably larger
person than a Frenchman, or a Belgian. If we add two
or three inches in height, and assume a proportionate
addition to breadth and thickness, we shall make out an
Englishman to be the far larger animal. It may be true
that we require a greater quantity of food in proportion
to our loftier stature, but the question here is, whether
the Belgian with meat every day would do more than he
does now. It is not certain that he would, but it is highly
probable. We are told that Irish reapers, when they first
arrive here, are incapable of performing the quantity of
work which they get through in the height of the season :
that they require some weeks of a hearty English meat
diet to make men of them. We are also told that the
Lincolnshire farmers, who pay their labourers good wages,
are discontented if a considerable portion of the wages is
not expended on meat for the labourer's own consumption :
this, of course, when the man is working by the day. I
have been told by Major Eyre that some of the Hindoos
have learnt from the Europeans to disregard the rules of
their race, and to eat animal food : he assures me that
the practice causes a wonderful improvement in their
appearance and bodily strength. I must do our Indian
fellow subjects the justice to add that these transgressors
are not of the best class of natives, but that the men of

high caste will wander famine stricken within reach of animal food and refuse to touch it. No doubt they feel as we should, if we were tempted to allay the pangs of hunger by the offer of human flesh. I have seen a Jew shudder at the thought of pork, and in the same way an Hindoo may shrink with disgust from flesh of any kind.

We are apt to forget that it is not easy in many parts of the world to obtain fresh meat during one half the year. It is a happy circumstance for us that we have no difficulty on this head; but we all know that two centuries ago even the rich were obliged to be contented with salt meat during many months. In the United States salt meat is greatly eaten, and this is supposed to be one of the many causes that make the Americans so void of flesh and substance, and so short lived as they are. The supply of cattle, and still more of sheep, is said to be very bad in the United States: mutton scarcely eaten; and cattle half starved during the long winter. Captain Barclay a few years ago gave a lamentable account of this branch of farming there. In the North and East of Europe, where the snow lies on the ground about half the year, people must be content during that time to dispense with fresh meat. M. Le Play mentions that the Cobalt miner he describes, who lives not far from Christiania, is in the habit of buying a cow every year and salting it for half the year's supply. It is true that the price of meat is very high in England, but the article is obtainable, fresh, at all times. The high wages of our mechanics generally, enable them to pay the high price. I wish I could say the same of our country labourers: there is hope, however, that causes now at work will in a few years put them also in as good a position as to diet. If labourers should become scarce among the farmers, it might be found advantageous to give a man half as much more wages and to require a proportionate quantity of work.

I will add to these remarks what M. Le Play says. He observes * that heavy labour is believed to require better food than grain and milk: that meat is supposed to be necessary, yet that many vigorous labourers live without it yet not without fat or milk. And in another place,† he attributes the indolence of a particular class to the want of meat and alcohol: though he adds that they are also in want of mental stimulus. He observes ‡ that in the South of Europe butter cannot be had during the greater part of the year, but that cheese is used as a substitute. He does not seem aware of the extent to which it is used in England by country labourers; not indeed because butter cannot be had but because cheese is far cheaper. Mr. M'Culloch § says, "The Arabs are the greatest consumers of butter in the world. Burckhardt tells us that it is a common practice among all classes to drink every morning a coffee cup full of melted butter or ghee! and they use it in an infinite variety of other ways. The taste for it is universal; and the poorest individuals will expend half their daily income that they may have butter for dinner and butter in the morning." We find few parts of the world except Ireland, in which an unmixed vegetable diet prevails.

If we are desirous of comparing the food generally of different countries, we may advantageously refer, as to

* Le Play, 33. 1.   † Ib. 248. 1.   ‡ Ib. 32. 2.   § Com. Dicty.—*Butter*.

Norway, to the volume of Mr. Laing, who gives us many and valuable particulars. Mr. Laing, from his actual residence in Norway during two years and a half, and from his having cultivated a small farm, is a particularly trustworthy authority. No doubt he was at the time of his stay, imbued with ultra-liberal and almost democratic notions, such as then prevailed among English politicians far more than at present. The Reform Bill had lately passed, after a struggle that had inflamed the minds of men : the liberals in the flush of victory anticipated little short of a millenium from the prevalence of the popular party : young men almost expected all the evils that afflict humanity to be corrected, and were disappointed to find that the very clouds and fogs could not be banished by Act of Parliament. I have a perfect right to smile at this exalted state of mind, because I must confess that I shared in it. Looking back now, when twenty years have passed, and reading Mr. Laing by the light of these recollections, I suspect that, in all possible good faith, he has drawn a very favourable picture of the Norwegians : and that while he lived among them, his fastidiousness as a gentleman was thoroughly controlled by his partiality as a politician.

I have heard from friends who have lately travelled in Norway, that the accommodations are of a very poor kind : that it is necessary to carry provisions for one's own consumption, even in travelling on the ordinary route. The roads are good but very steep, the little horses still trot full speed down declivities that are astounding to an Englishman : each traveller has his *carriole* with his horse in harness of a very rude and very flimsy sort. If this were all I knew I might have set the Norwegians down as a poor and uncivilised race of people. But referring to Mr. Laing I find that I should have been utterly mistaken : and whatever deductions I may be disposed to make as to the political state, and as to the refinement of the land-lords, I have entire confidence in Mr. Laing's narration of facts.

One of the first statements is as follows.* " I live here on strawberries and milk, and trout, or rather char, being pink, not white like fresh water trout. Fish appears everywhere the basis of a Norwegian repast. Meat, even at the table d'hôte at Christiania, seemed secondary. The river or lake is everywhere resorted to." Again,† "The standard of living with regard to food, appears to me also higher in Norway than in most of our Scotch highland districts, though I cannot yet form a decided opinion. The materials are the same, viz., oatmeal, bearmeal, potatoes, fish from the river, salt fish, and salt herrings, of excellent quality from the sea coast, also cheese, butter, and milk. Four meals a day form, I understand, the regular fare in every family ; and with two of these meals the labourers have a glass of home made brandy distilled from potatoes. It is usual, I understand, to have animal food, such as salt beef, or black puddings, at least twice in the week." It appears, however, that great want of food is felt at par-ticular times. ‡ " This mode of grinding or baking makes intelligible the use of bread of the bark of the fir tree in years of scarcity. Its inner rind, kiln dried, may un-doubtedly be ground, along with the husks and grain, and add to the quantity of meal ; it may even be nutritious.

* Laing's Norway, Ed. 1851, pa. 31.   † Ib. 37.   ‡ Ib. 41.

I had previously been rather disposed to doubt the fact, and to laugh at the idea of a traveller dining on sawdust pudding, and timber bread. In years of scarcity, however, this use of fir bark is more extensive than is generally supposed. The present dilapidated state of the forests, in districts which formerly supplied wood for exportation, is ascribed to the great destruction of young trees for this purpose in the year 1812." And in a later part of the work, * speaking of the Fjelde, " It is difficult to convey an idea of the dreary aspect of this plateau, and its utter solitude. . . . . Trees are sprinkled over the surface, but they do not enliven the scene, being the dark, stern looking pines which appear almost like a piece of the rock from which they are growing. Many were standing with all their branches dead, stripped of the bark to make bread, and blanched by the weather, resembling white marble, mere ghosts of trees. The bread is made of the inner rind next to the wood, taken off in flakes like a sheet of foolscap paper, and is steeped or washed in warm water to clear off its astringent principle. . . . . When dry it is pounded into small pieces, mixed with corn, and ground into meal in the hand mill or quern. It is much more generally used than I supposed. There are districts in which the forests suffered very considerable damage in the years 1812 and 1814, when bad crops and the war, then raging, reduced many to bark bread. The extended cultivation of the potato since that period has probably placed the inhabitants of the lower country beyond the necessity of generally resorting to it; but the Fjelde bonder use it, more or less every year."

* Ib. 219.

We see from these extracts that the food of many of the Norwegian labourers is tolerably plentiful, but that of others scanty. It appears also, from other sources, that the inhabitants of the coast are in a state of a good deal of wretchedness. It must be remembered that Norway is fully peopled, and that its population has long ceased to increase except very slowly. It is rather surprising that there should not be more distress than is actually found. The peculiar manners and customs that prevail must have the credit of this exemption from squalid indigence; and the advocates of a division of land into small properties may triumphantly point to Norway as a proof that such a division may under some circumstances be satisfactorily carried out.

As to the serfs of Russia the notion that prevailed among us a few years ago was, that they were badly fed and that their state altogether was one of misery. In the early part of the late war, when some Russian prisoners were found to be in excellent condition of body, it was rather supposed that this was exceptional, and that the majority of their countrymen would be found in a much worse state. Any one reading M. Le Play's cases will come to the opposite conclusion, and will find that in many parts of Russia, food is abundant, the land insufficiently peopled, and the serfs, therefore, well provided.

Indeed it seems a safe general rule, that under the régime of Patronage the working classes are well fed, and that as Individualism is substituted, food becomes more scanty. It does not appear that the slaves in the United States have generally any complaint to make of a want of abundant subsistence, except in a case here and there of a greedy ill-conditioned master. There is, I suppose, far more hunger felt in this free country than in Virginia and Carolina and their neighbours. The reason is obvious. It is not that masters are more competent to provide for their dependents than the dependents would be if they were free : but it is that slavery or serfdom generally prevails in countries that are thinly peopled. Of what advantage would a slave or a serf be in England, where every one can have as many labourers as he wants, and has to pay less for their services than it would cost him to maintain a slave ?   But if another fertile island ten times as large as this were raised close to us from the bottom of the sea, labourers would flock to this new land of promise, and there would be an outcry among employers for some arrangements equivalent to serfdom, that should give them the command of labourers. Concurrently with this newly demanded régime of patronage and dependence, there would be an abundant supply of food to the working classes.

It is not wonderful, then, that the serfs of Russia should be well fed : it would be contrary to analogy if they were not so. Hereafter, when the population has increased up to the limit of its food, the condition of the boor will be deteriorated : but the seigneurs, finding themselves burdened with too many people on their estates, will cease to value themselves on the number of their serfs, and will gladly set them free to get rid of the surplus. Freedom and hunger, apparently, go hand in hand. It is the business of the philanthropist and the statesman to guard against this conjunction, and so to cultivate the minds and habits of free subjects as to make them masters of their own destiny.

M. Le Play's statements are distinctly, that in Russia
there reigns among the serfs an abundance of food such
as is rarely found in Germany, or the Western states of
Europe. Thus, in the case of an agricultural labourer in
Armagnac, he says * " though belonging to the inferior
class of agricultural labourers, this man lives in a state of
abundance and well-being, such as the author of these
studies has observed no other example of in the West
of Europe, and which almost equals that which has been
recorded of the Russian and Hungarian peasants."

If we turn to actual cases of the Russian serfs, we find
their food good and plentiful. The *Englishwoman in Russia,*
visiting a monastery, found a number of peasants feasting
on buck wheat, black bread, and oil ; and drinking quass.
M. Le Play gives four Russian cases. In the first † he
describes the food as copious and substantial, consisting of
grain, fat of pork, meat and poultry. In the second, ‡ he
says that here, as in the greater part of Russia, the principal
articles of food are, first, a soup of pork, mutton, or beef,
with preserved cabbage ; secondly, a soup of fish caught in
the rivers ; thirdly, of porridge, &c., with milk, butter, fat,
or oil. The bread is made of rye, with part of the bran,
ground in a very simple and ingenious hand mill. The
drink is quass made of rye, in every household, once a
week. On feast days dishes of a better kind are prepared.
It must be confessed that our labourers, and even our
mechanics, would be glad of such fare. The third case §
is that of a man employed among iron works in the Ural
mountains. He consumes grain in two forms : as bread,

* Le Play, 213. 2.   † Ib. 60. 1.   ‡ Ib. 70. 2.   § Ib. 79. 1.

made of rye and wheat mingled : and as porridge, made of
a mixture of barley with other grain. Like the Cobalt
miner mentioned by Mr. Laing, he provides salt meat for
the winter, as well as salt fish. He enjoys the use of milk,
butter, fresh meat part of the year, eggs, game from the
forest, besides berries and mushrooms, which are much
eaten in the north of Russia. The fourth case * confirms
the previous ones.

Thus we see that in Russia generally the food of the
peasant is various and abundant, and very different from
the meagre fare which was formerly supposed to fall to
his lot. If plenty to eat and drink were the only thing
to be desired, the serf might be well contented with his
fate. But the nobler nature of man leads him to aspirations
after something higher than a mere animal existence, forbids
him to be content to eat, drink, and sleep continually at
the beck of a superior.

The Hungarian peasant seems to share the abundance
of the Russian. M. Le Play says † that the farming
labourer, with regard to abundance and quality of food
is in the very first ranks among the European labourers
who have fallen under his observation.

We find one peculiarity in the habits of an Austrian
mechanic whose case is given. ‡ He is a Viennese, his
circumstances are poor, his fare scanty ; but he drinks no
spirituous liquors, and supplies their place with coffee : he
never takes pure water, but always resorts to coffee. This
custom, it seems, is not uncommon among the Viennese
workmen of sober habits. Elsewhere § we find that coffee

---

* Le Play, 87. 1.   † Ib. 111.   ‡ Ib. 122, 2.   § Ib. 158, 2.

is much taken at meals, in Northern Germany, Holland,
Belgium, and the North of France. In England, so early
as the end of last century, we find not coffee, but tea, a
very common beverage in England. Thus, Sir F. M. Eden
tells us * that in some families in Kent, in 1795 or
1796, tea was taken with every meal. It is amusing to
find Arthur Young, in his usual rough undoubting way,
denouncing the practice. † He speaks of " several pernicious
habits, particularly the use of spirits, and what has of late
increased to a very injurious degree, of tea as a substitute
—bad indeed for almost all other support—being a vain
present attempt to supply to the spirits of the mind what
is wanting to the strength of the body ; but in its lasting
effects impairing the nerves, and thence equally injuring
both body and mind—and though perhaps beginning with
elevation, certainly ending in depression." Would our
modern teetotalers forgive this diatribe against tea, in
consideration of the accompanying condemnation of spirits ?

In Germany generally, we do not find that generous
diet which prevails in Russia. The peasants are free and
poor. The population is too thick on the ground to make
a serf of any value, and, as among ourselves, the aim
proposed is to lessen the numbers. The very large emigration that is constantly taking place, confirms that view.

Comparing France and England, the great difference is,
that the French like their food in a liquid state ; we like
ours in a solid state. This is not true only of the middle
and upper classes : among the labourers also, soup is in
France the principal mode of taking food. Our labourer

* Eden's Poor, 2. 280, and 2. 288.   † Young's Annals, 25, 367.

eats his bread and cheese without further preparation ; the French peasant makes his bread into a soup, adding what he can to make it palatable ; a little salt and butter, and some vegetables. The French, as is well known, are great consumers of bread. We are all aware that in Paris, and on the principal roads, this is tolerably good, though its sourness is not pleasant to our palate. In the country it is not used by labourers, made of unmixed wheat: in Auvergne * we find it of rye ; in Armagnac † of one-third wheat and two-thirds rye. In the latter case, this mixed bread forms the principal food. The state of the French labourer as to the quantity of food he enjoys seems far from satisfactory. In A. Young's time the same state of things existed, and to such an extent that he concluded the population to be too numerous by many millions. The French mode of making all food, including even bread, into soup, and the opposite English mode of taking most food solid, are not easily accounted for. Some one, noticing the fact, that solid food prevails more in some parts of England than in others, tries to explain it, by the scarcity or abundance of fuel. Where coal is accessible and cheap, a fire is readily obtained and a pot is boiled. The same is true Eden says of potatoes. ‡ In some parts of England they were formerly little eaten, because of the difficulty of finding fuel with which to boil them. But fuel is certainly as scarce and dear in France as in any part of England, and this explanation is not convincing.

On the whole, if we compare the condition of our working classes as to food, with that of other nations, we have

* Le Play, 249, 1.   † Ib. 237, 1.   ‡ Eden's Poor, 1. 152 and 2. 16.

no great reason for self gratulation. It is probably much
inferior to that of the negro slaves, and to that of the
serfs of Russia and Hungary : it is certainly inferior to
that of the free labourers of the United States. Taking
all parts of the kingdom together, it is difficult to make a
close comparison, since our mechanics are far better fed
than our farm labourers : the English farm labourers are
probably better fed than the Scotch farm labourers ;
and both of these are much better fed than the Irish
peasants. Malthus * contrasts the white wheaten bread
of the South of England with the coarser food of Scotland.
The number of wheat consumers in England has much
increased since the beginning of the century, but the
researches of organic chemistry appear to have shewn that
oatmeal, the common Scotch food, is far more nutritious
than we had imagined.

It will scarcely be disputed, however, that the English
country labourer is better supplied with food than the
Scotch, and I entirely sympathise with Malthus in his
hope that the fare of our men may not be brought down
to the lower level. He censures A. Young † for expressing
a desire that the English would adopt potatoes and milk
as their main food. This much must be remembered of
Malthus, when we are disposed to censure him for some
thoughtless and harsh expressions in his earlier editions :
that he was a constant and sincere friend to the highest
condition in which a labourer could be placed. His censure
of Young's recommendation of potatoes was not founded on
the uncertainty of that root, or on the great variation of

* Population 1. 331.   † Ib. 2. 383.

its price, but on the fact that labourers supported on it were in a lower economical condition than labourers who depended on bread for their maintenance. Now he regarded individual prudence as the only permanent safeguard against distress. He looked upon poor laws, erroneously, I believe, as promoting in the long run a lower and lower state of being. He contended that men made or marred their own destiny, and that government and private charity, might mitigate poverty for a time, but could do nothing to remove it. He therefore felt that the great problem was, how to stimulate the working classes to the exercise of prudence; and he believed that if they could once become determined to rest satisfied with nothing short of a high standard of living, they were then safe. That a people should sink from wheaten bread to oatmeal, or from oatmeal to potatoes, he would have pronounced a great misfortune, and he would have rejoiced to see every labourer in the kingdom enjoying a daily meal of meat. Few people now will be found to dispute the accuracy of this part of his opinions, though not long before he wrote A. Young * spoke doubtfully of what he called the luxury of the English labourers.

We shall not, however, be disposed to charge any great luxury against these poor people, if we look either at the wages they earned, or the commodities they were able to purchase. We have seen before, that a hundred years ago, the ordinary wages were not more than six shillings to seven shillings a week, though they rose one shilling or two shillings towards the close of the last century. Malthus, † quoting Eden as to this latter period, states

---

* Young's France, 1. 566.   † Malthus Pamphlet, 1814. 5.

that the farm labourers' wages might be divided into fifths, and were thus appropriated:—

Two-fifths were spent on meal or bread.

Two-fifths were spent on rent, fuel, soap, candles, tea, sugar, clothing.

One-fifth was spent on meat, milk, butter, cheese, potatoes.

Such a beggarly account needs no comment.

Sir F. M. Eden also furnishes[*] an account of the cost of food of a Cumbrian labourer:—

Breakfast—Hasty pudding and milk ... ... 1d.

Dinner—Potatoes $\frac{1}{4}$d., butter or bacon $\frac{1}{2}$d., milk
and bread $\frac{1}{2}$d. ... ... $\Big\}$ $1\frac{1}{4}$d.

Supper—Boiled milk and bread ... ... $\frac{3}{4}$d.

_____

3d.

This sum of 3d. exceeds the actual outlay.

I have often shared the wonder I have heard expressed, as to how a poor family lives. This short account has partially enlightened me.

_____

* Eden on Poor, 2. 74.

CHAPTER IX.

THE next topic I have to discuss is the dress of the working classes. In England it can scarcely be said that a particular costume is set apart for any class of society: and those who are much influenced by æsthetical considerations, feel that this is a matter for regret. Lady Eastlake, especially, in her witty and admirable essay on dress, points out how much the working classes lose in dignity, and how much the world generally loses in picturesqueness, when the peasant adopts an imitation of his superior's costume. I have heard a wish expressed in conversation, that we could go back to the ways of our ancestors, and that all men and women should carry on their backs an advertisement of the grade to which they belong.

It is, no doubt, true, that a distinct peasant costume is more picturesque, and, in point of beauty, far more desirable than the dress worn by our working classes. Lady Eastlake says that a peasant woman in her English Sunday clothes is only a coarse imitation, and a plain likeness, of a lady: whereas in a different costume the same woman would present an appearance that might be admirable in itself, and which would provoke no disparaging comparison. I have myself been struck with a similar circumstance. I noticed a plain farmer as a fine specimen of humanity; with sunburnt cheeks, bright eyes, and white teeth, with cutaway green coat, and broad brimmed hat, he looked a model of manly beauty. The same day, I dined in his company, and to meet the gentlemen he had imitated their dress. In his swallow tail Sunday coat and awkward black cravat, he looked plain and uncouth.

But however desirable as regards symmetry and beauty, a classified costume may be, it is not perhaps so feasible as some persons suppose. There may be reasons, I think there are reasons, why among ourselves such a distinct costume would not be tolerated for a day.

Nothing is more common than for a mechanic to become a master manufacturer: M. Le Play says that most of the considerable houses of Sheffield have sprung from working men : my own observation of traders in the midland counties has led me to the same conclusion as to them. Suppose, then, that a particular person was twenty years ago a workman : having saved a few score pounds, he leaves his master and starts on his own account: he continues to labour with his own hands ; but as he employs a capital, has other men working for him, and sells finished goods to merchants, he must be regarded as a master : after a struggle of ten years he has saved a thousand or two thousand pounds, and finds leisure to busy himself a little with the affairs of his town, perhaps as a guardian of the poor : in another five years he may find himself a member of the corporation, and in a few years more he perchance arrives at the dignity of the mayoralty, and is seen presiding during a whole year, on every occasion of public ceremony, and sitting on the bench to administer justice. We all know that this is no fancy picture, but that it represents what is daily going on. It is of such materials as this man that mayors, aldermen, and councillors, are commonly made, and very properly and wisely made.

Now the advocates for a peasant costume would of course have put that costume on this man, so long as he worked for a master. Would they allow him to leave it off when he commenced business for himself, or would they require him to retain it so long as with his own horny hands he continued to wield the hammer? Ought he to carry it with him to the parish offices, and to the council chamber? Should the alderman's gown cover the same peasant dress, and should the same dress be found under the Mayor's gold chain when he received the Prince Consort at an entertainment, or presided at the Quarter Sessions of the magistracy?

It is not so usual in the country for men to rise from the ranks to fortune. Yet examples of such an elevation are not wanting. The thrifty labourer here and there, invests his small savings in a shop, and before the close of a long life, becomes a freeholder. Shall such a man retain his peasant dress to the last: shall he leave it as part of his inheritance to his son and his grandson? If all the families whose progenitors were of the peasant class, were required to retain the costume of that rank, how many members of the House of Commons, how many Peers even, would be without it?

It has not been sufficiently remembered, how, among ourselves, one class runs into another, and how men are constantly shifting from class to class. A spendthrift master leaves his son a clerk or workman, but this man, discontented with his lot, aspires to rise again, and possibly leaves his son in a better position than the original one of the spendthrift progenitor. Sometimes in the course of a generation or two, families change places; the master's family sink into the ranks and the servant's family rise to command. Nor are such mutations confined to towns: even the landed gentry occasionally fall into the depths of poverty. Macaulay, with his usual felicity, relates how the ancestors of Warren Hastings had once possessed the Manor of Daylesford, and how faults and misfortunes had reduced the family so low that the boys became the associates and schoolfellows of the ploughboys of the parish. At what point in this declension of fortune should the falling family have been called upon to don the peasant costume? Hutton, whose life I have already sketched, relates an affecting incident that occurred to himself.* Presiding one day, the 21st July, 1786, in his favourite Court of Requests, among 170 defendants' names called, was one familiar to him, that of Henshaw Grevis. The man appeared; a meagre figure, nearly sixty years old; and " behaved with all the humility of manners that fancy could paint;" with apparel not worth eighteen-pence. Thirty years before, Hutton, a poor man struggling with adverse circumstances, had seen this person " completely mounted and dressed in green velvet, with a hunter's cap and girdle, at the head of the pack." Hutton was now a substantial citizen, and the presiding genius of the Petty Court before which this unfortunate was dragged in his tattered clothes. The poor wretch when asked how long the Moseley Hall Estate had been in his family, until it slipped through his grasp, replied, from the time

* Hutton's Court of Requests, 378.

of the Conquest. Would the advocates of a classified costume have required this spendthrift to retain the last rags and tatters of his green velvet hunting suit, or would they consent to leave every man to adopt at his own pleasure, that dress which is most pleasing to himself?

This absence of a marked distinction between one class and another is nothing new : Shakspeare makes one of his characters complain that the toe of the peasant galled the kibe of the courtier. It was not so in France before the Revolution of 1789, and any one reading Madame de Genlis' novel of *Les Parvenus*, will see how entirely separate and distinct the noblesse was kept from the bourgeois. Not that individuals of the bourgeois class were excluded from the society of the noblesse : there was, indeed, far more familiarity than at present between members of the different classes when they did meet on friendly terms ; for since marriage between a bourgeois and a noble lady was regarded as almost impossible, there was less jealousy than we feel of any thing like unequal intimacies.

In Russia, as is well known, this distinction is rigorously observed. A serf is frequently allowed to leave his village and to become a trader in one of the great towns. If he is prudent and lucky he accumulates a fortune. He does not by this means cease to be a serf, but during his absence from his seigneur's estate is required to pay the *abrok*, a capitation fee. In many cases he is allowed to purchase his freedom, but sometimes his superior is obstinate, and not wanting money, will not be induced to sell liberty to his serfs. It is said that there are in Russia traders worth £10,000., £50,000., £100,000.; (nay, I have been assured by a trustworthy friend, that he has known a man reported to be worth a million sterling), and many of these men are still in the condition of servitude. In principle, I believe, the property, as well as its owner, belongs to the superior, and the right to both might be here and there asserted but for the despotic power of the Czar, who by a threat of Siberia would soon effectually interfere. Under such circumstances a peasant costume is perfectly possible, because every one belongs to a particular class. A man was a serf yesterday, and to-day he is a freeman : he wore the serf's dress yesterday, but the dress of a freeman to-day. To attempt such a distribution where all are born free, and, in the eye of the law, equal, is simply impossible. Beauty and æsthetical fitness must give way to higher considerations.

M. Le Play illustrates this question by mentioning his having met a woman in England who was driving a cart, and who looked very ridiculous from wearing some cast off finery of a lady. This, he says, evidently did not arise from poverty. I should rather suppose that it arose from a penurious disposition on the part of the wearer, who had happened to pick up this finery at a less price than that of plain clothing. I have had an opportunity of noticing the ordinary dress of women who may be supposed to be in the lowest depths of poverty ; my daily walk into town taking me by the relieving offices of the parish ; and I constantly see the unfortunates who suffer the humiliation of applying for assistance. The dress of these women is decent, equally removed from the rags of an Irish beggar, and from the tawdriness observed by M. Le Play.

M. Le Play is disposed to regret that the dress of the Western States has not the durability of that of the East ; and that our clothes are not such as to last our lifetime, or to be handed down to a second generation. As there is a fixed costume in the East, and no change of fashion, this durability is rendered possible. Now there is certainly another and a very unpleasing side to this picture. In Morier's admirable *Hajji Baba in England*, the Hajji complains of the absence of personal cleanliness among us, from the want of baths. The Mehmandar answers that if the English leave their skins too much to nature, they constantly change their linen; even a mechanic indulging once a week in a clean shirt; but that the Easterns after their frequent ablutions always resume the same filthy dress. Since that book was published a great change has taken place, the daily sponge-bath having been adopted by all the educated classes. But the unchanging East still goes on with its perpetual baths and hereditary garments. How offensive this practice is, was proved to me by the whim of an old gentleman, who, some years ago, was in the habit of now and then going to visit some property he had at a little distance from his home: on these occasions he always put on a certain dress which had served the same purpose for years: his friends when they saw this well-known costume always endeavoured to keep to windward of him, though at other times there was nothing unpleasing about his society. If any one will invent linen, or some other fabric capable of being washed, which shall have the durability of a lifetime, he will be a benefactor to the race; but long may it be before our working classes adopt the long-wearing upper garments of the East.

M. Le Play says that in the East there is a strong sense of personal dignity, and that this causes a fondness for dress on the part of the men. He is also of opinion that the prohibition of usury, and even of interest on loans, leads to the exhibition of rich ornaments, and of coin as a decoration, which would be otherwise employed in producing an income.

As to the former notion, that there is a strong sense of personal dignity among the Mahometan populations, there seems much reason to doubt the correctness of the statement.   The Turks, no doubt, are manly fellows, with a good deal remaining of that haughty spirit which is commonly found in a conquering and dominant race.   But if we go to a neighbouring nation which also professes the faith of the Koran, this virile temper disappears.   Even in Constantinople there seems to be a familiarity with the bastinado which comports but ill with our notions of personal dignity: but in Persia, if we are to believe Mr. Morier, the stick is in perpetual motion as an instrument of punishment.   The Persian ambassador on his arrival in London is made to complain that among many other grievances, the crowds of people are allowed to laugh at his beard, and no police are employed in striking right and left on the heads of the offenders.   He would have been still more scandalised if he had remained long enough to find, that when the police do put out this kind of vigour the whole nation is in arms against them.

It is curious enough that this fondness for dress seems to flourish most where personal chastisement is in vogue. The American slave is cowhided to-day, and to-morrow he appears in the gaudiest colours he can find.   The Russian serf plying in the streets of St. Petersburgh, if he trespasses, or is supposed to trespass, one inch beyond his beat, is summarily knocked down by the policeman: he goes home uncomplainingly, and on the next feast day exhibits himself in a costume which delights the eye of the lover of the picturesque. The Persian, as I have already noticed, is caned, and bastinadoed, and beaten across the mouth with a slipper, on every frivolous occasion; and he too consoles himself with a slender waist, a splendid shawl for a sash, and gorgeous arms. If the régime of the stick be a proof of the personal dignity of the subject, then may it truly be said that the gorgeous dress which is commonly found in company with that régime, is the result of a sense of personal dignity on the part of the wearer.

Something of the same kind is to be found in our own history. The cane was formerly used more freely than it is at present, and in former times the dress of Englishmen was far more ostentatious than it is now. Hutton complained that the brutality of his schoolmaster was such as to cause a disgust at the sight of a book. Hutton went to work at a mill at eight years old, and therefore in his schooldays he was a mere child; yet his schoolmaster, not content with ordinary chastisement, was in the habit of seizing him by the hair, and thumping his head against the wall. Afterwards in the silk mill, his master caned him so severely as to cause a bad wound, and was guilty of striking this wound so cruelly as to cause imminent danger of mortification, and to disable the child from work. Still later, when he was a youth of eighteen, he was severely flogged by his master, who was also his uncle, for neglecting his work and giving a saucy answer. So strongly was he impressed with reverence of the power of the stick, as I have noticed before, that when he visited London for the first time, he expected to find the great openly flogging

their inferiors ; and standing at Westminster to gape at
the sights, he was astonished to see a poor woman thrust
her wares under the nose of a member of parliament,
without drawing down upon herself the gentleman's cane.

These circumstances carry us back a full century, since
Hutton was born in 1723, and paid his first visit to London
at the latter end of George the Second's reign. Few will
say that there was a stronger sense of personal dignity
then, than now. To say nothing of the fact that a master
who should now endanger his apprentice's life by beating him
on a previously inflicted wound, would now be in some danger
of the treadmill ; or of the fact that a master who should
break a thick stick over the back of his apprentice of
eighteen would probably get as hearty a thrashing as he
gave ; where was the sense of self respect in the masters
themselves : in the schoolmaster who would beat the head of
a mere child against the wall, in the large millowner who
would condescend to use his cane with habitual cruelty,
or in the uncle and master, a good man withal, who would
outrageously maltreat his dependent ?

Yet there was then, the same habit of ostentatious dress
which now prevails in the east. What would Chesterfield
have said, if he had seen a peer of ancient family lounging
about Whitehall in a dreadnought coat, or if a change of
fashion had required himself to appear at a ball in a suit
of plain black cloth ? The rapier, and ruffles, and wig,
have disappeared : the green velvet hunting suit has given
way to broadcloth and corduroys : the nobleman is no longer
to be distinguished by his dress from his house steward
or valet, except indeed that these are the better made up.
I recollect hearing that an old gentleman who has now

been dead nearly thirty years, was married in a coat of scarlet. This was rather before 1780. I believe the dress excited some amusement at the time, but the fact shews that there was a recent tradition of a costume very different from anything that now prevails. As the personal dignity of the English character has increased, the indulgence in ostentatious dress has diminished, and I suspect that this will generally be found to happen.

I imagined formerly, that when this pretentious costume prevailed among the educated classes, the working people must have been shut out from all participation in it. We find in the life of Hutton, some casual remarks about his dress. While he was apprenticed to his uncle, he was badly provided, and complains that during some intensely cold weather he had no great coat, and not even an ordinary coat, but only a thin waistcoat. Afterwards from resentment at the beating he had suffered, he ran away and carried his clothes with him. In the inventory he gives us, we find a best wig which he packed carefully lest it should be crushed. The old man, in his recollections of his youth, always speaks with much unction of this matter of dress, regards the passion for finery as something respectable even in a man, and is altogether in this respect a fair pendant to Pepys himself.

Hutton's wig, I confess, caused me some surprise. But I have since heard a gentleman say what is quite consistent with Hutton's statement, and what shews that I was quite wrong in my supposition that the working classes did not share the finery of their masters. Speaking of the present improvidence of the mechanics, he told me that their progenitors were just as bad: that in Birmingham formerly, the working men who had money in their pocket, used to amuse themselves by hiring horses, at the rate, as they expressed it, of three shillings a side, meaning six shillings the ride. He added that they arrayed themselves in knee breeches, and had their heads dressed out, and bragged that they never went to work till they had shaken the powder out of their hair. Many clerks at a hundred pounds a year, are now better dressed than their masters, except in the essential article of clean linen; and many mechanics on Sundays are at least as smart as their masters, though blind Willie in Redgauntlet would find out their condition by touching their hands.

We see then, that in towns, a community of costume is no new thing. Among domestic servants, indeed, there was formerly a broader distinction than there is now, as compared with the members of the family : the best men servants have an increasing dislike to livery, and the women servants have adopted a jaunty pretence of caps that would have astonished our grandmothers. In the country the farm labourers have not the means of imitating the middle classes, and the gaudy waistcoat that Hodge delights in is not a copy of that worn by the quality. The clean smock frock, too, still holds its ground. It was noticed in Paris at the late exhibition of cattle, that our drovers and herdsmen were the worst dressed, and the least picturesque in appearance, of all the motley crowd there present.

With regard to dress considered only for its utility, and not as a means of pleasing the eye, the greatest peculiarity that I am acquainted with is that of the Chinese; though whether it is found in the whole of that immense empire, or only in the portion visited by our informant, I cannot say. The Chinese, it seems, instead of warming themselves by fires as we do, have recourse to thicker clothing as the weather gets colder, and pile garment upon garment until the human figure is lost. An European in his moderate winter clothing is an object of astonishment to them.

It seems to me that we might take an useful hint from this custom. The variations of our insular climate, it is true, are not so great as those of continental countries : our thermometer does not vary from 100° in the shade, to the point below zero at which mercury is frozen. We imagine that for this reason we may dress as we please, and may dispense with the skeepskins and furs of the north of Europe. It is certainly true that the oscillations of the thermometer in England are confined within narrow limits : we do not experience such cold and heat, that by successive contraction and expansion granite quays and buildings are broken up, as in St. Petersburgh. But we ought always to remember that the effect of climate on ourselves is not measured by the thermometer. We have everywhere a moist atmosphere, and in many parts of the country we have frequent and heavy fogs. If any one wants to know how it is that a fog makes him shiver, let him on a winter's day plunge into a cold bath, and he will then easily conceive why an atmosphere loaded with vaporised water, carries the heat rapidly away from his skin. A fog is a mixture of air and water : it is a cold vapour bath. When with a moist air we have a wind that is constantly changing the atmosphere around us, and that carries off every moment the warmed particles to replace them with cold ones, no wonder we feel ourselves chilled although the thermometer may indicate a temperate state of the air. Arctic voyagers tell us that however low the thermometer may be near the pole, the dry air is not painful so long as it is calm.

When I see a youth walking on a raw day without a great coat, I understand that he thinks himself giving a proof of his virility. He proposes to harden himself. If he had a commission in the army, and were going out to command in the trenches, with the necessity of bearing cold, rain, and snow, his proceeding might be a judicious one. But if he is about to remain at home with no necessity for exposure to weather, I do not see what is gained. In the early part of winter, during the November fogs and Christmas hoar frosts, he suffers a good deal of pain, and probably some disturbance of the functions of the stomach : the digestion is disturbed or the liver is disordered. By the close of winter he is acclimatized; and his skin bears the cold and damp without much pain; and his functions cease to be deranged by it. He is now in an excellent condition for enduring severe weather; he can submit to it nearly as well without a great coat as his neighbour can submit to it with a great coat.

But in a short time spring begins to open : there comes a hot week in April. Your skin having been thoroughly trained to bear the cold is in a very unfit state for heat : you are oppressed and languid, and your stomach suffers again. I, who during the coldest weather mounted two great coats, now throw off one or both of them; and far from feeling oppressed by the heat, I bask in the sun with delight. In a week or two the cold winds come upon us : you want a fresh acclimating, while I content myself with an extra coat again. In short, you accomplish by constant changes of the skin what I accomplish by as constant changes of clothing.

When the heats of summer come upon us, the hardening process leads you to wear the same clothes that you had in the winter, and by the end of the fine season you will bear the heat as well as I do. I, during the same period, have not only cast my slough of over-coats; I have also reduced my other clothing to the most attenuated state that decency permits. Your skin has again to do a great deal of duty that my clothes do for me. Your hardening process is constantly going on, and will continue all your life, unless you change your practice: the result is that you suffer much unnecessary pain and considerable disturbance of all your bodily functions.

I know that in the minds of many people there is a notion of merit attached to every self sacrifice: that each voluntary pain seems to them deserving of praise. They are afraid of indulging in comforts, of wrapping themselves up, of lying on a soft bed, of lighting a fire in their chamber, lest they should become effeminate. I confess that I have a strong sympathy with this feeling: that I do respect persons who bear cold and heat without murmuring, who care little for what they eat and drink, who, with something of a stoical spirit, in all small matters, daff the world aside and bid it pass.

But it is clear that this temper requires to have a limit set to it, since if unrestrained it will lead us to the old folly of the anchorites: we shall retire to a cave and wrap ourselves up in the pharisaical self righteousness of asceticism. Far better is it to be a stoic than to be an epicurean, but far better still to be neither. The world is not so abounding in pleasures that we can afford to cast away those that are innocent: the world furnishes abundant opportunity for self denial without exercising it for its own sake. Few men are so fully masters of their appetites but that they indulge too much in sensual pleasures. If you want to practice self denial, practice it in such a way as to benefit your health: abstain occasionally from dining: drink water or milk sometimes instead of wine and beer: lessen your night's sleep: above all, take bodily exercise however distasteful it may be. All these acts of self denial tend to make life happier and longer, to clear your head, to improve your temper, and to enable you to perform the duties of your station.

I cannot help suspecting that working men do themselves some injury by a want of care as to wearing sufficient clothing. They are not aware that the absence of an over-coat makes a greater quantity of food necessary to supply the additional waste of internal fuel. When I see them with their hands in their pockets and their shoulders up to their ears, bending forward to the cruel east wind, I regret that they have not prudence enough to keep a heavy over-coat for the winter: it would cost no great deal and would last many years. It would save them from much pain, from some indisposition, and would probably be very economical in its results. It is quite true that the working classes are far hardier than we are. They eat greasy dishes that would turn us sick and give us a fit of indigestion; they live in small rooms the closeness of which would make our heads ache; they drink a gallon of adulterated ale at a sitting, walk home without excitement, and next morning are neither sick nor sorry; they work night and day upon occasion without sleep and without exhaustion. Their constant bodily exertion gives an alacrity to all the functions of their frame, such as we poor sedentary creatures of the middle class seldom enjoy. With their muscular system in full play, and their brain in constant repose, they smile at the petty troubles which make our lives miserable. But to these advantages, if they would only add that attention to the conditions of health which we give from necessity, they might enjoy animal life to a degree of which few of us have any conception.

CHAPTER X.

I will now make a few remarks upon the houses in which the working classes live. At a casual glance, it might be thought that the best fed people are also the best lodged, but this is far from being universally true. The Russian serf is well fed, and he is also well lodged: the Norwegian houseman is only moderately supplied with food, but his house accommodation is excellent: the Irishman formerly had an abundant supply of potatoes and milk, but his cabin was even then a disgraceful pigstye.

Other circumstances being equal, the cottages will be best where the building materials are cheapest. The bogs of Ireland furnish an excellent supply of fuel, but only poor means of constructing a house. The people having been despised and neglected for centuries, and allowed to remain in that half civilised state into which, unhappily, they had fallen, made little effort to overcome this difficulty, and sat down in a hut which would scarcely content a Red Indian. Selecting a dry ditch, as A. Young tells us, they would throw a few sticks across from bank to bank, cover these twigs with turf, and with * two slight walls added, a cabin in a couple of days, was ready for the reception of a family. If Ireland had possessed forests instead of bogs, the natives probably, would have been as well lodged as those of other countries.

---

* Young's Ireland, 2. 197.

Every one is familiar with the way in which a family is provided with a habitation in the back woods of America: the neighbours are collected, trees are felled and piled up for walls, branches and rough boards are stretched across, a floor is laid, and the family enters its home. To construct a cottage in such a mode in England, would be an act of extravagance: it is a poor hedgerow tree that is not worth £2.; and it would require a great many such trees to build in this hasty way. It is far cheaper to use brick and slate.

In the north and east of Europe houses are put together in a way similar to that of North America. The *English-woman in Russia* in the early part of her work, * speaks of many peasants as being miserably lodged. Afterwards † she mentions that houses are formed by laying beams horizontally one above the other, as we place layers of stone, or courses of bricks. When the joints of such walls are filled in, as boat builders caulk the seams of their barges, they make excellent houses, the thick wood being an excellent non-conductor of heat. The early remarks apply to the north of Russia, the authoress having landed at Archangel; and she does not say whether timber is scarce in those parts.

The same mode of constructing houses of all sorts, prevails in Norway, as we learn from Mr. Laing. He tells us ‡ that after the walls are constructed with thick beams, the joints are caulked with moss. The workmanship is rough, but efficient. We find § that the rooms are airtight and

* Pa. 24.   † 240.

‡ Laing's Norway. 28.   § Ib. 197.

free from draughts, besides * being well warmed with stoves.
He says that the Bonde † (the yeoman) is as well housed
as the gentleman ; and that the Norwegians generally are
the best housed people in Europe. He estimates that a
house may be built substantially, as described above, for
£10. : but we must remember that this is a much larger sum
than with us, the rate of wages and of commodities being
much lower there than here. What Mr. Laing under-
stands ‡ by a Norwegian house, we find to be one of four
rooms, with glass windows.

As the population of these countries increases and
encroaches on the forest, it is to be feared that it will
deteriorate in this important matter of warm lodging.
Even a great railroad or canal that intersected the country,
might so raise the market value of timber as seriously
to damage the peasants while it enriched the proprietor.
It too often happens that movements tending to increase
the greatness of a country, and to promote its civilisation,
begin with causing much misery to the working classes.

Mr. Laing contrasts the houses of Norway and those of
Scotland, and his comparison is very unfavourable to his
native country. §   " In the dwellings generally of the
labouring class (in Norway), the squalor, dampness, dark-
ness, and total want of accommodation and comfort of
the sod-built hovels which disgrace the face of the earth
in Scotland and Ireland, are unknown. The meanest
habitation has wooden floors, windows, apartments for the
family to sleep in, besides their sitting-room ; also fit
places for keeping their food. It is highly characteristic

* Laing's Norway, 268.   † Ib. 72.   ‡ Ib. 22.   § Ib. 187.

of Scotland, that within sight of its Parthenon, human dens may be found in which whole families—father, mother, and grown-up daughters and sons—are lodged under one roof, without other division into apartments for the decent separation of the sexes, than is made by a wooden bedstead placed in the middle, without other floor than the raw earth; the walls of sods and stones, not lined with wood inside; the roof a mass of damp rotten straw and decayed vegetable substances, supported by a few sooty rafters; the windows, a single pane or two of glass stuck in a hole in the thatch or the wall; the family provisions of meal, salt meat, herrings, milk, butter, all huddled together in the single room, in which all the wet stockings and sweaty shirts are fuming and drying, and all the exhalations of the crowded inmates cooking, eating, and sleeping, are poisoning the atmosphere."

This comparison reads a good deal like a satire on the Scotch, and it is possible that while the facts are accurately stated, the impression given to the reader may be false. It is true I have no doubt, that there are many persons in Edinburgh or its environs, ill lodged, disgracefully ill lodged: so there are in London, about St. Giles's, and within a stone's throw of Westminster Abbey. A few years ago there was in Liverpool a large population crowded together in cellars, until an Act of Parliament drove them out. Yet it would be a most incorrect inference, to say on this account, that the working classes of England are ill lodged generally. In the same way, the existence of a number of miserable huts such as Mr. Laing has described, proves nothing as to the general mode of lodging of the Scotch. The agricultural Norwegians who form the great body of the nation, have good houses and are altogether in an excellent condition : but Norway, like other countries, has its plague spots of misery ; for to say nothing of the Laplanders, there is the fishing population on the coast, which is said to be squalid in its habits ; and if we searched among them, we might find cabins as bad as those of Scotland.

I do not mean to assert that the Scotch are a well housed people. We have heard something of *bothies* in which the farm labourers live, and that something is decidedly unfavourable. Scott's pictures of peasant life, too, confirm the notions that the habitations are generally deplorable. With regard to Edinburgh, I have heard it affirmed by an excellent authority, that there has of late years been a decided deterioration in the habits of the people, in consequence of the large influx of slovenly Irish peasants.

Miserable house accommodation is not peculiar to Ireland and Scotland ; it seems to be the general rule in countries long civilised. As a nation advances in refinement, it might be expected to improve in the habitations of all classes. But as the land is more and more occupied, the materials for building become continually dearer, and in spite of refinement of taste, there is great danger that the working classes should become more and more straitened in their means of lodging themselves.

In going through M. Le Play's cases I have been struck with his statements of facts about habitations. In Lower Britanny, for instance,* I find a family living in a house of one room, which they share with the cows. We might say

---

* Le Play, 231. 1.

that they have no cottage, but live in the cowhouse. In the
towns we find * a Viennese mechanic with a family of
" children who have all feeble health and a lymphatic tem-
perament, owing, as it would seem, to their living on a damp
ground floor, in which the influence of the sun is too little
felt." In the next page we find that the family has only
two small rooms, looking on to the inner court of a large
house. The kitchen appears to be about $9\frac{1}{2}$ feet each way,
or what is equivalent to this: the bed-room about fifteen
feet each way, or its equivalent. This is narrow accommodation for a husband, wife, and five children, the eldest being
a boy of fifteen.

In the case † of a weaver of Rhenish Prussia, we find a
cottage of two rooms with a hayloft above, and with a cow-
house and garden attached. The hand-loom weavers here
are so unfortunate a race that we rather expect to find
them the same elsewhere, and this case taken alone might
not impress us much. But it does not stand alone.

Two other cases, both in Geneva, may produce a greater
impression. We expect to find in the metropolis of Switzerland and of Calvinism, a something of superiority in the
character and the condition of the working classes. In this
respect M. Le Play does not disappoint us. One of his
two cases indicates great decency of living, and the other a
high degree of refinement.

The first workman I have mentioned ‡ is a watchmaker,
working generally for one master, to whom he is bound by
no tie beyond that of habit, and with whom, as happens
among ourselves, frequent disputes arise as to the price of

* Le Play, 121. 2.   † Ib. 159. 1.   ‡ Ib. 170.

work. The workman is fifty years old, with a wife three
years older, and a son of thirteen.   The family might be in
easy circumstances, but that the parents incur considerable
expenses in the education of their son, instead of making
him a source of income.   At the age of thirteen the boy
might maintain himself, but we must sympathise with the
honourable efforts of a couple, who keep themselves poor
that they may raise their only son to a higher grade in the
intellectual scale.   The family suffers something approaching
to positive want whenever a commercial crisis happens, and
appears to be in a worse pecuniary condition than most of
the Genevese.   All the three members are Calvinists, and
zealous in their creed: they attend regularly to the practices of religion : the chief amusement of the father is the
reading of books of a pious sort : and far from being inert
and careless of what goes on around him, he shows much
interest in all the great discoveries of the day.   That he
and his wife set a high value on education is shown by the
sacrifices they make in conferring it on their son.

I should have hoped to find in a family of such high
respectability as this, a determination to live with decency,
and therefore in a house or part of a house which would save
their son from the blush of shame on entering it.   We find
this description of it, however. *   " The family occupies on
the third floor of a house, and up a dark narrow staircase,
a little apartment consisting of a kitchen which serves as a
dining room and sitting room, of a bed room for the parents,
and of a closet which holds the son's bed and a little book
case."   And in the previous page † we find that " The three

---

* Le Play, 171. 1.   † Ib. 170. 1.

members of the family have an excellent constitution of body ; and resist well the influence of the bad hygienic conditions that result from living in a confined apartment devoid of air and light." I think all will agree that such a habitation is far below what we should have expected in the case of a man of such a high tone of mind as this Genevese.

It may be thought, however, that as this workman is poor, his case may be exceptional, just as that of the Paris rag picker is found to be exceptional in the opposite direction. I will give some particulars of the second case I have referred to, and this will illustrate that point.

The case * is that of another watchmaker, and is similar to the former in many respects. This man, however, is in much better circumstances than the former, his income being nearly half as large again ; a difference that we shall realise better by supposing that the one earns seventeen shillings, the other twenty-four shillings a week. Our present workman is much younger, being only twenty-seven years old, with a wife of twenty-five years old, to whom he has been married three years and a half, and by whom he has one child of two years and a half. This family also is Calvinistic, and earnest in religion. Both husband and wife have great refinement of manners and language, and their intelligence is as remarkable as their morality. In no other European country has M. Le Play found examples more worthy of note in both these respects ; though he has met with similar ones in some great manufacturing towns of Western Europe, as Lyons, Paris, Liége, London, and Glasgow.

* Le Play, 164.

A happy influence is exercised in Geneva, as to the neatness of the houses, and generally as to the morality of the working classes, by the pastoral visits, which take place at no distant periods, and at least once a year.

The household furniture is not merely neat; it is elegant; and will bear a comparison with that of the lower middle classes.

And now as to the habitation of this family. We find a tolerably liberal income, a small family, something of a disposition to indulge in the comforts of life, a household overlooked and visited by the pastor of the church, great intelligence and refinement on the part of both husband and wife: here, of course, we shall find an excellent house or floor of a house. I will copy what M. Le Play says. " The house occupied by the family communicates with the road, and with a small court inside, by a long entry. On the ground floor are two shops, and a large room in which all the tenants of the house wash their linen by turns. On each of the three upper floors are two sets of apartments, all on the same staircase. On the fourth floor are attics, in which the tenants dry their linen. This arrangement which is very common at Geneva, is very advantageous for the neatness and health of the inhabitants: and is very superior, for instance, to what takes place among the working classes of London."

" The present family occupies a set of apartments on the second floor, looking on both the court and the road. There are a cooking kitchen, a sitting room, three alcoves, a dark closet, and a little light closet which is the wife's workshop. The communication with the staircase is by an open gallery, on the balustrade of which the wife keeps a few flower pots.

According to the season, the child plays in this gallery or in the sitting room."

We get additional information from this remark.* " The husband and wife are both of small stature and have every appearance of a lymphatic constitution; however, their general health is as good as could be expected from their residence in a 'populous quarter and in an ill-ventilated house."

This description altogether gives a gloomy, unpleasant, notion of a habitation, though it is not so precise as what I quoted before. The family seems to have a kitchen, a bed-room, one light closet, and one dark one. The bed-room has three recesses for beds, and in the day time, after the continental fashion, is used as a sitting-room. The whole house, of which these rooms form a part, is situated in a crowded part of the town and is ill-ventilated. The rent is £8. 8s. a year, or about 3s. 3d. a week, which seems a great deal for such accommodation. The furniture and clothes are estimated as worth the large sum of £92. This circumstance is explained by the fact that both husband and wife were very prudent before marriage, the one at twenty-three years old having saved £76., and the other at twenty-one years old having saved £40.

Now it seems to me that this case confirms decisively the notion that the European workmen are generally worse lodged than we should have expected. I think that among ourselves a couple possessed of such refinement and intelligence as are here described, spending an income of 22s. 6d. a week (after deducting the annual savings), with only

* Le Play, 164. 1.

one child and that one a mere infant, with no waste or
debauchery, or even dissipation, with a taste for a decent
appearance as shown in the rather extravagant clothes and
furniture, would certainly be quite dissatisfied with living in
two rooms up two flights of stairs, in a crowded ill-ventilated
house. On reflection, perhaps, this result of observation is
not surprising. Home is more thought of by ourselves
than by other nations, and we might be expected to spend
more than other nations in providing ourselves with houses :
and the same notions that prevail among the educated
classes, naturally descend to the lower. Educated families
in Paris occupy far worse habitations than families of equal
education in London : the Parisian spends more upon dress,
the Londoner more upon houseroom. The same rule may
naturally prevail among all classes, comparing France with
England, and even comparing the Continent generally with
England.

We naturally ask how the working classes were lodged
in former days. A. Young, speaking of the miserable Irish
cabins nearly a century ago, compares them with the cottages of English country labourers, in such a way as makes
us suppose that the English cottages then were about the
same that they are now. On the other hand, the information derived from other quarters leads to a different conclusion. I am not acquainted with any description of a
labourer's house in the last century : but I have met with
many notices of the rent paid. Eden gives many examples.
In one place,* we find a man of thirty, with a wife and
three young children, paying sixteen shillings a year, or less

* Eden, Poor, 2. 74.

than fourpence a week. In another place, * a miner, who with the help of his family, earns £44. a year, pays 1s. 2d. a week : another miner, of rather larger earnings, is also charged 1s. 2d. a week for his cottage. A mechanic, † whose income is 22s. 6d. a week, expends ninepence a week as rent. In Durham ‡ we meet with a weekly rent of five-pence ; in Kent, § of 1s. 4d. for a cottage, a garden, and right of common ; in Middlesex, of 1s. 6d. for a cottage with a small garden. These low rents indicate very poor accommodation. What room could be given for fourpence, fivepence, or even 1s. 2d. to 1s. 4d. a week ? The rent is low out of all proportion to the earnings. As to towns, going back another half century, we find Hutton mentioning one of his progenitors who lived in Derby in a house con-sisting of two rooms. The Hutton family appear to have belonged to the class of decent mechanics, and not to have been of that worst sort who end their days in jail or work-house. This man must have been contemporary with Pope, and no lines of his are much better known than those describing a house of the lower sort.

> In the worst inn's worst room, with mat half hung,
> The floor of plaster and the walls of dung,
> On once a flock bed, but repaired with straw,
> With tape tied curtains never meant to draw,
> The George and Garter dangling from that bed
> Where tawdry yellow strives with dirty red,
> Great Villiers lies.

This description carries us in imagination rather to an Irish cabin where potheen is sold, than to an English road

---

* Eden, Poor, 2. 88.   † Ib. 2. 98.   ‡ Ib. 2. 157.   § 2. 187.

side beer house : it leads us to suppose that an improvement has taken place in the habitations of the working classes, during the last century and a half. The satire of a poet, to be sure, is not much to be trusted, but so correct a writer as Pope would not grossly misrepresent what actually existed; his satire would consist in seizing the parts that suited his purpose, and neglecting others that would diminish the force of his colouring. The floor of plaster and the wall of dung, were no doubt drawn from observation. Eden mentions a workman in Leicester who, with earnings of eighteen shillings a week, spent 1s. 6d. a week on his house. With such an income a man now would spend 2s. 6d. to 3s. 3d. The proportion spent on rent seems very small in the Leicester case.

But whatever improvement has taken place in towns, and whether or not any improvement has taken place in the country, it is now strongly felt that an alteration for the better is needed. This is especially true of the country. Malthus observed the effect produced by the poor law on the cottage accommodation in rural parishes. The landlords of estates have been unwilling to build new cottages, and have frequently pulled old ones down, in order to lessen the number of persons chargeable to the parish. Malthus saw that the poor law had thus, indirectly, lessened the population : but he feared that this process of compression had sometimes been carried too far, and this has proved to be the case. Great complaints are now made of households so crowded that decency cannot be observed; and it is felt that when families herd together like pigs in a stye, the first step is taken towards female degradation. This necessity for sexual decency, however, is a notion peculiarly English, and does not seem to be understood by other nations. The French regard us as *furieusement pudiques*, and I conjecture that they suspect us of hypocrisy, and think with Swift that nice people are people with very nasty ideas. The Italians and the Germans, I am told, resemble the French, in these respects, far more than they resemble the English. A London lodging-house keeper was lately summoned before a magistrate, for allowing a number of persons of different sexes to sleep together in the same room. He acknowledged that such was the fact, but alleged that the lodgers were Germans, that they were accustomed to live together in this way, and that they did not like to be interfered with.

There seems to be a great difference among our own working classes in this respect. I have known great indignation expressed by a number of workmen, because a whimsical fellow chose to bathe himself in a tub, in such a situation that a number of men and women might see him if they chose, but were certainly under no necessity of seeing him. On the other hand we are told in the newspapers that it is not uncommon in some parts of the country, for a man and his wife, and his wife's sister, to occupy the same bed. Where houseroom is very much restricted, such promiscuous lying seems almost inevitable. I presume that our notions of decency have become much more developed than they were, or else the arrangements of our barracks never could have arisen. At the present day we could not have originated an organization by which married couples should sleep in the same room with unmarried men, with only an intervening curtain; or by which married couples should sleep in adjoining beds without even a curtain between. If, however, we have any doubt as to the change of feeling in these respects, we need only read over again a dozen numbers of Addison's Spectator, or remember that Lawrence Sterne read his Tristram Shandy to his own daughter to whom he was greatly attached. Our improved sentiments will doubtless lead to a supply of improved cottages.

One powerful reason may be alleged for the superior accommodation of modern times. If we go into the old parts of ancient towns, we find the streets narrow, the houses piled up towards the sky, and the upper floors projecting into the street. Even the bridges were built upon. In the days of fortified towns, when civil wars had not ceased, before the adoption of cannon had rendered the defences of a city useless, this crowding of habitations was more than useful; it was inevitable: the place must be surrounded with a wall, and therefore must be contracted as much as possible. Edinburgh, Bristol, Chester, are striking examples, though the picturesque portions are daily disappearing.

Newer towns have an appearance far less interesting, but they are more favourable to the health of the inhabitants. One cannot help regretting that beauty and utility should in this instance be antagonistic, but such is the case. I do not mean merely that the curious relics of our ancestors' street architecture are constantly dropping off; though this one regrets, just as one is grieved to see the rural lanes near a town being daily superseded by straight trim roads: besides this, the aspect of our cities is now deprived of the addition derived from streets of dwelling houses. The middle classes, with the exception of medical men, rush into the suburbs or environs. The villas that are dotted over the face of the country, if they were compressed into streets and squares would add greatly to the dignity and beauty of a town. We must be contented, however, with an arrangement that is highly favourable to the health of the middle classes, and which tends also to make men look for their evening amusements, to their own families rather than to the theatre and the club.

The working classes have participated in this change. They cannot generally live in the country, because they must be tolerably near their work ; though it is surprising what a distance many mechanics walk daily to and fro. Most working people live in the town, but the boundaries of the town are greatly enlarged. Land is of far less value therefore, and each house has a more considerable portion of breathing space assigned to it. In many places a large majority of families have each of them a separate house, instead of having a set of apartments as on the Continent, or a flat as in Scotland, or a cellar as formerly in Liverpool. In the census for 1851 we find all the particulars illustrative of this point, and an epitome of the results is given by Mr. Cheshire in a short pamphlet published in 1853. He says * " The possession of an entire house is strongly desired by every Englishman. This feeling is universal, but stronger in England than on the Continent. The crowding of the middle and higher classes, who sleep in flats, is carried to a great excess in the capitals on the Continent. The department of the Seine, for instance, in 1835,

* Page 21.

had, on an average, twenty-two persons to a house, whilst in densely populated London, in 1851, there were barely eight persons to a house."

It appears that during the last half century, the number of houses has not increased in England quite so much as the number of families, and that, therefore, there are rather more cases than there were in 1801, in which two or more families live under the same roof. This, however, seems to be accounted for at once, by the fact that during the fifty years, the town population has increased far more than the country population; it being in the towns generally that several families occupy one house.

We shall form some comparison of the different large towns of Great Britain from the following short abstract. The number of persons in a *family* in Great Britain, in 1851, was not far short of five, being 4·825. The number of persons living in each *house* was—

In Leeds,......decidedly less than 5, being	4·76
In Sheffield,...........very nearly 5, „	4·99
In Hereford, ... „ 5, „	4·99
In Birmingham, rather more than 5, „	5·07
In Manchester, (parliamentary borough) ....nearly } 6, „	5·94
In Manchester and Salford, (parl. bor.) together, under } 6, „	5·88
In Gloucester, rather more than 6, „	6·18
In Bristol, „ „ „ 6½, „	6·58
In Liverpool,................nearly 7, „	6·92
In Durham, ... „ 7½, „	7·45
In City of London, ... „ 9, „	8·77
In Plymouth, ...about 10, „	10·09

In Edinburgh, ...about 20½,   „   20·57

(In Department of Seine, 1835) 22

In Glasgow, ...about 27½,   „   27·58

* In the above returns it is remarkable that the one for Leeds makes the number of houses greater than the number of families, unless we suppose that the number of persons in a family is smaller in Leeds than in other places.

An attempt has been made of late years to prove by experiment that separate houses are, under some circumstances, disadvantageous; and that with judicious architectural arrangements, large buildings may be constructed so as to give to each family a flat containing all the accommodation required. The model houses do not appear at present to have made much way, and even less elsewhere than they have in London. I do not, however, mean to allege this fact as disproving their utility. In places where each working man has been accustomed to have a separate

---

* Mr. Cheshire, page 23, speaking of the midland counties, says, " a large proportion of the people lived in separate houses (in 1851), with the exception of Bristol, Clifton, Gloucester, Hereford, and Birmingham." It will be seen above that Birmingham is far from being an exception, as a great majority of families have separate houses. A Fellow of the Statistical Society should be more accurate, unless he desires to justify the sarcastic remark attributed to Canning; that nothing is so false as figures, except, indeed, facts. To say even of Bristol and Gloucester that a large majority of the people do not live in separate houses is a careless mode of expression. The statement as to Hereford is peculiarly unhappy, as in that little city nearly every family has its own house. I should imagine that Hereford has been confounded with Hertford, where the population is more crowded : but such a blunder makes sad confusion in geography.

house with his kitchen on the ground floor, it would imply a considerable change of daily habit to live on a flat up two or three flights of stairs : and to cook and wash in an attic would seem almost an inversion of the order of nature.

At present in Birmingham, and I suppose elsewhere, the majority of houses are not built fronting to the street, but with the windows looking on to a narrow strip of ground dignified with the name of a court. This furnishes the means of drying the clothes, and these are washed in an outhouse which is used by the different tenants of the court in turn. If each family had the means of washing and drying separately, while there would be a considerable loss of out-lay in brick and mortar, there would be a great saving of temper, and no small reduction of fees to magistrates' clerks ; as many disputes and assaults arise out of the use of the wash-house. Still, this is far better than having to wash in the kitchen.

It is said that the model houses pay the proprietors ; but an experience of many years will be required to test the assertion. It is very likely that no sufficient allowance has been made for loss of rent. No property, it is said, yields such high interest as small houses, if only the pro-prietor can get his rents, but the deduction for bad debts is something considerable. A dishonest tenant frequently makes a midnight flitting ; another dies ; a third is out of work, or sick. A hard landlord will take the goods of the widow or the disabled, but a humane man hesitates to seize the bed from the children, or the chairs of the kitchen ; and therefore to a kind hearted man small houses are the worst of property. The result is that cottages are let at an advanced rent to cover these defalcations, and the apparent rate of interest on them is high. I am not aware whether the model houses can be put up so as to yield the same rate: if not, they can hardly be expected to spread. They may be very well as toys for philanthropists, but they will not take root in the rough world of every day life.

One disadvantage might arise from the adoption of many-storied, lofty houses. The courts into which the present cottages look are already gloomy enough; but if the buildings were doubled in height, they would be still gloomier. It is true that a much larger court might in that case be afforded, but it is very doubtful whether it would be afforded, because it would not be absolutely necessary. It would be a melancholy result of the efforts of the benevolent, if the working classes ended with a diminution of one half of the small share of sun and air that they now enjoy. This contraction would be welcomed by the governing powers of boroughs; for the present plan of separate houses causes an extension of the boundaries, and an addition to the streets, that causes a vast expense in lighting and watching. But this expense must be more than compensated, by the advantage of space and elbow room for the multitude of human beings that constitute a large town. Since we cannot get rid of smoke and worse effluvia, it is better that these should be mixed with as much air as possible: if we were compelled to swallow poison, we should prefer it diluted to the utmost. It is objected to the small houses, that they are built back to back without the possibility of a thorough draught at any time; but if we look at the construction, we find only one or two small rooms on the ground floor, each having a door, a window, and a chimney. Upstairs every room has a window and door and ought to have a chimney, and I cannot conceive that more ventilation than this can be necessary : the case is entirely different from that of a building with long rooms and passages. On the whole I lean to the opinion that the English custom of separate houses is advantageous, although it robs the streets of all pretensions to dignity, and converts a manufacturing town into something little better than an aggregation of cottages.

CHAPTER XI.

With regard to the furniture found in the houses of working people, M. Le Play gives us a number of details that are sufficient to supply the means of very exact comparisons. He is not contented with telling us that such a cabin was found bare of furniture, while in another place he met with as much as would content a French peasant. Such general remarks do not satisfy him. He gives us the particulars, and writes out an inventory with far more care than is employed by an appraiser who is paid for his task.

I will take the first case; that of the Mahometan half-migratory herdsman, living on the Asiatic slope of the Ural Mountains.

	£.	s.	d.
The bed of the chief: one mat, 11d.; one woollen carpet, 3s. 7d.; one feather bed, 18s. 1d.; one woollen mattress, 11s. 9d.; three down cushions, 12s. 3d.; one counterpane of quilted cotton, 4s. 6d.; cotton curtains, red for winter, white for summer, with rod, 12s. 8d.	3	3	9
Children's beds: three little felts and three cushions, 1s. 10d.; one cradle and ring with rod, 1s. 4d.	0	3	2
Carried forward................	3	6	11

	£.	s.	d.
Brought forward	3	6	11
A glazed wardrobe with two shutters and table, 13s. 8d.; a wooden table painted red, 2s. 2d.; two chairs with backs, 3s. 7d.; two benches, 2s. 3d.	1	1	8
A brass tea-urn *á la Russe*, 23s. 6d.; one brass kettle with handle and spout, 4s. 1d.; one porcelain tea pot, 1s.; four porcelain tea cups, 1s; one japanned iron tray, 1s. 9d.; one iron candlestick, 4d.; one lamp, 5d.; one hatchet, 5d.; one lance of painted wood, 1s. 5d.	1	13	11

6 2 6

It will be remembered that I have already referred to this case, as an illustration of the patriarchal mode of life. In the present instance, a younger brother and his wife lived with the chief of the house. The furniture used by them together with sundry utensils not already mentioned, are put down as worth   1 14 5

Making the total value of the furniture to be   £7 16 11

This is no very large sum for the entire worth of the furniture of two families, but it is quite as much as I should have expected to find.

I do not propose to go all through M. Le Play's thirty-six cases, stating particulars as I have done above; though any one desiring to become familiar with the daily habits of people of different races, might obtain a great deal of information from these inventories. The first item that occurs in the next case that I shall give, reminds us strongly of the marked distinction between the almost idolatrous saint-worship of the Greek Church, and the pure, untainted, veneration displayed by the Mussulman, for the Great Spirit who is not to be symbolised by human hands.

This case is the second given by M. Le Play, and is that of a peasant in the south of Russia. His furniture is as follows :—

	£.	s.	d.
Six holy images with niches to hold them	0	7	3
Mats, sheepskins, cushions, &c., two cradles ...	1	18	10
Table, bench, four boxes, one small looking glass and sundries	1	11	11
Pots, knives, candlestick, &c., &c.	0	17	9
Total of furniture..............	4	15	9

The household here consists of the elderly head of the family, who is a widower; three married sons with their wives and two young children; and an unmarried daughter. The furniture seems scanty enough; and the more so when we remember that this is one of the parts of Russia in which the peasantry are in the best condition. This family is abundantly fed and well housed. As we might have anticipated, the taste for better furniture follows a higher state of civilization.

It is worthy of remark, however, that the Russian peasant frequently takes pleasure in adorning his cottage. This is noticed by M. Le Play; * and also by the *Englishwoman*

* Le Play, 36. 1.

in Russia, * who speaks of the villages as consisting of a long
line of wooden houses on each side of a road, with usually
a row of birch trees in front; with some of the peasants'
houses ornamented with a border of wood so light as to
resemble lace. Such peasants will soon, probably, acquire
a taste for a better class of furniture.

We will now visit the Norwegian mechanic described in
case seven. We learn from Mr. Laing,† that in Norway, the
furniture even of the better classes is antiquated, and that
the peasants, excellently as they are lodged, are but scantily
provided with furniture. It is interesting to compare this
general statement, with the exact account of the precise
French engineer. The particulars are not given in this instance in the same detail as in the other cases I have referred
to. We are told that the house is well provided generally
with wooden furniture, worth about £7   4   0
and with cooking and other utensils, many of ⎱
them of wood .... ⎰ 1   8   0
                                                    _____
                                                      8 12   0
                                                    _____

It is probable that the farming peasants, or housemen,
up the country, are worse off in these respects; and we
have no inconsistency to complain of on the part of our
two authorities.

If we now proceed to the Viennese mechanic in case
eleven, we find some advance on the Norwegian; and we
must observe that this Viennese is a man in rather poor
circumstances, and scarcely able to keep his head above
water. He is found possessing—

---

* Englishwoman in Russia, 27. 28.   † Laing's Norway, 47. 106. 107.

	£.	s.	d.
Three common wooden bedsteads with mattresses filled with chips, feather coverlets and pillows, sheets and pillow cases......	6	6	0
Other furniture, cooking utensils, &c..........	3	5	0
	9	11	0

In Geneva the two mechanics we have already met with both possess furniture of considerable value. The one man,* in rather poor circumstances as to income, is set down as having beds, tables, chairs, linen and utensils worth £31. 5s. The other,† a man of the very highest grade of mechanics as to refinement, though with only a moderate income, is estimated as having furniture worth not less than £78. 5s.

M. Le Play observes that in towns there is generally a tendency to superfluity in this respect, with something of an inclination to rival the lower *bourgeoisie.* Even the rag-picker of Paris, one of the lowest class of human kind, is found less destitute than we might expect. We see ‡ that he possesses—

	£.	s.	d.
A crucifix, four religious pictures, and a vessel for holy water	0	4	9
Two beds with spare linen for them..............	4	5	0
Sundry furniture	1	19	0
A bookcase with some thirty volumes, either religious or adapted for the little girl......	1	5	4
Cooking utensils, &c..................................	1	2	10
	£8	16	11

* Le Play 170.   † Ib. 164.   ‡ Ib. 273. 1.

If we compare this considerable value of furniture, with the £7. 16s. 11d. of the patriarchal household containing two families on the Asiatic Ural Mountains, or with the £4. 15s. 9d. of the Russian household, containing a grandfather, three married sons, and others, we shall agree with M. Le Play, that in the article of furniture there is a tendency to superfluity in inhabitants of towns. It is understood that it is intended to represent the rag-picker, not as a fair specimen of his class, but as a man of a certain natural refinement, who, by his wandering tastes, and vacillation of character, has been driven down into the abyss of the prolétaires of Paris.

I will conclude by quoting the estimate given us of the contents of the four English houses which are described.

The first is that of a London cutler, who earns thirty-five shillings to forty shillings a week. His furniture is estimated at about £30.

The second is that of a Sheffield cutler, who earns twenty-two shillings to twenty-four shillings a week. His furniture is estimated at about £14. This man is an Irishman by birth.

The third is that of a Sheffield box maker, who earns twenty-five shillings to twenty-eight shillings a week. His furniture is estimated at about £35. This man is a mechanic of the best class, who saves money, and is preparing the timber of a house which he hopes to build for himself by the assistance of a land society.

The fourth is that of an ironfounder of Derbyshire, who earns thirty shillings to thirty-two shillings a week. His furniture is estimated at £24. This man is a native of a manufacturing district of Yorkshire, where the habits of the workmen are of an unfavourable kind. He married without any savings for the purchase of furniture. But on his migration to Derbyshire, finding better habits prevailing among his new companions, he gradually provided himself with decent furniture.

On the whole, there is nothing in these four English cases of which we have any reason to be ashamed. Fortunately for our reputation among all M. Le Play's readers, he did not penetrate into Ireland. Had he done so, I fear we should not have seen without a blush, the description which he would have had to give (and which he certainly would have given without exaggeration or extenuation) of the utter destitution of the Irish cabin.

I confess that I am rather surprised to find the contents of an English working man's house set down as worth so much as we find above. I do not pretend to cast any doubt on the statements made; I only mean that I had a general impression that the value was less than we find it. A few years back, a man who had been at first a mechanic, but who for a good while had occupied the position of a small master, determined on emigrating; and his wife assured me that the furniture being nearly all sold, did not realise much more than £5. The man, no doubt, was very poor; he had kept house many years; his wife's interest had led her to understate the amount of the proceeds: but with all allowances that can be made, I can hardly put the saleable value of this furniture including utensils, at more than £10. or £12. M. Le Play, however, does not tell us by what scale he has set his value, whether by the price which was originally paid for each article, or by the price for which it would now sell. This is an important question

in estimating the accuracy of the inventories; for we know
that furniture after a few years' wear, will not sell for more
than a half or a third of its prime cost. But the inventories
are, no doubt, all framed on one principle; and in comparing one with another, it is of little importance what that
principle is. It is only when we compare M. Le Play's
inventories with others made by ourselves, that it becomes
essential to ascertain the principle.

I should be glad to make a comparison of the value of
the furniture possessed by English mechanics, now, and
formerly; but I have scarcely any data. One circumstance
may be worth mentioning, however. Old Hutton, in his
Court of Requests * says that in his time, eighty to one
hundred years ago, the landlords of mechanics' houses in
Birmingham, could not frequently distrain for rent, because
the furniture was insufficient to cover the expenses of the
legal procedure. No doubt there are plenty of such cases
now. But from the manner in which Hutton mentions
the fact, I gathered, when I read the book, that this absence
of furniture worth a few pounds, was more common then
than now. In the present day, I am sorry to say, the constant *midnight flittings* that take place, shew that the
mechanics frequently have enough effects to cover their
arrears of rent and the expenses of a distress, but that the
men are unprincipled enough to reward in this way the
forbearance of the owner of the house. I must repeat here
what I have said before. Working men generally will not
wrong each other: but they regard landlords and masters
as too many of the middle classes regard the government.

* Hutton's Court of Requests, 190.

There is the same absence of sympathy, the same want of conscientious scruple as to wronging their superior in pecuniary matters.

M. Le Play does not say much that is striking about the fuel used in the houses of different countries : though he insists strongly in many places on the great effects produced by the adoption of coal for manufacturing purposes. Mr. Laing,* in his work on Norway, has some remarks that are worth noting.

He shews very forcibly the great saving to the nation, arising from the use of mineral fuel. He says that " England is the only country in the world which draws its whole supply of fuel from below the soil. In all other countries the extent of land producing fire-wood is very large. It has been estimated that one-fifth of France is so occupied. When we consider that a crop of trees can scarcely be cut oftener than once in twenty years, so that the wood consumed by twenty-five millions of people in a year is but a twentieth part of what necessarily occupies the soil, the proportion of one-fifth seems not over-rated."

This is a matter of high importance to the greatness of a nation. If we take Great Britain, as maintaining, in round numbers, twenty millions of people, independently of importations of food ; and if we suppose that the supplies of coal had ceased a hundred years ago, it follows, according to Mr. Laing, that we must have had one fifth of our fertile land occupied with firewood, in order that we should be warmed even as well as the French are. This would cause a reduction in our population to the extent of four millions of

---

* Laing's Norway, 104.

people.   To say nothing of the hindrance to the development
of our manufacturing system, a hindrance that some persons
would rejoice in ; our population, our power of paying taxes,
our means of maintaining fleets and armies, in short our
national greatness, would have been lessened in the proportion of four millions to the number of our entire population :
i.e., in the proportion of four to twenty, if we exclude
Ireland, though in a less proportion, if we include Ireland.
That very numerous class which believes that it is the
extension of our manufactures which has given us our
present preeminence in national wealth, will see in the
hypothetical cessation of a supply of coal, a still heavier
misfortune.

We are apt to suppose that a population living in the
midst of lands uncleared of timber, must be better off for
firing than we are.   But according to Mr. Laing, " Wood
is very expensive firing, even if got for nothing.   The labour
and expense of preparing it for fuel, the perpetual chop,
chop, chopping, all day long in every family, amount to
a tax heavier than a poor rate.   In this neighbourhood,
where every farm has either wood within itself, or has the
right to take it from the common forest within a mile's
distance, the fathom of six cubic feet of billets for the fire
costs six orts, or 4s. 6d. sterling.   This value of coals in
a coal country would go further than the same of wood here :
that is, if coals are used in stoves, and with the same
economy."

This statement is rather a surprising one ; but Mr. Laing
goes on to give other facts in support of his opinion.   I
could readily believe that in a southern country, in which
the weather is open all the year round, and in which, there-

fore, labour is always in demand for the ordinary purposes of life, the cost of felling trees and of chopping them up, would be something considerable. I should have supposed however that in a country which is ice-bound several months in the year, labour during the winter time would have been a drug; and that fuel for the whole year would have been cut and stacked during that period, at a price almost nominal. I do not pretend to set this conjecture against Mr. Laing's distinct statements.

But if we are fortunate in the possession of our coal pits, when we compare ourselves with people who live in the midst of forests at their disposal, how much more fortunate are we in comparison with those among whom even wood is scarce, or entirely wanting. In Ireland, indeed, an excellent substitute is found in the peat cut from the bogs; and Arthur Young was of opinion, a hundred years ago, that an extension of cultivation, by diminishing these bogs, would seriously injure the peasant. Other countries, or provinces, are not provided with this resource. We find * in Central Hungary, the peasants using reeds and straw for fuel, though they seem † to have some wood also, happily for them. Arthur Young tells us ‡ that in one part of France, neither wood nor coal being procurable, broom was grown to supply their place. On a cold winter's day even in temperate England, it makes one shudder to think of a crackling fire fed only with sedge, straw, and broom twigs. I wish I could believe that the unfortunate families so ill provided with fire, were rich and provident enough to imitate the Chinese. They, as I have mentioned, being

* Le Play, 101. 1.   † Ib. 110. 2.   ‡ Young's France, 1. 365.

unable to obtain fuel, fence out the cold from their bodies by additional clothes; adding garment after garment until in the depth of winter they present as shapeless an appearance as the Turkish women present at all times. The Chinese are astonished to see an European in the winter preserving the manifest figure of a man. There must have been a long continued want of fuel to have fostered such a practice; and to the unfortunates who are deficient in clothing the sufferings of winter must be intense.

We have, therefore, great reason to rejoice in the possession of our coal fields; as setting free a large proportion of our fertile land which, but for our coal, would be necessarily applied to producing fire-wood; as furnishing us with fuel at a cheaper rate than that of wood even to the Norwegians and Russians; and as putting us very high above those unfortunate tribes who are driven to the use of such substitutes as straw, reeds, and twigs.

But Mr. Laing stâtes rather too generally, that England consumes coal alone as fuel. This is more nearly the truth than it was when Mr. Laing wrote, twenty years ago; and far more nearly than it was fifty years ago. Before the canals were made in the latter half of the last century, coal cannot have been used except in places either near the mines, or accessible by water; and even now, the country parts which are far removed from both canals and railroads, have to pay a great price for wood as fuel. The last twenty years have done much in this respect, by covering the island with arteries and veins of railway communication; and the annual sufferings of the poor have thus been greatly relieved. We hear much of the improvident way in which our railroads have been laid down, and we are told that two-thirds, or one-half, of our actual lines, might have satisfied the needs of the nation. It is perfectly true that the North Western Company supplied all that was necessary for the interchange of persons and of goods between London and Birmingham; and that the broad gauge line might have been dispensed with so far as those great towns are concerned. If, then, the two lines ran side by side, little or nothing would have been gained by the second, and there would have been the needless expense of keeping up two establishments. But any one who will run his eye over the map, will find that the two lines diverge very much from one another. Starting from Birmingham, the one, in its first twenty miles reaches Leamington; the other, passing through Coventry, goes towards Rugby. The country places through which the two run are quite different. And this is a matter of very high importance as regards the supply of fuel, even in the heart of the kingdom. I myself am familiar with a parish in Warwickshire, which, quite recently had no railway within seven miles of it; and which had no immediate canal communication; where, consequently, the poor suffered greatly from the price of fuel during winter. Yet the country is flat and free from engineering difficulties. A new railroad that should have a station in this place, would be a great boon to the inhabitants, however ruinous it might be to the proprietary.

One other advantage arises incidentally from our supply of coal: I mean the absence of stoves in our rooms. This, no doubt, is caused very much by the moderation of our climate, and by the brevity of our winters. But if fuel were very dear, as it would be among us in the absence of coal, stoves would have been forced upon us. It is impossible to say how much of the superiority of English health and longevity is owing to the use of open fire-places : probably a considerable part is owing to it. We all know how close and stifling is the atmosphere of a room heated by a stove; and how much more difficult it is to keep a room perfectly ventilated in summer, than it is in winter, when the fire is constantly changing the air. It may be true that three-fourths of the heat of our fire-places passes up the chimney and is lost to us; but we gain far more advantage by the fresh air constantly introduced into the room.

CHAPTER XII,

I HAVE, thus, given a number of facts relating to the food, clothes, houses, furniture, and fuel, of the working classes in many parts of the world. These heads seem to include all that is necessary to the support of the material frame of men, so long as they are in health. But perfect and unbroken health is not the lot of humanity: all men are sometimes sick; most women and young children are frequently sick. The provision made for medical attendance is therefore of great importance.

Our friend M. Le Play is aware of the scepticism felt by many persons as to the efficiency of medicine. But he observes that even in a moral point of view medical services are highly to be desired. He says * " the organisation of medical services is indispensable to every civilised society; less even to mitigate physical suffering than to satisfy the moral needs of the highest order. Every one endued with sensibility who sees one of his kind, and especially a member of his family, overpowered by illness, must be greatly distressed by inability to procure the aid of art. This is felt most acutely, perhaps, by the highest natures; and, on the other hand, it is easily shown that families accustomed to leave their sick devoid of assistance, are by that very practice tainted with a real moral degradation. Remembering

* Le Play, 43. 2.

even the doubts that have been expressed of the practical usefulness of medicine as it is frequently administered, we cannot shut our eyes to the unfortunate moral results that follow from its absence."

Besides this reason assigned by M. Le Play in favour of the importance of medical attendance, there are others which weigh with me. It may be true that the routine of many apothecaries, and that the routine even of many physicians, is so unscientific and absurd, that more persons are injured than are benefited by their intervention. There are too many Sangrados in the world. But even if I believed that the licensed medical practitioners killed more persons than they cured, and permanently injured more than they permanently relieved, I should still regard it as a misfortune if the licensed medical profession ceased to exist. For it is certain that sick people will not be content to do nothing towards obtaining relief; and that if a licensed practitioner be not at hand, an empiric will be called in to supply his place. Neither the sick man nor his friends will trust to nature. However futile, therefore, may be the remedies administered by an apothecary, however injurious even they may be, the alternative is not between these remedies and no remedies, but between these remedies and the still more futile or injurious ones of the quack. If the licensed practitioner does nothing more, he occupies the place of the quack, and at the worst does far less harm than the quack. I do not mean to state it as my own opinion that the practice of the regular medical men is either futile or injurious. That they kill many patients is unquestionable; that they injure the frames of many whose lives they spare is not to be doubted: but I am convinced that the most skilful of them save more lives by far than they cut short; and even as to the least skilful I am far from certain on which side the balance lies. When, however, we take into account the fact I have suggested above, that but for the interference of these men the crop of quacks would grow in rankness without disturbance, we may fairly put to the credit of the qualified practitioners, not only the lives which they rescue from disease, but also those which they snatch from the clutches of the old woman and the herbalist.

The most valuable service rendered by medical men is, perhaps, not the administration of drugs, but the general regulation of the mode of life. Among the lower classes, especially, the great difficulty of a physician is not to induce his patient to swallow the necessary medicine, but to induce him to abstain from improper food during illness. A poor man feels languid from the effects of fever: he thinks himself weak and swallows as much meat as he can get, and as his want of appetite will allow. Among the more educated classes, such gross mistakes as this are less common. But it requires far more skill than most unprofessional persons possess, to recognise even the ordinary symptoms of disease; to distinguish the throb of fever from the rapid but feeble pulse of inanition: especially in families where the health has generally been good, and little attention therefore, has been directed to the interpretation of nature. Even if I were convinced that medicine is unnecessary, I should still call in a medical man when I was ill, in order to consult him as to the meaning of the symptoms I displayed.

The advantages, then, that I attribute to the services of educated medical men, are three: first, that they shut out the injurious interference of less qualified doctors: secondly, that they interpret the symptoms of disease and regulate the regimen of their patients: and thirdly, that in many cases they administer medicines which are positively beneficial. I have said nothing of surgery, because no one entertains a doubt as to its efficacy.

It is, therefore, painful to be reminded by M. Le Play,[*] that "the regular aid of medicine is still wanting, in the greater part of Europe, to the scattered working populations; and especially to the agricultural labourers who lie outside the radii of towns." This is the more to be regretted in cases where people are ignorant of the first principles on which disease should be treated. As, for example, in the South of Russia, where [†] "the care applied to children, whether in or out of health, is far from enlightened: thus it is the custom to expose children to the air, even in the coldest days of winter, when they are suffering the most from the fever produced by measles and other eruptive disorders. The practice of surgery is still more defective: the accouchements, in particular, are entrusted to ignorant incapable women, who receive one penny or three-half-pence for their trouble." It is no wonder that with such practices, there should be only found five families in the place mentioned, "who claim the exemption from labour granted to those who have more than six children living."

In many manufacturing districts of Europe, medical attendance and drugs are furnished at the expense of the masters, and this is especially the case among miners.[‡]   M.

---

* Le Play, 43. 2.   † Ib. 59. 1.   ‡ Ib. 43. 2.

Le Play is of opinion that there is an increase in this intervention on the part of the masters, even in those places where in other respects there is a tendency to leave workmen to their own unaided exertions. Particular mention is made of the mines of Siberia ;* of the celebrated iron mines of Danemora in Sweden ;† and of many others besides.

In Vienna,‡ we find a workman attended during sickness at the expense of the guild to which he belongs. In many other places men make some provision by subscribing regularly to a fund for this purpose.

In England, as we know, clubs for providing against illness are very general. But the principal object proposed is to furnish an income during incapacity for work : the services of the *club-doctor*, are also given. I was not aware till recently, that these provident institutions are far from being of recent origin. In Hutton's *Court of Requests*, however, we find that of the numerous cases brought for adjudication, those brought by stewards of sick-clubs against members, and by members against the stewards, formed a very considerable portion. Since these institutions, nearly a hundred years ago, were so numerous in Birmingham, they must have had their origin much earlier. Hutton says § elsewhere that some of the clubs were formed in the seventeenth century.

The *Club-doctor* is very often a rather unpopular man among the working people. He is poorly paid and cannot afford much time to each case, and he is therefore supposed

* Le Play, 44. 1. † Ib. 92. 27. ‡ Ib. 121. 2.

§ Hutton's History of Birmingham, 217.

to do his work negligently. It may be imagined, in truth, that he does not administer any unnecessary medicines, and that he thus gives nature a chance of exerting her curative power : but the ignorant are dissatisfied, unless they see and taste that something is being done. The fancy of many an old woman converts a dose of assafœtida into a gratifying draught.

One reason, no doubt, why members of a sick-club are suspicious of their medical man, is, that they have no choice after he is once elected. The minority of the members, those who opposed his election, will feel this dissatisfaction the most strongly. To remedy these evils, a scheme was set on foot in Birmingham, some twenty years ago, for a self-supporting dispensary. Another object proposed was, to supply the wants of a class of persons who shrink from asking for the gratuitous services and medicines of the public infirmaries and hospitals, and who yet cannot afford to pay the ordinary charges of a qualified practitioner. I have known a mechanic, earning from thirty shillings to forty shillings a week, who has had to pay £20. to £30. to a surgeon for one year's bill.

This scheme has taken root, and there are several such dispensaries in existence in Birmingham. Any one may get a ticket by paying the stipulated price : the choice is open to him of several regularly educated surgeons. These are not necessarily young men without experience. Though the remuneration in each case is small, it answers the purpose of a surgeon to fill up his spare time in this way, with the expectation that he shall thus obtain clients who will pay him better. It is on the same principle that many physicians and surgeons, in order to promote their practice, set apart one or two mornings a week for seeing poor patients gratuitously.

The charge for a ticket in this self-supporting dispensary is 3s. 6d.: the patient is visited at home as often as is necessary: the ticket is available for three weeks: the 3s. 6d. includes the charge for medicine. M. Le Play * tells us that in a particular case in Sheffield, the charge to a man was 1s. 6d. for each visit, including medicine. This is far dearer than such a ticket as I have described; since the holder of a ticket would hardly be satisfied with less than three or four visits, and would frequently require ten or fifteen. In Geneva, we find † the watchmaker paying tenpence a visit, besides buying his own medicines. Elsewhere the same rate seems to prevail.

On the whole, it is far better that the working classes should, wherever it is possible, provide themselves with medicine and attendance, whether by sick-clubs, or self-supporting dispensaries, or by a small payment for each visit. But where the labourer is so poor, or so improvident, that he does not accomplish this, the want should be supplied. If we lay down as a principle that no one, however extravagant or vicious, shall be allowed to perish for want of food, clothes, or shelter; much more should we take care that no one dies, or falls into permanent ill health, for want of medical care. If improvidence as to the certain want of daily food is not to constitute a disqualification for parish assistance, much less should improvidence as to the uncertain and varying want of medical attendance, not be regarded as a disqualification. Every labourer feels that

* Le Play, 194. 2.   † Ib. 164. 1.

he shall want food, clothes, and shelter: but in health, he may be almost excused if he forgets to make provision for the uncertain day of sickness.

Where provision is made by any of the modes mentioned above, it may be questioned whether the labourer is not in as favourable a condition as to medicine, as is the richer man. In the highest classes of society, the very anxiety of the practitioner defeats itself by disturbing the judgment. Even among the middle classes, the physician or surgeon would often be more successful, if he could act more as a man of science and less as a friend. A question of importance, a close examination of the person, will be omitted through considerations of delicacy, in the case of an educated and fastidious patient, but will be pressed home without shrinking in the house of the peasant. The peasant is a great gainer.

One serious obstacle to a sound practice has now nearly disappeared: I mean the custom that formerly prevailed among apothecaries, of charging for every box of pills and every draught. The necessity of making a bill at the end of every year, was a sore disturbance to the man of honest principle, and often compelled him to send medicines which he knew to be needless. The custom of charging in the lump for visits and medicine, or of charging for visits only, leaving the patient to buy the medicine, has put an end to a world of quackery. I was surprised to find within a very few years, that the old custom of charging for each article of medicine had not disappeared. In my own neighbourhood the custom has been abandoned by all reputable practitioners thirty years or more.

After enquiring as to medical services, we naturally ask what are the results : what is the comparative mortality of different times and places. Fortunately, we now possess the means of replying accurately to many questions about mortality. This was not the case formerly ; and the absence of precise information led, as usual, to gross misrepresentation and exaggeration. Dr. Price, in particular, arrived at the conclusion that the deaths, towards the close of last century, were so numerous as to more than equal the births ; and therefore, that England was in the course of depopulation. This is the more curious as having preceded, by only a few years, the exaggerated statements of Malthus, who led the world to regard increase of population as the bugbear of society.

Dr. Price founded his opinion on an examination of facts, and not on mere conjecture ; and it is no wonder that he felt alarmed, and expressed himself strongly, when he saw the national debt fast increasing, at the same time that the persons who were to pay the interest were, as he believed, yearly diminishing. If the facts had been as he supposed, Great Britain would have been at the present day, a very inconsiderable power ; and the taxes necessary to furnish the interest due to the fundholders, would have been intolerably oppressive.

The source of Dr. Price's error is well known : and one of the Registrar General's Reports contains a full investigation of the subject. At the present day, we have two modes, independent of each other, by which we estimate the movements of population : we have the census, or enumeration, taken every ten years ; and the registers of births and deaths, which proceed from day to day. Former

inquirers had no such means at command. Dr. Price, in
the absence of these, resorted to certain parish registers,
and especially to those of a portion of Northampton : comparing the births with the deaths there set down, and
finding that the recorded deaths exceeded the recorded
births, he concluded that the population of that district was
diminishing.   And as he could find nothing in Northampton
to distinguish it from other parts of the kingdom, he set
it down as an established truth, that depopulation was going
on in England generally.

It no doubt seemed to him, as it must occur to all of
us, that his inference was too wide for so narrow a basis :
but he took the best materials within his reach ; and those
who have ever been at all concerned in the investigation
of facts and numbers, will be the last to complain of his
inaccurate results.   It is very easy for men who sit at
home and do nothing, to censure errors which the idle avoid
only by their apathy and uselessness.

It is certain enough that Dr. Price's error was the one
into which it was most likely he would fall.   He had no
means of going from house to house, and counting up how
many persons had died and how many children had been
born.   He relied on the parish registers.   Now the register
of deaths might be presumed to be very nearly complete :
for every dead body must be buried, and few indeed are
placed in unconsecrated ground, or deprived of the ceremonies
of interment.   But the case of births is a very different
one.   Many parents, and especially among the lowest class,
are indifferent about the rite of baptism, many are procras-
tinating, and some are hostile to the rite.   Every corpse
is buried, but many infants miss the sacrament of baptism.

Besides these grand causes of inaccuracy, it appears that there was a special cause at Northampton, in the existence of a large number of Baptists, who reject infant baptism altogether. It is no wonder then, that Dr. Price's estimate was incorrect.

It is not to be supposed that this notion of depopulation was universally, or perhaps, generally received. It was loudly protested against by many writers, and among them, by Arthur Young and his correspondents, in the *Annals of Agriculture*. The prosperity of the country, also, after the peace of 1783, the growth of shipping, and the augmented returns of exports and imports were protests against the doctrine. Then came Malthus, who gradually making his way in public estimation, led men to fear, not a decrease, but an excessive increase of numbers. The census of 1801 laid the foundation of certain knowledge on this important subject: that of 1811 established the fact of a large increase of numbers; and each succeeding enumeration has exhibited steady progress in the same direction. During the fifty years that followed the first census, the inhabitants of England and Wales doubled their numbers; having been nine millions in 1801, and eighteen millions in 1851.

But the census alone was insufficient to determine questions relating to health : for it is an old observation that the most unwholesome countries are the most populous. The following conversation occurs in the life of Dr. Johnson. " *C.* It is remarkable that the most unhealthy countries, where there are the most destructive diseases, such as Egypt and Bengal, are the most populous. *Johnson.* Countries which are the most populous have the most destructive diseases. *That* is the true state of the question. *C.* Holland is very unhealthy, yet it is exceedingly populous. *Johnson.* I know not that Holland is unhealthy. But its populousness is owing to an influx of people from all other countries. Disease cannot be the cause of populousness, for it not only carries off a great proportion of the people; but those who are left are weakened, and unfit for the purposes of increase."

Men might have gone on disputing in the same strain till the present day; and if even one writer nearly arrived at the truth by imperfect observations and doubtful conjecture, another writer of apparently equal ability might have made a great show of probability on the other side. So late as 1831 the following remark was made by Mr. Rickman, a man eminent for his ability and his experience in statistics. He says,[*] in his remarks on the Population Abstracts of 1831, " the great increase in the town of Liverpool is attributed to the salubrity of the air, and progressive improvement in its trade," &c. The salubrity of the air! in a borough remarkable, as it has turned out, for a rate of mortality that exceeds by far even that of the worst of the great manufacturing towns: in a borough where the number of deaths is twice as great as it is in the healthy country places. When such an authority could err so grossly, there was a pressing need for more precise information.

Exact registers of births, marriages, and deaths, have long been established in several countries, and especially in Sweden. It was discreditable to Great Britain to be behind hand in such a work, but we did nothing till about twenty

---

* Registrar General, 8vo., 5. 34.

years ago. The wars of Napoleon, and afterwards the pro-
tracted wars of domestic parties, left no pause for less ex-
citing topics. At present, as to England and Wales, we have
regular and minute returns on most of the points which
interest even the most curious inquirers into statistical
matters. Each quarter of the year the public is put in
possession of the numbers of births, marriages, and deaths
that have taken place ; together with a good deal of information relating to them : and at irregular intervals there
appear bulky blue books, which contain a vast quantity of
miscellaneous matter bearing on the same subjects. There
are given the number of legitimate and illegitimate births,
the proportion of the sexes born, the number of illegitimate
births in each county, the total number of marriages, distinguishing the modes and places in which they are celebrated,
the ages of the new married persons, the deaths in every
quarter of the year and every locality, the ages of the
deceased in every county and every town, and the nature
of the deaths, whether violent or natural ; with a very
elaborate classification of the diseases of which people have
died. To these returns are added, from time to time, information of a similar character as to foreign countries, besides
many valuable essays and tables relating to the laws of
health and disease, the expectation of life, the principles of
life assurance, and other cognate subjects. It is only a
matter of regret that such a mine of information should
require a good deal of repulsive labour to bring the pure
metal into light. A score of heavy folios will scarcely find
a score of regular readers.

A good many of the facts, however, find their way to
the public by the means of other publications. And the

registers, far from being useless, have certainly done much to stimulate the adoption of sanitary measures. By showing the numbers of persons who die of smallpox, they have led to compulsory vaccination : by exhibiting the excessive mortality of towns as compared with that of the country, they have promoted the improvement of drainage, have caused the prohibition of the use of cellars as habitations, and have induced legal restraints on the crowding of lodging houses.

I am not about to give an abstract of the facts contained in these registers. A slight inspection of them will show the superior healthiness of the country as compared with the town; and will convince us that cold weather is far more fatal than mild or hot weather. The numbers of deaths of a particular winter quarter, may be less than those of a particular spring, summer, or autumn quarter : but on the average, the deaths of the winter quarters predominate.   It must be observed that by the winter quarter is meant the three months from Christmas to Lady Day; the three months from Michaelmas to Christmas being called the autumn quarter. Any one who consults the earlier registers should also bear in mind that at first, the year was reckoned from one Midsummer to another; but that afterwards, the natural mode was adopted of taking the year from the first of January to the thirty-first of December. In comparing the returns of early and of later years, this alteration causes some confusion; but some of the more important tables have been corrected, and are given under subsequent years.

No one doubts that the number of deaths in the world might be greatly diminished. Many lives are shortened by vice, many by sloth and gluttony, many by want and hardships. The mortality of England is less than that of other countries; and in one point of view this is singular. For the mortality of towns is far greater than that of country places; and therefore, the nation that has most towns, and great towns especially, might be expected to enjoy a bad preeminence of deaths. But England with its half town, half country, is nevertheless more healthy than the agricultural nations. In a late report we find the five great powers thus arranged * as to annual deaths among every thousand persons living: England $22\frac{1}{4}$, France nearly 24, Prussia $26\frac{1}{4}$, Austria $30\frac{1}{4}$, Russia 36. The temperate climate of England, the superior means of living of our labourers, and their greater cleanliness, more than counterbalance the destruction of life caused by our great towns.

An opinion is expressed in the same volume that "the natural deaths in our present imperfect state" may be regarded as seventeen in a thousand of the population, annually. The actual deaths in England and Wales on the average of the fourteen years from 1838 to 1851, were rather more than $22\frac{1}{4}$ in a thousand; and therefore, the excess above the deaths assumed as natural, was $5\frac{1}{4}$ in a thousand. This excess, and not the actual numbers, is what we should always look at. If we find that during ten years, the average deaths of the kingdom were twenty two, those of Birmingham twenty-six, and those of Liverpool thirty-six, we must say that the excess of Birmingham was four, while that of Liverpool was fourteen: and therefore, that the excess of Liverpool was $3\frac{1}{2}$ times as great as that of Birmingham.

* Registrar General, 8vo., 16. Q. R. 122.

No greater mistake can be made on this subject, than the coming to a conclusion as to the healthiness of a place, from the observations made during a short period. It is not uncommon for a local newspaper to lay hold of a quarterly return of deaths, and to denounce destruction on a town because the mortality during three months, has been unusually large. No trustworthy conclusion can be arrived at from one quarterly return, nor even from one or two years' returns. The Registrar General himself was too hasty in his inferences in his early reports. I will give an example of the different results that arise when we take different periods of time.

Number of deaths annually in one thousand of the population :—

	Whole Kingdom.	Birmingham.	Leeds.	London.	Manchester.	Liverpool.	Sheffield.	Cornwall.
1838-39 two years.	22	25½	24½	28	30½ with Salford.	29 with West Derby.		
1838-40 three years.		27	27	27	35½ without Salford.	35 without West Derby.	30	
1838-44 seven years.		26	25½ with Hunslet		32½	33		
1841-50 ten years.	22	26	30	25 all metro- polis.	33	36 omitting year 1847.	27	19

It is noticed as remarkable that the density of population is far greatest in Liverpool, next greatest in Birmingham, and next in London : also that it is greater in Salford than in Manchester, though the mortality of Salford is something less than that of Manchester.

In comparing the returns of 1841—50, it must be observed that London is made to include all the metropolis, whereas in other places only the town is taken, and the suburbs and environs are left out. For example; the return of Birmingham for 1851 applies only to a population of 174,000 persons, whereas the census makes the numbers 232,000. Most of the middle classes live at Edgbaston, a suburb within the borough but out of the parish. If the mortality-return extended to the whole borough, the twenty-six would fall to twenty-five,* as far as we know: this is exactly the rate of the metropolis.

By a comparison of the above columns it will be seen that short periods are insufficient to prove any thing. In the first line, that for 1838—39, Liverpool occupies a not very disreputable position, as being better than Manchester, and not much worse than London. But in the last line, that for 1841—50, the Liverpool mortality for the ten years is frightful. It is set down as thirty-six, but if we include 1847, it rises to thirty-nine; that year having been omitted because the Irish famine drove over thousands of unfortunates to find a grave in Liverpool.

Then as to Leeds. In the first line it appears as the best of the towns I have given: but during the ten years from 1841—50, it occupies a far worse place than Birmingham or Sheffield, though it still stands much above Manchester, and still more above Liverpool. It is plain that no inferences can safely be drawn from returns, until they have continued for a great number of years. It is very likely

---

* Aris's Birmingham Gazette, 27th October, 1856.

that the results for 1851—60 may be very different from those of the preceding ten years, because between 1841 and 1850 there occurred two disastrous years, that of 1847 when influenza raged all over the kingdom, and that of 1849, when Asiatic cholera decimated the people. The deaths in each thousand of the population of England and Wales were—in 1845, 21; 1846, 23; 1847 (influenza), 24½; 1848, 23; 1849 (cholera), 25; 1850, 20½. It will be seen that the influenza year was nearly as bad as the cholera year.

The small mortality of 1850 is remarkable, and may naturally be explained by the common notion, that a year of unusual mortality cuts off all the persons of tender health, and leaves fewer of such precarious lives to terminate in the year following. That there is some truth in this hypothesis cannot well be doubted; but whether it is so far true as to account for the very low mortality of 1850 is not at all certain. The Registrar General remarks that there is one circumstance which militates against the hypothesis. It is well known that Birmingham is one of a very few favoured places which escaped the horrors of the cholera; so that while the male deaths in Manchester, from all causes, rose from the rate of about 3500 in ordinary years to 4161 in the cholera year of 1849; and while the male deaths in Liverpool, from all causes, rose from the rate of about 4500 in ordinary years to 6457 in 1849; the male deaths in Birmingham, from all causes, instead of rising in 1849 were decidedly lower than usual. The male deaths, from all causes, in Birmingham were—in 1845, 1909; 1846, 2381; 1847 (influenza), 2758; 1848, 2405; 1849 (cholera), 2009; 1850, 2127; 1851, 2489.

According to the hypothesis I am discussing the mortality of the kingdom in 1851 was low, because in 1849 it was

high. But the mortality of Birmingham in 1850 was also
low : and why ? Because it was high in 1849 ? Not so ;
for it was remarkably low in 1849. And just as it is argued
that a high rate of mortality in one year, is naturally followed by a low rate the next year, because the frail plants
have been weeded out; so may it be contended, as a consequence, that a low rate one year, by failing to weed out
the frail plants, leaves a large crop of deaths for the next
year. Therefore, the Birmingham mortality of 1850 ought
to have been high ; but it was low : a shrewd argument
against the truth of this hypothesis. Birmingham, and the
whole kingdom, were both of them healthy in 1850. We
may fairly suppose that this common condition was the
result of a common cause : and this common cause is not
found in the mortality of the year before ; since in that
year, the kingdom was frightfully unhealthy and Birmingham was singularly healthy. We must attribute the
healthiness of the year 1850, to the ordinary favourable
causes.

The returns confirm the known facts, that while the births
of males exceed those of females, the deaths of males also
exceed those of females. During fourteen years, from
1838 to 1851, the number of deaths to every thousand of
the population of England and Wales, was, of males 23·15,
of females, 21·54, average 22·34, or 22$\frac{1}{3}$.

The few facts I have here mentioned, are very trifling
extracts from the contents of nearly a score of bulky
volumes : any person who has a taste for dry research,
will find a multitude of other facts in these reports ; though
without considerable care he will be apt to be bewildered by
the multiplicity of the records.

Elaborate as are the returns, valuable as is the occasional information, and able as are the disquisitions of Dr. Farr, I cannot say that I think the system is perfect. I find especial fault with the arbitrary way in which the boundaries of the districts have been fixed, and with the obstinacy with which they are adhered to. In the course of twenty years, a town overflows its parish, runs into what was the country, and even invades another county. The registers should be varied accordingly; but in fact no change is made. A town does not consist of a certain number of square acres, which happen to constitute a parish or a dozen parishes: a town consists in an aggregation of people. To confine the registry of a town within certain ancient, unchangeable, boundaries, is just as wise as to confine the municipal authority within the same boundaries. Instead of adopting the obsolete divisions into parishes, the more natural mode, as it appears, would have been, to adopt the municipal divisions where they exist, and to form similar divisions where there is no municipality. The registrars' districts were, I know, arranged before the new corporations were formed; but the materials out of which the corporations were formed, existed and might have been used. It is high time that a change should be made.

The four following examples will illustrate my meaning:—

Population in 1851.	According to Registers.	In the Municipal Borough.	Deficiency in Registers.	
Liverpool	258,236	375,955	117,719	or more than $\frac{1}{3}$
Manchester without Salford	228,433	303,382	74,949	„ „ $\frac{1}{4}$
Birmingham	173,951	232,841	58,890	or nearly $\frac{1}{4}$
Leeds	101,343	172,270	70,927	or more than $\frac{2}{5}$

If a borough were fairly divided in these registry districts, so as to include a due proportion of good parts and of bad ones, the result would be the same as if the whole borough were included. But the case is just the reverse. For example: the register for Birmingham is confined to the parish and does not include Edgbaston, nor that part of Aston which is within the municipal borough. Edgbaston is used principally for houses of the middle classes, and the mortality of the parish is very low. Aston is more varied in its occupants, containing many manufactories and small houses: the mortality, however, is moderate. In 1855 the mortality [*] of Birmingham (as registered) was 25·460 in the 1000.

Of Aston within the borough 22·179   „   „
Of Edgbaston .... 17·387   „   „
Of the whole borough......... 24·359   „   „

The mortality of Birmingham, therefore, as registered, was about $25\frac{1}{2}$; while that of the municipal borough was under $24\frac{1}{2}$. It follows that the excess in 1855 above the average rate of the kingdom for fourteen years (22·34)[†] was really two in a 1000, though it is set down as three in a 1000.

It will be understood that the registrar's district, while it leaves out the parts occupied by the middle classes, includes the parts occupied by the very lowest classes: that it avoids the parts where the mortality is lowest, and includes those where the mortality is highest. In the old parts of every town, in close lanes and among decaying houses, are found a large proportion of thieves and prostitutes, of low lodging houses and tramps, of barefooted

[*] Aris's Gazette, 27th October, 1856.   [†] Registrar General, 8vo., 14. xvi.

children and of squalid destitution. Such are the places
where death riots. But if a fair comparison is to be made
of one town with another, or even of towns with country
parts, these hotbeds of pestilence and death should be
taken together with the more favoured and healthy parts.
In London, while the deaths in Whitechapel are thirty-
nine in the 1000, those in St. George's, Hanover Square,
are only eighteen in the 1000.* But these and similar
districts are thrown together, and as a result, the mortality
of the metropolis is set down as being twenty-five † from
1841 to 1850. I have already shewn that for the same
period the registered mortality of Birmingham was twenty-
six, against twenty-five in London; and I have since shewn
that the mortality of the whole borough in 1855 was one
less than the registered mortality: we may conclude that
from 1841—50, the borough of Birmingham was about
as healthy as the metropolis.

This unfairness is constantly increasing. Since the
registry was first established, twenty years ago, Birmingham has increased from 170,000 to, perhaps, 270,000. Of
course the centre of vice and misery has increased in proportion, while the more prosperous parts of the people
have escaped out of the parish. This process is still going
on; and even though the whole borough should improve in
salubrity, the parish may be expected to get worse and
worse, in consequence of the increasing preponderance of
the filthy centre. In some places this might not be true,
because there might happen to be a quantity of land
remaining to be built on. But the density of the popula-

* Registrar General, 1. 78, and 2. Appendix, 11.   † Ib. 8vo. 16. 144, &c.

tion shows the truth of what I say in this instance. Birmingham is rather remarkable, when compared with old towns, for the reasonable breadth of its streets, and the absence of height in its houses : the census shows that each family has generally a separate house. Yet, according to the Registrar General,* in 1838—40, while the density of population was highest in Liverpool, Birmingham stood next in order, London (not the metropolis) was third, and Bristol fourth. This shows that the parish of Birmingham was greatly covered with houses twenty years ago.

It is by no means necessary that I should assign a motive to the Registrar General, or his advisers, for continuing arrangements that are manifestly incomplete and unfair. I say unfair, because boroughs as well as persons should have justice done them ; and a healthy town has reason at least to rejoice in its good fortune. A dislike of the trouble that would attend any alteration of boundaries may seem a sufficient motive for avoiding a change : but I can fancy one that appears more creditable, though I believe it would be a very mistaken one.

The burden of the reports from first to last has been the great mortality of the towns as compared with that of the country, with regret that little has been done to mitigate the evil. Any thing that tends to impress this fact on the minds of citizens is welcome to the humane Dr. Farr : any thing that weakens the impression is to be avoided. But the present practice with regard to boundaries, in exaggerating the evil, is so far advantageous that it creates a louder call for sanitary measures ; while to represent the

* Report, 4. 11.

mortality in its true light would be to give up a hold on the
sympathy of the benevolent. It may be thought that men
must be sometimes deceived for their good.

I do not presume to say that Dr. Farr, or any other
person, has entertained such notions as these; I draw
purely from fancy. I know that men accustomed to public
affairs often do act with similar dissimulation, though more
often from a wish to " make things pleasant," than from
the promptings of benevolence. I am convinced that the
policy of such diplomacy is stupid as well as wrong. I will
not say that it is the duty of every person, at all times, to
speak the whole truth. I may happen to see two parties in
a town council disputing about the propriety of obtaining
power to raise additional rates for sanitary purposes: the
one party urging the fact of an increasing mortality, the
other tacitly confessing the alleged increase. I may know
that both are wrong in this respect. Yet it may not be my
duty to rush into the strife and set them right. If I think
the additional rates desirable, I may hesitate about taking a
part which may prevent the acquisition of the power to
raise the rates.

But if I occupied a prominent position in such a council
I should probably feel it my duty to speak the whole truth.
Much more, if I held the responsible situation of Registrar
General, should I think myself bound to represent facts
exactly as they are, and to avoid all arrangements that tend
to deceive the public. I should hold my business to be,
the collection of statistics; and I should regard the drawing
of inferences as altogether a subordinate duty. For this
reason I should feel it incumbent on me, I hope, from time to

time, to revise the boundaries of my districts, with a view to equalise the nominal and the real town populations. Independently of the general principles of truthfulness and good faith, I see one strong practical reason for this course. The Registrar General, or his assistants, are fond of repeating that the towns are doing little to improve their sanitary condition. Now, I can point out a borough in which a great deal of money has been laid out in sewerage, though the mortality was previously light by comparison, though the rates are commonly seven to eight shillings in the pound, where a single shop assessed on appeal at £1200. a year, pays annually £450. as rates, a borough in which the population is constantly outgrowing the limits of the registrar's district. The tendency of the ill-drawn boundaries is to exaggerate the apparent mortality. What is the natural inference that the inhabitants will draw from the facts before them? " Our mortality was originally low : we were told by authority that improved sewerage would render it lighter : we were justly proud of the healthiness of our people, and we took a pleasure in labouring to secure and extend that healthiness : we were heavily taxed before, but we increased our rates with a view to secure so beneficial an object. What has been the result ? That the mortality has been increasing : that the more money we have spent, the more the people have died. We fear we have been deceived ; and though we know our sewerage to be still incomplete, we will raise no more rates for such purposes, but we will fold our hands and wait on events." It is in vain for one person, or a dozen persons, to point out the fallacies of the register. Members of a town council cannot be expected to investigate principles, or to discuss the accuracy of the legally formed returns.

There is one other matter in connection with this subject which has long attracted my attention ; but as it leads to no practical result, and merely gratifies a natural curiosity, I banish my remarks to a note at the end of the volume.*

* See Note at end of Volume.

CHAPTER XIII.

I HAVE now given a short account of the state of the
working classes, as regards those things which concern
their physical needs; as regards their food, clothes, houses,
furniture, fuel, and medicine. These things are required
to satisfy our bodily wants. The cravings of hunger, the
sensation of cold, the pining of disease, are common
to us with the lower animals. But there is in man a principle which the brutes have not, or which, at the most,
they have in a very small measure. Bishop Butler may be
right in assigning to the dog, the elephant, and the mouse,
an immortal soul; Buffon may be right in denying them
even the power of thought; Kirwan may be right in the
ingenious notion grafted on his humane sympathy, the notion
that all animals are mere machines, preordained to start
at the lash, to shrink from the spur, though really devoid of
sense and feeling. But Butler, Buffon, and Kirwan, all
agree in regarding man as a creature of higher destinies,
of nobler capacities, of more various requirements. When
we have given our domestic animals an abundance of food
and water, we have satisfied their principal want; and if
we add shelter and occasional medicine, that is the most
we can do for them. But where our care for the lower
animals ends, our care for our own species may almost
be said to begin; since the instinct of those, wants no

cultivation, while the reasoning powers, and the moral sentiments of our race are dormant, until they are developed.

Most persons in the present day agree in regarding religion as the first and most necessary food for the mind of man; and in placing the instruction of the understanding in the second place. Some thinkers will say that moral excellence after all is the sole aim of religion, and that they who attain to such excellence, possess all the piety that is needed. But the world at large is not satisfied with so rationalistic a maxim, and is apt to believe that moral excellence is not to be found, out of the domains of positive religious habit and culture. Besides, there are few men of any reflection, who are altogether free from occasional apprehensions of the future. Sometimes their minds are ruffled by the probability that pain and grief may be their lot in this world; or by the contingent unhappiness and misconduct of those they love; or by a fruitless endeavour to peer through the curtain that shuts us out from the last act of this drama of our being. Though under the pressure of sickness, or adversity, or domestic grief, death may have few terrors, and the grave may be regarded as a place of repose; yet in health and prosperity, when troubles have been forgotten, and the current of life runs freely, the recollection that all must have an end, throws at times a dark shadow on the strongest mind, and bends the weaker mind to asceticism or superstition. General interest is therefore felt in the enquiry, what is the state of religion among the working classes of different countries?

M. Le Play furnishes much information on this subject, giving a few paragraphs upon it in each case. He does not confine himself, however, to religion, but under the same head notes down his observations as to the moral habits. Indeed, whatever may be the relation between religion and morals, that they are closely connected is doubted by few persons.

I have already alluded to M. Le Play's tolerant appreciation of the excellences found in professors of the Mahometan faith. If he had met with only a single instance of their good qualities, we might have suspected him of fancy or exaggeration. But he tells us the same tale in different places.

First,* among the half no made tribes living on the Asiatic side of the Ural Mountains, under the shadow of the Czar's throne, we find that "all the inhabitants of the village belong to the Mussulman faith: about one half obey the main precepts of the Koran; the remainder neglect or openly break them. Kourama, and under his influence, the other members of the family, are distinguished by their fervour, and especially by their punctuality in performing the duties of ablutions, prayers, &c. This disposition has raised the family above the moral level of the rest of the inhabitants, especially in pecuniary transactions. . . . The principal vice of the population is an inveterate propensity to idleness." . . . We see afterwards, that the moral tone of the tribe is by no means high. "The Bachkir exercise a certain degree of self restraint in their pecuniary transactions with each other, but in dealing with the Russians they have little scruple in practising fraud. The least scrupulous among them go so far as to traffic in false evidence, with a view

* Le Play, 49. 2.

to extort money from the rich by charging them with
scandalous offences." The distinction of honesty in transactions among themselves, and in transactions between themselves and the Russians, is similar to what I have noticed
as regards our working classes; who will not generally
rob each other of a trifling tool, but who will waste
the property of their employers without scruple. The
workman has little sympathy with the master who lives in
comparative superfluity or luxury: the Bachkir has little
sympathy with the Russian who is to him an alien in blood
and in religion. In both instances the men are guided by
a feeling of sympathy and not by a restraining sense of
duty. But the chief, Kourama, says M. Le Play, elevated
by the sincerity and fervour of his piety, rises above this
low, coarse, bifaced morality.

In another case given by M. Le Play,* we see a
Christian workman in the service of a Mahometan master;
and it is agreeable to find that the relation between them
is of a highly satisfactory character. Far from oppressing
his dependent, the master assists him when he is in want,
and shows the kindest consideration for him. M. Le Play
speaks in one passage, of the charity that eminently distinguishes the Mussulman law. In the present example he
says † " In principle, the organization of agriculture, like
that of trade in Turkey, is founded on the system of forced
engagements: in reality, the manners and particularly the
excellent habits of patronage maintained by the Turkish
seigneurs, confer on the permanent relation that exists
between the masters, and their tenants or workmen, the
character of permanent voluntary engagements." After

* M. Le Play, 104. &c.   † Ib. 109. 2.

explaining that the workmen are bound to their master by a debt, incurred when they are in want of assistance, M. Le Play explains that this debt might be paid off in many cases: but that if any workmen were to do this "the circumstance would not give rise to a notion of quitting an occupation in which they, and their fathers before them, have found a happy existence. This state of things, too, is maintained by the conservative spirit which reigns over the population, as well as by the kindly disposition and the religious sentiments of the patrons. These, for example, scrupulously observe those precepts of the Koran which forbid loans on interest: and however large may be the debt of the workman, no stoppage is made from their wages without their consent."

The same belief in the existence of Mussulman excellence is expressed by Mr. Morier * " Although it may be urged that such characters as my hero and heroine are not known in Persia, yet let me say that there is no good reason why they should not. It has been remarked that the principles which actuate them are not likely to be produced by the doctrines of the Koran; but we often see in the votaries of a false religion an excellence, however produced, which seems to be guided by the true one. Let me ask those who have lived in the East, and particularly in Turkey, whether they have not been acquainted with Mahomedans there, whose conduct in life would have done credit to Christianity?"

Having finished this pleasant sketch of the happy influence exercised by the religion of the great impostor, I come to

* Preface to Zohrab the Hostage, 1856. viii.

the Greek Church, and I will quote a few of the notes given us on the state of religion among the peasants professing the Eastern faith. During the late Russian war, some persons were so shocked at the mummeries of the Greek Church, that they boldly professed their belief in the superiority of the Mussulman practice. They saw the Turk bowing down reverentially, and worshipping the Great Spirit, while the Greek Rayah servilely prostrated himself before an image. So far is this veneration carried, according to the *Englishwoman in Russia,* that a servant girl bent on some petty offence, laid hold of a counterfeit presentment of her saint, and turned its face towards the wall, that it might not see her sin. The pure worship practised by the Mahometan, the bowing of the mind and body before the Creator, is refreshing in comparison with this grovelling superstition. It is true that the educated classes in the East, like educated people everywhere, rise above these gross forms; and the more easily because they are allowed, as it seems, * to read the New Testament, except the Book of Revelations: but this does not in the least modify the coarse and palpable superstition that weighs down the souls of the peasantry who cannot read. One regulation in the East tends, however, to prevent many scandals, that in earlier ages, and in remote places, have arisen from the celibacy of the clergy. In Russia, † a priest cannot take a cure of souls until he is married. Another rule is, that a widowed priest cannot marry again: a third is, that a widower cannot have a cure any more than a bachelor: he generally retires into a monastery.

* Englishwoman in Russia, 133.   † Ib.

M. Le Play's second case * gives us an exact account of the religious rites practised by a particular family in the south of Russia. " The † whole family has been brought up in the orthodox Greco-Russian church; it fulfils its religious duties with exactness, yielding obedience in this respect to tradition, to the impulsion of a lively faith, and to the requirements of law. In this respect it follows precisely the customs which are almost universal in Russia. This disposition is the result rather of an instinctive faith than of a reasonable development of religious sentiment : it does not restrain the family from a certain tendency to intemperance, dissimulation, tricksiness, or even fraud in pecuniary matters ; but it confers a stoical resignation under physical and moral sufferings ; it helps to maintain a profound respect and absolute deference towards parents ; finally, it inspires, in the presence of death, an assurance and a serenity which have a real character of grandeur."

A few pages further on ‡ we have some interesting particulars given us. We find that the family in question incur the following expenses : and we must remember that a shilling in a Russian village represents a great deal more labour, more food, more of every thing that we value, than it does among ourselves. " These expenses are partly caused by the religious fervour of the family ; are partly imposed by the regulations of the public administration ; are partly due, and especially as to those relating to marriage, to the urgent demands of the clergy."

---

* Le Play, 58, &c.   † Ib. 58. 2.   ‡ Ib. 67. 2.

	Annual.	
	s.	*d.*
1. Permanent Expenses—		
For masses, &c..............................	3	0
For confession of eight persons	0	10
For the pascal collection	1	9
For the services of three anniversaries		
of the dead	0	11
	6	6

	Annual Average.	
	s.	*d.*
2. Occasional Expenses—		
Baptisms	0	8
Marriages	1	3
Funerals	1	7
	3	6

Total of the average annual expenses		
for a family of eight persons, about	10	0

An interesting and exact account is added,* of the ceremonies of marriage, and of previous betrothal.

The next case † is that of an emigrant porter, a native of
Central Russia. We are told here that the family brought
up, like the last, in the orthodox faith, " brings to the
fulfilment of its religious duties, in the absence of an
ardent zeal, an exact adherence to the requirements of
law."

" The principal vice of the population is a want of
uprightness in pecuniary affairs. Intemperance, though
diminishing, is still a great obstacle to the prosperity of

many families. Chastity is tolerably well observed among young women, less by the sentiment of honour than by the precocity of marriage, and by the favourable influence of family life. The habits of migration, however, which have become a local necessity, cause unhappy consequences in this respect, through the prolonged absence of husbands."

" The leading qualities of the population, the love of family life, respect for paternal authority, resignation under misfortune and suffering, serenity in the presence of death, are no less developed in this neighbourhood than in the greater part of Russia."

The annual expense of this family for religion is set down at about fifteen shillings.

In another case * selected from the North of Russia, (the two former ones having been taken from the south and centre), the family is, like the others, of the orthodox faith. " The conduct of the chief, and of the other members of the family, is regular ; these moral habits, however, result less from any energy in religious sentiment than from the influence exercised by the assistance rendered towards the support of the family, from the laborious habits imposed by custom, from the watchfulness of seignorial authority ; in a word, from the entire circumstances under which the family grows up."

The annual religious expenditure is estimated at about eight shillings.

In another Russian case, taken from Western Siberia, we meet with a similar state of things, though with shades of

* Le Play, 78. 1.

difference : rather severer morals running into something of austerity ; with a hatred of innovation, and a consequent distaste to education of children.

We find in all the Russian cases, an habitual attention to the outward forms of religion. Besides attendance at mass and confession, the peasants on every important occasion of meeting, commence* or conclude with prayer. Thus, in the account given us of the artèles,† or associations of emigrant labourers, the meeting held for arranging preliminaries, " terminated with an official proclamation of the association, followed by a prayer made in common," &c. At another preliminary meeting at the native place, prayer was made in common. This habit of solemnising, or sanctifying all important undertakings by prayer, or by other religious forms, seems to diminish as civilisation advances. The French are not a religious nation, and we do not wonder that this habit has ceased among them. But the English middle classes are unquestionably religious ; and yet we should be greatly surprised, perhaps scandalised, by a proposition to commence a railway meeting, or a free trade gathering, with prayer. The custom of saying grace before and after dinner, holds its ground in England. But in the last century many other equally significant forms were prevalent.

I have been told by an old person that one of these obtained in Birmingham. The factors there are middle-men, who buy goods from the manufacturers and sell them again to merchants at the ports, and to a greater extent to the ironmongers scattered over Great Britain and Ireland. The

* Le Play, 76. 2.   † Ib. 76. 2.

factors are really inland merchants, and are called merchants
when they extend their operations into foreign parts. It
is their custom to make journeys either in person, or by
paid travellers, to collect accounts and orders. Formerly,
before the factor mounted his horse and saddle-bags, (the
only conveyance in those days whether for factors, or judges
of assize, out of certain great lines) he sent a circular to
each of his customers, announcing his approach. These
circulars commenced with the words, *God willing;* and in
the language of the countinghouse the circulars were
called *Godwillings.*

The same piety, or superstition, appeared in Bills of
Lading. I have before me two of those documents, both
dated 1820. The one commences, " Shipped, by the grace
of God, in good order and well conditioned by Campbell
Bowden and Co., in and upon the good ship called the
" Melantho," whereof is master, under God, for this present
voyage Robert Porritt, and now riding at anchor in the river
Thames, and by God's grace, bound for St. Thomas," &c.
There is a surplusage here, of words of piety, that remind
one unpleasantly of Praise-God-Barebones.

The other bill is of a different tenor. " Shipped in good
condition, by John Tennent and Co., in and upon the good
ship called the " Laurel," whereof Thomas Tummon is master
for this present voyage, and now lying in the port of Liverpool, and bound for St. Domingo," &c. The London bill of
lading makes a great profession; the Liverpool one makes
no profession : but no one will therefore attribute to this
London shipper, or to the London shippers generally, a
superiority of piety over their Liverpool contemporaries.
When we read in the obituary of a newspaper, a notice

written with a fulsome superfluity of admiration and regret, we are apt to suspect the survivors either of hypocrisy or coarseness.

We need not, therefore, condemn ourselves as inferior to the Russian peasantry, because the name of God is not always in our mouths, and because it does not now head all our mercantile documents. It would not even be difficult to make out a charge against the Russian peasantry of habitual immorality, very inconsistent with these professions.

Thus, Malthus,* fifty years ago, accused the Russian servants of gross licentiousness. He mentioned a particular case of a female servant, who, living under a mistress accounted a strict one, gave birth to six illegitimate children in succession, all of whom were sent to the Foundling Hospital. The *Englishwoman in Russia* † attributes great immorality both to the upper and the lowest classes. She says that the marriages of the serfs are generally arranged by their seigneurs, or by the land-stewards, for reasons which are obvious. However, the next page of the book seems to contradict this assertion; for we are told that a master one day calling his men servants together, told twenty of them that he wished them to marry; and that they asked leave to go to their native village to choose their wives. It does not appear that there was any dictation as to the choice.

Besides, it must be observed that the authoress speaks only of the people she knew, and that she puts together in the same category, the domestic servants and the country serfs. But there appears to be a marked distinction between

---

* Malthus, Population, 1. 312.   † *Englishwoman in Russia*, p. 103.

the two classes of peasants. I am informed that practically, the servants are slaves. An English gentleman assures me that he has known a Russian under the excitement of gambling, lose at a sitting all his money and valuables, and then stake his carriage with the coachman and footman. But in the country, the peasants cannot be sold from the estate they live on.

M. Le Play tells us there is a marked distinction between these two classes.* " Independently of the peasants, the seigneur maintains on his estate a particular class of people called dvarovié, who are attached especially to the farming of his domain, and to his personal service; viz., the shepherds who have the care of his flocks, the mechanics who work up the wood, iron, leather, &c.; the civil officers who manage the administration of the village, the manufacture of spirits, and the seignorial magazines; and lastly the domestic servants of the seigneur's house. This class of dvarovié, which has always a tendency to increase unnecessarily, is a burden, and almost always a cause of embarrassment to a great Russian estate."

" There exists a marked distinction between the habits of the peasantry and those of the dvarovié. The leisure of a life of indolence, an over intimate contact with the seigneur's house at a time when the morals of the nobility were less regular than they are now, have injuriously influenced the dvarovié. In truth, the common interest of the seigneur and of the peasants maintains between these two classes of peasants an almost absolute line of demarcation. The seigneur, fearing to lose an useful member of

* Le Play, 58. 1 and 3.

the community, will not authorize the marriage of a son of the dvarovié with a peasant girl; and on his side, a peasant shrinks from introducing into his family, habits of demoralization, or at any rate of indolence: and therefore, would not accept a girl of dvarovié as a daughter-in-law."

It seems, therefore, that the *Englishwoman* may be perfectly right in her remarks as far as her own observation extended, but that she was wrong in supposing that the peasant class generally resembled, in regard to morals, the domestic servants with whom she was acquainted. It does not appear that the slavish superstition is a mere cloak worn to conceal immorality of habits; and this would be the case if the *Englishwoman's* statements were generally applicable to the peasants.

I now turn to Austria, a country in which the Roman Catholic church retains a greater influence than we find conceded to it in many other countries. Case eleven is that of a mechanic living in Vienna: we find the following notes. * " Husband and wife have both received in their native place the elements of primary education: they received their first communion as early as seven years old. The boy when he became an apprentice, was required, in conformity with the rules of the corporation, still to receive instruction in the catechism and to observe his religious duties. When he afterwards became a companion, he could not commence his tour of Austria, or receive the passport authorising him to travel, without first exhibiting certificates attesting his regular fulfilment of these obligations during his entire apprenticeship."

* Le Play, 121. 1.

" Attracted to Vienna by the desire of improving their circumstances, the two young people appear to have led a sufficiently regular life. They yielded indeed to the influence of the relaxed morals of this great centre of population, and of the local regulations which throw obstacles in the way of marriage; but the irregular connexion they formed at first, has since been legitimised. Since that period, the family may be classed, as to moral habits, with the most estimable of the population of Vienna. The anxiety of husband and wife is entirely concentrated on the interests of the community (guild); they labour with sustained zeal, without ever being led astray by the love of pleasure; they live soberly, abstaining from all spirituous liquors: their only recreation consists in the care necessary to their children."

This is a very pleasing picture of the life of a rather poor mechanic, and it would be agreeable to be able to believe that the family is a type of the class to which it belongs. But M. Le Play does not seem to regard it in this light; and the accounts we receive from other persons generally represent Vienna as a city in which immorality abounds. It appears, therefore, that comparing Vienna with towns in the west of Europe, the working classes are compelled to attend on the ordinances of religion, while our people are left to their own discretion. It appears, also, as we might have anticipated, that this compulsory attendance fails to secure a high moral condition.

Vienna is generally set down as an unusually corrupt city; on the ground that the number of illegitimate births there, is frightfully large. It is well known, however, that this circumstance is very much owing to the difficulties thrown in the way of marriage. M. Le Play's observations on this point are very valuable. "In Vienna,* as in Southern Germany generally, the administration lays down as a principle, that authority to contract a marriage can be granted to none but those who can secure to a family the means of subsistence. The workman who proposes to marry, must obtain from his patron a certificate attesting that his day's wages are not below a certain sum: he must also obtain from the communal authority a certificate of good morals." Besides these obstacles, another arises from the considerable expense that is unavoidable.

"The illicit unions that these regulations provoke, are severely repressed by the police of Vienna; the laws of this kind which had fallen into disuse, have been rigorously enforced since the events of 1848. In no case is toleration extended to the cohabitation of a couple that cannot exhibit a marriage certificate: persons convicted of an infraction of this law are locked up, either with a view to marriage if they can shew the possession of means of existence, or to a return to their native places."

"As it is remarked elsewhere, the régime of restriction does not appear so efficacious as the German administrations suppose: it is difficult also, to harmonise it with the rules of morality, and with the just claims of the dignity of men."

In another place † M. Le Play shews us the way in which the regulations fail. After saying that among the Hartz miners a man may not marry before he is twenty-five years old, and that in Carniola the legal age is about seven years

* Le Play 127. (c) † Ib. 139. 1.

later still, he goes on; "these regulations not only involve the evil of being contrary to morality : they fail to attain the end proposed. Thus the workmen of the guild of J................., all of them while very young, contract illicit unions, most of which are legalised at the allowed age of marriage. By an unhappy dereliction of duty, the parents are obliged, under pain of condemning their daughters to celibacy, to connive at these relations, and to establish in their own houses a kind of regular concubinage. In studying the morals of this neighbourhood, in enquiring, for example, how so singular a state of things can be reconciled with the earnestness shewn by most of these young mothers in the practice of the duties of the Roman Catholic religion, one is painfully impressed with the serious scandal brought upon public morals and upon religious sentiments."

If we now turn to Prussia, we are furnished with two Roman Catholic cases. In the former* " the family fulfils its religious duties, and is distinguished by the excellence of its morals. The wife who is very industrious and of a firm disposition, exercises a preponderating influence in the management of family affairs ; it is to her especially that are owing the prevailing temperance and frugality. The incumbent who has been established twenty years in the parish, contributes on his part, by his private advice and his sermons in church, to repress all tendency to immorality. The scandal of illegitimate births is very unusual : and besides, is soon followed by marriage or emigration."

* Le Play, 146. 2.

The second Roman Catholic case * in Prussia, notices the question of religion shortly but decisively. "The family professes the Roman Catholic faith: all the members fulfil their religious duties; the wife, however, attends church more assiduously than her husband. Both husband and wife are remarkable for the excellence of their morals."

One other Prussian case † is given, that of a cutler at Solingen. "The family is of the Calvinistic persuasion. Without exhibiting any extraordinary fervour, it performs its principal religious duties: all the members attend church on Sunday, and receive the communion once a year. The morality is consistent with this state of things: illegitimate births are rare and are generally legalised by marriage. There is much honesty in pecuniary transactions. A love of good cheer and of fermented liquors is the only striking fault of the family: intemperance is peculiarly the vice of the eldest son who served many years in the Prussian army."

These habits are common to most of the population of Solingen; however, there are notable distinctions between the three classes of workmen. It is remarked that the most dissolute men belong to the class of grinders, whose wages, always very high, are at times, (in 1851 for example) ten times the average wages of the trade. It is in the class of moderate wages that are found workmen of the most temperate habits; men, therefore, the best fitted to rise gradually by frugality to the condition of manufacturers and merchants."

* Le Play, 158. 1.   † Ib. 152, &c.

The last remark of M. Le Play is one often made, and is generally true, I believe, but with many exceptions. Of course, if there are two reckless sensual workmen, the one who gets £5. a week has the means of greater dissipation than are within the reach of the one who gets only ten shillings a week. The latter must work regularly or starve, while his richer companion may live in sensual luxury by working two days a week.

In the case of the Solingen grinders there is another mode, in addition to the high wages, of accounting for their ill morals. It is observed that needle pointers in England are a race who earn high wages, and who spend their earnings coarsely. The trade is a very unwholesome one, and the grinders know that they shall soon be diseased and shall die early. It is said that this consciousness makes them reckless. The effect, I suppose, is something like that of the skeleton in the Egyptian feast : let us eat and drink, for to-morrow we die. This recklessness is not found among English grinders of edge tools ; but neither is their occupation any thing like so injurious as that of the other class. Needles are pointed on dry stones ; English edge tools, sword blades, cutlasses, gun barrels, are ground almost entirely on wet stones. The possible danger, also, arising from the risk of the breakage of a rapidly revolving stone, is greatly diminished in this country by the arrangements made. The grinder sits behind his grindstone, astride a heavy wooden *horsing*, which is fixed to the ground by solid chains and which advances considerably towards the spindle : if the stone breaks it must fly forwards, and cannot strike the workman. In every decent mill, too, each workman is out of the range of any other projected stone. I have been informed that in Solingen there is a great deal of dry grinding of edge tools, and that the men work in front of their grindstones instead of behind them : if this information is correct, it is no wonder that they earn high wages and spend their gains dissolutely.

As far as these notices go, then, I think they are favourable as to the moral state of Prussia. I will conclude my remarks upon Germany by quoting from the interesting book, the *Englishwoman in America*, a work that must not be confounded with the *Englishwoman in Russia*, being written by a different lady, and having little resemblance to it except in the title. We are told * that in Cincinnati, " The Queen City of the West," there are " nearly 50,000 Germans, and I believe 40,000 Irish, who distinctly keep up their national characteristics. . . . . The Germans, as at home, are a thinking, sceptical, theorising people : in politics, Socialists—in religion, Atheists. The Irish are still the willing and ignorant tools of an ambitious and despotic priesthood. And in a land where no man is called to account for his principles, unless they proceed to physical development, these errors grow and luxuriate. The Germans, in that part of the town almost devoted to themselves, have succeeded in practically abolishing the Sabbath. . . . . The creeds which they profess are ' Socialism', and ' Universalism,' and at stated periods they assemble to hear political harangues, and address invocations to universal deity. Skilled, educated, and intellectual, they are daily increasing in numbers, wealth, and political im-

---

* *Englishwoman in America*, 119.

portance, and constitute an influence of which the Americans themselves are afraid."

This passage is a very interesting one as showing the tendencies of the Germans when they are left to themselves. At the same time I do not regard the account given us, as by any means a statement of the whole facts of the case. I have the highest respect for the accomplished and most benevolent writer of the book; but I must be excused if I remember that her stay at Cincinnati was but short, and that she received her first impressions there from the Bishop. I have often heard ladies and clergymen speak of classes of men as Atheists; but when pressed to explain themselves, confess that they only meant to say unbelievers in Christianity. There is something worse than carelessness in this slipshod way of talking.

It must be remembered with regard to the observance of Sunday, that the Germans were not accustomed in their native country, to see it kept with English and American strictness. It is deeply to be regretted, even as a social question, that they should work on Sunday; but I have no sympathy with the Judaical sabbatism which condemns one day of the week to sloth and sensuality.

The neglect of religious ordinances by the American Germans, seems a not unnatural consequence of the severe imposition of those ordinances by the laws of the country from which they have escaped. Take a boy to church three times every Sunday, overwhelm him with long daily prayers, bore him with the Catechism, the Westminster Confession, or the Whole Duty of Man; and make up your mind that at the University, or in the Mess Room, he will be the fastest, the loudest, the wildest, of his set. Force religion upon people by law, fine them for absence from church, compel them to produce certificates of religion and morals before they can act as carpenters or shoeblacks, and as soon as they can escape from your clutches, they will be found wildly rushing into " Socialism and Universalism." It is to be hoped that the tyrant majority of the States will not interfere. Then, as the Germans acquire property they will cease to bawl for Socialism : as their circumstances improve they will learn to prize the leisure of Sunday : when the first ebullition of a licentious freedom has subsided, unbelief will cease to content them, and scepticism will give way to reverence and faith.

Before I remark upon the religious and moral state of the working classes of any country that is what the English commonly understand by purely Protestant, I will refer to the Norwegians, who live under a Lutheran Church. I say purely Protestant, although I have discussed the state of Prussia. I am not aware of the exact profession of that kingdom at present. But in 1817, * the royal family was Calvinistic, while of the population of Berlin, the Lutherans were eleven times as numerous as the Calvinists, the Roman Catholics and Jews being both of them very few. The Evangelical Church is the state union of Lutherans and Calvinists. †

Mr. Laing ‡ says " The Norwegian Church is an establishment not uninteresting in the present times. In principle

---

* Jacob, 1819, 207.

† Ib. Population of Berlin, 1817, not including suburbs ....

‡ Laing's Norway, 119.

Protestants...	174,428
R. Catholics ...	4,258
Jews	3,690
Memnonists .	2

182,378

and doctrine it is more purely Lutheran, perhaps, than the Church of England," &c. Mr. Laing, in speaking of the English Church as Lutheran, seems to have forgotten the saying attributed to Lord Chatham, to the effect that that church in his time, had a Roman Catholic ceremonial, Calvinistic Articles, and an Arminian clergy. "There are in Norway 336 prestegils or parishes. Many of them are exceedingly large, extending in this part of Norway, from the sea coast up to the Swedish frontier; and containing from 5,000 to 10,000 inhabitants. In considering this low provision for religious instruction, it must be remembered that the pure Lutheran Church, as it exists in Norway, is essentially ceremonial; as much so almost as the Roman Catholic. The altar is decorated with crosses and images. The priest, arrayed in embroidered robes of velvet, on the back of which a large and rich figure of the cross is conspicuous, celebrates high mass under that name, which sounds strange in a Protestant Church, before the altar, on which candles are lighted, as in the Roman Catholic Churches. . . . . It is also to be considered that, although the country be poor, the property is distributed among the people. . . . . Hence in Norway it is, perhaps, necessary that the income of the clergyman should be decidedly high, to maintain him in a suitable station in society; and that could not be the case, from whatever source his income was derived, if his parish was small."

Another peculiarity in Norway is the great importance attached to the rite of Confirmation, which is not, as it is among us, a ceremony forgotten as soon as performed, or at the most, regarded as a passport to Communion. The

Norwegians regard confirmation as a sort of diploma, which affects the status of the receiver. We are told * that advertisements are commonly seen " A confirmed shopboy wants a place:" " Wanted a confirmed girl who can cook:" and that the absence of confirmation is equivalent to the want of a character.

In Norway, as in other Lutheran countries, the Sabbath consists, not of the whole of Sunday, but of Saturday evening and of Sunday until the evening. " A Lutheran minister gives a party on Sunday evening at his house, at which you find music, dancing, and cards, without scruple," &c.

It is singular that there should be no dissent from the church in Norway. How this unanimity has arisen I am not aware. Mr. Laing assigns as a principal reason, that the clergy have no political power, but this seems to me inconclusive. Where the minds of men are at work on the great problems of our existence, where they are constantly labouring to fathom the unfathomable mysteries that surround us, where they habitually meditate on the recondite questions which have perplexed the limited faculties of humanity since the days of the Sophists, and probably, since the creation of the world, dissent is natural. The minds of men will not run on the same line of thought, as Charles V. discovered too late. The absence of dissent seems to imply an apathetic state of the understanding. It must be remembered that Norway, until a recent date, was an absolute monarchy; and that it was only on its disruption from Denmark, and its union with Sweden, that its govern-

* Laing, 125.

ment became free. It is a singular anomaly that being an absolute monarchy one year, it became the next year, the most democratic state in Europe; and this, without bloodshed or violence. But I cannot help suspecting that the uniformity in religion is part of the legacy bequeathed by the old monarchy. Whenever greater intellectual activity springs up, dissent will doubtless follow.

It is interesting to enquire what moral condition of the working classes follows this formal and sluggish state of religion. Mr. Laing's account is highly favourable. He describes the people generally as living together on the most amicable terms: the rich without ostentation; the labourers without discontent. As a Presbyterian himself, he is not likely to attribute undue excellences to the influence of a ceremonial church. He says * that there is a singular equality among all classes, and that the standard of habits and manners is far from being a low one. He speaks of " the self-respect, the moral restraint, the independence of spirit, and the amiable manners and consideration for others in domestic intercourse, even among the lowest of the people, which in other countries are found only among the classes in easy circumstances. The cause seems to be that between the distribution and general dissemination of property by their peculiar law of succession, and the general simplicity of the way of living, a greater proportion of the people really are in easy circumstances than in any other country in Europe. . . . . All have the ideas, habits, and character, of people possessed of independent property, which they are living upon without any

* Laing's Norway, 215.

care about increasing it, and free from the anxiety and fever of money-making or money-losing."

I have quoted at some length from Mr. Laing, both because from his residence in Norway he is a high authority as to the actual state of this part of the world's population, and also because the Norwegians are a singular people, who enjoy much happiness in an almost stationary state, and in an old-fashioned way. Mr. Laing, no doubt, is something of an enthusiast on this topic, and fails to insist strongly on the fact that there are portions of the working population in a very inferior condition to the one on which he dwells: we learn incidentally, and from other sources, that the agricultural labourers living on the out-lying lands, and the fishing population on the coast, are in a much less satisfactory state than the *housemen* whom Mr. Laing delights in.

M. Le Play has one Norwegian case,* and it is interesting to note what he says, and to compare him with Mr. Laing. The man described is a miner in Southern Norway. " The family professes, without any particular appearance of zeal, the reformed faith of Luther. The manners are generally rough and unpolished; but the course of life seems to show a rather decided development of the moral sentiments. . . . The women are generally distinguished by beauty and grace as well as by morality : they exercise great authority in the family, and assist very much in raising its moral tone."

The rough, unpolished manners complained of by M. Le Play, do not agree very well with the urbanity and courtesy

---

* Le Play, 98, &c.

described by Mr. Laing. Both authors agree in ascribing moral habits to the population, though M. Le Play's eulogy in this respect is not greater than he utters as to many other people. It may be that the mining population with which M. Le Play became familiar, is inferior in manners and morals to the agricultural people among whom Mr. Laing lived.

An impression has existed that the very slow growth of Norwegian population has been accompanied by the usual results: frequent celibacy; late marriages; and numerous illegitimate children. Mr. Laing rather confirms this impression. But stubborn facts show it to be incorrect. The Registrar General * tells us that the proportion of illegitimate births is about the same in Sweden, Norway, England, Belgium, France, and Prussia; being $6\frac{1}{2}$ per cent. of the whole births in Sweden and Norway, and 7 per cent. in Prussia; while the other nations I have enumerated have something more than Norway and something less than Prussia. It is remarked, however, that in a country like Norway, where a great number of persons are unmarried, a given amount of illegitimacy proves less immorality than it shows where persons generally marry early, as for example, in the United States.

With respect to the morality of the working classes of Protestant countries, as we commonly understand the word Protestant in England, if I wished to draw a favourable picture, I should only have to copy what M. Le Play says of the two watchmakers of Geneva in cases XVIII. and XIX.† As to the less favourable of the two, ‡ we find

* 6th Report, xxiii.   † Le Play, 164 and 170.   ‡ Ib. 170. 1.

" The family professes the Calvinistic faith; and exhibits much religious zeal, which is kept up by regular attendance at public worship, and still more by reading books of piety, an occupation that is almost the only recreation of the father of the family. This singular piety colours all the habits of a family, always pinched, and sometimes indigent: it imparts something of distinction to the man, and gives him a touching air of resignation." We find also that this mechanic takes an interest in what is going on in the scientific world, and makes great sacrifices to give his son a superior education; sacrifices which are shared by the wife.

In a note on this case * we have a comparison of this mechanic with labourers of other countries. " It is especially by the depth of religious sentiment, and by the moral consequences which follow, that the Genevese workman, and many other types of western workmen, rise above even those eastern workmen who are the most inclined to yield to the influence of Mahometanism or of the Christian religion." . . . .

" The favourite recreations of the Genevese workman are, perhaps, the detail of his existence which best exhibits the distinction of his tastes. During fine weather his principal pleasure is a walk, with his wife and children, in the picturesque environs of his town. The demeanour of the families who meet for conversation, or pleasure, is remarkable for propriety; and exhibits a striking contrast with that of the populace in many other countries. During the winter the respectable workman passes a part of his leisure

* Le Play, 174. 2. (B.)

time in a certain society to which he is regularly affiliated, and in which lectures are given gratuitously by persons desirous of benefiting the lower orders. Reading aloud at home is regarded as an indispensable recreation, particularly by women and young persons of both sexes. Most households have some books; and procure others by a small payment. . . . . This habit of reading, if the choice of books is not altogether irreproachable, proves at least that the workman of Geneva is already to a great degree freed from the slavery of bodily appetites; that is, from the inclinations which in the greater part of Europe degrade the workmen properly so called below the middle and higher classes."

This is a very favourable statement of the condition of the Genevese mechanics. Many persons may doubt whether M. Le Play is not guilty of an unintentional exaggeration, in attributing the superiority to the strength of religious sentiment. Many very religious mechanics may be found who are entirely wanting in the refinement found at Geneva; and in many other cases, considerable cultivation of manners, and of tastes, is possessed by mechanics entirely destitute of outward profession of religion.

In the other Genevese case, * we see more clearly the way in which, as M. Le Play conceives, religion has exercised an unusually salutary influence as to external and secular habits. " Pastoral visits, made frequently in every family, and at least once a year, have a happy influence on the neatness of the houses, and generally on the morality of the working classes. In many respects, the clergy of Geneva

* Le Play, 164. 1.

exercise over the workmen of this town, the patronage which in the ancient European polity, belonged to the employers of labour." Another note* enters on further particulars: " the utility of these visits consists less in the relief conferred as to bodily wants, than the moral effects produced. The presence of the pastor raises the workman in his own eyes; it relieves him from the feeling of isolation and neglect; it inspires new strength for his struggle with the difficulties of his situation. Pastoral visits also stimulate qualities that poverty tends to deaden. Thus the expectation of these visits at times not fixed, keeps the wife always on the watch, and influences her favourably as to cleanliness in house, furniture and clothes."

" On the whole, the pastoral circuits of Geneva, should be quoted among the most efficacious means of assistance and improvement, by which is exercised that patronage which is springing up under new forms in the midst of the modern institutions of the West. Established already by a tolerably long continuance, this custom is quite in harmony with the physical necessities and moral aspirations of the labouring populations crowded together in towns."

Having now said something of the nations living under Mahometan institutions in the Ural, under the Greek Church in European Russia, under strict Roman Catholic rule in Austria, under the same rule in a milder form in Prussia, under a ceremonial Lutheran Church in Norway and in Prussia, as also in Geneva under Calvinistic Communion, there remain France and England for me to notice. Not that the countries I have mentioned are the only ones

---

* Le Play, 175. 2.

with which we are concerned, but that they are the only ones about which I have anything interesting to offer.

M. Le Play's French cases are, naturally, more numerous than those of any other country; being eleven out of the whole thirty-six. We may suppose also, that more reliance may be placed on their accuracy. I will first quote what he says about the religion and morals of the French country people, and I will then refer to the rather astounding disclosures he makes as to the dissipated, disreputable life led by the Paris workmen.

The first French case * is that of a labourer in Armagnac. " He and his wife are of the Roman Catholic religion, and fulfil the duties of piety with regularity; although their religious sentiments are neither enlightened nor deep. The moral habits are good both before and after marriage."

The second French case † is that of a labourer in the Nièvre. This family, like the last, is Roman Catholic, but with more fervour, especially on the part of the women. The morals of the neighbourhood are good, and illegitimate children are almost unknown. The most common offence is the pilfering of wood in the forest. It is remarked that the number of derelictions of this kind depends very much on the direction given to the religious sentiment: insomuch that an old servant who had long had the forests under his care, after commenting on the various priests who had succeeded each other in the parish, ended with saying that one good priest is worth four keepers.

The third French case ‡ is in Maine, and is not so favourable. The family is still Roman Catholic, but the

* Le Play, 212, &c.   † Ib. 218, &c.   ‡ Ib. 224, &c.

neighbourhood is one of so little fervour, that not more than half the women and a fourth of the men attend regularly to their religious duties. The morals are indifferent: illegitimate births not uncommon: and these not always legalised by marriage. The ordinary character is indolent: quarrels are settled, not by violence, but by law. Lying, cheating, and perjury, seem to be too frequent. The husbands are often guilty of a selfish neglect of their wives.

The fourth French case * gives a favourable and pleasing account of the morals of Lower Britanny: the fifth † confesses a good many illegitimate births, which, however, are always followed by the marriage of the parents. It must be observed that in most parts of the world, marriage renders legitimate, the children previously born. Our law has in this respect, an austerity not generally found elsewhere. The sixth case is satisfactory both as to religion and morals.

The seventh French case ‡ is one in Auvergne, and the account varies a good deal from the previous ones. The family is religious, without superstition: the man of a mild temper, but with something of a habit of dissimulation in the deference paid to his superiors. This character seems much like that of the Irish of the present day; and another circumstance strengthens the resemblance. In the North of France, when peasants quarrel, they resort to the law-courts for the settlement of their dispute: but in Auvergne there commences the tendency to private bloodshed. This is found so great an evil, that the priest of the parish §

* Le Play, 230, &c.   † Ib. 236.   ‡ Ib. 248, &c.   § Ib. 249. 2.

has forbidden the amusement of dancing, in consequence of the sanguinary quarrels that are caused by it.

The eighth French case * is favourable. The ninth † is less so. The man is a blacksmith, of a hard, coarse, character: he is steady and regular in his habits, through a desire for acquiring property. M. Le Play fears that something of sordid avarice is rather prevalent in this part of France.

This finishes the cases taken from the provinces: the two remaining ones are taken from Paris. Of these two, one is that of the rag-picker whom I have already described. The other is that of a man who has a washing establishment near Paris. He and his family, as it appears, are altogether irreligious as far as outward forms are concerned. But they are correct in their morals, frugal, and withal kindhearted. They are hard working people who live well and dress well, but who regularly save a part of their income, and are ready to assist the distressed. The most unpleasant feature of this case is the custom of working on Sundays with nearly the same regularity as at other times. ‡ Setting aside the religious aspect of the question of Sunday work, the custom is much to be regretted. I am not one of those who approve the English habit of making Sunday a day of gloom and austerity in outward appearance, of sloth and sensuality in private. But I should much regret the adoption of continental customs in this respect. The majority of Englishmen of the middle classes work too hard already, and if they added

* Le Play, 254, &c.   † Ib. 260.
‡ Ib. 267. 2.

a seventh day of labour, incalculable evil would follow both to mind and body.

Under this case, we find many remarks on the general moral state of the neighbourhood of Paris. It * varies very much according to the pastoral care or negligence that has prevailed. M. Le Play speaks highly of the influence exercised by the lay society of Roman Catholics known as the Conference of St. Vincent de Paul ; a society mentioned in the notes on the rag-picker. In the neighbourhoods where neither lay nor clerical influence has been exerted, there is said to prevail an avaricious, selfish, hardhearted tone of feeling ; such as leads men to acts on the very verge of what is punishable by law, to an entire absence of public spirit, and to an odious envy of the higher classes of society.

We find afterwards, a note on the habits of Parisian workmen generally : first of those of the migratory class ; secondly of the permanent residents. As to the permanent residents, the account given is very unsatisfactory, not to say frightful. We have often been told that one third of the births in Paris are illegitimate, one third being really a slight exaggeration, † but a considerable portion of these irregularities has been attributed to the difficulties thrown in the way of celebrating a marriage. In truth we have seen in the example of the rag-picker that some force must be allowed to these legal difficulties : the rag-picker could not celebrate his marriage until he had obtained certain documents from his native place, and this he could not have done without the aid of a charitable society. However,

* Le Play, 271. 2.　　　† Registrar General, 6. xxiii.

after reading the note I have mentioned, * we may cease to wonder at the irregularities practised.

The resident Parisian workmen may be divided into two classes; the grossly sensual, and the refined: but both classes are equally improvident and dissolute. The sensual workmen have nothing in common with the middle classes. They wear a blouse, vest, or paletot. Their principal desire is to get outside the barriers into taverns frequented by their own class. They scarcely read the newspapers, and trouble themselves little about politics, except when they are directly affected by them. They envy their employers, not as desiring to share their power, but as wishing that they could work less, and could prolong their weekly debauch beyond Monday. They lead a dissolute life, and continue bachelors, till old age comes upon them; though it sometimes happens that they marry a steady, industrious woman who effects a reform.

The second class of resident workmen approach more nearly to the middle classes, as to furniture, dress, and recreations: they are led to this by the nature of their employments, or by a certain intellectual culture, which is developed by the circumstances in which they are placed. They frequent the theatres, the little cafés, and the public balls in the interior of Paris: and they there meet the young people engaged in trade and belonging to the lower middle classes.

Like the workmen of the sensual class, these men are indisposed to marriage; but their connexions are more permanent, and many of them require as much respect to

* Le Play, 277. 1.

be paid to a mistress as if she were a legitimate wife. The household is carelessly conducted ; the furniture is neglected ; the clothes are worth two-thirds of the whole effects ; the most available articles are generally at the pawnbrokers.

Taking into account the annual slackness between the seasons, the Parisian workman can seldom accomplish more than 280 full days' work. However pressing may be the demand, Monday is always devoted, not to rest, but to pleasure. Of the annual receipts, one-half is spent in eating and drinking, one-fourth for rent, and the other fourth for clothes and amusements.

The spirit of religion is extinct, not only among the workmen in general, but even among the women : they never go to church or observe any forms of worship. Too often both men and women are unfaithful to each other. The woman has charge of the household, and she sometimes contrives to regulate the expenditure of the gains. She has no part in the selection of recreations, and sometimes she is excluded from them. If marriage takes place, the wife secures greater influence, and adultery appears to be very rare.

These men are not indifferent to sentiments of generosity, compassion, enthusiasm : but there follows no wholesome fruit. Spending their gains from week to week, devoted to selfish pleasures, they neglect even to assist their old parents, at the same time that they recognise their claims.

A great portion of these workmen consists of modellers, draughtsmen, chasers, and engravers, who play an essential part in the production of articles of taste and luxury, for which Paris is renowned throughout the world. It may be doubted whether residence in great cities produces in the masses, the artistic aptitudes and the eminent qualities which spring up spontaneously, by meditation and leisure, in the isolation of a pastoral life, or among imperfect modes of civilisation. But it is certain that the taste and manual skill furnish admirable means of carrying into effect those artistic conceptions which are the principal element of success in the manufactures of Paris.

It must be added that this unfavourable account does not apply to all the Parisian resident workmen. There is a numerous and estimable minority, who are improvident indeed, but not immoral. The rag-picker whom I have mentioned, is a type of this minority. It often happens that such men have great difficulties to contend with, both from the evil example and the raillery of their companions, and also from the unhappy influence of masters who retain the sceptical tendencies of the last century. Men who resist these evil influences, and the temptations to criminal pleasure which assail them on all sides, are unquestionably, more hardened in goodness, and more adepts in virtue than others elsewhere, who only share in habits of piety or morality which are common to themselves and their companions.

This concludes the remarks I have to make on the religion and morals of the French working classes. In the country parts, as far as we see, the labourers are pretty much what they are elsewhere. They attend on the established public worship, are more or less immoral before marriage, settle down into decent characters afterwards, vegetate a certain number of years, and die with the consolations of religion. But in Paris the condition of the mechanics is far different

from this. The bricklayers and many other labourers are
a migratory race who share the qualities of the country
parts from which they come. But the resident workmen,
the real Parisians, have a code of morals, or habits of immorality, peculiar to themselves. Either coarse and sensual,
or aping the manners of the middle classes, these men
seem in both cases ready for any mischief. Devoid of the
restraints of religion, abandoned to criminal pleasure, with
little or none of the wholesome soothing influences of
home, envious of the superior wealth and leisure of their
employers, they are ready instruments in the hands of
any one who can arouse them to violence. With such a
population, Paris is a volcano, bursting from time to time
into an eruption: and we wonder no longer at the periodical
revolutions, nor at the anxious solicitude shewn by Napoleon
to mitigate the consequences of a bad trade or of dearness
of bread.

Having thus run over several of the principal States of
Europe, it only remains for me to notice our own country.
The distinguishing moral peculiarities of Great Britain I take
to be these: first, that in only one other great country
is Sunday observed with any thing like the strictness that
we practice; and secondly, that in no other country is there
so large a class of entirely irreligious persons. In the
rural districts, perhaps, our peasantry may have as much
of the sleepy devotedness to forms as is found in peasants
elsewhere: but in our own large towns the majority of the
working classes systematically absent themselves from
public worship, while they abstain on Sundays from the
performance of all ordinary occupations. Yet the habits
of our mechanics are not to be confounded with those of

the Parisians, so severely described by M. Le Play. The Parisians, we are told, live in a state of vicious celibacy: our mechanics generally marry very early. There is among us a good deal of drunkenness and much improvidence; but the number of mere pleasure seekers is comparatively small.

One great reason, no doubt, of the irreligiousness of towns, is the very rapid growth of the population. In the last quarter of a century, a manufacturing town has doubled its numbers: what was 120,000 has come to be 240,000. The educated classes have slumbered over this increase, opening their eyes dreamily from time to time, and making a feeble effort in a desultory way, to build a church or a school in some neglected corner. In the mean time, however, a generation has grown up with little attention paid to its education. Till the last fifteen or twenty years, the political bitterness that existed, the constant struggle going on between the democratic and the conservative elements, presented an obstacle to any amalgamation of the different classes of society.

The result, however, has been far less unfavourable than might have been anticipated. We might have expected to find around us, a fierce, lawless, people; envious of their superiors, and hating the laws; accustomed to avenge themselves when injured, and disposed to protect delinquents, from the quest of the police. The reverse of all this is the case. To whatever cause we may attribute the facts, it cannot be denied that English townspeople are a quiet, orderly, race, addicted to any thing rather than violence. Some miserably superficial observers, noting their greasy appearance in their working dress, hurt at the rude indifference with which they go straightforward to their destination through the streets, and catching their coarse familiar expressions, enquire no further, but set them down as degraded specimens of humanity. But let us try to penetrate beneath the surface : let us dig through the rugged crust of rude independence : let us overlook for a moment the irritating facts, that men in their shirt sleeves and apron will not touch their hat to a good coat, and that they will obstinately regard a clergyman as a man like themselves.

If we go to the Police office, we find nothing to indicate anything like turbulence of character. Among a quarter of a million of people, you will find a murder a very rare occurrence; stabbing very unfrequent; and even the savage use of fists quite an exceptional case. We hear a great deal of the excellent education given to the Scotch: but it is remarkable that instances of personal violence, and of ferocious assaults, are far more frequent among the instructed Scotch than among the comparatively neglected English.

Then again, we may take the degree of reverence that exists towards the law and its administrators, as one severe test of civilization. In Ireland, that test condemns the population, but in England it more than acquits it. To me nothing is more surprising than the authority conceded by a crowd to a policeman. Knowing, as I do, the class from which policemen are taken, I am astonished at the peaceable way in which a score, or a hundred, men and women, submit to his dictation. The common policeman is a very inferior man to a skilled mechanic. Very often he comes from the country as a discharged gamekeeper, or a servant out of employ. He brings a written character from his late master, from the clergyman of the parish, and from as many of his friends as can write their names. Neither the master, nor the clergyman, nor any one of his friends, is known to the authorities who have the appointment. The precaution is taken of writing by post to one or two of the principal referees, and if a satisfactory reply is obtained, the applicant, if otherwise suitable, takes a long oath of office, and dons his blue livery. Such is the man at whose presence a crowd ceases to squabble, and to whom an alleged criminal is quietly surrendered.

Cases of severe assault on a policeman certainly occur sometimes; I will not say that the policeman is in such instances always in fault: but more often than not, such an assault is provoked by the undue display of authority, or by the exercise of unnecessary violence. If an officer lightly draws his staff, uses irritating language, or resorts to brutal violence, he may make up his mind to a broken head. But if he performs his duty simply and quietly, he may arrest any man, anywhere, without danger of injury. The criminal will escape if he can, but even a mob will seldom rescue him, and a crowd of decent mechanics almost never.

The same conclusion is arrived at if we count the military force employed. In Paris you can hardly stir out without meeting troops marching, and in every direction you see barracks with sentinels posted: in London you might live for weeks in the city, and the populous suburbs, without being reminded that an army exists. In Lyons the working classes are intimidated by thousands of men, and by cannon pointed towards the workmen's quarter: in Birmingham a quarter of a million of people are watched by a troop of cavalry, and sometimes a company of infantry.

Nor is this reliance of the government on orderly habits any thing new. The only formidable riot that Birmingham has ever seen, occurred in 1791, and was caused by the bitter animosity of the Church-and-King party against the French revolution and its abettors. The population even at that time was very considerable, yet not a soldier was posted in the neighbourhood: several days elapsed before any could be brought, and their appearance in the town at once put down the mob. What would happen in many countries, with a town of 50,000 persons, and no soldier within a day's march?

Up to the year 1839, I believe, Birmingham was favoured with one troop of cavalry and no other soldiers. Till the same year the police force consisted of twenty-two runners, or detectives, besides a number of old men employed at night as watchmen. A riot in 1839 caused the establishment of a regular police of some 300 men, who took the place of the old watchmen.

If we compare this small force with that which is found necessary in continental towns, we cannot resist the conclusion that our mechanics, rude as they are to the eye and ear, are a very peaceable race, far indeed from being addicted to violence. The comparatively equal laws and mild rule of hundreds of years have gradually produced a reverence for law and a willing submission to its administrators, that in my opinion are infinitely more valuable than the greatest refinement of manner and high cultivation of intellect. The Frenchman may vent his politeness, and the Scotchman may even talk metaphysics; but until the one has learned submission, and the other has laid aside his ferocity, I shall put both far below the rough, but peaceable, Englishman, in the first quality necessary to civilisation.

If, indeed, this substantial gentleness had been gained at the expense of manly qualities, I should be the last to admire it. A man, says the peaceable Adam Smith, who can neither defend nor avenge himself, is scarcely worthy the name of man. Men must be prepared to defend their own honour, to vindicate their own liberty, to protect their own soil from the foreigner. A habit of submission to the law would be ill purchased by an effeminate and unwarlike spirit that shrinks from danger. I am not afraid that such a spirit should be imputed to my countrymen. Even the Russians who satirised our commanders as asses, eulogised our soldiers as lions: and the Russian serfs, docile and disciplined as they were, showed beside the fiery, but stubborn, spirits of our army, like schoolboys among grown men.

The way in which criminals in our towns sustain their trial, and listen to their sentence, is indicative of the self-possession of freemen, accustomed to do and to bear. A woman convicted and sentenced, may whine; a boy may shed tears; a hardened man may look obdurate; a young offender may look downcast: but put a Pole or a Frenchman in the same situation; he gesticulates, raves, tears his hair, throws himself on the ground, and shouts or screams till he is carried out of hearing.

I conclude that our town population, though decidedly irreligious, is submissive to the law, and is little disposed to revolution: that it is kept in order by a moderate police, and with only an occasional exertion of a small military force. With regard to morality it is difficult to draw any comparison between one country and another. Offences against law are certainly very numerous among us, but it is generally believed that the greater part of these offences are committed by a criminal class, and not by the ordinary population. A tenderness, perhaps a squeamish tenderness, of the liberty of the subject, prevents us from sweeping our streets from this criminal pollution; and makes us almost sigh for one year of the irregular vigour of old Harry the Eighth, who would have made the gallows and the hangman give us a ready deliverance.

But though the results are not so fatal as might have been anticipated, two questions naturally present themselves: How the lower classes have become so irreligious; and how it is that more harm has not arisen.

As to the first question, it is generally said that the Church of England is not the church of the poor, but of the middle and upper classes. No doubt this censure is partly justified, by the fact that the churches are divided into pews, which are assigned to houses of some pretension; and that in many cases the pews are let for money: while those who cannot pay, are thrust into the aisles, or stuck in corners where they can barely see or hear. In one respect, however, during the last thirty years, the church has reclaimed her right to be called the friend of the poor. She has been stimulated to become the educator of the masses, and in few places is the parish school found wanting. Unfortunately, no provision has been made for meeting the wants of increasing populations: while in the great towns, every ten years, an addition is made of one fourth to the men, women, and children existing, there are nowhere any funds with which a proportionate number of churches and schools can be put up.

It has long been a subject of remark, too, that a Protestant country is in one respect worse off than a Roman Catholic country. A Protestant clergyman must have such a provision as will maintain, not only himself, but also a wife and children. A Roman Catholic priest may therefore be supported on a third of what is necessary for a Protestant. If our clergy were trebled, I fear that some of us might rather complain of an excess, than of a scarcity, of the theological element.

The dissenters, no doubt, have done a good deal; and the Wesleyans, in particular, have produced great effects among the working classes. But then, the dissenters depend for their means of action, on the voluntary contributions of their members. When methodism was a new creed, it was aggressive, and imbued with a missionary spirit at home as well as abroad: but now it seems to have lost that disposition to make proselytes, and is satisfied to confine its exertions within the limits of its own members. From time to time it builds new chapels, as the natural increase of population requires them: but it does not go into the coal fields of Staffordshire and reclaim the rugged pitmen, as it went into the copper and tin fields of Cornwall to convert the neglected miners there.

What we want then, is some means of systematically supplying moral and religious instruction, as soon as it is wanted. If a town is found to increase steadily at the rate of one fourth in ten years, the means ought to be at hand to add one fourth, during the same period, to the places of instruction. We ought not to wait like overgrown children, until mischief is done, and then set about to correct the evil: we ought to look forward and endeavour to anticipate the coming evil. But if I were asked how this could be done, I am obliged to reply that it is much easier to point out a blot than to find out the means of removing it. The spirit of free inquiry, that has given to the English an unusual freedom from degrading superstition, and from the dominion of priestcraft, has also given them jealousy of the predominance of any sect, and an utter indisposition to submit to taxation for the purposes of religion. But without the aid of Government, any systematic provision for mental wants is, I fear, impossible.

But how is it that so little harm has been done by the neglect that has taken place? How is it that the mechanic who seldom enters a place of public worship, who is visited by no minister of religion, who reads no books of piety, is nevertheless, as peaceable, as moral, as submissive to law, as the church-going farm labourer: and far more upright and truth-speaking than the devout Russian saint-worshipper, or the pious priest-ridden Irishman?

One great fact must be remembered, in explanation of this phenomenon. The English mechanic, while he is devoid of religion, is also singularly free from superstition. It cannot be denied that the greater part of what is called religion, throughout the length and breadth of the world, is really superstition. The pure flame of religion burns faintly, and is in most places utterly discoloured by the impurities of superstition that are mixed with it. In some places these impurities flare out in their true colours. The peasant prays to a block of wood carved into a rude resemblance of a saint; and if the ligneous counterfeit disappoints him, he beats it as an infant beats the toy that has offended him. The illiterate Roman Catholic reverences his priest, and regards him as the anointed of God, who has authority to bind and to loose; as a man who has power, by genuflections and muttered charms, to determine the weal or woe of the members of his flock, for hundreds or thousands of years; as one who by performing masses for the souls even of the departed, can release them from the fires of purgatory. In the eyes of the superstitious believer, the efficacy of these incantations is quite independent of the character of the priest: he may be a drunkard, a cheat, a blasphemer, but he is none the less an agent between man and the Almighty.

In reading early European history, nothing is more striking to me than the gross superstition that prevailed almost universally. We forget what it was, because the most unblushing form of it has almost disappeared from the countries with which we are familiar. But here and there we meet with something to refresh our memory. The following passage may act in this way.

" The town (of Santiago) is full of priests—the people are consequently indolent and immoral; and I certainly never saw more sad examples of the effects of bad education, or a state of society more deplorable. The streets are crowded with a set of lazy, indolent, bloated monks and priests, with their heads shaved in different ways, wearing enormous flat hats, and dressed some in white serge coats and gowns, and others in black. The men all touch their hats to these drones, who are also to be seen in the houses, leaning over the backs of their chairs, and talking to women who are evidently of the most abandoned class of society. The number of people of this description at Santiago is quite extraordinary. The lower rooms of the most respectable houses are invariably let to them, and it is really shocking beyond description to see them sitting at their doors, with a candle in the back part of the room burning before sacred pictures and images."

" The power of the priests has diminished very much since the revolution. They are not respected; they have almost all families, and lead most disreputable lives. Still the hold they have upon society is quite surprising. The common people laugh at their immorality, yet they go to them for images and pictures, and they send their wives and daughters to confess to them. Three times a day the people in the streets take off their hats, or fall down on their knees. Every quarter of an hour during the night the watchman of each street sings as loud as he is able a prayer of ' Ave Maria Purissima,' and then chants the hour and a description of the night."

" During the day one constantly meets a calesh drawn by two mules, driven by a dirty boy in a poncho, and followed by a line of inhabitants with their hats off, each carrying a lighted candle in a lantern : every individual in the streets kneels, and those who have windows towards the streets (who are generally the females I have described) are obliged to appear with a lighted candle. In the inside of the carriage sits a priest with his hands uplifted and clasped. In this system of depravity the great sinner pardons the little one. Sins are put into one scale, and money into the other; and intent upon the balance, both parties forget the beauty and simplicity of the religion which they nominally profess." *

There is nothing new or unheard of in this picture of a miserable superstition, not hidden in corners and concealed from the gaze of men, but stalking forth in the full blaze of noonday. We may well thank God that our countrymen, imperfect as they are, have yet escaped from the mummeries and immoralities of such a religion as that of Santiago. Better to be as we are, with little thought of religion, than to be the grovelling slaves of priests, who, stained with lust and impurity themselves, yet presume to traffic between man and his Maker.

But there is another abuse from which our citizens are generally free: I mean fanaticism. Time was when the Wesleyans must have been distinctly excepted: but at the present day, when the Conference finds it necessary to utter a decree condemnatory of the practice of dancing, we may believe that the old spirit of methodism has deserted the younger members. A Wesleyan dance! A ball given by the Communicants of a Methodist Church! And a resolution of the Conference found necessary to prohibit such practices! Fanaticism surely has departed from the followers of John Wesley.

It may be thought, indeed, that however much true philosophy must condemn fanaticism, as carrying men far away from that ideal of excellence to which we should desire to attain, yet that as regards the immediate interests of society, fanaticism must be beneficial. It is true that one

* Sir F. B. Head, Pampas, 1826, page 191.

poison is less mortal than another. It is better that a man should be a mystic than that he should be a drunkard: better that he should foam at the mouth and stagger under religious madness, than that he should reel home heavy with beer. It is less injurious that he should wildly denounce war against innocent amusements, than that he should attend prize-fights, or join in burglaries and swindling.

Among a very rude and immoral population, therefore, it is conceivable that even the false heats of wild fanaticism, may act as an useful medicine. But among those of a somewhat higher level the advantage is not so manifest. John Wesley himself found a difficulty that perplexed him. He succeeded in reclaiming a man from gross vice; he infused into him a spirit that led him to abandon the gin shop, and the brothel; he substituted the love of mental excitement in the place of love of bodily excitement. The convert became grave and thoughtful, industrious and sober. He worked harder and spent less: he ceased to suffer the evils of penury. By degrees the fumes of spiritual excitement passed away, and were followed by habits of piety, of industry, of temperance. The convert found that his worldly condition was greatly improved, and that he might aspire to rise even to a higher class of society. Then came a love of money, a worldly spirit, avarice and ambition.

If the observations current in society are to be trusted, it is not among the stricter sects of religion that we are to look for a conscientious spirit with regard to money. There seems to have been a time, if we may trust old Hutton, when the Quakers were distinguished for their moral excellence. Hutton says * that he cannot recollect ever finding one of them doing wrong, and he speaks of their nearness to perfection. Now, it must be conceded that the sect is still worthy of high praise, for its distinguished support of works of benevolence. If nothing else were known, we must place the Society of Friends very high in the social scale, when we remember that in the United States none of its members ever hold a slave. What a disgrace, by comparison, to the Episcopalians, and Presbyterians, and Congregationalists, all of whom vie with each other in pandering to the selfish determination of the slaveowners to hold fast their human cattle. Yet with all this admirable philanthropy, there is a taint of worldliness, and of something like cunning in money matters, which unpleasantly marks the Quakers as men of business. Many of the sect, no doubt, are as upright, as honourable, as liberal, in all their transactions, as men can be. But, unless the world at large is deceived, the majority of the sect are apt to palter in a double sense, to equivocate, to deceive by implication, to take advantage of an agreement framed with craft, to resort to those little shifts and expedients which we suppose to be the peculiar heritage of the Hebrew race. It must be remembered, too, that in spite of Hutton's eulogium, the Quakers had earned a reputation for cunning before his time. Pope's well-known lines prove this :—

> " Is he a Churchman ? then he's fond of power :
> A Quaker ? sly : a Presbyterian ? sour :
> A smart free thinker ? all things in an hour."

---

* Hutton's Court of Requests, 282.

The Wesleyans are by many persons charged with the same vice. The severer sects generally, the Evangelical Church, the Independents, the Baptists, do not escape from this blame. I will not affirm that the censure is deserved : but I must say that in my own experience I have not found men of the stricter sects by any means more worthy of confidence than other men of less profession. I have known them, as I have known other men, selfish, avaricious, grasping; combining, as other men do not, the grave vices of the world with extravagant pretensions to piety. Such professors are either hypocrites or self-deceivers. To which-ever class they belong they are much worse men than those who make no religious profession : their moroseness is destructive to good fellowship, and often ruinous to their children, while their pharisaical spirit cries to Heaven against them.

I think, therefore, I am justified in saying that it is a happiness in our working classes to be free from this fanatical spirit, just as it is a happiness in them to be free from the gross superstition often palmed off on the world as religion. And the absence both of superstition and of fanaticism may partly compensate for the evil of an absence of religion generally. The working classes of towns seem to offer a singularly fair field for rational missionary enter-prize : since their minds are in an unoccupied state, unem-cumbered with error, and therefore ready for the reception of truth without the previous process of clearing away obstructions.

CHAPTER XIV.

NOTHING is more common than to hear men rail at the improvidence of the working classes. Let a labouring man, they say, exert the same prudence that commonly prevails among the middle class; let him remain single a few years after he is of age.; let him live as frugally at twenty-one, as he will be compelled to live afterwards, if he marries early; let him save two-thirds of his wages for ten years, and thus become possessed of a house and furniture of his own, besides such a sum of money as will keep him out of want for the rest of his days. A man who earned eighteen shillings a week, and saved two-thirds of this sum, would be possessed of £30. at the end of a year; and if we allow him to spend the interest on his savings, he would still, at the end of ten years, be the master of £300. If he married at this time, he would not have remained single longer than the men of the educated classes. During the earlier years of his married life he might still add a little to his accumulations; and at the age of forty, when his family might be numerous, and none of them perhaps would be assisting to maintain themselves, there would be enough income, barring accidents, from wages and interest on property, to support the family, without drawing on the principal saved.

It is agreeable enough to draw a sketch of this kind. Nothing is more pleasant in the placid intervals between

our own misdoings, than to point out to others their
obvious duties. It may occur, however, to the minds of
some persons, that there are difficulties in the steep and
thorny path of self-denial : that an uneducated man cannot
be expected to look forward so far as another person of more
cultivated mind. We may remember, too, perchance, that
men of the middle classes have not always, perhaps not
generally, any great merit in postponing marriage till they
are of a mature age. Professional men seldom establish a
practice, or secure a living, till towards middle life. Men
of business seldom earn a competent income before they
are thirty, and it is even a matter of common remark
that few do much for themselves before they reach forty.
But the case is quite different with a mechanic or farm
labourer. I will not say that such men earn as much
at twenty-one as at forty ; and yet in many cases the
difference is not great. In an ordinary trade, a mechanic
at twenty-one is as skilful as he will be at forty ; and if he
is incapable of working quite so many hours, he has some
advantage in activity and in quickness of sight. At any
rate, a young man whose apprenticeship has just expired,
is perfectly competent to support a wife; whereas an
educated man of the same age must generally have the
prospect of waiting ten years before he can earn any thing
considerable. When we are told, then, that the working
classes, by deferring marriage for ten years, might generally
secure their future lives from distress, we must grant that
this is true ; when we are told that the middle classes do
actually defer marriage, we concede that point also : but if
it is intended to imply that on this ground, the middle
classes may claim great superiority of prudence as compared

with the lower classes, I demur to that inference, because I see that the postponement of marriage on the part of the middle classes is the result of necessity rather than of prudence. We, of the educated class, therefore, are justified in shewing those below us what prudence requires; but we have no right to claim any superiority over them, so far as the date of marriage is concerned.

Every one is aware that we are very apt to be unduly impressed with the circumstances immediately around us, and that we commonly neglect to inquire whether similar circumstances are not found elsewhere. We indulge in foolish tirades against the want of foresight and self-restraint on the part of those among whom we live, without taking the trouble to ask whether the rest of the world is any better than our portion of it. M. Le Play gives us an opportunity of amending our practice. He furnishes us with a number of facts, which throw much light on the general character of working people in various countries, as regards prudence. I will take, one by one, some of the examples given.

First, in Northern Russia, * we are told of a smith, that " This workman being very skilful, obtains in working by the piece at the rates fixed by his master, very high wages; he never saves, but spends his gains for the advantage of his children." And again it is said of the same man,† " In the family here described, the man furnishes an excellent specimen of the natures, laborious, but imbued with little foresight, which are employed in forges." The next example

* Le Play, 78, 2.   † Ib. 84. 2.

to this is that of a man who is of a different sort, but whose case I will defer.

Under case v.* we have these remarks as to the peasantry of Western Siberia. " The greater part of the workmen are contented with the well-being secured to them by the social organization of the country, and especially by the ties which unite them to their family, their commune, and their seigneur: they make no effort, and practice no self denial, in order to rise above a condition which satisfies their desires, and which they enjoy quietly in every period of their existence.

If we now go to Norway, we meet with these remarks as to a skilled labourer in a cobalt mine. † " This workman is entrusted with a task that requires peculiar skill, obtained by a long apprenticeship: he therefore belongs to a class superior to that of a mere labourer. On the other hand, being deficient in any inclination to save, he has no chance of rising above his present condition."

The same character is attributed to the agricultural labourer of Central Hungary.‡ " Little disposed to pru- dence, families placed in the same condition would most of them fall an easy prey to usurers, if it were in their power to mortgage their property ; so that it may be truly said in this point of view, that the well being of many families is still dependent on preserving the last traces of the feudal system." And of the same case M. Le Play says,§ " The inclination to save, which forms in the West of Europe, the

* Le Play 87. 2.   † Ib. 98. 2.   ‡ Ib. 110. 2.
§ Ib. 111. 2.

surest protection of individual existence, is almost entirely
wanting among all the members of the family here described.
Nevertheless, maintenance is sufficiently guaranteed by the
abundant produce derived from cultivation of the land."

Again as to the Solingen mechanic, we are told,[*]
" reckoning from the date of marriage, the households in
which order and prudence prevail, rise gradually to affluence.
Unfortunately, these qualities being absent in the greater
number, the families remain in the medium state described
in the present case. They eagerly snatch all the bodily
pleasures consistent with an active attention to their
business, bearing with resignation the privations which, in
times of commercial crises, attend the want of a reserve
fund."

In France, we find the same recklessness of the future.
M. Le Play says of an agricultural commune in the Nièvre,[†]
" A most careful enquiry has shewn that of fifty labourers
of this condition living in the commune, only five had any
inclination to save, and had therefore a prospect of improving their condition. In order to represent in the present
case, the prevailing habits of the country, it has been
necessary to describe a family altogether without foresight,
and consuming all its earnings."

These examples taken from different nations, and consisting both of country labourers and of mechanics, may
convince us that England has no monopoly of improvidence ;
and that the working classes throughout Europe, have
generally a strong tendency to enjoy the present day and to
neglect the future. But we are naturally curious to see in
what terms M. Le Play describes our countrymen in this

[*] Le Play, 153. 2.   [†] Ib. 218. 1.

respect: whether our working classes appear to him worse or better than those of other countries, as to the quality in question.

In the case of the London cutler,* we find that the family is moral and temperate. " Still, the inclination to save is almost entirely wanting : the family never makes a deposit in the Savings' Bank. The most that is done is for the wife to hoard £2. or £2. 10s. during an unusually sustained briskness of trade, as a provision for a slack season. An abundance of food and excellent house accommodation are the comforts that the family craves, and these keep the expenditure always on a level with the income."

Of the Sheffield cutler it is said † that he is improvident, like English workmen generally ; and that he spends all his earnings.

In Derbyshire, the forgeman is described as a man of very decent conduct. Yet " the family gives way completely to the usual desire among English workmen for physical enjoyments ; and all the surplus earnings are employed in providing abundant food : a third of the income is expended on meat, spirituous drinks, tea, coffee, and sugar ; whilst in France, ·among men ambitious of rising to possession of property, these articles do not swallow up a tenth, or even a twentieth, of the income."

This concludes the English cases, except one of a joiner, who is represented as an exception to the rule of improvidence.

We see, then, that according to M. Le Play's observations, improvidence prevails generally among the working

* Le Play, 188. 1.   † Ib. 194. 1.

classes of Europe, just as it prevails among those of England. In Russia, Hungary, Norway, France, the labourer lives from hand to mouth, and intent on present enjoyment, leaves the future to take care of itself. Such is the rule, although there are in most countries many exceptions.

This want of prudence produces injurious effects in more ways than one. The most obvious result is, that it leaves the workman exposed to want, when sickness, failure of employment, or old age, comes upon him : he has exhausted in superfluous gratifications, during a time of prosperity, the fund which in time of distress would have supplied his pressing necessities.

But a second result follows, which is familiar to all who have thought on these subjects : I mean the high price which the labouring classes pay for their purchases. I say nothing of those cases in which the extravagance of a workman, and his wife, puts them in the power of a grasping creditor, or of a hard-hearted master. There is a great waste even where no unfair advantage is taken. M. Le Play gives an example, which is very creditable to his kindness of heart in trying to amend this fault, in a Viennese family.*

" One of the most characteristic details of the economical régime of this family, is the habit of buying separately for each meal the portion of food which is to be eaten. This leads to a considerable increase of expense, into which the author, in concert with the mother of the family, enquired carefully. It turned out, for example, that the fifty-six grammes of sugar bought for each breakfast, and for each supper, cost 0·090, while the same quantity bought in

* Le Play, 128. 1.

quantities of 560 grammes (a Viennese pound) comes to only $0 \cdot 075$. The mother clearly understood that she would save in this article of food seventeen per cent. if she could make up her mind to reform her habit of buying. The author proved this to her, by comparing, with the help of a pair of scales, the weight of ten of these small purchases with the weight of one larger purchase : he then advised her, first, to buy a whole pound of sugar and to make it last five days ; secondly, to set aside each day the sum she had been in the habit of spending in sugar ; thirdly, at the end of the fifth day again to buy a pound of sugar, and to put the money saved into a savings' box.'' For the result of this experiment I must refer to M. Le Play's work. The experiment failed from the want of a habit of self-denial on the part of the family.

The whole case is a very interesting one, both as exhibiting the feelings of a labouring family, and as revealing a kindness of heart on the part of the author. At the same time, I conceive that this amiability of feeling has blinded M. Le Play to a part of the facts. It may be true, as he says, that in the actual state of intelligence, something like hardness of character would be necessary, in order to secure frugality. But it should be added that a higher cultivation of the understanding would render frugality possible, without injuring the affection of the mother. The children having been once accustomed to eat all the sugar in the house, would with difficulty be taught to refrain from the same indulgence. But a little more intelligence on the part of the mother would have introduced this providence in the first instance, and would have educated the children in the habit of abstinence. When the eldest child had become knowing enough to ask why some of the provisions were kept back, it would have been told that without this foresight there would be none left for the following days. This first instruction in voluntary self-denial, this habit of thinking of the future as well as of the present, is one of the most weighty lessons that a child can learn, a lesson of far more importance than any that a school can give. The power of self-control is the foundation of all virtue.

It may strike some persons as unfair, that small buyers should pay more for their purchases than is paid by larger buyers; and it may even be thought that there is on the part of the shopkeeper in this case, something like a taking advantage of the necessities of the poor. But such notions are quite unfounded. The small buyer gives a great deal of trouble, and must pay accordingly. The woman goes twice every day to buy a spoonful of sugar: if she went only once every five days to buy ten times as much, that larger purchase would give no more trouble than one of the small purchases, and only one tenth part as much of the seller's time would be taken up. But the retail dealer charges for his goods, partly according to what they cost him wholesale, partly according to the time required to distribute them. A chemist sometimes dispenses a draught, or a box of pills, of which the materials may have cost him a farthing, but for which he asks a shilling: and the charge is reasonable if the time required for compounding the medicine is at all considerable. A man standing behind a counter must charge for his time, just as a man working in the fields charges for his time. Where a woman buys only an ounce of sugar at once, instead of buying a pound and herself dividing it into ounces, she employs a shop-keeper to do part of her household work; and she can no more expect the man to do this for nothing, than she can expect a charwoman to come and clean her house for nothing.

It seems, then, that wherever we go, we find the working classes generally improvident. But there are many exceptions to this rule: many working men make a provision for sickness and old age; many even rise by industry and frugality, to a higher position in society. All of us must be acquainted with cases of this kind among ourselves; and we find scattered notices of similar cases in the work I have so often quoted.

Thus in Western Siberia, we are told,* "industrious and clever workmen, who have their bodily appetites under command, and in whom are found, in a word, the inclina-tions and sentiments which raise men above an ordinary condition, find here, as elsewhere, the means of establishing an exceptional position. They commonly attain this end by applying to some occupation which their intelligence renders lucrative, the time at their disposal after they have fulfilled their duties to their seigneurs." . . . .

" The head of a family here described, having already succeeded in procuring a horse, a sum of £9., and some credit, finds himself in a position to carry on a considerable trade." . . . .

" Many men in this locality have pursued with success the career on which this man is now entering; and have acquired fortunes of many hundred thousand francs."

---

* Le Play, 87. 2.

So we find the Spanish miner * described as a man little imbued with religious sentiment, possessed of scarcely any education; but "the regular habits of husband and wife arise principally from their energetic disposition to save: in this point of view, the love of work is a tolerably good substitute for moral qualities of a higher order."

This man is a native of Galicia, and is one of a class who migrate temporarily into other provinces, as the Irish reapers come over into England. Some particulars are given † of the earnings of these Galicians, and of their mode of life. They begin their migrations at about eighteen years of age, and save at this time about £5. a year. The workman here described, had saved by the time he was twenty-six, a sum of £54. (a very large sum in that country): he then married in his own province. During the last eight years, he had lived altogether in Andalusia: he now spends five months of the year at home : his earnings after marriage are about £14. a year. By the time he has amassed altogether, £100., he will probably live at home the whole year.

In " Lower Britany, ‡ the majority of the labourers, having saved enough to enable them to marry and commence housekeeping, make no efforts to improve their condition. But those who are frugal and temperate, are able to save about £4. a year, and by the time they are thirty-five years old, may take a farm. The ordinary mode of employing the savings is to lend them out at five per cent. interest, with the right to recall them at three months notice. Some-times a man buys cows, and hires them out to other

* Le Play, 182. 1.   † Ib. 183. 2.   ‡ Ib. 231. 2.

labourers who have none of their own, the charge being five shillings a year for each cow, or else an equal division of the improved value of the cow. A labourer who pursues this career of frugality, may save £300. by the time he is fifty.

We have in another place, * the case of a working owner of a washing establishment near Paris. Not only is this man frugal himself, but as we are told, a large proportion of the inhabitants of the village have more than a competency.

In Paris, M. Le, Play says, † the mere labourers are to a great extent strangers, who migrate from Auvergne principally; these men are frequently frugal: probably it is just the ambitious and enterprising, and therefore saving, natives of Auvergne, who migrate to Paris. The improvident, reckless, dissolute, character of the permanent Parisian men, has already been described. As to that minority ‡ which consists of men of decent habits, even they are far from practising frugality.

These few exceptional examples of prudence taken from several countries, remind us of what goes on at home. Here also, many of the working classes save money, and a considerable number of them rise to a higher condition. Of the four English cases described by M. Le Play, one of them is that of a very prudent carpenter of Sheffield. This man is described as so entirely careless about religion as to be unable to say in what persuasion he was brought up, whether as a churchman or as a dissenter. But the family is remarkable for temperance, order, and even a certain elegance in the manner of living. The man is a subscriber to the

* Le Play, 266. 1.   † Ib. 277. 1.   ‡ Ib. 278. 1.

funds of a land society, and employs his leisure hours in making furniture, and preparing wood-work, for the house that he hopes to build on his allotment.

We must all be aware that the case of this Sheffield carpenter is not an uncommon one. We know that many mechanics save money. M. Le Play was informed that most of the Sheffield manufacturing and mercantile houses had their origin among the working classes; and the same may be said of other towns. In Birmingham, a large proportion of the manufacturers have been once workmen, or are the sons of men who were once workmen. Such an one, beginning at the anvil, died at sixty, leaving £25,000 : such another, commencing as a tool maker, leaves £50,000 : while a third is pointed out who began his trade with his own hands in his garret, and now possesses landed property worth a quarter of a million sterling. In Manchester I have heard the same thing : I have been informed that an eminent trader commenced his career in Manchester as a labourer seeking employment; and I believe it is not at all uncommon there for a man to rise first to be an overseer, next to be a junior partner, and lastly to be a trader of wealth and importance.

But if these things really are so; if it is true that in all the great towns of England, a large number of manufacturers and other traders have sprung from the working classes; if, as is alleged, a great part of the large capitals employed have had their origin in the industry and frugality of workmen; it must be utterly false to assert that the labouring classes are universally improvident. The capitalists to whom I have alluded, have, indeed, ceased to be workmen : but their savings for many years, that is before the rise of condition took place, were made from wages, and there are, no doubt, other workmen who are now following the same provident career, and who are themselves destined to be hereafter masters. Besides, there are a great many of the labouring classes who do not aspire to any change of condition, or who are not fortunate enough to have such a change within their reach, or who are unfitted by nature to fill any situation to which they have not been brought up, but who, nevertheless, have so much industry and self-denial as to enable them to save. The Sheffield carpenter mentioned above is an example of this class. If a land-society and a building-society are brought within reach of men of this class, they are eagerly made use of, although the same men, in the absence of such opportunities, might spend every thing they earn. If it is true that the sight of means to do ill deeds makes deeds ill done, it is equally true that the opportunity of doing prudent deeds makes deeds prudently done. However true it may be, then, that there is a great deal of improvidence among our working classes, it is not less true that among a considerable minority of them there is a great deal of prudence.

But more than this. We condemn the majority for imprudence; but we must remember that that imprudence is very often qualified by a considerable degree of foresight as to a provision for illness. The number of men who subscribe to sick-clubs is very large indeed. What has surprised me most in this respect is the long period during which such clubs have flourished. I had imagined that they were rather a recent institution; but I find that a hundred years ago they were very common. We find some curious information on this point in *Hutton's Court of Requests*.

Nothing seems to have been more common in that court than for the stewards of a sick-club to be summoned by a member for non-payment of the stipulated allowance during illness. This would be nearly a hundred years ago. We find * that scarcely a court-day passed over without a case of this kind. From some remarks in another place, † we gather that the stewards were sometimes very slippery in their conduct. According to certain statutes of a club, a member lost his right to relief if he were seen intoxicated during his illness ; and this ground of disqualification seems to have been pleaded. ‡ We find afterwards § that to evade payment in a case of permanent sickness, the stewards of the club surrendered their offices, and two new stewards were elected who lived outside the jurisdiction of the court. At the same date there were female sick-clubs : for in one place ‖ we have an example of the summoning of the stewardess. These disputes were, no doubt, aggravated by the high rate of allowance during sickness : this appears ¶ to have been seven shillings a week ; which was nearly the wages of unskilled labour, such wages being at that time ** about eight shillings.

But there were in those days other kinds of clubs among women, such as gown-clubs, stays-clubs : some of young girls, some of wives, some of widows. †† Among men there were two-guinea clubs at public-houses. ‡‡

The institution of clubs being of such long 'standing it is the less surprising that it should be widely spread.

---

* Hutton's Court of Requests, 160. 161.

† Ib. 324.   ‡ Ib. 325.   § Ib. 327.   ‖ Ib. 264.   ¶ Ib. 324.

     ** Ib. 190.   †† Ib. 263.   ‡‡ Ib. 154.

M. Le Play tells us * that in 1850 there existed in the United Kingdom of these islands 33,000 societies for mutual assurance, with three millions of members, an annual income of four millions sterling, and accumulated funds of eleven millions sterling. Three millions of members give us one member in every second family of England, Scotland, and Ireland: i.e., there are half as many members as families. But if we took England alone, we should find far more than one member of a club for every two families. There is a qualification to be made, however. Many men belong to more than one club, just as many of the middle classes pay premiums to several Insurance Societies. The Sheffield carpenter mentioned above † belonged to three sick clubs; he received, during the first ten weeks of illness twenty-five shillings a week from the three together; and half that sum afterwards. Similar societies exist in other countries. In France they are tolerably numerous and are increasing. I need hardly say, that medical attendance and drugs are furnished, as well as an allowance in money.

I repeat then, that it is very unjust to charge the working classes with extreme improvidence. It appears that many save so much as to raise themselves into a higher class of society: that more effect such savings as to secure them from want: and that a very large number indeed, make a weekly provision by means of sick clubs, against a time of illness.

Still, it cannot be denied that, among a large number of the working classes, there is great room for improvement; and we naturally enquire whether it is possible to adopt

* Le Play. 199. 1.　　　† Ib. 201. 2.

any means to lessen the improvidence of these thoughtless people. The favourite remedy of half a century ago was, the abolition of the poor law. It was contended that a working man who knew himself to have no resource but his own labour and foresight, would certainly, in a time of prosperity, lay up a provision for a time of illness or distress: and it was thought that the certainty of relief from the parish, accounted for the improvidence that was found to exist. It cannot be disputed that the poor law was greatly abused, before the reformation of it twenty years ago. But the writers I allude to, were not satisfied with calling for an amendment: they denounced the law altogether as false in principle. Arthur Young, an accurate observer, a great student of social economy, and a copious writer on such subjects, clamoured loudly against the parish relief system. Malthus echoed the cry in much milder language. Continental authors have continued generally to condemn the system.

It is worthy of note, however, that Malthus in his later editions, acknowledged the existence of provisions in the old poor law, such as to mitigate, if not to counteract, its evil results. What Malthus principally censured, was, the encouragement given by the law to early and improvident marriages, and the tendency to promote an undue increase of population. But he subsequently observed that the law of settlement, by its operation on parish officers, and on owners of estates, acted very strongly in the opposite direction to the law generally, and by limiting the number of cottages, neutralised the supposed tendency to encourage early marriages.

There are some well known, undisputed facts, which are hard to reconcile with the statement that our poor laws have corrupted the working classes. England has had a poor law nearly three centuries, a period long enough to allow a full development of the supposed effects. Scotland, during the same period, has had a very small provision for the destitute. Can it be truly said that the Scotch peasantry is in a better condition than the English? The Scotch, since the time of William and Mary, have educated their poor far better than we have educated ours. If a liberal poor law be indeed a bad thing, we might have fairly expected that the Scotch peasantry, free from the cruel kindness of this incubus, and elevated by superior instruction, would have risen far above the level of the English peasantry. Yet when an enquiry was made, some years ago, the result was so unsatisfactory, that it was thought necessary to enact a more stringent poor law for Scotland.

If we cross the Irish Channel, a still stronger case presents itself. While the English had a very liberal provision for the destitute, and the Scotch a very narrow one, the Irish had no provision at all. We ought to find, then, on the supposition that a poor law corrupts the people, that the Irish peasant was a superior being to the Scot, and still more superior to the Englishman. Let the notorious facts of the case answer if this is so: let the rags, and filth, and destitution, and famines, of Ireland, reply to the question.

If we go to other countries, we do not find any evidence in the opposite direction. Germany, or parts of it, has some provision for the destitute, and there is no doubt, a good deal of poverty. But France has no poor law. And what do we find? A thrifty peasantry carefully saving up a fund for sickness and old age? inspired with such resoluteness, that they will rather emigrate than starve? a population setting to the world at large an example of universal co-operation by means of benefit societies? Nothing of the kind. On the contrary: in the provinces, general improvidence: in Paris a population immoral, dissolute, reckless; spending every week the gains of the preceding week, in dissipation or coarse debauchery: every where a people so devoid of resolution that they will make any sacrifice rather than leave their native place: a population following with feeble steps the example long set them of co-operation for mutual benefit.

Of all the fully peopled and considerable countries of Europe, England is the one in which the people at large enjoy the greatest well being; in which they are best paid, best fed, best clothed, best housed. And this is the country in which the poor law has been in operation for centuries, with great generosity of administration. This liberal provision for the needy is no experiment set on foot by a revolutionary government, no attempt by a timid despot to pander to the corruption of the populace: it is an institution that has stood the test of civil war, that has survived the reconstruction of our monarchy, that has lasted long enough to engrain itself in the character of all classes. Let those who still chant the old song, down with the poor laws, ponder the facts of the case, and say whether they desire to reduce our labourers to the level of the Scotch, the French, the Irish.

I see no reason, therefore, for believing that the abolition of our poor law, without the substitution of another
efficacious provision for the destitute, would cure the improvident habits that we regret. And I even greatly fear
that the absence of systematic relief for distressed persons,
would allow those unfortunates to fall so low in the social
scale, that there would be little hope of their rising again
to their old position.

But it is supposed that if we could by any means induce
the working classes to defer their marriages a few years,
so that they might start with a house of their own, plenty
of furniture, and a sum of money in the savings' bank, there
would be no danger of any want of prudence afterwards.
It is disappointing to find that in practice, this remedy is
not so efficacious as we might suppose. In many parts of
Europe, custom does not allow a young couple to marry,
until considerable savings can be shewn. But it does not
appear that this habit of frugality universally, or even
generally, continues after marriage. It would seem that
in most places men have a strong desire to marry, and that
in order to accomplish this object, they will make considerable sacrifices of labour and frugality: but that when this
point is gained, sloth and self indulgence again assert their
rights.

Thus, we find as to the Hungarian peasants, * that they
are often the proprietors of the houses they live in: having
acquired them sometimes by inheritance, sometimes by buying them with their savings; but that when they have

* Le Play, 117. 2.

accomplished this object, they generally make no efforts to increase their property, but content themselves with what they have acquired. In Rhenish Prussia,* the first thing a man does is to serve as a soldier for a few years. Afterwards, towards the age of twenty-five or twenty-seven, he marries. He and his wife, for some time, save part of their earnings to buy a cow. Having done this, they abandon themselves to habits of improvidence; spending the whole of their earnings, and running into debt as far as they can get credit. Neither the postponement of marriage beyond the ordinary age, nor the temporary self-denial for the purpose of procuring a cow, forms in this case, a permanent habit of prudence.

In Lower Britany a singular old custom still prevails. Every youth living in the house of a farmer as a servant, has the right of keeping two heifers with his master's herd, and at his master's expense. This privilege may be regarded as part of the wages, but it can be used only by those servants who possess two heifers. Here is a great inducement to save money for the purchase of the heifers; and the arrangement seems well calculated to initiate youths in habits of prudence, and to inculcate that self-respect which is supposed to attend the possession of property. It does not appear, however, that the good effects produced are spread very widely among this population. M. Le Play certainly says, † that three out of ten succeed to some extent in improving their circumstances, but he also says, ‡ that " The greater part of the labourers, who have married and become day labourers, make no effort to improve their

---

condition; but that those, on the contrary, who preserve their habit of frugality and who abstain from drinking, may succeed in saving about £4. a year, and by the time they are thirty-five years old may be able to take a farm."

I could produce other examples, all, like the above, tending to shew that young men who save with a view to marry, or who, after marriage, save for some particular object, do not therefore become permanently frugal, so often as we should suppose. I will shortly allude again to a Genevese case, to illustrate this, and also another principle.

No doubt it would be a great point gained, if our mechanics generally owned the houses they lived in; if they possessed a larger stock of furniture, on which they might borrow money at need, without depriving themselves of the necessary clothes and beds; and if they habitually kept a reserve fund in the Savings' Bank. But if this could be accomplished only by deferring the date of marriage, it is worth while to consider carefully what consequences would probably follow.

It cannot be doubted that some increase of vice would result from any postponement of marriage. Even among the middle classes, the comparatively late date of marriage leads to much that is to be regretted : far more of the same vicious practices would ensue among the labouring classes. For imperfectly educated as the middle classes are, and defective as they are in real refinement, the lower classes have both less education and less refinement. The education of the middle classes, limited as it is, furnishes them with many occupations and amusements; and their refinement, though far below the level of a high standard, restrains them to a considerable extent, from gross vice. But the working classes have at present few recreations beyond the pleasures of sense; and it is vain to expect from them such delicacy as would shield them from temptation to illicit gratifications. Marriage, a home, a wife, and children, are more necessary, therefore, to a working man than to his employer : necessary, I mean, as a protection from vicious habits. It is to be feared that if our mechanics commonly remained bachelors till twenty-eight or thirty, many of them would form habits of irregular indulgence that would not easily be abandoned. Even a great deal of saving would be ill purchased by such a consummation as this. Nor is it pleasant to reflect what disturbance to the peace of towns might arise, if men under thirty were generally unmarried, living in lodgings, and constantly herding together in their amusements. We might find ourselves after a time, in the same volcanic state that is so alarming a feature of the condition of Paris.

If we were here discussing Malthus's Principle of Population, the question would assume a very different aspect. But the numbers of people in England have no appearance of being greater than can obtain a competent living : the condition of the lower classes has certainly not deteriorated in the last hundred years; nay, it has unquestionably improved. If the case were the reverse of this, if the working classes had become poorer, worse fed, worse clothed, and worse housed, the gain of a ten years' postponement of marriage would be so great, that we might willingly run the risks I have pointed out. The evil, however, we are now considering, is not excess of numbers but improvidence; and it seems to me doubtful whether, in the present mental condition of working men, an early marriage is not

almost necessary as a protection.   Better have a good deal
of needless destitution, than a great deal of vice.

The situation of things may hereafter be very different.
It is ably contended by Mr. Mill, in opposition to a long
received opinion, that a stationary state of population is
not necessarily a state of misery.   I believe it to be true
that with advanced intelligence and refinement, a country
may learn to merely reproduce its numbers, without being
driven to this prudence by the pressure of actual necessity.
Such foresight implies a long postponement of the time of
marriage on the part of the working classes; if, as it is
assumed, emigration has ceased to be advantageous.   But
for a community to practice so much self-denial, it is necessary that it should have far more intelligence than is now
common, as well as far more self-command.   The possession
of these qualities would give, in all probability, an increased
degree of delicacy.   The lower classes might very well be
then as refined as the middle classes are now; and in that
case the lower classes might then safely marry as late as
the middle classes marry now.   All I maintain is, that in
the present state of the lower classes, considerable danger
might arise from such a postponement of marriage.   And I
fear that those who should use their influence so as to cause
such postponement, would lead us to fly from evils that we
know, to others that we know not of.

Another remedy for improvidence is supposed to be the
adoption by working people of a high standard of living.
It is, no doubt, much to be regretted that a man should sit
down contented in poverty without making any effort to
escape from it.   Few spectacles are more to be deplored
than that of a people cheerfully living in cabins formed out

of a dry ditch with two days' labour, clothed in picturesque but filthy rags, and sharing their meal of potatoes with the pig and the beggar. The contented disposition that sweetens such a life may be worthy of our love : but a community constituted of men of this sort has small hope of well-being, and no hope of greatness. The contrary temper, which leads men, at whatever cost of personal hardship, to exert themselves for a rise out of this slough of destitution, which induces them to remain for years unmarried, which urges them on to change their abode, and even to cross to the antipodes ; such a temper, though it may sometimes run into hardness and austerity, is far more favourable to the permanent well-being of mankind.

A determination, then, not to sit down contented in a state of mere existence, devoid of the comforts of life, is highly to be commended. So far a high standard of living is advantageous. But even this may run into an extreme. While in Ireland, and perhaps in the country parts of England generally, there has hitherto been too tame and resigned a disposition of mind, in the towns of many countries, the working people have often hurt themselves by an ambition of imitating the habits of the middle classes.

This fault is not a new one. In the chapter on dress, I have quoted from old Hutton, to show that 120 years ago, the working men indulged in the adornment of a wig : and I have stated what I have heard from one who knew a good deal of the Birmingham mechanics of the end of last century, that at that time those men used to wear powder on Sundays ; and that it was a saying that they would not go to work at the beginning of the week, until they had shaken the powder out of their hair. They were accustomed also to hire horses for riding. Such men would not easily resign themselves to the destitution of an Irish cabin : but on the other hand, their indulgence in expensive pleasures kept them poor, and prevented them from laying up a provision against times of distress. I remember the case of a mechanic, in my boyhood, the husband of one who had been my nurse. He was a man of sober, steady, habits, and was very industrious. But he had notions of refinement, and of pride, that, while they saved him from vice and gross misconduct, greatly interfered with the well being of his family. When trade was good, he earned high wages, but these were only enough to maintain him in the way he thought suitable to his position. Unfortunately, there came a great slackness of business, extending over several years. The pride of the man would not allow him to descend to an inferior occupation. He was a jeweller, and he would not take a situation as porter or servant of any kind. Much less would he ask for relief from the parish. The result was great suffering to his wife and family.

One of M. Le Play's cases is somewhat similar. I have alluded to it more than once before ; and especially I have already mentioned it in this chapter, as another example in addition to those I have given, to show that the saving of property before marriage, does not necessarily secure habits of frugality afterwards.

The man and his wife here described, * possessed when they married, nearly £120., deposited in the savings' bank :

* Le Play, 165. 2.

£40. of this sum having been accumulated by the young woman from her wages, in five years. " The annual savings commonly diminish after entrance on housekeeping, . . . and is still further lessened on the birth of children. This is especially the case where there is a tendency to super-fluity in furniture and clothes. . . . . Many workmen who enter on married life with as much affluence as is described above, are obliged in their old age, to demand assistance from the public."

M. Le Play remarks also " When we consider the rather large outlay in this family in obtaining superfluous articles of furniture and clothes, we conclude that the possession of these articles is an object of great desire to the workmen in towns. The present example shews us, that this desire, excited by contact with the middle classes, prevails, even among the most provident workmen, over considerations of prudence and foresight."

It appears, therefore, that a high standard of living on the part of workmen, is, up to a certain point, advantageous; because it leads them both to industry and self-denial: but it appears also, that if this standard rises above a certain level, it is injurious, by causing workmen to spend the whole of their income, and even to trench on the fund accumulated in early life. Every virtue carried to excess becomes a vice.

But too ambitious a mode of living is not the only fault into which decent, well-conducted, labouring men fall. It is with these men as it is with the middle classes : many are improvident, some are parsimonious. The respectable vice of avarice is one that by no means disgraces a workman in the eyes of his employer. It leads the man to be regular in his hours, sober, industrious; ready at all times to work overtime if the state of trade requires it. But avarice is not the less a vice, because it makes a man respectable. If a workman choose to deny himself Sunday clothes, reasonable indulgence, moderate recreations, no one has a right to complain. But if he extends the same hard measure to his wife, if he feeds his children scantily, and allows them to go in rags, if he sells their infancy to work, and fails to give them education, if he refuses his contribution to brother workmen in distress, if he squeezes out of his apprentice the utmost work that the law allows him, he may be a treasure to his employer, but he is really more odious by far than the thoughtless fellow who never saves, but who is ready to share his last shilling with distress.

This hypothetical sketch is no invention, but is drawn from the life. I remember a conversation that I had, many years ago, with a borough magistrate. He said that master manufacturers required as much legal restraint as the men. He acknowledged that he spoke of the smaller manufacturers. I objected that these small manufacturers had generally risen from the ranks : that they were, in fact, workmen who had risen by their good conduct : that they surely, therefore, must be superior to those they had left behind. This reply might pass in conversation, but on reflection, I saw it to be sophistical. Workmen rise, not because they are better men than those they leave behind, but because they are more prudent. Now prudence is an excellent quality, but it is not a virtue of a high order, much less is it the only virtue. The same prudence that enables a man to rise to be a master, may readily be pushed so far as to become a vice. A workman who has exhibited such industry, and such frugality, as to raise his condition, will, in many cases, be a man likely to be severe in his dealings with his workmen, and harsh towards his apprentices. The virtue has, by excess, run into a vice.

M. Le Play remarks,* " In domestic communities, so favourable to the development of free will, we see a multitude of individuals rise by labour and frugality from the lower ranks of the working classes. Many may rise to wealth without being placed, by public opinion, at any rate at first, in the highest ranks. In truth, the qualities which have secured their success are commonly the reverse of those which deserve such an elevation. A sustained application to manual labour, an incessant desire for gain and for saving, are opposed, up to a certain point, to the most simple development of intelligence, and of moral sentiments. They generally impress on the mind a character of harshness and selfishness, such as none but the finest natures can resist. It is from such circumstances, and especially among the middle classes, that spring the miser and the usurer."

In another place we are told † " The moral imperfection of those who rise immediately from the working classes, results from the very nature of man. Foresight, and a habit of calculation, are the only things which can raise a workman from the rank in which he was born. These oblige him incessantly to resist the inspirations of his heart; and the first movement of the man who submits himself to their government, is, to resist the disposition which leads

* Le Play, 294. 1.   † Ib. 278. 2.

us, at a certain cost, to gratify our senses or our moral sentiments. If, then, such a man is not disposed, by an exceptional organization, to the love of his neighbour, or if he is not regularly influenced in that direction by the sovereign influence of religion, we are sure to find in him all those faults that are engendered by an excessive devotion to self-interest."

We find in some of the cases given, traces of this hard, unfeeling, disposition, caused by an excess of frugality, that runs into parsimony. In the case of the Auvergne miner * it is said, " The whole population shews a decided tendency to saving: unfortunately, this virtue often degenerates into a sordid avarice, which leads to the use of insufficient food, which prevents the education of the children, and which too often interferes with the attentions due to the sick and infirm."

It is pleasing, however, to find that this censure is not passed on industrious, enterprising people, but on a people sunk in sloth. I should be glad to believe, that though an individual here and there, throughout the world, may be at once industrious and mean, yet that in comparing one community with another, the most industrious, will usually be also the most open handed. In this instance, " The farmer works with little energy, and often indolently. This inert condition may certainly be attributed partly to the insufficiency of the food; meat and spirituous liquors being almost entirely wanting: but the leading cause, unquestionably, is the absence of intellectual culture, and the slothful habits

* Le Play, 248. 1.

contracted in infancy, from the necessities of a pastoral life, and from the custom of passing the long winter evenings in the gentle warmth of the cow-house."

If we turn to the blacksmith of Maine, M. Le Play gives us the following unpleasing observations:* "Perhaps we must consider it proved, that the virtue of frugality, which is the means the workman possesses of passing the barrier that separates him from the proprietor, has frequently a predominant influence over the character of the people of Maine. In the case of many children it corrupts the sentiments of respect and affection for their parents: in some instances of older people it degenerates into a sordid parsimony that destroys every social relation: too often it extinguishes all enthusiasm, and all disposition to self-devotedness, and to personal sacrifice."

These cases given by M. Le Play, and the remarks that he has founded on his observations, must make us painfully aware of the danger, that the working classes, in curing themselves of improvidence, should rush into the opposite vice of avarice. I fear that if this were to happen, our last state would be worse than our first. Imprudence and carelessness are faults much to be deplored; but a cold, hard, selfish, parsimony, is destructive of every amiable and generous sentiment. A people among whom such parsimony generally prevailed, besides being detestable in private life, would be devoid of public spirit, and would be deficient in the virtue necessary to preserve the political freedom which was their heritage.

* Le Play, 260. 1.

While we acknowledge, then, that there is a good deal of improvidence among the working classes, we cannot deny that there is a considerable admixture of prudence, as proved by the large number of persons who are members of sick-clubs and other provident societies. It seems, also, that the various remedies proposed for the cure of improvidence, have their dangers as well as their advantages. A postponement of marriage on the part of rather coarse natures, implies a lamentable amount of gross vice: an adoption of a high standard of living may be carried to such an extreme as to cause as much imprudence as it cures: frugality itself may easily be pushed into parsimony.

But no one proposes that these remedies should be applied by the strong hand: it is only desired that the working man should be enlightened as to his true interest, and should be furnished with the opportunity of pursuing that interest by readily investing his savings in a safe and lucrative manner.

When, however, we propose to teach the lower classes their real interest and their duty, we should be tolerably sure that we know what the interest and the duty of men, really are. There is a strange misapprehension current in the world, as to the worth of money. Men will acknowledge on Sundays, that riches have no great value, that they make themselves wings and flee away, that they cannot bring any real happiness to the home or the heart; but on week days their creed is altogether different, and their practice is in accordance with their week day profession.

Nor is this error altogether one of the heart: the head has its part in it too. Few men even of the middle classes, are born to riches: the greater part have their own fortunes to make. Now it is the duty of every man to labour, and even to make great sacrifices, in order to secure a competent provision for himself and his family. But a man commonly arrives at middle life before he has secured this provision, and in a majority of cases he goes far beyond middle life before he does this. During the twenty, thirty, or forty years, applied in this way, the habits are completely formed, and a man cannot alter his mode of life, but goes on to the last, striving to accumulate money. Nor is a man censured for this course. The world makes little distinction between the industry applied to securing a competency, and the industry applied to enlarging a store that is already sufficient. The energetic, laborious, man, is an object of admiration, whether his efforts are directed to securing a competency, or to raising a competency into an unnecessary fortune. Yet there is, in fact, a very broad distinction between the two things. The man who labours for a competency, is striving after that which is necessary to his happiness, and is equally necessary to the happiness of his children. But the man who goes on adding to a sufficient fortune, is doing that which may gratify his passions, which may satisfy his love of luxury and his desire for distinction, but which, as far as we can judge, can add nothing to his happiness.

I am aware that men, individually, are not guided by truths however clearly proved to them. But communities, I think, are, in the long run, very much influenced by the truths that are current in them. Once establish in any nation this truth, of the distinction between labouring for a competency and labouring for superfluous wealth; let the truth embody itself in a proverb, and be pointed as the moral of popular tales, and it will then tell on the actions even of men of business.

But the same distinction ought to be explained to the working classes and impressed on their minds. It would tend to make them more prudent up to a certain point, while it would tend to save them from pushing frugality into sordid parsimony. By all means encourage them to become members of sick-clubs and provident societies, to save something before they marry, to become possessed of a house of their own, to accumulate a little fund in the savings' bank; but teach them at the same time that the object of this prudence should be to secure a competent provision against want, to furnish a fund for their support when they are out of work, and to secure them from the danger of passing their old age in the degrading position of paupers. Endeavour, at the same time, to impress upon their minds, that though to rise in life is a legitimate object of desire, yet that to labour beyond their strength, or to abstain from temperate enjoyments with this view, is to make a sacrifice of present happiness, for what, after all, is a doubtful future good : and that, for such a gratification of ambition, to deprive their wives and children of bodily comforts and mental education, is an inhumanity that it is impossible to defend.

CHAPTER XV.

If improvidence is the principal weakness of the working classes, drunkenness is their principal vice. Many people believe that the drunkenness is the cause of the improvidence, and that if we could only make people sober, we should at once make them also prudent. Now, it is well known that in some southern countries sobriety does prevail; and that among all Mahometan populations, spirituous liquors are abstained from in public, although they are taken to some extent, just as opium is taken among ourselves, as a secret indulgence. If, then, drunkenness is really the cause of improvidence, we might expect that among the temperate populations of the south and east, foresight and prudence would be characteristics of the working classes. But foresight and prudence bring prosperity and well-being : and on this reasoning we ought to find Spain, Italy, and Turkey, far before the more northern countries as to the well-being of the labouring class. It is notorious that this is not the case.

But the latter part of this reasoning may be objected to : it may be thought that in Spain, Italy, and Turkey, the prosperity that would naturally follow foresight and prudence, is prevented by other causes, and particularly by the defective character of the governments of those countries. I will endeavour to show that the supposed foresight and prudence do not exist.

Thus, in the Viennese case * already cited, the husband and wife are both of them people of singularly temperate habits : " they live with sobriety, and abstain from all spirituous drinks." Yet " in their improvidence they adopt the usual habits of the workmen of Vienna. In accordance with a disposition common enough among the labouring classes, the wife, before marriage, had a decided tendency to frugality : but the discouragement produced by a bankruptcy which deprived the family of its little principal, and the frequent increase of family, have gradually effaced all traces of this inclination." This is the household in which M. Le Play noticed the loss caused by daily purchases of small quantities of provisions, and which he vainly endeavoured to assist, by offering inducements to buy provisions in larger quantities and on better terms.

Here, then, is a family in which the strictest temperance reigns, but in which improvidence is as strongly marked as in most families in which a good deal of drunkenness takes place. It is true that the wife showed originally a considerable power of self-control, and that she saved a sum of money much of which was lost by misfortune. But at no time did the husband exhibit the same disposition. After he had served as an apprentice, and had made his tour of Austria, he worked twelve years with plenty of employment, but without making any effort to rise, and without saving any thing. During the latter years of celibacy he earned 2s. 2d. a day, but he spent his surplus gains on agreeable food and smart clothes. This man's sobriety entirely failed as a preventive of improvidence.

* Le Play, 121. 1.

In Castille, it is said, * " Under the influence of these
sentiments the Spanish workman is observant of decorum
just as the superior classes are. His extreme sobriety, due
to the threefold influence of race, climate, and education,
protects him from submission to material appetites, which
constitute the bane of workmen of other regions of Europe."
Here, then, if any where, we might expect improvidence to
be banished. Yet we are told † that while the prudent
part of the peasantry may arrive at a competency, " the
greater part of the *métayers*, devoid of order and foresight,
do not rise above the condition of working tenants, leaving
their children to begin life as day-labourers."

We must not suppose, therefore, that drunkenness is the
parent of all the faults of working men ; nor must we
indulge the hope that by curing them of this vice, we
should set them free from all the ills to which they expose
themselves.

But though the evils of drunkenness have been exaggerated, they are yet very great. If any one is desirous
of refreshing his memory on the subject, let him read again,
the early history of old Hutton. His father was a man of
good prospects as a mechanic, a man of skill in his trade as
a woolcomber ; of ability beyond his station, with acute
reasoning powers, an excellent memory, a good deal of
knowledge, and a fluency and eloquence of language. Yet
he was so carried away by his love of convivial society, that
he slighted his family, left them at times without bread,
neglected the education of his sons, and put them to trades
in which, as he declared, they could not get a living. He

* Le Play, 181. 1.   † Ib. 177. 2.

was, at one time, a man commanding a certain degree of respect, since he was made constable of Derby ; and a hundred and thirty years ago, a constable must have been a man of decent reputation. But his passion for the tavern was irresistible. In his pocket was found this written resolution, which there is no reason to think that he fulfilled :—" O Lord ! by thy   assistance, I will not enter into a public-house on this side of Easter."

Such a case as this is certainly exceptional. As a rule, men do not go to the extent of utter recklessness. Far too much money is spent in drinking, but men generally do make some provision for their families. They do not, like Hutton, sell their furniture and go to lodgings, as soon as they lose their wives ; they do not let their children want bread. Many men, no doubt, do this, and do a great deal worse: for the sake of drink, they cheat and rob and murder. Mr. Chesterton, in his book relating his experience of prison government, speaks of confirmed drunkards, as being, like confirmed gamesters, quite incurable.

But drunkenness generally shews itself in a much milder form. Indeed the habit which commonly prevails is rather that of drinking than of drunkenness. Labourers now, do what the middle classes did a generation or two ago: they get intoxicated on high days and holidays, and take more than does them good, whenever they can get it without inconvenience or disgrace. The quantity, however, that a working man can drink without excitement, appears marvellous to our unseasoned heads. A mechanic at a feast thinks himself scurvily used if he is supplied with less than a gallon of strong ale. He dines early, to be sure, and sits soaking all afternoon, as our progenitors did. But when the gallon of ale is exhausted, he very likely gets more at his own expense, or finishes with a glass or two of spirits. After all, this is no more wonderful than the habit of the two or three bottle men of the last generation.

Most of us know very little about what goes on among workmen in the evening. We see them in their places during the day, we find them always ready to labour when they are called upon, and we set them down as men of temperate habits: inferring from their regularity that they are not guilty of excesses in their leisure hours. It is sometimes startling to find that we are entirely mistaken. A young man once worked for me, having been brought up from childhood in my service. He was a person of great skill in his trade, had several men and boys under him, and earned from thirty shillings to fifty shillings a week. He was regularly at his post, and ready at all times to do any quantity of additional work that might be required. I supposed him to be as temperate a man as I knew him to be a steady one. However, he fell ill, and then, to my astonishment, it came out that his liver was diseased in consequence of the quantity of spirits he had habitually taken. His medical man warned him, that unless he gave up this indulgence, he would soon die. As he lived many years since that time, and apparently in good health, he probably attended to the warning he received. This man's regularity at work was probably owing in part to his having been brought up in a forge. Men so brought up are taught the necessity of being always at work when the steam engine is going; whereas men who work without machinery, are able to pull up at the end of the week the time they lose at the beginning. The man, too, was a bachelor, and had therefore an unusual sum of money to spend every week. In another case of a steady, hard working man, I was surprised to find the same habit of regular drinking. He fell ill and went into a hospital, and the surgeon who attended him there let me into the secret. I rather believe that this man, too, was a bachelor.

This daily habit of taking too much is far more dangerous, and to me, far more offensive, than an occasional indulgence. If a man is usually abstinent, but occasionally, when in the society of his friends, goes a little beyond the bounds of moderation, this excess is certainly to be regretted, and yet it has the excuse of good fellowship. Mr. Macaulay tells us that in the good old Stuart times, grave peers of the realm, men of reputation as to morals, thought little of drinking to positive intoxication. If our working classes, when they meet for conviviality, err only as much as these grave men did, we must let the excuse of sociability pass current as a decided palliation. But the habit of constant drinking, of beginning early in the day, and keeping up the stimulus from hour to hour, has no such excuse. It is at once expensive, and injurious to health. It is a mere sensual indulgence, inconsistent with vigorous exertion, and destructive of sustained industry.

In comparing different countries, as to the habit of drinking, we must remember the well known truth, that the great difference between one climate and another accounts for much of the variation between one people and another. We have seen that M. Le Play confirms the opinion that the Spanish are very temperate. We shall see that he equally confirms the opinion that more drinking takes place among the northern nations. But it is certain that if the Spaniard swallowed as much alcohol as the Scandinavian, he would be far more injured by it: the greater cold of the north carries off the heat generated by the spirit. But the comparative cold is not the only ground of distinction. We all know the chilling effects of a fog. It is remarked by Arctic voyagers that the dryness of the climate when they have wintered on the ice, allowed them, when the weather was calm, to walk about with very moderate clothing. I have heard an officer say the same of Canada, referring to a time when the thermometer was 20° lower than we dream of in England. A foggy atmosphere is a modified cold bath, and carries off the heat from the skin at a great rate. The moist air of Scotland justifies the use of alcohol, as does the moist air of England in a less degree. This distinction, though well known, is liable to be forgotten. I lately saw a remark on the supposed superiority of the Red Indian over the white man, as to strength of constitution. The alleged reason for believing in this superiority, was the fact, that you may see an Indian on a winter night, lying intoxicated without any protection from the intense northern continental cold, and this without injury. I scarcely doubt that, under Indian training, the tender shoots die off, and the hardy shoots become hardier than the scions of the English race; just as would happen among ourselves, if we brought up our children according to the severe process recommended by Locke. But the writer who brought forward the fact that Indians do lie intoxicated in the cold of winter, forgot, apparently, that the quantity of fire-water swallowed is a great protection against the inclemency of the sky. For the same reason, we must make allowance for variety of climate: we must not charge intemperance against a Scotchman who

takes a dram to fortify himself against the fog of his mountains; though we might severely censure a Spaniard or an
Italian, who habitually indulged in spirits during the summer.

In no country, we are told, is drinking carried to a
greater excess than in Russia: but the imperfect information we possess, is insufficient to establish this charge.
Malthus * said that the immoderate use of brandy in that
country shortened the lives of the population. The *Englishwoman in Russia* tells us, † that the lower classes have the
curious privilege of being allowed to get intoxicated during
Easter week, with impunity; and that a great number of
drunken persons are seen in the streets during that period.
She says that the better classes generally are very temperate. M. Le Play, as far as I am aware, gives no
information that confirms Malthus's severe censure.

As to Sweden, we learn in the Danemora case ‡ that
there is a tendency to an excessive use of spirituous
liquors; but that the influence of the employer is success-
fully exerted to maintain order and decency, even in this
respect.

Of Norway we learn something in the case of the man
employed in Cobalt works. § " . . . . the disposition
to drunkenness so decided among northern nations is controlled in this family by the influence of the temperance
societies. Under the influence of the societies many of the
men employed in these works have given up the use of
spirituous drinks, even in the most moderate quantities.
The family here described makes use occasionally of small

---

* Malthus, Population 1, 305, 306.

† Englishwoman in Russia, 221.   ‡ Le Play, 92. 1.   § Ib. 98. 1.

beer, bought at the tavern, or brewed at home. But it is in some degree influenced by the employer, so as to yield to the temperance society to the extent of altogether abandoning the use of spirits."

We hear a good deal on this topic from Mr. Laing. It appears that a great deal of beer and brandy is taken daily. The first thing in the morning, the family of the proprietor of a farm takes coffee; but * " the workpeople have a cake of oat or bear meal with butter, and a dram of potato brandy." This is very early in the morning. Then, about nine, comes breakfast, and at this meal the Norwegians generally take a glass of potato brandy. Ale makes its appearance, and sometimes tea. No spirits are taken at dinner or supper, the entire allowance being two drams a day.† In the afternoon the workpeople have another substantial meal like the breakfast, and again have a dram.

Mr. Laing says of the Norwegians, ‡ " They are not a sober people; but I have remarked that I never saw one of them drunk when he was especially required to be sober. I never saw a man at work, or a soldier in regimentals, in liquor. It is not common, as in Scotland, to meet a person in the streets or on the roads in a state of intoxication. They take convenient times and places for their potations; and weddings, baptisms, burials, besides the Christmas, Midsummer, hay and corn harvest home, and other festivals, give times and places enough without much alehouse or spirit-shop meetings."

Mr. Laing says also, § " nor can I admit that the common people are more addicted to drunkenness in Norway than

* Laing's Norway, 189.   † Ib. 191.   ‡ Ib. 190.   § Ib. 254.

in Scotland. They use more spirits undoubtedly, but they spread it over a greater portion of time. If their two glasses of raw spirits daily, which is perhaps the average consumption of each of the labouring class, were taken all at once, or in two evenings of the week, they would lose two, or perhaps four days of that week, from the effects of excess; but divided as they generally are in fourteen portions at intervals of twelve hours, it is the physician rather than the moralist who can speak to the effects. The ordinary observer can only remark that in spite of this poison they are a very athletic, healthy-looking set of men, carrying the bloom of youthful complexions to a much later period of life than other nations: they have particularly well-made limbs, in which respect the English peasant is often deficient, and their children are uncommonly and strikingly fine looking little creatures."

Of Germany I have heard different and inconsistent accounts, and this of the same provinces. One traveller says that the beer commonly drunk is of so very mild a kind that it has hardly any intoxicating power; and that this circumstance accounts for the absence of drunkenness which is observable. Another tells me that though the Bavarian beer is often very weak, yet that other German beer is very heady: and that besides this, spirits are drunk in great quantities. How, otherwise, it is added, can we explain the habits of drunkenness that certainly prevail?

I am glad to turn to M. Le Play, and to note what he says of the particular cases that fell under his observation.

I have already made many remarks on a Viennese family which he examined, and in which he found an union of perfect temperance and decided improvidence. In Rhenish Prussia, the account as to sobriety is less favourable. At Solingen,* " the ordinary drink of the household is coffee : no fermented liquors are used at meals. On the other hand, the men drink much at other times, and especially at the tavern." Apparently, a man ordinarily consumes a bottle of brandy a week, besides a liberal quantity of beer and wine.† The brandy seems to be taken as in Norway, by a dram morning and evening.

We generally regard the French as a sober people, and think of them as worthy of imitation in this respect. It is a great mistake, however, to suppose that none of them drink too much. We find M. Le Play ‡ censuring the farm labourer in Maine, on this point. " The labourer's principal recreation is the consumption of coffee, wine, and brandy, in the taverns of the village and of the neighbouring villages, whither he loves to go on market and fair days. The women, who have generally no taste for spirituous liquors, do not possess influence enough to restrain their husbands from this practice, which is often the principal cause of the misery of a family."

In the account I have already quoted, of the habits of Parisian workmen, we have seen that a large class of them spend their evenings in sensual gratifications ; passing the early portion of the week in taverns outside the barriers. We may be sure that drinking is one of the gratifications in which they indulge.

I am not sufficiently familiar with the French to be able to give an opinion as to the quantity of spirituous liquors they

* Le Play, 153. 1 and 2.　　† Ib. 155.　　‡ Ib. 225.

generally consume. But every one who has been in France must be aware that among the middle classes a great deal is drunk. Some people shut their eyes so close, as to come away with the belief that the French drink little but coffee and *eau sucré*. Yet if they even entered a *café*, they must have seen the *petit verre* handed to every one, as a matter of course, with his cup of coffee: and they must have very little observation if they do not see that a great many persons frequent the *cafés* in the morning and fore- noon, as well as later in the day. The truth is that the French middle classes are greatly addicted to brandy. What should we think of an English merchant, or manu- facturer, or professional man, who walked into a spirit shop or tavern, at eleven or twelve o'clock, and took his dram ? Or rather, what do we think of the small class which follows this custom ?

Many people in Paris, no doubt, take a forenoon meal which is half breakfast, half lunch, and which includes wine, and perhaps, a dram. Then, it is said, English people, who dine in the evening, also take a similar lunch. But the Englishman's lunch is taken much later, and as a means of maintaining his strength till dinner time : while the Frenchman's meal is a late breakfast, taken before he has exhausted himself with work. This custom is not peculiar to Paris, but, as I understand, is common among private families in other parts of France. At Evreux, in Normandy, when I was breakfasting late one morning in the public room, several scores of men came in from the town, and took as hearty a meal as might have served for dinner, with large draughts of cider. An Englishman of the middle class, would feel himself very unfit for business after such a meal.

In dining, too, at the *restaurants*, and *tâbles d'hôte*, of
Paris, I see no signs of that abstinence which is attributed
to the French. It is quite a mistake, of course, to suppose
that the dinners eaten at those places, by the Parisians, are
such as are usually taken every day : but even regarding
them as occasional indulgences, I see no ground for calling
the Parisians a very temperate people. I do not mean to
suggest that they often get drunk, but I believe that during
an ordinary day they swallow quite as much wine and
brandy as is good for them, and far more, apparently, than
is swallowed by the educated classes in England.

This French habit of drinking in the morning, and of
getting through a good deal of wine and spirits during the
day, without ever getting intoxicated, resembles what happens in the United States, far more than what happens in
England. The many alluring beverages introduced to us
by our American cousins, fully establish the superiority of
invention on the other side of the Atlantic ; and prove that
a great deal of attention is there applied to the supply of
agreeable modes of quenching thirst. A very temperate
people would not be successful in this department of industry. Indeed, every one who is at all familiar with
American habits, knows that a visit to the bar of an hotel
is as usual among the men of the middle classes, as a
visit to a tavern is usual among working men here. The
Americans do not first perform their day's work, and then,
having dined quietly, draw round the fire to enjoy a sociable
glass of wine. They snatch their drink from time to time
during the day, just as, at a certain hour, they snatch their
dinner. It is acknowledged that during the day they get
through far more spirituous liquors than we do, and far

more than is good for their health. They take very little time about their drinking, and this brevity they may regard as an advantage: but it appears to me that the day is quite long enough for the performance of every duty, and that the rest which we take after dinner is a positive gain to mind and body. The French, indeed, are by no means addicted to hurrying their dinner, as though it were an affair of small importance: the habit in which they resemble the Americans is that of drinking wine and brandy at times before dinner.

When we come to England we cannot deny that there is great excess in the matter of drinking, although we may feel that that excess has been much exaggerated by the over-zeal of philanthropists. It is extremely difficult to form a fair estimate of the habits of workmen in this respect, both because we have no exact standard to measure them by, and because masters and philanthropists are apt to agree in censuring too bitterly every supposed deviation. Drinking is the coarse pleasure of coarse men. Educated and refined men have other pleasures of a more decent kind. The middle classes, having outgrown the sensual habits of their progenitors, are too apt to look with contempt and loathing on those same habits still existing among the labouring population. Yet we have other faults and vices in the place of those we have cast off. Our delicacy is apt to run into fastidiousness, our frugality into parsimony, our sobriety into moroseness, our decency into ostentation, our morality into a pharisaical self-esteem. Under the influence of these evil tempers, which are scarcely less censurable than the sensualism we have abandoned, we are too ready to set up a high ideal standard for our uneducated neighbours, and to blame with unsparing severity every departure from it.

The declamations of unreflecting orators of temperance societies, have magnified the excesses of our workmen. Among all nations we are stigmatised as drunkards. The habits of the educated English of the last century, justified this reputation at that time; and it was not to be supposed that domestic servants would be behind their masters, or workmen be behind their employers. A great change, however, has taken place in the middle and upper classes. Men are no longer looked upon as effeminate because they refuse a second or third bottle; and to be drunk at a dinner party, even though no ladies are present, is as disgraceful as it was formerly disgraceful to be sober. The French still shrug their shoulders, and call us a barbarous people, because we allow the ladies to precede us in retiring from table; but the short time we outsit them, and the apathy with which the bottle is passed, give no pretence to charge us with excess. A man in good health may now dine out day after day, without suffering even a headache as the consequence.

I am by no means so clear as to the improvement of the working classes. I can hardly doubt that there has been an improvement, but I cannot appeal to any facts in support of my opinion. In the case of the middle classes, the change is evidenced, not only by the experience of all of us, but also by the circumstance, that while the population of the country has doubled, the quantity of wine consumed has scarcely increased. Nor do I see any reason to think that this diminished proportionate consumption has been caused by the adoption of other liquors on the part of those who were wine drinkers: on the contrary, we have it in evidence that large quantities of wine are now sold retail in spirit shops, and to a class of people lower, as I should suppose, than those who habitually took wine, fifty years ago. I wish I could advance reasons as valid for believing that an equal diminution has taken place, in the consumption by the lower classes, of beer, porter, gin and brandy.

M. Le Play gives only four English cases, and I will mention his remarks as to the habits of all of them with regard to drinking. The first man is remarkable for temperance, and never drinks spirits: the second is extremely moderate in the use of fermented liquors: the third, a rough, improvident man, never takes spirits at home, and seldom takes them elsewhere: the fourth is not in the habit of frequenting taverns, but passes his leisure hours at home.

Yet M. Le Play still speaks of English workmen generally as addicted to drinking: he regards all the four men I have mentioned, as exceptions to the rule. There is something remarkable in this inconsistency between the general opinion entertained, and the facts in every case quoted. M. Le Play, indeed, tells us that he has published only a selection from the cases he actually observed; and it may be that in other English families he has found that habit of drunkenness which he attributes to our workmen generally. But it is also possible that the general opinion has been formed from communications made to M. Le Play by Englishmen of the middle classes, who are too much addicted to speaking ill of those below them. That there is in England far too much money spent in drinking, no one can doubt: but if we could make an accurate comparison with other countries, we might find a more pleasing result than we anticipated.

This contradiction between M. Le Play's opinion and his facts, is the more striking, when we compare it with the perfect consistency that prevails, on another subject, between his opinion and his facts. Just as he accuses our working classes of being addicted to drinking, so he accuses them of being nearly destitute of religion. But there is this broad distinction. The English workman is a drunkard, says M. Le Play : we turn to his four English workmen, and we find that so far from being drunkards, they are decent, temperate men. The English workman is irreligious, says M. Le Play : we turn again to his four English workmen, and we find that every one of them is an irreligious man. In the matter of drinking, M. Le Play's opinion is altogether at variance with the facts he gives us : in the matter of religion his opinion is altogether at one with the facts he gives us. Under these circumstances, we cannot accept his opinion that our workmen, when compared with those of other countries, are addicted to drinking.

I have quoted Mr. Laing's observations as to the habits of the Norwegians. He seems to have a notion * that an artificial dearness of spirituous liquors, caused by the interference of government, is not beneficial. He would let things alone to take their natural course.

I have heard a still broader opinion expressed : that the best way to cure drinking, is, to make the means of drinking

---

* Laing's Norway, 254.

cheap. The propounder of this dogma had a notion, that people value liquor, as they value diamonds, according to its rarity. If people drank to gratify their vanity, this might be true: and when they do actually consume the high priced Clarets, or Tokay of a hundred years old, or Madeira at five dollars a bottle, they do this to gratify their vanity principally; since few men have sufficient delicacy of palate to appreciate the superiority of such wines. But most men drink from motives quite different from that of vanity: from the desire for the genial warmth that fermented liquors diffuse through the frame; from the love of sociability and good fellowship; from the agreeable anticipation of excitement in this dull world; from a wish to forget for a moment the carking cares of a troublous life. These effects follow from a cheap stimulant as well as from a dear one. And if we, of the middle classes, refuse the strong ale, and the fiery spirits, that working people consume, we do so, not from vanity, but because we dread the headaches that follow. The working classes, with frames hardened by labour, can take these rough stimulants with comparative impunity; and the cheaper they find beer, and rum, and gin, the more they will take.

The facts Mr. Laing adduces, illustrate this argument. The Norwegians are at liberty to distil as much spirit as they please; and every family avails itself of this licence, and produces potato brandy without fear of exciseman or informer. But this facility of distilling, and consequent cheapness of spirits, has not extinguished the love of drink: on the contrary, as we have already seen, a great quantity of this home made spirit is taken.

Mr. Laing, therefore, disproves this extravagant notion, that the cheaper the liquor, the less of it will be taken. Yet he himself declaims against " legislating for morality by distillery laws," and compares it to the " Penal laws against sabbath breaking." Yet on Mr. Laing's own facts it appears that our distillery laws produce two good effects. First, they raise a revenue of a great many millions sterling, without interfering with the necessaries of life. Secondly, by making spirits dearer, they diminish the consumption of them; and thus diminish the tendency to drunkenness in a country where the comparatively high wages give a great facility to indulgence. A legislator would be mad indeed to give up such a revenue, with no probable result but that of demoralising the people. Let the ultra-temperance people talk as they please of the abomination of raising a revenue from the vices of the people. If the consumption of fermented liquors is in itself vicious, let the government absolutely forbid the use of them, so soon as it can do so effectually. But if, as I believe, the moderate consumption of such liquors is innocent, or even beneficial, and if it is only the excess against which we have to guard, let government continue to lessen the consumption by a considerable weight of taxation; taking care, as is now done, that the impost shall not be such as to cause any extensive illicit distillation.

M. Le Play, under the head of the Norwegian cobalt melter, notices the existence of temperance societies, and attributes to them excellent and wonderful results: he states that communities which have adopted the custom of abstaining altogether from spirituous liquors, are most favourably distinguished from the rest of the nation. We know that similar effects have been produced in Ireland, and, to a smaller degree, in England. Father Mathew, the Apostle of Temperance, is now dead; but doubtless, he will live in history as a great reformer of men's manners. The success of his self-imposed mission, was in Ireland, very extraordinary; and for a time, seemed almost to open a prospect of regeneration to that miserable people. It is painful to know that the reformation has not been so permanent as it was extensive; and that the promises, and oaths, made in haste, have been repented of as violent and vain. For my own part, I was never a convert to the practice of total abstinence, except in the case of confirmed drunkards, who were incapable of attaining to the virtue of moderation. While the temperance societies confined themselves to the enforcement, by argument and instruction, of decided moderation, and in the case of drunkards, alone recommended total abstinence, I entirely approved of their proceedings. I saw that, among the middle classes, they did much good, by calling attention to the evils of habitual drinking, on the part even of people among whom drunkenness was unknown. Many persons, I knew, permanently diminished their daily stint of wine, or abandoned the pernicious habit of a nightly glass of grog. But when I found the temperance societies, in the flush of victory, rushing into the extreme of denouncing as ruinous the use of any spirituous liquors whatever, I strongly suspected that they were wrong. Time has confirmed my opinion: I am convinced that it is better to be moderate than to abstain altogether; and that the general adoption of total abstinence would lead to deplorable consequences.

Many persons of scrupulous, or rather of squeamish consciences, are made uneasy by the declamations of teetotal orators. When accounts are given of drunkards who have been reclaimed, of wives who have thus been restored to well being and domestic happiness, of children who have thus been saved from rags and vice, these tender consciences reproach themselves for not joining in so excellent a work. The same scrupulosity would make men close all the theatres, because many evils attend them, would lead them to denounce all gypsey parties, or other gatherings of work-people, on the ground of the irregularities that will follow: would cause them to abandon the evening services of churches and chapels, seeing that those sacred edifices become, in many instances, places for foul assignations. A more robust conscience is not satisfied with slavish submission. A man of a well balanced mind resolves to know what effects are produced on the whole, and in the long run; and will not lend himself as an instrument for effecting a temporary and partial good, until he satisfies himself that there is no danger of causing a permanent and wide spread evil.

Those who visit among the poor, indeed, or who are in the habit of using their influence with their dependents to promote sobriety among them, must feel the personal argument more strongly than others do. You press me to become a teetotaller, says a drunkard; are you one yourself? If you answer, no; wait till you are one, and then urge me, is the reply. You may tell the man that such abstinence is unnecessary for you, because you find no difficulty in restraining yourself from excess. The answer is ready at hand; the man will try to imitate your moderation : and so will he " resolve and re-resolve, then die the same." But if you can say at once, I am a teetotaller, and have long been such, that is an intelligible reply, and more convincing than a hundred sermons.

I cannot wonder, therefore, that many philanthropic persons adopt the practice of total abstinence; and I have little doubt that they often accomplish much good by this self-denial. But this concession of mine does not at all settle the general question, as to the advantages of total abstinence generally : much less does it justify the self-righteous temper which animates some professors of temperance principles, and which leads them, in their pharisaical zeal, to a dogmatism so fierce as to resent every doubt of the sacred principles of teetotalism, as though such a doubt were an insult to their hearts and understandings. Not more intolerant is the Roman Catholic with his infallible Pope, nor the Mussulman with his one God and Mahomet his Prophet.

I do not, then, dispute the advantages derived from the exertions of temperance societies : I only conceive that their zeal has pushed them into an extreme. So long as they confined themselves to explaining, and enforcing, the evils of drunkenness, and of habitual excess short of drunkenness, the good they accomplished was almost unmixed. Even when they went a step farther, they were still in the right. They found that, up to this time, they had induced many men to lessen their potations, a reduction very beneficial to health and pocket. These, however, were not the drunkards, but rather, men who had thoughtlessly followed the example of their forefathers, and of their neighbours, without being at all aware of the injury they were inflicting on themselves. Another, and a smaller class, was found deaf to instruction and admonition. These men, with whom the love of drink was a passion, were taught, and declaimed at, in vain. They knew their folly, they felt their misery, but they had not resolution to shake off the chains that bound them. They tried to be moderate, but under the first temptation their resolution gave way. Then came the notion of inducing such men to do generally, what Dr. Johnson, a century earlier, had done at the prompting of his own mind. They should resolve, and promise, and even asseverate as in the presence of God, that they would henceforward abstain from all spirituous liquors whatsoever. Whether it were right to induce men to make such solemn declarations, many persons have doubted. But that a great deal of immediate good was done can scarcely be disputed : and that the practice of teetotalism is the only cure for a confirmed drunkard, I will not dispute.

The leaders of the temperance movement however, now pushed matters to what I conceive to be an injurious extreme. Instead of resting contented with teetotalism as a cure for drunkards, they desired to impose the practice on all persons, however sober they might be. They argued as the Puritans did about theatres and promiscuous dancing ; that practices very liable to abuse, and which in fact are daily abused, ought to be stopped. They tried to show that the money annually spent in the British Isles on spirituous liquors, was as much as the annual taxation. They contended that if all drinking were abandoned, the health of the nation would be improved, crime would disappear, and poverty would be almost unknown. Surely, they said, it is the duty of every one to put his hand to so good a work. Every intemperate man ought for his own sake to give up drinking, however painful the first effort : every temperate man ought for the sake of others to give up drinking ; especially as to him the sacrifice is a slight one.

I do not wonder that these declamations made many converts, and particularly among those sincerely bent on improving the condition of the working classes. There can be no doubt that if the working classes would voluntarily give up drinking spirituous liquors, a great improvement would be effected in their condition ; and that if the middle classes, by setting the example, could induce the working classes to do this, they were bound to set the example. But I believe the whole structure of well-being thus proposed to be built up, to be just as substantial as the baseless fabric of a dream. My gardener, or porter, being himself a temperate man, accustomed to supply his wife and family with all the means of living they require, making provision against illness by a sick-club, and saving annually something for maintenance in old age, would certainly demur to any proposition I might make to induce him to forego his daily pint of ale. From the few pleasures he enjoys, he could not afford to surrender this one which he feels to be innocent. He might very fairly tell me that there was no comparison to be made between me with my comfortable carpeted rooms, and my refined amusements, and my enjoyment in books, on the one hand, and him with his brick-floored kitchen, and want of recreations, and uncultivated mind, on the other hand. The truth is, that men must have amusements of some kind, and to men of coarse natures, moderate eating, drinking, and smoking, are nearly the only innocent amusements at hand.

But if you cannot hope to extirpate drinking from among the best of the labouring classes, much less can you hope to extirpate it from among the more wretched and vicious of them. A remonstrance addressed to one of these, may well be answered by the eloquent passage put by Scott into the mouth of Maggie Mucklebackit, in the Antiquary. Monkbarns has been hoping that the distilleries, which have been shut up, will never work again in his time. " Ay, ay—" says the fish wife, " it's easy for your honour, and the like of you gentlefolks, to say sae, that hae stouth and routh, and fire and fending, and meat and claith, and sit dry and canny by the fire side; but an ye wanted fire, and meat, and dry claise, and were deeing o'cauld, and had a sair heart, whilk is worst ava' wi just tippence in your pouch, wadna ye be glad to buy a dram wi't, to be eilding and claise, and a supper and heart's ease into the bargain, till the morn's morning?" Most persons will say with Oldbuck. " It's even too true an apology Maggie."

I believe, therefore, that if the educated classes were entirely to abandon the use of spirituous liquors, the lower classes would not follow the example : that the more decent and temperate workmen would refuse to surrender the innocent gratification of their daily pint of ale; and that the more miserable could not generally cast off the use of that which, for the time, relieves them from their distress, and puts them on a level with the highest. A drunken beggar is just as happy as an intoxicated king.

It must be remembered also, that excess is not as injurious to a labourer as it is to an educated man. Scanty fare and hard work are excellent curatives: and the constitution made robust by steady labour, shakes off with ease, a debauch that would throw one of us into a fever. I do not mean to defend drunkenness on this ground. I cannot forget, that a working man who spends his wages at the alehouse, selfishly neglects his family, and that a drunken husband is likely to be a brutal husband. But still we ought to remember that the entire results, mental and bodily, of occasional excess, are not nearly so fatal to a working man as they are to his employer.

However, if these apologies were all that could be said against the teetotallers, they might fairly claim, if not a victory, yet a drawn battle. But I am quite convinced that while their aim is altogether visionary, the consequences of success, if they obtained it for a time, would be positively disastrous. And I could wish that all persons disposed to join the teetotallers, would consider seriously what effect is likely to be produced upon their own families.

A majority of men are married, and have sons to educate. All such men should hesitate before adopting the extreme measure of banishing fermented liquors from their table: and I suppose that few teetotallers take the milder course of abstaining themselves, while they furnish a moderate supply of wine and beer to their sons. But I augur very ill of the prospects of boys brought up to enforced abstinence. I am myself acquainted with the case of a family of boys so brought up, who contracted the habit, during the holidays, of running about to the neighbouring farmers, and of accepting by stealth the tankards of ale that were proffered to them. The unnatural restriction at home inflamed the boyish desire until it led to this discreditable irregularity.

The subsequent effects would probably be still worse. It is notorious that in the college, and in the mess-room, the wildest lads are generally those who have been educated by strict parents. An amiable boy is brought up at home with his sisters, kept in the country out of the way of temptation, and is wonderfully innocent of the wicked ways of the world. Or even in a town, by constant watchfulness, a boy may be kept in a condition of considerable ignorance of evil. But such a boy, whether town or country bred, must at last go from home. He is persuaded to visit a theatre: he feels that he has committed a great sin: his exalted self respect is thrown down; and he goes from this supposed offence to other offences which are but too real.

Now what is the difference between this youth, and another who has been to a public school, or who has had a great deal of liberty at home? The difference is a very simple, but a very important one. The innocent, home-bred youth has had no experience of evil; he has not suffered temptation; he has not gone through those gymnastics of the mind which harden it into fortitude; he is still in the gristle; and when he is called to fight the battle of life, he is stricken down by the temptations which he has not learned by experience to combat.

But I conceive that a boy brought up in the practice of total abstinence, is exposed to the dangers I have pointed out. He has been accustomed to abstain from drinking, but he has not undergone the temptation of drinking too much. So long as he usually lived at home, shame would prevent him from taking wine or beer, when he was visiting his friends. His companion in the visit, lying under no restriction, takes, perhaps, rather too much: but he pays the penalty in a headache next morning, or in a rebuke from his father. The next time he goes out he is more cautious, and effectually resists temptation. This is just the training that most of us have gone through, and with most of us the training has ended by giving us a power of self-restraint, that enables us generally to achieve moderation. But the unfortunate youth who has been cut off from this process during his boyhood, enters on real life under the necessity of learning in manhood the alphabet of practical morality.

Many teetotallers talk as if total abstinence were the highest virtue. To my judgment it seems that there is a higher virtue than this: I mean moderation. Dr. Johnson could abstain from wine altogether, but could not achieve moderation: for that reason he abstained. And this is the essential advantage of teetotalism as applied to drunkards: these men can abstain, but they cannot be moderate. It seems then, that abstinence is less difficult than moderation. And which virtue will you rather inculcate in your son: the more easy or the more difficult? For my own part, I answer, I will teach my son the more difficult. When a man is being prepared for the performance of a feat of bodily strength or activity, he is taught to do something more than the required feat. He is exercised in running up hill, although the contested race is to come off on level ground: he takes his training walk, encumbered with heavy clothes, although he will be allowed to cast these off in his final contest. A tutor at Cambridge, preparing a man for his final examination, will set him a heavier paper than he is likely to have in the Senate House. So, it is far safer to train a youth to the more difficult habit of moderation, leaving open to him to adopt afterwards, if he pleases, the less difficult habit of total abstinence.

It may be objected, that I am training my son to drink, while you are training your son to abstain. This is specious, but false. It is not true that I am training up my son to drink: to learn to drink requires no training: your son who has never tasted liquor, will take to it as kindly as if he had sucked it in with his mother's milk. The taste for wine is not like a taste for olives, or a taste for smoking. Most boys do not like olives or cigars, and it does take some effort on their part to eat the one and puff the other. But unfortunately, this is not true of wine and beer. Some children, indeed, and even some boys, have an original distaste to wine and beer. But then, this is not a question merely of the palate. People drink, not so much because they like the flavour of their liquor, as because they feel themselves soothed and cheered by it. It requires no practice to enjoy the genial sensations that follow a glass of wine.

It is not true, then, that I train my son to drink: what I do, is, to train him to moderation in drinking, to teach him to exercise self control, to accustom him to confront temptation and conquer it. You, on the contrary, train your son to run away from temptation: and as the temptation will follow him through life, you expose him to a contest which he cannot avoid, and for which he is unprepared.

It may be contended that if all men did their duty, this difficulty would cease, because spirituous liquors would disappear from the society of educated people. Let us suppose that this actually happened, and let us see whether one very unpleasant consequence would not follow.

There is about the English, something of a severity of character that leads them to undervalue the lighter moral excellences. They at once recognise the excellence of the solid qualities; justice, veracity, fortitude, benevolence; but as to the lighter qualities, such as good humour, cheerfulness, facility of temper, they hardly admit them to the dignity of virtues. They dislike austerity and harshness in other people, but they scarcely rank them as vices. Call these latter qualities, however, by what name we please, they must be confessed to be very undesirable, and to greatly detract from the happiness of our race: and therefore, it must be allowed that an antidote to them is much to be wished for. Now I do not hesitate to affirm, that the moderate use of wine, by promoting social intercourse, and by giving a happy easy tone to it, tends decidedly to brighten the face of society. A man returns from his daily task harassed with losses and perplexities. He unwillingly dresses and dines out. He comes home at night refreshed and cheerful, and wondering that the ordinary casualties of the morning should have so disturbed him. But for his visit he would have been discontented, querulous, and the plague of his family. The slight stimulant he took, made him capable of enjoying the conversation, and of contributing to the merriment of his friends. I remember that once, at the conclusion of an illness, I went to dine out, perhaps rather rashly. My medical man, next day, said on seeing me, that the cheerfulness of my face told him at once what I had been doing. If we had physicians who attempted to minister to the mind diseased, though they could not pluck up a rooted sorrow, they would certainly prescribe society, and a temperate use of wine, as an excellent means of mitigation.

I have not a sufficient acquaintance with teetotallers to enable me to say on what terms they live with their wives and children. Among the lower classes, it may very well happen that they are more amiable and conciliating than their neighbours, because a large number of working people drink to excess, and suffer all the irritability of a crapulous state. But I am persuaded that among the temperate educated classes, the entire abandonment of drinking would be followed by a great increase of moroseness and ill temper in domestic life. I agree with the old Greek notion that the leading fault of old age is austerity, and that that austerity is softened by wine as iron is softened by fire. And what is true of old age generally, is, I believe, partially true of the English character at all stages of life. We have a nearly parallel case in the stricter sects of religion; in the Congregationalists, the Presbyterians, the Wesleyans. Men of these sects deny themselves many pleasures that other persons consider innocent. Eating and drinking, indeed, they do not deny themselves. But on the whole they enjoy far less of the lighter pleasures of social intercourse than fall to the lot of other men. I am assured by one who knows them well, that many such men are, in their families, intolerably morose and exacting. Depend upon it, we cannot afford to lose any innocent pleasure.

It is always well to remember what has been thought by other nations in other ages. We find in the historical records of the Old Testament, that wine was used and abused in a very early stage of the world. We know that the supposed inventor of wine was honoured in the East, as a God. We find Jesus Christ partaking of wine and miraculously adding to the provision of it.

As to the Greeks, a man would be very bold, if he held them up as examples for imitation. Yet we cannot but wonder, with David Hume, that so eastern, and so southern, a people, should be notoriously addicted to drinking: that Plato should even approve of the formation of clubs for taking potations pottle deep; and respecting which clubs he especially provides that their president shall be a man not in the habit of getting drunk: that in the Banquet, Alcibiades should be described as coming in intoxicated, and the virtuous Socrates as sitting soberly drinking all night, and then walking out to his daily avocations, leaving all his companions under the table.

One other remark, and I have done. It has been broadly stated that in places where teetotalism prevails, the sale of opium has greatly increased; and it has been inferred that persons oppressed by an obligation contracted publicly, and with God to witness, have resorted to the use of narcotics as a solace under a deprivation which they have found intolerable. I have no means of verifying either the statement or the inference; and I have learned to look with much suspicion on alleged facts advanced to maintain a controversy. My intercourse with the advocates of total abstinence has been much too limited to allow me to express an opinion as to the results of their practice.

But in one instance I have been very much struck with a circumstance that occurred. A workman was absent from his duty. He was a man of undeviating steadiness, a sincere teetotaller, and a rather intolerant advocate of the practice of total abstinence. I found on enquiry, that this absence of his was caused by his oversleeping himself; and it was explained to me that he had been unwell the evening before, that he had a habit of taking opium as a medicine, and that, probably, he had on this occasion taken an overdose. I have at other times observed the same man in a strange, dreamy, state, as though he had been unwell again. I confess that my confidence in the man was a good deal shaken, and that I should have thought better of him if he had taken a sociable glass of brandy and water.

We must all, I think, feel that this resort to narcotics is a not improbable consequence of teetotalism. If we had been told that men died young, or became deranged, or lost their power of work, or committed suicide, in consequence of total abstinence, we should have smiled and disregarded the statement. But the resort to opium we feel at once to be likely enough. We remember at once that Eastern people who do not drink, do smoke and chew opium or bang. And then the disagreeable recollection comes upon us, of what the consequences of opium-eating are. The temptation, how powerful! the opportunities, how frequent! the restraint, how small! the cure, how impossible!

Let those who are temperate in their drinking, who have learnt the difficult practice of moderation, be well content; and let them not be persuaded to sink into the lower class of teetotallers. Let those who have families, try to prepare them for the conflict that they cannot avoid, by training them to the art of self-defence. Let the educated classes place before the less refined, the example of undeviating moderation. Let it be well understood that total abstinence is an useful medicine for the weak and sickly in mind, but that it is no fit regimen for the robust and healthy soul.

CHAPTER XVI.

It is not possible to be indifferent to the habitual manners of the persons with whom we live: real politeness adds a great charm to social intercourse. Nor can we altogether disregard the demeanour of those who are our dependents, or who hold an inferior rank in society. It is not an agreeable thing to find a porter rudely pushing by us, or to have a butcher's boy thrusting his tray of flesh into our faces. But as in all similar cases, we are apt to be unduly impressed with the superficial evil, and we often fail to inquire into what is concealed below.

We constantly hear complaints of the rude behaviour of our working classes in towns; and the comparative civility of the village population is placed in favourable contrast. It is acknowledged that the mechanic is far more quick witted than the ploughman; that he is cleverer in his talk, and as to substantial services as obliging. But the country labourer touches his hat to every gentleman he meets, whereas the mechanic has as little reverence for a good coat as for a flea-bitten horse.

I have, myself, no liking for the careless disrespect that prevails in towns: I feel that the English dislike of ceremony, often runs into boorishness. But I believe that the town rudeness is the result of a higher social advancement than the servility of the country. The mechanic has shaken off the unreasoning reverence for his superiors, and he has not yet learnt that politeness is compatible with in-dependence. Nor, as I shall afterwards remark more fully, have the educated classes done their part in setting a just example in this matter.

I have been alternately amused and angry at remarks made upon this subject: amused at the folly and angry at the injustice. One writer, with more of the fastidious-ness of a polished gentleman, than of the kindness of a Christian priest, condemns the working people around him, because they shove him from the wall, and habitually use language unfit for chaste ears. While I can readily forgive the one offence, I much regret the other. But I cannot help remembering that a comparatively few years have past, since the middle and upper classes indulged in offensive and profane expressions. I appeal to any reader of Sir Charles Napier's life, or of Lockhart's memoirs of the exemplary Sir Walter Scott, in proof of this assertion, if indeed, any proof were needed. The popular expletives at present are no doubt singularly offensive, but are used with as little meaning, as were those profanities in which our progenitors delighted. I will not sully my paper with a record of the particulars which would be necessary for a satisfactory contrast; nor will I presume to decide on the comparative turpitude of indecency and blasphemy.

Every reader of Addison's Spectator must remember the censures that occur there on the habit of swearing which prevailed among our forefathers. The present genera-tion is the first which, even among the educated classes, has learned to speak strongly without resort to an oath; and the French still apply to us the uncomplimentary soubriquet of *les Gottams*. Yet in practice, the French appear to be far more profane than we are; since every trifling surprise is marked by the interjection, *Mon Dieu!*

But putting aside this question of language, and regarding only the outward manifestations of gait and gesture, there must be confessed to exist a certain rudeness of manners on the part of the English. This censure is confirmed by M. Le Play, a man who has been familiar with many tribes and nations, and who is unusually free from prejudice.

The constantly taking off the hat to a lady, or the touching it to a stranger, is the ceremony which distinguishes other nations from the English. Even in England, a gentleman doffs his hat to a lady of his acquaintance. But in France a man does not enter any place where a petticoat is visible, without going through the same ceremony: and if there be any one thing that, more than another, has discredited the politeness of the English among the Parisians, it is the forgetfulness of taking off the hat to the presiding goddess of the restaurants. The Speaker of our House of Commons is not more inexorable on that point, than those wax dolls are. I have amused myself, as I have sat in the room of a Consul, by watching the pantomime of a foreigner who has gone in and out repeatedly. At each entrance there has been the military salute, not addressed to any one in particular, but practised under a strong sense of self-approbation. Touch the hat on every occasion, is the foreigner's eleventh commandment.

Nor is this shibboleth of the gentleman, at all peculiar to France. In Germany it prevails to a harassing extent. Murray's handbook tells us that in some public places, there is a notice placarded, that gentlemen are there absolved from this onerous duty. In Norway, as Mr. Laing informs us,* the schoolboys are carefully trained to touch their caps to each other. It would be found difficult to induce our University undergraduates, grown men as they are, to be equally ceremonious towards each other. The *Englishwoman in Russia*, censures the servility of the serfs towards their superiors, but admires the politeness of the serfs in taking off their hats to each other. Sir Francis Head, thirty years ago, was surprised to find the rough Gauchos on the Pampas, retaining so much of European civilisation, as to doff their hats on entering a neighbour's cabin.

I am disposed to believe that the absence of formality on the part of the English, is more than skin deep : that there is a degree of roughness in trifles, which it would be well to correct. A person who has had competent opportunities of judging on this subject, assures me that this is far more true of the middle and lower classes than of the higher classes : that though the women of the educated middle classes are little inferior in gentleness and polish, to the wives and daughters of the aristocracy, the men of the educated middle classes have far more asperity of manner, and far less polish, than the men of the aristocracy. But we must go further. We must confess that as mere acquaintance, or as stranger travelling companions, we generally prefer an Irishman, or a foreigner, to one of ourselves. The facility of a casual acquaintance is agreeable, though we do not altogether rely on it. In

* Laing's Norway, 78.

our hearts, perhaps, we have rather more respect for the gravity and hardness of the chilly Englishman; and indeed, I have heard a gentleman maintain, though not perhaps with great earnestness, that a man who is very pleasing on first acquaintance, is seldom acceptable in the long run.

It is manifest, however, that the bluntness of our manners is not altogether owing to peculiarity of original character, but is partly the product of recent circumstances. When we meet with any one of an unusual formality, we call him a man of old fashioned politeness. In days gone by, a son was not allowed to sit in the presence of his father; and according to Morier, such is now the case in Persia. It is said that even in France, a great deterioration has taken place; and that in the Faubourg St. Germain, regrets are still felt for the chivalry which made a gentleman stand hat in hand, while he addressed a lady in the Tuilleries gardens, or on the Boulevards. Should such self immolation again take place, I trust that wigs will again protect the head from cold. In England, the habit of addressing parents as Sir, and Ma'am, has ceased only in the present generation; and in some families the custom is hardly yet extinct, of requiring children to drink the health of every one at table.

Ceremony is fast losing its hold in England, but it keeps a tighter grasp elsewhere. In France, we are told, marriages are arranged with as cold a formality as ever; and men in that country who marry for love, are regarded with as much contemptuous pity, as those among ourselves who marry their housemaid. In case of death too, there is an amount of formality that is surprising. I lately saw an engraved circular to this effect.

" M,—Madame Vve. Sowlasse, Mademoiselles Marie et Anne Sowlasse; Madame Vve. Schmidt; M. et Madame Haye et leurs enfants; (with six or seven more lines of names and relations) ont l'honneur de vous faire part de la perte douloureuse qu'ils viennent de faire en la personne de Monsieur Victor SOWLASSE, &c., &c., leur époux, père, frère, beau-frère, oncle, grand-oncle et neveu, décédé en son domicile le 23 Mai, 1857, à l' âge de 72 ans.

" Dieu est non aide, le Seigneur est de
" ceux qui soutiennent mon âme
" P. S. LIV. 6."

The recapitulation, " husband, father, brother, brother-in-law, uncle, grand uncle and nephew," savours of a climax of eloquence; and the entire document has something of an old world solemnity.

Ceremony, then, though still lingering in France, has departed from England. But it would be rash to conclude that because a people is more formal, it is therefore more polite. I have lately noticed, in walking the streets of Paris, that in no place is there less consideration shewn for the feelings of others. To say nothing of the general indecency practised by well dressed men, an indecency more offensive to me than the idle unmeaning ribaldry of our working people, I observe that a Parisian turns off the causeway, every one he meets. With a lady on my arm, I have again and again been thrust into the carriage way by a man having the look of a gentleman. Indeed, I have heard it stated by an Englishman who has resided a great deal abroad, that the English are the most polite people in the world. I am afraid there is some John Bull prejudice implied in this assertion, even though we take politeness to mean, not external polish, but kindness in small matters. Undoubtedly, there is still some truth in the comparison made by Goldsmith in the *Citizen of the World*, as to the manners of rival nations. The Frenchman, says Goldsmith, walking with an acquaintance, and caught in a shower, offers his great coat, with the remark that there is no sacrifice too great to make for so dear a friend. The Englishman under the same circumstances, pulls off his coat and makes his companion take it, on the plea that he does not want it himself, and even finds it oppressive. If we suppose that the Frenchman performs his part with grace, and that the Englishman performs his uncouthly, and even with the garnish of an unnecessary oath, we shall see the difference between polish and politeness.

It is impossible, however, to disengage ourselves from the influence of urbane manners, even when we know that they are merely superficial, and mean nothing. The smiling face and the ready salute are always welcome : while to meet a mechanic in whom you feel a real interest, whom you know to be substantially obliging, but who slouches by you without the slightest recognition, is decidedly unpleasing. The importance of such peculiarities is, no doubt, exaggerated. I have heard an Irish gentleman, accustomed to much deference at home, complain of the surliness of our people, and boast that in one village he had cured it. But when we came to particulars, I found that the only change he had effected, was, that he had induced the men and boys to cap the clergyman, and to take off their hats when he called on them. I had a friend who so strongly distrusted first appearances, as to maintain, that whenever he found a stranger's manners particularly pleasing, he expected to dislike the man on further acquaintance. In another instance, a stranger, discussing the characters of my neighbours, expressed his particular liking for two of them, who to me, knowing their real tempers, seemed conceited and offensive. The forward, cordial, manner, that puts the stranger at his ease, is distasteful to others who have learnt that it is hollow and almost hypocritical.

If we get below the surface, we are often surprised at the result. A manufacturer had always thought of his mechanics as men with greasy jackets, smirched faces, and mouths full of ribaldry. On the opening of a new factory, he gave an evening entertainment to all his people. Their conduct astonished him. He found that with their Sunday clothes they put on civilised demeanour; that they could behave with propriety, dance, sing comic songs void of offence, and laugh at them. Soon afterwards a large meeting was held of another body of mechanics, for the purpose of discussing with the employers, certain trade regulations: the gentleman who took the chair, assured me that he felt proud of the orderly and considerate behaviour of the men.

It appears that in the United States, the outward appearance of mechanics is pretty much the same as in England. But the universal sentiment of political equality, considerably modifies the demeanour of the different classes. We are told that if a merchant in New York stops to speak to his carpenter or baker, he shakes hands with him on parting. I presume that, on the whole, there is on this account more sympathy among people of different classes, than there is in the old country. A labouring man among ourselves fears to give offence if he tenders his services;

but the *Englishwoman in America* tells us that a mechanic of uncouth appearance offered her his arm across a railway, and was not regarded as having done any thing singular or presumptuous. She mentions other circumstances confirming the well-known fact of the great consideration the Americans exhibit towards ladies, and showing that the labouring classes share in this chivalrous habit. Particularly, she says that when she was worn out with continued travelling, two working men spontaneously gave up their seats to her, and stood up for more than an hour that she might lie down. This kindness to the weaker sex is the most singular, and the most hopeful, of the characteristics of our cousins. Little as I like their tyrannical democracy, I wish we could get rid of the aristocratic *morgue* that taints our upper classes and their legion of imitators, and could attain to a republican simplicity of manners, without surrendering our constitutional subordination of ranks.

With regard to our town population, I do not see any immediate prospect of improvement in mere demeanour; nor am I even very desirous of observing a great increase of outward reverence to the middle classes. I have a considerable sympathy with the late Hugh Miller, when, speaking of his old confraternity of stonemasons, he says that they are a fine manly race of fellows, and seldom touch their hat to a gentleman. The *Englishwoman* seems to have been surprised at hearing the saying of an emigrant, that he was no longer obliged to touch his hat to a good coat. To one who regards all men as originally equal, any mark of social inferiority is galling. A negro slave, we are told, always salutes a white man, though he is ignorant what he may be; and this servility is a natural result of a base condition. But among free men, such a distinction of rank should not exist. An English manufacturer who employs a number of French immigrant workmen, at very high wages, was told that it would conciliate them very much if he returned their salutations on equal terms. But it did not seem to occur to him that it would be a graceful thing to do the same towards all workmen. I cannot help thinking that this is a point of some importance. The working classes know little of their superiors, except from their outward behaviour. If a mechanic caps his employer and receives an ungracious nod in return, he is apt to dispute the pre-eminence so assumed: he remembers, perhaps, that the great man was himself once a workman, or that his father or grandfather was such: or at any rate he reflects that the employer and the labourer are both of them men, deriving life from the same source, fed with the same food, subject to the same diseases, destined to the same death. Christian and Jew, labourer and master, have a common origin and a common end. Granting a more exalted rank, a longer purse, a greater political influence, superior refinement of education, a wider extent of knowledge; how should the man of better taste shew his higher worth, but by more marked politeness? No man, according to Christian morality, should assume even the place he knows to be his due. Let the educated classes abandon their assumption of superiority, and the working classes will abandon their envious and rude demeanour.

CHAPTER XVII.

I PROPOSE in this chapter, to consider the relation in which the working man stands to his superior in Europe generally. We are so accustomed to see the labouring classes among ourselves employed by capitalists, and paid wages either by the day or by the piece, that we are apt to lose sight of the fact that the organization elsewhere is quite different. One circumstance, indeed, we do not forget; that multitudes of human beings, in other countries, are in bondage, and work, not as among ourselves in the hope of earning a subsistence, but upon compulsion and under fear of stripes.

We are told, however, that when labourers are not slaves they often work, not for wages, but under inducements of a different kind. We are assured that running over the principal countries of the world, we shall find the relation of capitalist and labourer, with wages as the reward, to be the exception and not the rule.

Russia forms a large portion of Europe. The towns there are few. In the country the labourers are not slaves, but serfs: they generally work for their seigneurs under an arrangement like that of the old French Corvée. In France the townspeople, no doubt, are paid as ours are: but the towns are not populous like ours. In the country, a good many work for wages, but the land is so split

up into small properties cultivated by the owner and his
family, that the organisation of farmer and labourers is
comparatively rare. In Germany, too, it appears that there
are a great many small properties. In Spain we shall see
that the ancient *metayer* system still exists. If we go to the
United States and confine ourselves to the north and west
where slavery has been abolished, we find men cultivating
their own farms with the help of their sons, and to some
extent, no doubt, with the help of labourers on wages. We
may conclude that in towns, men generally labour for wages,
as is the case even in Russia; but that in farming pursuits
many other arrangements prevail.

I have no wish at present to say anything of mechanics
or other workmen in towns: I will confine my remarks
to the organization of labour in rural pursuits among
persons employed on the land.

The country with whose former state we are best
acquainted, is France. The Revolution of 1789, with the
discussions that preceded and followed it, brought into
a strong light the condition of the working classes, the
oppressions heaped upon them, the misery they suffered.
The schedules of grievances sent up to the Assembly in
Paris, revealed the evils that existed, and the remedies that
suggested themselves to the minds of the sufferers, and
their friends. The aggregate of these schedules furnished
a detailed picture of society in every corner of France. It
happens also, that some other information of a very trustworthy kind, is added to this. Most persons have heard
of Arthur Young, the Suffolk farmer, but few persons know
much more than the name. He wrote a very valuable
work, relating an agricultural tour that he took in Ireland,

another similar work on the North of England; and just at the date of the Revolution of 1789, one on France. The French themselves fully appreciate the value of the tour in France; and M. De Tocqueville in his recent work has made good use of Young.

We find that up to the year 1789, a very small portion of France was cultivated on the principles that prevailed then among ourselves, just as they prevail now. An English gentleman having bought, or inherited, an estate, does not think of farming it himself, or of furnishing capital to another person as a means of farming it. He may, as an amusement, hold a hundred or two hundred acres in his own hands; or he may establish a model farm with the hope of improving the agriculture of the district. But if he wishes merely to get an income from his land, he lets it to one or more farmers, and these find all the cattle, implements, seed, and other floating capital. In France, however, the custom was quite different. A landowner who was desirous of adopting the English practice, was unable to do it, because he could not find tenants. France did not possess a race of substantial farmers with capital of their own; and the peasants who saved money were afraid of using it in stocking a farm, because this visible property would have been exposed to all the rapacity of the farmer of taxes. It was inevitable therefore, that French land should be cultivated on different principles.

The prevailing system, we find, was that of the metayers, by which the landlord furnished the capital and the metayer furnished the labour : the landlord and the metayer dividing the produce between them. Arthur Young gives an interesting account of the results.*

" Metayers. This is the tenure under which, perhaps, seven-eighths of the lands of France are held; it pervades almost every part of Sologne, Berry, &c., &c. . . . . In Champagne there are many at tier franc, which is the third of the produce, but in general it is half. The land-lord commonly finds half the cattle and half the seed; and the metayer finds labour, implements, and taxes; but in some districts the landlord bears a share of these. Near Falaise, in Normandy, I found metayers, where they should least of all be looked for, on the farms which gentlemen keep in their own hands; the consequence there is, that every gentleman's farm must be precisely the worst cultivated of all the neighbourhood : this disgraceful circumstance needs no comment. At Nangis in the Isle of France, I met with an agreement for the landlord to furnish live stock, implements, harness, and taxes; the metayer found labour and his own capitation tax :—the landlord repaired the house and gates; the metayer the windows :—the landlord provided seed the first year; the metayer the last; in the intervening years they supply half and half. Produce sold for money is divided. Butter and cheese used in the metayer's family, to any amount, compounded for at 5s. a cow. In the Bourbonnois the landlord finds all sorts of live stock, yet the metayer sells, changes, and buys at his will; the steward keeping an account of these mutations, for the landlord has half the produce of sales,

* Young's France, 1, 403.

and pays half the purchases. The tenant carts the landlord's half of the corn to the barn of the château, and comes again to take the straw. The consequences of this absurd system are striking; land which in England would let at ten shillings, pays about 2s. 6d. for both land and live stock."

This account given by Arthur Young is a very striking one, and seems decisive against this former system. It must be borne in mind, however, that Young had the fault which is very common among practical men: he was rather one sided. We may suppose it possible, therefore, that something might be said on the other side, so far at any rate, as to qualify the statement he makes. For instance, he leads his readers to suppose that the difference of rent in England and in France, is owing to this practice of farming by metayers: but no one knew better than he did that at this very time the whole social system of France was out of joint; and that the exaction of feudal rights, the oppression by the farmers of taxes, and many other causes, concurred in hindering the progress of industry, and therefore in reducing the productions of farming and the income from land. Young himself states elsewhere * that the real deficiency in France, was as to men capable of becoming tenants, such as are found in England. If a race of substantial farmers could have been created, with sufficient capital to stock the land, the owners would have been glad to give up the farms to them. We are apt to imagine of this old metayer practice, that it was the result of ignorance and prejudice on the part of the

* Young's France, 2. 165.

landlords: but it appears that it was the result of necessity. If tenants possessed of capital had been at hand, and had been refused the use of farms, that would have been the fault of the landowners: but as no such tenants were within reach, the landowners had no alternative but to find capital for the best peasants at command, or to find part of the capital for such peasants as had some of their own.

I do not doubt that our own system of tenant farmers on money rents, is a far better one than the old system of metairies: that it results in far higher farming, in greater productiveness, in an increased net produce, in more independence on the part of the tenant, and in an augmented income to the landlord. But with regard to the principle on which the metayer system is founded, I cannot join in the ridicule which has been lavished upon it by many writers. A French gentleman of the old régime was desirous of letting an estate, which, perhaps, he had reclaimed from the waste. He had no means of obtaining by advertisement, or through private channels, farmers possessed of sufficient capital and enterprise to take the land on a money or corn rent. He must either farm his estate himself, or arrange with a metayer, according to the custom of the country. Suppose he determined to hold the estate in his own hands, and to have a bailiff under him. He might find, after a time, that the bailiff took less interest in his business than might be wished; that he performed his duty in a perfunctory, slovenly, manner. It might suggest itself, that if the bailiff had a money interest given him, this would sharpen his attention. The landlord might say to his bailiff; I will continue to find live stock, implements and harness, and to pay the taxes: but instead of giving you a franc a day for wages, I will divide the produce of the farm with you: as I find the land, buildings, and floating capital, while you only give your labour, I will take two thirds of the produce for rent and profit, while you shall have the remaining third as wages. Afterwards, if the bailiff saved money, or if another person possessed of some money, offered to take the situation, the arrangement might be so far altered, that the landlord and the bailiff should each find half the stock; that the landlord, in consideration of his furnishing the land and half the stock, should take half the produce, while the bailiff, in consideration of his furnishing his own labour and half the stock, should take the remaining half of the produce. But the bailiff is now become a metayer: and this division of capital and of produce is precisely the metayer system. Young says that under this tenure " the landlord commonly finds half the cattle and half the seed; and the metayer finds labour implements and taxes; but in some districts the landlord bears a share of these. In Berry, some are at half, some one third, some one fourth produce."

Now what is this but a partnership? The principal partner finds land and capital, and takes two thirds of the profits: the working partner takes the remaining third of the profits as compensation for his labour. Or in another case the principal partner finds land and one half of the capital; the working partner also finds half the capital; the profits are equally distributed between the two partners: the land of the one is set against the labour of the other.

I repeat that in principle, the arrangement seems fair, and one that under some circumstances might work well enough; though I have no doubt that for ourselves, the ordinary mode of letting land on a money rent is a far better one. All I contend is that there is nothing absurd in the metayer system. Indeed, it is quite in conformity with a practice much recommended by a large class of foreign writers of the present day. It has been strongly urged as a cure for the improvidence and misery of the town population, that every working man should have a share assigned to him of the profits of the business in which he is engaged. A manufacturer employing a hundred workmen, would have a hundred partners, among whom he would distribute the greater part of the profits of each year. The metayer practice was far less bold than this. The landlord had only one metayer on every farm, and therefore in each separate business he had only one partner. I can just conceive that a manufactory might be carried on in this way, and I can well understand that land might be well cultivated on the metayer system.

I have supposed above, that a French gentleman having some land to cultivate, agreed with a bailiff to take a share of the profit; and I have pointed out that the bailiff then became a metayer. If the landlord desired to live part of his time in Paris, he would then require some one to look after his interests; to see that the metayer fulfilled his agreement; to check the sales and purchases; and generally, to see justice done in the partnership. But even if the landlord lived in the country, he would probably prefer to employ a steward, in order to save himself the trouble of constant attention to details; and the more, because, as

I apprehend, an estate was commonly cut up into a number of farms with a metayer on each. A seigneur with an extensive estate, divided among a large number of metayers, with each of whom he was in partnership; and with a steward presiding over all of them, was just in that condition, I fancy, to which A. Young's remarks have reference.

Young's Tour in France took place just about 1789; and the Revolution that followed swept away most of the old and peculiar customs of the country. More than sixty years have since passed away, and have led to further changes. But this metayer system has still held its ground in many places. Feudal rights were swept off, many properties have been divided into small portions, but still the metairies continue to exist. M. Le Play, in his twenty-seventh case,* speaks of proprietors, farmers, and metayers as living together in the Nièvre. It is true that the word metayer has a secondary sense equivalent to our small farmer; and if this were the only instance in which I found it in this book, I should have doubted what was meant. But in another place,† speaking of the course of life of boys and youths, M. Le Play says, "Those whose intelligence and good conduct recommend them to the proprietor, are raised to the position of a metayer, and carry on farming operations for the joint advantage of themselves and the proprietor." The peasant boys have no capital, of course, and all the stock must be furnished by the proprietor. M. Le Play's Index ‡ confirms this construction of his meaning: he defines a metayer as a

* Le Play, 218. 1.   † Ib. 213. 2.   ‡ Ib. 299. 1.

colon partiaire. It is worthy of remark, that the metayer in Armagnac (the second mentioned above), is described as living in a state of abundance and well-being very unusual in the West of Europe, and more resembling that of the Russian and Hungarian peasants; a picture that will surprise many persons who think of Russian serfs as of overworked, ill-fed slaves.

M. Le Play gives another example of a metayer, and that is in Old Castille. He speaks of the system as still existing there just as in France. In A. Young's time it prevailed, not only in France, but also in Piedmont, and the Milanese, as well as in Castille; * and Young generally speaks with contempt of the results, though he confesses that here and there the metayers were well off.

On the whole, it seems to me a great mistake to confound the system of metayers, with feudal exactions and other ancient practices of France. Where a race of capitalist farmers is wanting, this system may be useful as a means of introducing them, and as a substitute in the mean time.

But there is another engagement under which peasants have formerly laboured for their superiors, and under which they still labour in countries where little advance has been made in civilisation: I mean the Corvée. The exaction of the Corvée was one of the grievances of the French peasant, and yet if we look at it as it really exists at present in the East of Europe, we shall find that, when properly regulated, it may become a fair arrangement.

It is in the East of Europe that the Corvée is now principally found. I will give a quotation from M. Le

* A. Young's France, 1. 402; 2. 151; 2. 153; 2. 156.

Play, showing how labour is organised generally in Russia.*
" In the west, the centre, and the north, of Russia, where
the soil has little fertility, and where the population, already
crowded, applies with success to manufacturing, mining,
and the timber trade, the seigneurs abandon to the peasants
the whole soil and the complete disposal of their time, on
condition that the peasants should pay a certain annuity
called the *abrok*. This *abrok* may be considered in many
respects equivalent to the rent paid in the West; it differs
from it, however, in being imposed not on individuals, but
on the community: the community being empowered, without the interference of the seigneur, to divide the claim
among the different heads of families."

" The Russian workmen employed in business, the
mechanics, the carriers, the tradesmen, the builders, &c.
in towns, almost all belong to the class of emigrants on
abrok. The prolonged absence of the workman, the considerable gains he can realise, do not wean him from his
family: the authority of his father, the right of his seigneur,
the enlightened sense of his own interest, a sort of instinctive fear of becoming isolated, as well as an affection
for his native place, all draw him back towards the little
community of which he makes a part."

This account of the *abrok*, or capitation tax, I will just
observe, puts the matter in a point of view very different
from the one commonly presented. It seems that the
seigneur gives up his land to a community, and receives
an annuity, or rent, in return. The community apportions
the claim to the different families according to their means

* Le Play, 66. 2.

of payment. A member of one of these families migrates
to St. Petersburgh or Moscow. If he should fail to remit
to his father, or other head of the family, the portion of
the money which he ought to pay, then his brothers or
cousins will have to make up his deficiency. If his family
should fail to make up his deficiency, the other families
of the village must make it up; since the bargain is made
between the seigneur and the collective village, and not
between the seigneur and the individual members. The
abrok then, paid by a trader in St. Petersburgh, goes
immediately to the relief of his village, and only indirectly
to the seigneur. Nor is this payment a mere arbitrary
imposition: it is a payment in consideration of which the
land is surrendered to the village. The emigrant member
hopes to return and share the land, or may be, he takes
a pleasure in assisting his family, even though he may have
but a faint expectation of returning to his native place.

M. Le Play goes on; " In the rich agricultural provinces
of the south and east, where men are wanting to till the
land, it is the interest of the seigneurs to give up only
part of the soil to the peasants, and to keep the rest in their
own hands, applying to it labour furnished by the peasants
as payment for the land conceded. This is called Corveé.
The general principle that regulates the Corveé, is, that
the peasant should divide his time equally between his
seigneur's land and his own. This régime is exactly the
one that prevails in the particular case here described."

We see, then, that in the south and east of Russia, the
peasant has allotted to him, a sufficient portion of land for
the maintenance of his family; that half of his time is at
his own disposal for the cultivation of his own little farm;

and that, instead of paying a money rent, or a portion of his produce, for the use of the land, he is bound to work half his time for his landlord. This is the corvée. We see that, as in the case of the *abrok*, it is not an arbitrary exaction, but a payment in return for a concession of land; a substitute for rent.

If we suppose that the population in these provinces went on increasing, until they bid against each other for the means of subsistence, and that the seigneurs took advantage of this distressful condition to claim this corvée without giving land in return, we can then understand what were the feelings of a French peasant of the last century when the word was mentioned in his hearing. The population of France had greatly outrun the means of subsistence, the nobility were generally absentees, living in Paris, and no doubt constantly pressing their stewards to send them the means of supporting their luxury and extravagance. The feudal rights generally, and the corvée in particular, supplied the means of squeezing the wretched peasants to furnish the palaces and gambling-houses of their lords. So long as the corvée was a payment for advantages rendered, it was no oppression: but as soon as it became a mere right on the part of the seigneur, without any corresponding benefit conferred, it became an exaction and a cruel grievance.

This corvée at the present day, is not confined to Russia: it is found also in Poland and Hungary. In Poland it has one peculiarity. I was talking lately to an English gentleman who has a large manufactory in Poland, and who is joint owner, with his partners, of an entire village. I jestingly charged him with being a slaveowner, a character detestable in the ears of an Englishman. He answered, that he was more like a slave than a slave owner; for that in Poland the peasants were free: that they can leave their village when they please, without any restraint on the part of the landowner: but that the peasant can insist on remaining in possession of his little farm as long as he pleases, the landowner having no power to displace him. This arrangement is highly favourable to the peasant, and makes him singularly independent. All that is required of him is to pay his customary corvée, his fixed number of days' labour, and after that he can go or stay as he pleases.

In Hungary, it appears, the peasants who were serfs, are now become free, the Austrian government having compelled the landowners to sell the small farms on which the peasants were living. The Magyars complain, however, that a great injustice has been committed in the mode of payment, the sellers having been obliged to take the depreciated government paper.

The quantity of labour given by the corvée, varies, of course, very much. The peasant has a farm, or a mere plot of ground, assigned him for the support of his family. If the soil is fertile, and the climate mild, a moderate portion of labour will be sufficient to raise the necessary maintenance: but under less favourable circumstances, the greater part of the peasant's time might be necessary in order to obtain the needful produce for his family. In the former case the landlord might fairly claim a large share of the peasant's labour, because he gives up to him fertile land of great value: and after the man has, by moderate exertion, satisfied the wants of his family, he may reasonably be required to devote his surplus time to his landlord. I have already noticed, that in the fertile provinces of the south and east of Russia, the seigneur claims one half of his peasants' time. M. Le Play tells us that in these parts of Russia the population is well provided with the means of living, and in the enjoyment of far greater abundance than is found in the more civilised countries of Europe. It seems, therefore, that the terms of agreement between landlord and peasant, are not hard ones.

It must not be supposed, however, that the landowner gets all that he claims as corvée. The year, after deducting Sundays, contains 313 days, and half the peasants' time would amount to 156½ days. But the number of holidays in the Greek Church is very great, varying from thirty three to forty in the course of the year: * the working days are therefore reduced to about 273 or 280; and the corvée is reduced to 137 or 140. In practice the corvée is still further reduced to 125 days, † which is a reduction of thirty one days from our number of working days in a year. Besides, we cannot imagine that a day's labour given to the landlord's estate, is equal in value to a day's labour given to the peasant's own farm. We all know that men paid by the day are listless and sluggish in their work, and we must feel that we could not work on such terms, with the same pleasure and energy that we exhibit when we are stimulated by the hopes and fears which attend us in our own business. My Anglo-Polish friend, who is familiar with the energetic, sustained labour, of Englishmen, speaks of corvée labour as comparatively valueless. Yet

* Le Play, 67. 2. † Ib. 58. 1.

I have no doubt that the well fed Russian or Polish peasant works with good will and patience on his own farm, and that he reserves his listlessness for his days of corvée.

One reflection suggests itself here, as to the effects that follow from different forms of government under varying circumstances. We have seen that the Austrian Emperor has interfered between the Magyars and the peasants, and at the expense even of some alleged injustice, has compelled the landowners to convert the serfs into freemen. I am not sufficiently acquainted with the recent history of Poland to be able to say at what date the peasants became free; but we must all remember what was said of that country before the detestable partition took place: that the aristocracy had a freedom verging on license, but that the lower classes were kept in miserable slavery. I can hardly doubt that the peasants owe their freedom to the Czar, the oppressor of Poland as we must call him. This liberation of the peasant is consistent with the policy pursued in Russia itself. We are told that at the accession of the late Czar Nicholas, an ukase was issued, forbidding the sale of the peasants from one estate to another, and thus converting them from slaves into serfs. We know that of late years the serfs on the Crown domains have been set free. In the history of the middle ages we often find absolute monarchs protecting the working classes against the barons. Like those monarchs, the Emperor of the Russias apprehends danger to his throne, not from the peasant, but from the prince; and he would be glad to elevate the serf into a freeman, the freeman into a substantial citizen. These modern facts confirm the truth of what Adam Smith said: " *That the condition of a slave is better under an arbitrary than under a free government, is, I believe, supported by the history of all ages and nations. In the Roman history, the first time we read of the magistrate interposing to protect the slave from the violence of his master, is under the emperors. When Vedius Pollio, in the presence of Augustus, ordered one of his slaves, who had committed a slight fault, to be cut into pieces and thrown into his fish pond in order to feed his fishes, the Emperor commanded him with indignation, to emancipate immediately not only that slave, but all the others that belonged to him. Under the republic, no magistrate could have had authority enough to protect the slave, much less to punish the master." So says Adam Smith; and the conduct of the despotic Czar in the East, compared with the conduct of the democratic government of the United States, furnishes a melancholy comment on this passage. The efforts of the Czars have been directed to the setting free the peasants: our cousins in the West, unworthy descendants of Washington and Franklin, are yearly rivetting the fetters of the negroes, enlarging their numbers, throwing obstacles in the way of their ultimate emancipation, and perpetuating that institution which is the foulest blot that has ever stained the name of the Anglo-Saxon.

I have thus brought forward the principal relations which are found to exist among the working classes and their employers. First of all in our eyes, there are freemen who are at liberty to work for whom they please, and to go

* A. Smith, 4. 7. 2.

where they please. At the other extremity there are slaves
as in the United States, who can be sold like cattle, who are
subject to all the caprices of their masters, who have no
power of appeal to a higher power even against the most
intolerable cruelty, and for the treatment of whom the
master is not answerable to any court of justice, so long as
he stops short of putting to death. Between these two
extremes we have serfs, some approaching more or less
nearly to freemen, others approaching more or less nearly to
slaves. We have seen that formerly, the ordinary condition
of a farmer in France, and I might have added in Spain and
Italy, was that of a metayer, who was a working partner in
a small farming business, in which his landlord was the
principal capitalist and the sleeping partner. This relation
also, still exists in France and Spain. Then we have the
more primitive relation of landowners with peasants working
for them on corvée : the landowner furnishing a plot of
ground, and the peasant paying for this little farm by working for his seigneur during a certain portion of the year.
This is the ordinary condition of the fertile parts of Russia,
of Poland, and till lately, that of Hungary. This arrangement might continue if the serfs were set free, only that so
long as there is a superfluity of land, the peasant would be
apt to leave his little holding and squat in the forest; or to
make terms with his seigneur, and perhaps get one landowner to bid against another for his services. At present,
the serf cannot leave the estate on which he is born, but
neither can his seigneur sell him from the estate. Besides
this, we have seen that in the less fertile provinces, situated
in the north and west of Russia, there is another organisation : the seigneur gives up his land to a community, in

consideration of a rent, for which the whole community is responsible : the members of the community determine among themselves how much every one shall pay; and the proportion allotted to each, and called the *abrok*, is payable even by those who migrate to the towns in search of employment.

But there is one point of general interest on which I desire to say a few words : I mean the right that is assumed by men, of appropriating the land to themselves. I have heard it contended by a gentleman of excellent education, that every appropriation of land by an individual is a robbery of society ; and that rent is enforced only by that right which springs from might. It is vain to say that the present possessor of an estate has come by it honestly : that he has inherited it from his father ; or even that he has bought it with the proceeds of his own labour. The question goes back further than this : how did the father become possessed of the land ? How did the seller become possessed of it ? If the father, or the seller, made the land, in the sense that we make a house by building it; if he obtained it by damming out the sea, or by embanking a river, few will dispute that he has a right to it. But what as to land that the hand of nature has given to men, fit for cultivation, fertile, requiring no labour to prepare it for the plough : what right have I to sit down on such soil and call it my own ? Now we shall find that this latter case is what happens exactly, or nearly, in most countries. As to the present time, among ourselves, it is useless to plead prescription in favour of actual possessors : if the broad acres of England were first appropriated by force or fraud, no length of time can bar the rights of society to reclaim them.

If the first owner had no just title to the land, he could give no title to the second; nor could the second give a title to the third. No one can communicate a title that he does not possess: and though it is quite right that in the eye of the law, long possession should be the best of all titles, it is equally right that in the eye of·natural justice no length of possession should bar the claims of society. Slavery, for example, is in some countries legal, but cannot be right. Is the appropriation of land in the same category with slavery?

If to appropriate land be a wrong committed by a landowner against society, then, to demand payment of rent is a wrong committed by a landowner against a farmer. But this can only apply to that part of rent which is payable for the bare unimproved land as it came from the hand of nature. If a man seizes upon a portion of a prairie, plants hedges to divide it into fields, cuts drains to carry off the surface water, builds a log house and cattle sheds, all these hedges, drains, and buildings, being the work of his own hands, are as much his own as anything can be. Few persons can be found to approve of the maxim that all property is robbery: few will be found prepared to deny that what a man makes, that is his own. It will be granted that the maker of hedges, drains, and buildings, has a right to use them as long as he lives. It will also be granted that if he becomes incompetent, or unwilling to use them, he has a right to sell them, or to let them on rent. No right can be clearer than this; that what a man makes, that he may use, sell, or let on rent. The question is only as to the right of appropriating the land on which these effects are produced.

I can conceive a case in which the appropriation of land is unjust, because it is palpably opposed to the public interest. A good many years ago, when the Swan River Colony was founded, a grant was made to Mr. Peel, of a large tract of country. He found that he could not cultivate it, but he did not surrender his title to it. We have since been told that this district of uncultivated ground has been a great hindrance to the progress of the colony, because it has interposed itself between the settlers whose farms were placed north, south, east, or west of it: they must cross this neglected tract to communicate with each other. To the natural isolation attending recent colonization, is added the additional isolation caused by this huge uncultivated estate. Such appropriation of land as this, is indeed a wrong done to society.

But such a case as this is not applicable to a well peopled country like England. And of the rent paid in England, how much is paid for the mere soil as it came from the hands of nature: how much for the outlay in enclosing, planting, draining, and building? I have not the least notion what are the proportions, but it is certain that of the seventy or eighty millions sterling paid annually in the British Isles for rent, a very considerable proportion is paid for the use of results of labour applied to the permanent improvement of the land.

Now this notion that land ought not to be appropriated to individuals, is not a new one, or peculiar to theorists of the West. In other countries it has been put in practice. M. Le Play tells us * that in Mahometan countries, it is

* Le Play, 24. 2.

held that the land belongs to God : that the occupiers of it are not owners, and have no title to any thing beyond the usufruct : and that the occupiers are entitled to continue in possession, only so long as they cultivate the land, and pay the taxes due to the government and to the priests. He elsewhere gives a case of a smith living under Turkish rule in Bulgaria; and he takes occasion * to state what he found to be the tenure of land in that neighbourhood.

We find, first, a remark that the tenure varies in different Mussulman countries, according as they were the original seat of the Moslem, or were conquered provinces. In the present case there are two classes of land, the dead and the living. The dead land is that which is divided into small plots with a cottage and garden. The holder of one of these little properties has not the disposal of it like the owner among ourselves of land held in fee. The Bulgarian peasant cannot sell or mortgage his holding. But he cannot be dispossessed of it unless he allows his cottage to go to ruin, and leaves his garden uncultivated for three years.

Farms requiring plough cultivation are called living land. Here, personal appropriation is less decided than in the case of dead land. In principle, this living land is the property of the Almighty, and cannot become the object of any kind of traffic. Yet in practice, a rent is paid by the occupier to a Turkish family, part being paid over to the government; and the right to receive the rent is hereditary. This rent is of fixed amount. It must be observed also, that the farmers of the land are Christians, while the receivers of the annuity are Mahometans. No doubt, in

* Le Play, 109. 1.

the first instance, this payment was a tribute; because we know from other sources that the Mahometans gave to the nations they conquered the alternative of the Koran or tribute. It seems that this tribute has now become fixed on the land instead of on the person. It is remarkable that the Turkish seigneurs have no right over the land beyond that of receiving the tribute and retaining a part of it for themselves. They cannot turn out the cultivator, they cannot prevent his son from succeeding at his death. On the other hand, the farmer cannot leave his land to go elsewhere: he is bound to remain and pay his tribute. It is agreeable to find as to the neighbourhood in question, that the Mussulman superior and the Christian serf are on the most harmonious terms. The Mussulman's hatred of apparent idolatry does not lead him to oppress his inferior, and does not even prevent him from exercising great kindness towards him: while the Christian cultivator has not the least wish to escape from his easy and nominal bondage.

Thus we see how the grand principle of the Mahometans, that the land is the property of the Divine Being, and cannot be allotted to individual men, is greatly modified in practice. And society could scarcely have existed without some modification, and without something very much resembling the assignment to individuals of property in land: For who would build a cottage and lay out a garden, unless he could be secure of enjoying them? Who would break up fresh land, construct fences and cattle sheds, unless he were persuaded that so long as he paid his tribute his farm would be his own?

It seems, however, that this difference exists between the Bulgarian tenure and ours: that the holder cannot sell, or

mortgage his possession.   M. Le Play is not very explicit on
this point.   And, indeed, among ourselves a tenant cannot
sell or mortgage his possession.   In the north of Ireland,
it is true, what is called tenant right is saleable; and I
remember being once told by a landlord, that one of his
tenants desiring to leave, asked permission to put up his
tenant right in the farm to auction : the landlord refused,
although he did not dispute the customary right to sell by
private contract.   But though the Christian occupier cannot
sell his possession, there seems to be nothing in the tenure,
as far as it is stated to us, to prevent the Mussulman
superior from selling his right to tribute.   So with regard
to mortgaging, it must be remembered that according to
the Mahometan law, the taking of interest is forbidden, as
it was forbidden by the ancient Hebrew law, and by the
human laws of the early Christian times.   M. Le Play
seems to believe that this prohibition is really observed
by the Mussulman populations which he has visited.
However inconvenient it would be among ourselves, to
forbid the payment of interest, however destructive even
of that extended commerce which is fast turning Europe
and America into one vast republic, which, as I believe, is
extending a civilising influence over Asia, and even into
Africa, which bids fair to abolish the cruel practices of
privateering, as it has already abolished the horrors of
piracy; however unfortunate might be the effects of ob-
structing commerce, by prohibiting the receiving and paying
of interest; it is yet very probable that Mahomet was
right in copying that Eastern law which made the receiving
of interest a penal offence.   M. Le Play has found that
among the small proprietors of Europe, the existing facility

for borrowing money, is one of the greatest curses which afflicts them.

We see, then, that even in Mahometan countries, land is really made to a considerable extent the property of individuals, in spite of the distinct prohibition of the general law. In England, and in most Christian countries, the landowner has still more control over his estate: he can sell or mortgage it: he can cultivate it himself, or let it to farmers: he can turn one tenant out and put another in.

The question is, whether this nearly absolute power over the land is properly assigned to the owners of it. Putting aside the difficult problem of abstract right, I ask, does the arrangement work well for society? Suppose that there were a different organization; that all farming land had been retained as the property of the government; and that the cultivators took leases, or held from year to year, as they do now hold of the landlords. We see at once that a serious obstacle would be thrown in the way of all advance. Where would be all the buildings, the drainage, the permanent improvements, that have multiplied the produce of the soil, and have made it support twenty-five millions of people, at least as plentifully as it once supported five millions? If any lover of centralisation imagines that the government itself might have done, what individual landlords have done, let him look to the crown lands, and see whether, even with the example set by private persons, the government has succeeded in making the most of its domains. I believe that there is but one way in which men can be induced to improve their estates to the utmost. Make them secure that whatever they lay out shall be their own as long as they live, and shall go to their heirs after them. Give to a nation perfect security of property, and that nation will flourish. But if a government retains the power of meddling with the possessions of its subjects, and of reclaiming them after a given period, that power will prevent the nation from advancing in the career of material prosperity.

I must guard myself, however, from being misunderstood on one point. I am no advocate for the extreme notion that a man may do what he will with his own : on the contrary, I accept, and entirely approve, the maxim that property has its duties as well as its rights. And of all its duties, none is more binding than that of assisting the sick, the impotent, and the distressed; the widow, the orphan, and even the able bodied man out of work. I entirely approve the fundamental principle of the English poor law; for this principle is, that no man however extravagant may have been his expenditure, that no woman however dissolute may have been her career, that no child though convicted a dozen times of the offences possible at its age, shall be allowed to die of want; nay that no human being, how detestable soever may be the character, shall be without such food, clothing, and shelter, as are necessary for life and health.

But this law is a very serious drawback from the absolute control which a landowner is supposed to possess over his estate. It has been justly observed that in Scotland, where indeed there is a poor law, but a far less stringent one than in England, a landlord may do things which are impossible in this country. If an English landlord takes any step that throws labourers out of work, those unfortunates fly to the relieving officer: the parish rate is raised: the tenants complain: and in the end the rents of that landlord are lowered. If a nobleman were to convert an English parish into a deer park, he would have to provide for all the working people. If he induced them to migrate to towns, he would have them returned on his hands whenever they became chargeable in their new abode. The law of settlement is a large deduction from the landowner's power; and is a very important feature in the English tenure of land, as well as in the relation that exists between the working classes and their superiors.

I have thus endeavoured to sketch the relation which exists in different parts of Europe between the labouring classes and their employers. I have pointed out that between the entirely free labourer and the degraded slave who is treated as the mere chattel of his master, there exist several classes of working men, enjoying different degrees of liberty and of well being. There is the metayer who is really the working partner of the landowner: the serf who is tied to the land, and who pays for his allotment by working a nominal half of his time for his landlord on corvée: the serf who in common with other members of his village pays for the use of land by the *abrok*, or capitation tax: the Bulgarian christian peasant who is tied to the land, but whom his Mahometan master cannot displace. I have pointed out that in spite of the Mahometan principle which assigns all land as the property of God, land is partially appropriated even where the Koran is adopted as the law. And I have tried very shortly to answer the question, whether the more stringent and permanent appropriation that obtains among ourselves, is advantageous

to the community. I have remarked besides, that the
English poor law limits very considerably the absolute
powers of the landowner, and carries into practice the
admirable maxim, that property has its duties as well as
its rights.

CHAPTER XVIII.

IN concluding my sixth chapter, I stated my intention to inquire what substitutes our own régime of Individualism supplies, in place of the advantages conferred on the working classes by the other régimes. Having now in several chapters given a selection of the facts within my cognizance, as to the wages, food, clothes, houses, and habits of the working classes, I proceed to fulfil my intention as to the inquiry I proposed.

First, as to the patriarchal system. Under this, the various members of the household have their tasks allotted by the chief. Every man, woman, and child, is supposed to be thus set to do the thing which can be best and most conveniently done at that particular time. If this arrangement were accurately carried out by a chief of experience, of intelligence and of impartiality, perfect cooperation would be secured, a proper division of labours would take place, and great productiveness would be the result. Every thing, however, would depend on the good qualities of the patriarch. If it happened that he were dull or partial, the advantages would be lost. We are familiar with a very ancient example of such a household, in which the natural partiality of the chief towards the son of his old age, kindled a jealousy in the other sons, ending in an intended murder, which accident alone prevented from being accomplished. Joseph's life was not saved by any relenting on the part of his brethren: they were guilty in intention though not in act. No doubt, such partiality on one side, and such jealousy on the other, are often repeated.

Now, cooperation and division of labours are certainly not unknown in our own organization: they are certainly carried to a much greater extent under our Individualism, than they are under the patriarchal system. The capitalist has taken the place of the chief. There, every man and woman among fifty persons, may be supposed to be set to work at that which is most suitable: here, every man and woman of a hundred thousand, or of a million persons, is actually singled out and employed on that which experiencè and special instruction have made most advantageous.

We are told that the patriarchal system has its superiority as to the weak in body or mind, as well as to the incurably vicious. If a woman among ourselves is unhappy enough to have married a man who is imbecile or reckless, she and her children are sometimes without resource. But under a more primitive organization, the wife of every member has been adopted into the whole household, and is not dependent for subsistence, altogether on the caprice of her husband. Whatever may become of him, she is secure of the means of living so long as she does her duty. In England, it is true, a woman deserted by her husband is not left to absolute want: and humiliating as is recourse to the workhouse, it may perhaps, after all, not be more humiliating than dependence on those who are strangers in blood, and who, one would think, would be apt to grudge the expense of maintaining the wives and children of others. But in most countries, workhouses and a system of parish relief are unknown; and a, neglected wife has no resource but the precarious one of private charity. I cannot but think that the European system of Individualism requires the modification which, in England, it receives by the poor laws. I agree with Dr. Farr, * that these laws may be regarded as an insurance of life against the danger of death by starvation. In other countries, Dr. Farr maintains, the absence of such a provision, causes anarchy, riot, insecurity of life, and communism. He even goes further, and maintains that our own poor laws should receive an extension of liberality: that in the case of persons of decent station who have fallen into destitution, something more than mere maintenance should be given: that in doling out relief, regard should be had to the previous position of the applicant. It might be contended, that a distinction should be made between those who have formerly paid poor rates, and those who have never paid them: that a more liberal relief should be granted to those who have paid them; and that such persons should be exempt from the necessity of becoming inmates of a workhouse. The payment of poor rates would then become an insurance against the extremity of destitution, as well as a contribution to the relief of the distress of other persons. I have not the means of judging how far such a scheme could be safely and advantageously carried out.

The patriarchal system, no doubt, affords also a protection to wives against the brutality of their husbands. A woman living in a lone cottage, may be habitually maltreated, and occasionally half murdered, without having any one within

---

* Registrar General, 8vo. 12. Farr, xxxv.

hearing of a call for protection. In an extreme case, she may afterwards apply to a magistrate to avenge her; but the rather frequent instances which become public, in which husbands have been guilty of outrageous inhumanity, prove that the fear of punishment is an insufficient safeguard. In a patriarchal household, the chief is the champion of the wife against such brutality. A few years ago, it is true, there prevailed a notion that the Russian serfs, notwithstanding such restraints, habitually beat their wives: but recent writers, even though unsparing satirists, have acknowledged the falsehood of the charge. If, then, our individualism raises men higher in many respects, in the social scale, it also fails in some cases to secure due protection to women, and is so far inferior to the patriarchal organization.

The régime of patronage also, has its advantages. Even slavery, the most intense form of patronage, does with facility what is accomplished imperfectly and with difficulty among ourselves. The children of a slave are a valuable property to the master: they are nourished and cherished just as a flock of lambs and a litter of pigs are fed and tended by a farmer. But in free countries, the children of the poor are generally a burden to their parents, and never can be regarded as a source of profit. They are dependent on their parents, who must deny themselves in order to maintain their offspring; and in the too frequent cases where the parents are deficient in natural affection, or in a power of self-control, where they are either dissolute or avaricious, the children are neglected and wretched. Old Hutton and his brothers, after the death of their mother, furnish a type of a large class: though they had a father of skill and intelligence, their occasional destitution, and the harsh treatment they suffered, are shocking to think of.

There is, however, another side to this picture. Our notions of slavery are derived principally from the United States. Now for a good many years past, there has been an immense extension of cotton cultivation in that country, and this has caused a wonderful increase in the value of the slaves. A child at present is worth as much as a youth formerly, and a youth at present outweighs a man of thirty years back. No wonder the young Sambos are made much of. A master can afford to be tender to the young and considerate to the old. But this state of things is only temporary, and is not a fair representation of natural tendencies. Even twenty years ago it was said, (slanderously no doubt) that there was gaining ground, a detestable notion to the effect, that the most profitable mode of using a gang of slaves was to feed them parsimoniously, to drive them severely, to work them out quickly, and to replace them. There is little reason to fear that such a scheme should be generally adopted, and still less probability that it should be openly avowed. Yet the time may come when such a scheme will be politic, however inhuman.

All will agree that slavery in England would be unprofitable. A farmer who secures the services of a free labourer for ten shillings a week, for just so long a time as he wants him, would be sorry to have to substitute a slave, whom he must buy for £150. or £200., whom he must keep at all times, and whom he could not stimulate to work by threatening to discharge him. The English abolitionists, seeing these facts, contended that the same rule would hold good in the West Indies, and sometimes denied that slave-owners were entitled to compensation for being compelled to do that which would increase their gains. These humane persons did not, or would not, see the difference between the West Indies and Great Britain: they kept out of view the fact that here the land was fully occupied, while there, millions of acres were inviting cultivation. If a wall could have been built round the appropriated portion of every island, and the negroes could have been kept within that circuit, they must then have laboured for the owners of the inclosed land: and in that case, the planters might perhaps have obtained free labour at a less cost than slave labour.

But the same state of things is being gradually produced in America by the process going on. To talk of North America as a country destined to be fully peopled, seems at first sight quite Utopian. Yet when we remember that in eighty years the population has increased tenfold, and when we run our eye over the map and observe that a very large proportion of the whole continent is occupied, we may conceive it possible that in another century, slave labour may cease to be advantageous, because free labourers will no longer be tempted by unappropriated land, to refuse to work for capitalists. Whenever this time draws near, slaves will cease to be a commodity of great value. The masters will grudge the cost of rearing the children, and of maintaining the aged: the supply of food, and other necessaries of life, will become more scanty: and slaveowners will then be unable to boast that their born thralls are in a better physical condition than the freemen of the old world.

This change, indeed, may arise in another way. The great value of the slave, and his consequent careful rearing, are results of the constantly augmenting demand for cotton, beyond the possible supply of it. But in these days of activity and of incessant change, it is impossible to say how long the United States will retain the monopoly of cotton growing that they have, in practice, enjoyed. It is said that there is far more cotton produced in India than in America; and that the real obstacle to an Indian supply is not the present inferiority of quality, but difficulty and expense of carriage. If such be the case, the railroads in prospect may render the East a formidable rival to the West. If any considerable supply should be furnished from this, or from any other of the possible sources, there may follow, a cessation of the constant extension of cotton cultivation in the States, a diminished demand for slaves, and, unhappily, a less careful treatment of slave infancy and age. No doubt, there would be preponderating advantages in this change. For the area of slavery would cease to be extended, the possibility of emancipation, or of mitigation, would be acknowledged, and the odious practice of breeding people in one state for sale in another, might cease. Our transatlantic brethren might perhaps be induced to discuss the feasibility of turning their slaves into serfs.

But what I want to point out is this: that in considering what substitutes we possess in place of the physical comforts alleged to attend upon slavery, we must remember that the good condition of the negroes' at present, as to food and shelter, is probably only temporary. It may be true that the American blacks are better fed than European whites. But when the demand for cotton diminishes, when additional cultivation is no longer possible, when the price of negroes falls to two thirds, to half, to one third, of its present rate; when planting ceases to be profitable, and thousands of capitalists fall into embarrassment: what will then be the physical condition of the slaves? Will these unhappy beings then be fed better than European whites? Still more unpromising is their prospect at that period, still distant, when the land of the North American continent being generally occupied, free labour will fast encroach on slave labour, though as yet the masters have perhaps not had the courage to set their slaves, or serfs, free.

The régime therefore of slavery, and even of serfdom, is in its nature transitory: and its advantages, such as they are, seem to be very varying in degree. There may be times and places in which the material comforts of a slave are superior to those of particular classes of freemen. But to make a fair comparison we must take a considerable period of time: and then we shall perhaps come to the conclusion that even as regards bodily wants, the freeman is in the long run, better supplied than the slave. We shall say that a man is more securely protected from want by his own industry, foresight, and resolution, than by the varying self interest and uncertain benevolence of an owner.

Besides this; when the relations of slave and his owner, of serf and his seigneur, successively cease, distinct institutions spring up, to supply the deficiencies that arise. In Great Britain we have a poor law, by means of which every parish becomes the patron of persons in destitution, and saves their infancy, their old age, and even their manhood, from the extremity of want. In parts of Germany too, a similar law exists in a modified form. We find some scanty information on the subject in the works of Mr. Jacob. Writing in 1819, he said that there was no compulsory poor law in Prussia; and he takes occasion to speak with condemnation, in the prevailing tone of that day, as to the practice of relief that unfortunately existed in England.* He adds that the absence of compulsory relief in Prussia caused an abundance of spontaneous charity. In the same volume † he says that there was at that time no legal provision for the poor in Germany generally ; although he speaks of workhouses.

In the year 1825, Mr. Jacob was sent to Germany under instructions from our Privy Council, to inquire into the existing supplies of corn. In the short volume which gives an account of his proceedings, he says ‡ of Prussia, that support for the aged and infirm did not press on the consideration of the government till after the abolition of the feudal tenures ; because before that measure had been adopted, the seigneur was bound to do what was necessary in that respect. At this time, 1825, regular taxation for such relief had not been introduced, though it was contemplated. Mr. Jacob adds that the recent practice of relief by government, had not yet lessened the sympathy felt by the needy towards each other, nor the benevolence of the rich towards the poor.

This case of Prussia seems to be one peculiarly fitted to illustrate the subject of the present chapter. During the

* Jacob, 1819. 217.   † Ib. 410.   ‡ Jacob, Corn, 2nd ed., 1826. 45.

subsistence of the feudal tenures, i.e., under the régime of Patronage, the seigneur provided for the aged and infirm. When the dependence of the working classes on a patron, was removed, i.e., when Individualism was established, the government was obliged to provide a substitute in the form of a poor-law.

It has always been the fashion among political economists, to clamour against our English parish system, and to denounce it as causing that indigence which it professes to relieve. Continental writers, many of them, still follow the same cry. But if they had regarded the system in its true light, as merely a substitute for the old feudal mode of relief, they might have taken quite a different view of it.

Prussia, as we have seen, found it necessary, thirty to forty years ago, after the abolition of feudal tenures, to put the government in the place of the seigneurs. France, in the last century, omitted to take this step, and allowed its working classes to fall into a state of misery something like that which the Irish fell into under the same neglect. M. De Tocqueville in his recent work, on France before the revolution of 1789, says * that, " under the ancient feudal state of society, the lord of the soil, if he possessed important rights, had at the same time, very heavy obligations. It was his duty to succour the indigent in the interior of his dominions." He adds that in Prussia the lord was bound to see to the education of his vassals, in some cases to provide subsistence, and to assist those who fell into want. But unfortunately, in France no such laws existed.

* De Tocqueville, 71 of Translation.

The nobles, deprived of their provincial power by the cen-
tralised bureaucracy which ruled then as now, were relieved
at once of their authority and of their obligations. Even
in France, however, this obligation to provide a substitute
for the abolished seignorial benevolence, was acknowledged.
It seems * that the General Government sometimes furnished funds to the provincial intendant, for the purpose of
erecting *ateliers de charité*, and of furnishing work at low
wages. What degree of competency a central government
possessed, for supplying the pressing wants of a starving
province, may be judged of by other examples of its prompt-
itude. A parish meeting, for instance,† was desirous of
repairing the church steeple, and again of replacing the
gable of the parsonage. Nothing could be done without
the consent of the " King's Council" in Paris. It actually
happened that a year, and even two or three years, passed
away before such consent could be obtained. A localized
and efficient system of parish relief, if it could not, by preventing discontent, have warded off the revolution, might
at least, have robbed it of half its horrors : it might have
saved the country from *jacquerie*, the châteaux from plunder,
the nobles from exile, the ladies from dishonour.

Just as a poor-law is the substitute for the patron, so
are friendly societies and sick clubs the substitutes for
communism. In another chapter, in treating of the improvidence or foresight of the working classes, I have
pointed out that such clubs are very numerous in Great
Britain, and that they have long existed. It is worth

---

* De Tocqueville, 72 of Translation.   † Ib. 91. 92. 114.

remembering, that every second family in these islands, has at least one member of a club for mutual assistance.

And these institutions have not been forced upon labourers. Of late years indeed, they have occupied much of the attention of benevolent persons; and the results have been an improvement of their constitution, and an extension of their sphere. But in the first instance they seem to have sprung up spontaneously, and to have flourished with a certain rude health and with little refinement. Any one who will wade through Sir F. M. Eden's rather heavy volumes on the poor, will meet with many rules of Friendly Societies; some of them furnishing instances of bad grammar that would have attracted attention even in late government examinations. I quote one example. It is remarked of it,* that it consists of forty-six heads, of which fifteen or sixteen relate to eating and drinking: and that " the order of the annual feast is set down with as much precision as the ordinances of the royal household."

" 1. Every member at entrance shall pay 2s. 6d., and 1s. 2d. every meeting night after, that is to say, every four weeks. One shilling shall go towards raising a fund, and twopence to be spent in drinking and tobacco.

6. No person shall receive any benefit from the box until he is free, which shall not be before he has been in the society twelve calendar months : if any person or member of this community does receive any pay before he is free, he shall be excluded.

7. Every free member being sick, or lame, so as to render him incapable of working at his trade or calling, shall receive

---

* Eden, 2. 210.

seven shillings a week of the box, but if he be able to go to work sooner than a week, he shall receive 1s. 2d. a day (Sunday excepted) for every day during his illness.

8. For the better regulation of the Society there shall be a clerk appointed, which shall act in conjunction with the stewards in conducting their affairs, and to attend every meeting night, who shall receive one penny of each member every quarterly night; and if there be not enough members to raise five shillings it shall be made good to him from the box.

9. If God is pleased to take to his mercy any free member of this Society, there shall be allowed out of the box £6. to his wife, or to whomsoever he shall please to leave it, to bury him decent, and in a christianlike manner, towards which each member shall contribute one shilling the next quarterly night following: and the friends of the deceased shall acquaint the stewards of the funeral, who shall attend at the funeral with twelve of the members, according to their turns, as they are enrolled on the register book.

10. If any free member's wife dies, he shall be allowed out of the fund £3. to bury her, and the same attendance to be given by the stewards and members as to a man. Whosoever refuses shall forfeit one shilling or be excluded; towards which every member shall contribute sixpence the next quarterly night.

11. If it please God to take to him any member of this Society before he be free, there shall be a contribution of one shilling from each member, and the same attendance as if he had been free; whosoever refuseth shall forfeit one shilling or be excluded.

15. Since vice and immorality abounds in this age, even to the profanation of the Sabbath, it is agreed that, if any member of this Society shall, on the Sabbath-day, play at peck and toss, marbles, shake in hat, coits, or any other gaming, he shall forfeit 2s. 6d. or be excluded; and if any brother member sees him so doing, and gives information thereof to the Society, he shall receive one shilling and the other eighteenpence go to the box.

19. If any member shall continue sick or lame, after he has lain on the box twelve months, he shall be reduced to half-pay for twelve months more, if he continues sick or lame so long; and at the end of twelve months, he shall be given a sum of money, according as the above committee shall think proper, and then be excluded the Society. Likewise, if the fund should be reduced to £10. it shall be shut up for six months, and all payments stopped.

27. There shall be a feast held once a year, which shall be on Whit-Monday, towards which every member shall pay 1s. 6d. on the meeting night before, or on the morning of the feast-day before he goes to dinner, on the neglect of which he shall pay 2s. 6d., or be excluded.

28. That the stewards then acting shall take care to order the feast decently, and they shall be allowed one shilling each for their trouble: likewise in the morning of the feast-day the stewards shall attend at half-past eight of the clock, to provide breakfast for the members, and to serve them with drink, on the forfeit of one shilling, or be excluded.

29. That the members shall be allowed no more drink at breakfast than twopence per member; whosoever calls for any unknown to the stewards shall forfeit one shilling, or

be excluded ; and if the stewards have any more than each man's twopence amounts to, they shall pay it themselves, or be excluded.

30. That all and every member of this Society shall attend at the house where the Society is held, on the morning of the feast-day, in due time, to walk in procession to hear divine service, except sickness, lameness, or being at the distance of twenty miles, on the forfeiture of ten shillings, or be excluded.

31. If any member refuses to follow the procession to hear divine service, hides himself, or stays behind, not keeping his rank when commanded by the stewards, he shall forfeit one shilling for every such offence, or be excluded.

32. If any member behaves himself disorderly going to church or returning from the same, to any member or members of another society, by pushing his stick at them, cursing or guiling at them, or challenging them to fight, or do strike any or either of them, he shall forfeit the sum of 2s. 6d., or be excluded.

33. If any member behaves himself disorderly in the Church during divine service, by talking, swearing, or laughing, he shall forfeit 2s. 6d., or be excluded ; and if any member stay behind drinking, and will not keep his place in following the procession home to the house, but come to dinner drunken, and not in his time to dine with the rest, he shall forfeit one shilling, or be excluded.

34. If any member, during the whole day of the feast, shall fight, or challenge to fight, strike, or throw down, wrestle, or challenge to wrestle, or cause any disturbance in the Society, while at dinner, or after dinner, till all the

company are dismissed, with any of his brother members, he shall forfeit 2s. 6d., or be immediately excluded.

35. No member on the feast-day shall provoke another, by calling him nicknames, or by guiling at him, or casting meat or bones at another, or about the room : neither shall any member feed another by way of fun, and wasting the victuals, to the shame of the company : any such things being done, those that do them shall forfeit one shilling, or be excluded.

36. That there shall be allowed no more than sixpence each man in drink, the first day of the feast ; whosoever has more shall pay for it himself, or be excluded.

37. That the stewards take care not to have more drink than each man's sixpence amounts to, otherwise they shall make it good themselves, or forfeit one shilling each, or be excluded; and if any private member fetches any drink unknown to the stewards, they shall forfeit 2s. 6d., or be excluded.

38. That no woman whatsoever shall be allowed to enter the Society-room on a feast day during the time the Society drink holds, whosoever introduces any woman into the room shall forfeit one shilling : neither shall there be any victuals given away the first day of the feast ; whosoever carries or conveys away any victuals out of the club-room on feast days, or hides or pockets any with a design to carry it away, shall forfeit 2s. 6d. or be excluded.

39. That no steward nor private member shall be allowed to give any victuals away on the feast day, but the reserve shall be kept till the next day for as many as please to come to breakfast; and then the stewards shall have liberty to give a slice of bread and meat to any member's wife

or child, or to any friend, using discretion, as they think fit; and each member that comes to breakfast shall pay threepence to be spent in drink; whosoever refuseth shall forfeit sixpence or be excluded."

Trades' Unions, Combinations, Strikes for Wages, form another substitute for communism. Political Economists have condemned these, just as they have generally condemned the poor-laws. In a previous volume, on the *Science of Social Opulence,* I expressed my dissent from these philosophical opinions; and my belief that men are justified in combining together, and in using all peaceable means, to keep up the rate of wages. I adhere to that opinion: I still believe that notwithstanding many absurdities and consequent failures on the part of workmen's associations, the rate of wages is kept higher than it would be if each man made his separate arrangement with his employer: and I rejoice that we have, in Great Britain, arrived at such a condition of political stability, that we can safely allow our workmen to meet together when, and as often as, they please, to fix the rate of wages they will accept, and the rules to which they will submit. I trust that as our workmen become more enlightened, the follies that have frequently disfigured their associations, and the violence that has occasionally disgraced them, will recur less often, and will finally disappear.

I need not pursue the subject of this chapter any further. I have pointed out only a few substitutes by means of which Individualism has tried to supply the loss of those advantages which attach to earlier organizations. It must be confessed that. the principle of Individualism has by many persons been much exaggerated. Such persons seem to suppose that it is a good thing for every man to act with perfect independence of every other man; and that all infringements on this isolation are derogatory to the dignity of manhood. They condemn, not only poor-laws, but every other institution in which the better classes give assistance to the poorer and less intelligent. It can scarcely be denied that Malthus, especially in his earlier days, gave countenance to this hard philosophy: and that even in his latest edition he reconciled himself with difficulty to the notion that private charity could on the whole be beneficial. The experience of half a century has placed this question on a footing quite different from that of the date when Malthus's opinions were formed: and I doubt not that if he had been born in the last forty years, his narrow creed would have been greatly modified.

This exaggerated Individualism seems to err, just as an exaggerated Protestantism errs. Some persons say, let every man read his Bible, and construct his own system of divinity: other persons of more judicious minds, prefer that while every man reads for himself, he should enquire how other men have interpreted revelation, and should not presume to suppose that his own unassisted mind could arrive at the whole truth, and could succeed in building up a system of divinity. So with regard to social economy: let no man attempt to go alone, and affect to despise the co-operation of his fellows. Let him rejoice as he pleases in the modern organisation, which leaves him to arrange his household as he pleases, without the interference of his relatives; which sets him free from dependence on a superior; which saves him from being hampered with common rights; which, on the whole, surrenders to him the most entire independence, and unlimited freedom of action. Let him, however, understand that man is not fit to go alone, but that he requires the cooperation of his fellows; and that he cannot dispense with the affection of his kindred, with the friendship of his neighbours, or with the beneficial influence which public opinion exercises on his conduct. The asceticism of many religious persons, and the exaggerated individualism of many thoughtful persons, lead alike to egotism and moroseness; and are equally unfavourable to that social sympathy, and that public spirit, which are essential to the progress of mankind.

During the last thirty years, there have been many attempts to adopt plans of cooperation among the working classes of England. Owen of New Lanark, Fergus O'Connor, and a host of imitators, have no successes to boast of. They seem to have all committed the same fundamental error, of assuming, that with the general notions of individual right that now prevail, it is possible to resort to institutions that require quite a different set of notions. It is the peculiar characteristic of our days to set man above the community; and to hold that state necessity is the plea of a tyrant. But this notion of individual right, and of individual importance, is quite incompatible with socialism, and still more with communism. In the East the head of a household labours, not for himself, but for all his little tribe; and each inferior member does the same: nothing belongs to the individual beyond arms and clothes. In the republics of Sparta, and even of Athens, the interests of every citizen were subordinate to those of the republic: it was thought no injustice to call on an Athenian citizen to spend a large share of his fortune for the protection of the state; or to banish the most just man if his influence with his citizens seemed dangerous to the public liberty. Among ourselves such proceedings would seem arbitrary and detestable. And the same ideas that make us condemn them, also render it impossible for men to throw their possessions and abilities into a general stock, with a view to share every thing in common, and to labour for all instead of for one.

We must be contented in our days with cooperation of another kind. The most hopeful feature of modern society, is the disposition on the part of the educated classes to assist those below them. No doubt, our religious and benevolent societies have much that is objectionable. There are too many trading philanthropists: men who use benevolent associations for their own private purposes. Some, with no real desire to see instruction extended, are forward in the work of education: others, with no religion in their hearts, are loud in the support of church extension and missions. Subscription lists, with every giver's name blazoned abroad, advertised in newspapers, and annually circulated, become mere vehicles of ostentatious vanity. We look in vain for the anonymous subscribers who obey the precept, that their right hand should be ignorant what their left hand doeth. All these abuses make some men sick, and others cynical. But persons of a more vigorous mental constitution, shut their eyes to the evils which are incidental, and accept the good which is real and permanent. Reflecting men, conscious of the mixture of motives in their own minds, hesitate to condemn others even when the apparent motives are of no pleasing kind. They are satisfied, if on the whole, a certain society is of a beneficial tendency: and they will not refuse their cooperation because some of their associates are open to suspicion or even censure. They will remember that a feigned and self-seeking interest in a benevolent object, is, after all, the tribute paid by vice to virtue.

On the whole, while I acknowledge that each organization of labour has its merits that adapt it to a particular time and place, I cannot say that I have any wish to see Great Britain retrace its steps, and resume either the patriarchal régime, that of patronage, or that of communism. For most of the benefits of those modes of existence, we have our substitutes; and if in some minor points those modes have the advantage of us, we are constantly advancing in our efforts to correct the evils under which we suffer. In one highly important point our régime has a great advantage over them : our condition is comparatively permanent, theirs is temporary. It is tolerably certain that Russia is destined to cast off serfdom, just as Prussia and the rest of Germany, just as Poland and Hungary, have cast it off within the memory of living men. Family communism will come to an end in the East of Europe, just as it has finally ceased in France within the last ten or eleven years. The nations, therefore, in which these primitive organizations exist, have yet to pass through a change, or a series of changes, before they arrive at the state in which we find ourselves : that is, before every labourer will be at liberty to establish his own household, to choose his own master, and to fix on his own associates in labour. We may well rejoice that, deficient as our working classes still are in education, in providence, and in self-denial, they are nevertheless so far advanced as to be safely entrusted with entire freedom of action.

APPENDIX.

NOTE ON CHAPTER XII.

NEARLY twenty years ago, when our registers were first established, the high mortality of towns attracted a good deal of attention. That deaths were far more numerous in towns than in the country, had long been known or supposed. Dr. Price's remark has often been quoted :* " it appears with how much truth great cities have been called the graves of mankind." It does not appear however, that the causes of this great mortality, were correctly appreciated by him; since he sets them down † as " the luxury, licentiousness, and debility, produced and propagated by great towns :" though in another place he mentions the dirt and crowding of Edinburgh as tending to the same results.‡ No doubt, the same general notion of the unhealthiness of towns, was commonly received; although as I have already pointed out, the eminent Mr. Rickman chaunted the praises of unhealthy Liverpool on the score of its salubrity.

Our systematic registry has nearly put an end to all conjectures on this subject : we know now that great towns are far less healthy than ordinary country parts. But one

* Price on Reversionary Payments, 2. 243.   † Ib. 1. 280.

‡ Ib. 1. 289.

objection long ago occurred to me, though I never fairly investigated it till lately. Manchester has far more deaths per cent. than Cornwall: but are the populations of the two localities similarly situated? That of Manchester has long been fast increasing; that of Cornwall has been increasing but slowly. Manchester has been constantly receiving recruits from the surrounding country, while Cornwall probably, has been sending out recruits to other places. But these Manchester immigrants are generally vigorous persons; commonly young persons; and scarcely ever are they old or even elderly. It will happen in many cases that these immigrants are married, or soon marry, and have families. The question then, is, how this movement of population affects the comparative ages, and therefore the deaths, of the Manchester or Cornish inhabitants.

Since the immigrants are generally young persons, and are scarcely ever old persons, the old persons in Manchester will be comparatively few. The Registrar General * in his first report, founded an argument on this paucity of the aged in great towns. He gave examples of the number of persons who died at 70 and upwards in different places: he inferred that where there were a great many deaths at an advanced age, there must be a great many inhabitants at an advanced age; and that as there were few such deaths in the great towns, there could be but few old persons there. That great towns actually contain few old persons is best proved by the census.

Number of persons who died at 70 and upwards, out of 1000 who died at all ages :—

Registrar General, 1. 15.

Average of England and Wales	...	...	145
"	Agricultural parts of Yorkshire and Durham	...	...	210
"	North Cumberland, &c.	...	198
"	Cornwall	...	188
"	The Metropolis and Suburbs	...	104
"	Birmingham	...	81
"	Leeds	...	79
"	Liverpool and Manchester	...	63

The Registrar stated these figures as a proof that London was more healthy than Birmingham, Birmingham than Leeds, Leeds than Liverpool. He assumed that the fewness of old deaths in Liverpool arose from the fact that nearly every one died at earlier periods of life.

Two years later * however, we are told that the above inference is fallacious; because many persons leave the great towns in their old age, and retire into the country to die. That the inference is fallacious I am convinced, but I think a far better reason may be assigned for its being so.

It is not disputed that the immigrants into towns are generally young people, who swarm off from the villages in search of a new hive. A youth of 20 comes into Manchester: it will be fifty years before he can attain the age of 70. At the date of the first report (1839) the Manchester immigrants who had come in at 20, must have migrated in the year 1789, in order to have attained the age of 70: and all immigrants of 20, since the year 1789, would be under 70 years old. But most of the

* Registrar General, 3. 13.

increase in the population of Manchester has taken place since 1789, and therefore most of the immigrants of 20 years old, would in 1839 be under 70. I am not aware of the precise numbers living in Manchester in 1789; but only 16 years earlier, in 1773, they are stated * as 27,000, including Salford; and it cannot be doubted that in 1789 the population of Manchester itself was only an eighth or tenth of what it is now. A large proportion of this extraordinary augmentation is owing to immigration of young persons, and of immigration at so recent a period that those young persons have not had time to become elderly. This accounts for the low numbers of people of 70 and upwards, in towns that have increased rapidly.

There may seem to be another reason why the population of such towns should on the average be far younger than that of the country parts. If it is true that most immigrants are young persons, there will be a large proportion who are either married when they arrive, or who marry a few years afterwards. It might be expected therefore that there would be a great many children in growing towns. Besides this : an increasing population is generally a prosperous one ; and for that reason early marriages and numerous families might be looked for.

On these grounds, the statement as to the unhealthiness of towns might to some extent be impugned. It might be contended that the different ages of the town and country population, throw a doubt on the inferences drawn from the registers of deaths. True, it may be said, more persons die in a town, than in a country parish, con-

* Eden, Poor, 2. 356.

taining an equal number of souls; but the different ages of the inhabitants of the town and of the country parish, may account for this without supposing greater unhealthiness. For no fact is better established than this: that there are far more deaths among a thousand infants than among a thousand adults. If then it be true that there are more children born in a town than in a country parish of equal numbers, it must be expected that there should be a greater mortality in the town, even though it were as healthy as the country. Particular cases are conceivable, in which a great difference in the number of deaths might be thus accounted for. The deaths among young children are in truth, very numerous even now, in spite of increased care and improved medical practice. According to Simpson,[*] the deaths formerly, in London, among 1000 infants during their first year, were no less then 320, or nearly one-third of the whole: according to Price, similar deaths at Northampton, were 257 in a thousand: according to Heysham, they were at Carlisle only 154. In the Registrar General's 5th Report,[†] Dr. Farr makes the infant deaths 174 in the 1000 during the first year. This number is very high if we compare it with the number of deaths at other ages:[‡] with 5 to 10 years old, 9 in 1000; 10 to 15 years old, 5 in 1000; 15 to 25 years old, 8 in 1000. We may imagine a particular colony in which there were 1000 infants under a year old, and 3000 other persons. According to our English rate, out of the 1000 infants 174 would die in a year; and if none of the other colonists

---

[*] M. C. Commercial Dictionary, 1840. 725.

[†] Registrar General, 5. xii. [‡] Ib. 8 vo., 14. xvi.

perished, the deaths in the community would be **174** out
of 4000 persons, or about 43 in the 1000: a mortality
exceeding that of our worst districts except under peculiar
visitations. Another colony having also 4000 souls, might
possibly for a short time be without young children, and
might consist of persons from 5 to 30 years old. If this
second colony lost during a year only half as many lives as
the former colony, it would naturally be set down as far
healthier than the former. The second colony loses 87
out of a population of 4000, or something under the English
rate for the whole kingdom. But in England a community
aged from 5 to 30 would not lose on an average more than
8 or 9 in a 1000, and at that rate the second colony ought
to lose in a year only 34 instead of 87 that it does lose.
Therefore, judged by the English standard, the first colony
losing 174 infants and no other persons, is remarkably
healthy; and the second colony losing only half 174, but
losing that number from adults, is very unhealthy.

I have given this case simply as an illustration of a
principle. I have been desirous of shewing that the ages
of the deaths, as well as their number, ought to be taken
into account, in comparing place with place, or year with
year. I by no means assert that the two colonies represent town and country among ourselves. Even if it were
true that infant deaths were far more numerous in towns,
we should still have, in estimating comparative healthiness,
to take into account the superior numbers of aged deaths
in the country. We have already seen that in Liverpool and
Manchester, only 63 persons of 70 years and upwards, die
annually, against 210 of a certain agricultural district. But
at an advanced age, life becomes as precarious as it is in

infancy: a death at 85 years old ought to count for about as much as one under a year old: a death at 72 ought to count for about as much as one from 1 to 2 years old. And the number of deaths at 70 and upwards is far more considerable than we should have thought, if it is really true that in the agricultural parts of Yorkshire and Durham already alluded to, more than one-fifth of the whole deaths take place at 70 and upwards.

This comparison of town and country could only be made formerly by estimate and conjecture. Dr. Price * thought that the real mortality of towns was greater, and not less, than that indicated by the number of deaths: he imagined that deaths on the average took place at a more vigorous age in towns than in the country. He stated that in consequence of the migration of young persons, the number of deaths in the London Bills from 20 to 30 is generally above double, and from 30 to 40 nearly triple the number from 10 to 20.° He appears to have thought that the flocking to London of people of robust age, raised the numbers of deaths above 20 years old, when compared with those before 20.

At the present day however, we have no excuse for trusting to conjecture, since we have elaborate observations to guide us.. First, we can appeal to the census, for the actual ages of the inhabitants of town and country; and by this means we can partly determine whether there is such an excess of young children in great towns, as to modify materially the mortality returns. From the census

* Price's Annuities, 1. 336.

of 1841, we know, that at that time, out of a thousand persons living, the numbers under 5 years old, were :—

In England (not including Wales) ...	76
„ Cornwall	71
„ Liverpool	76
„ Manchester	76
„ Birmingham	72
„ Leeds	70
„ *London*—	
Bethnal Green (very unhealthy) ...	70
Whitechapel (ditto) ...	82
Spitalfields (ditto) ...	73
St. George's, Hanover Square ...	116
„ Bath	102
„ Brighton	87
„ Leamington	85
„ Cheltenham	84

I have extracted these figures from the tables very carefully, and yet they are so surprising that I almost suspect my own accuracy. That St. George's, Hanover Square, should have a preponderance of infants, is astonishing: and the similar predicament of the old half-pay officers, dowagers, and spinsters of Bath, is marvellous.

This return is, no doubt, inconclusive: for it may be argued that the paucity of children living, is the result of the great mortality among them, and not of the paucity of births. It may still be true that the number of young married couples, and of children born, is greater in Liverpool

than in St. George's, Hanover Square, but that the higher
mortality reduces their numbers in Liverpool. This objection appears to have weight as regards any inference drawn
with reference to the results of migration: but it assumes
the truth of the opinion about which we are now interested;
it assumes that the number of children who die in Liverpool
is greater than the number who die in a country parish
of equal population. It leaves us, therefore, to conclude
that the real mortality of Liverpool and other great towns
is not so great as is indicated by the number of deaths.

But there is another point on which the census gives
us no information. We learn from it, the number of
persons living, and their respective ages, at periods ten years
apart; but it tells us nothing as to what happens in the
intervening years. Now we know that the marriages and
births fluctuate very much from year to year; and consequently that the ages of the population fluctuate very much.
On the average of the whole country, of course, there would
be far greater steadiness than in any particular place. If
then, we find an increase in the returns of mortality of a
particular town, we naturally ask whether this increase has
taken place among the young, or among those of robust
ages. During a time of prosperity we may expect more
marriages, more births, and therefore a considerable increase
of young deaths, and an apparently unfavourable mortality
return. Do young deaths preponderate in such a case, to
such an extent as to add to the numerical more than to
the real mortality ?

The following is a return of births, marriages and deaths
during some years, for the whole kingdom, and for Birmingham.

	ENGLAND AND WALES.			BIRMINGHAM.		
	Marriages.	Births.	Deaths.	Marriages.	Births.	Deaths.
1843	123818	527325	346445	1130	5161	3342
1844	132249	540763	356933	1222	5328	3885
1845	143743	543521	349366	1426	5646	3604
1846	145664	572625	390315	1623	5952	4684
1847	135845	539965	423304	1560	5949	5404
1848	138230	563059	399833	1572	6128	4658
1849	141883	578159	440839	1638	6389	3942
1850	152744	593422	368995	1745	6590	4056
1851	154206	615865	395396	1983	7157	4989
1852	158782	624012	407135	2006	7563	4567
1853	164520	612391	421097	2074	7546	4949

Observe the order; that the first column contains the Marriages, the second column contains the Births.

In comparing these returns, it must be remembered that an annual addition would naturally arise from the increasing population; and also that the rate of increase is very different in the whole kingdom, and in Birmingham. To make this correction, we shall not be far off the mark if we add $\frac{1}{7}$th. for the increase, during ten years, of the kingdom, and $\frac{1}{4}$th. for the same increase of the town.

It will be observed that the marriages were very numerous in 1845 and 1846; that the births of 1846 were very numerous throughout the kingdom; that the births in Birmingham increased steadily during the whole ten years, until 1853, and that 7546, the last return I have given, exceeds by far more than $\frac{1}{4}$th.- the return of 5161 for 10 years earlier. It would require much consideration before we could determine what effect would thus be produced on the mortality. The large number of infants would swell the returns of deaths: but on the other hand, the infants that had survived would, in the course of 5 years, have entered on a robust age: since it appears that of 1000 children from 5 to 10 years old, only 9 die on the average every year; against 174 who die in the first year of their existence.

We evidently want therefore, some mode of exact comparison. When we find that in a particular place 1000 deaths have occurred, and in another place of equal population 1100 deaths have occurred, we have need of some process by which we may determine the real value of the 1000, and of the 1100 deaths: we should be glad to put the respective deaths into a scale and fix their just weight. A sharp wind in autumn, may cut off all the dahlias, or even the chrysanthemums; but if it destroys the cabbages and turnips, we regard it as something portentous. So, an unhealthy season may be fatal to a great number of infants; but if it reaches to the destruction of many adults, we regard it as very severe. We want to find then, some means of distinguishing between the *number of deaths*, and what may be called *real mortality*.

In the course of English nature, out of 1000 infants born, 174 die the first year. Of 1000 children living from 5 to 10 years old, only 9 die annually: of 1000 from 10 to 15 years old, only 5 die annually. If it happened, therefore, in a particular place, that within a year 174 infants died under one year old, and 9 children died from 5 to 10 years old, I should say that the 9 would count for as much as the 174. So, 5 deaths from 10 to 15 years old should count as equivalent to those of 174 infants, or of 9 children from 5 to 10 years old. For what we want to know, is, not the number of deaths that take place, but the excess of deaths above the average of the kingdom.

If then, 174 infant deaths count as much as 9 deaths from 5 to 10 years old, we may express each infant death as $\frac{1}{174}$, and each death at 5 to 10, as $\frac{1}{9}$. So, we may express each death at 10 to 15, as $\frac{1}{5}$.

Then, 174 deaths of infants under a year $= 1$

     9 deaths from 5 to 10 .... $= 1$

     5 deaths from 10 to 15............ $= 1$

     348 deaths of infants under a year $= \frac{348}{174} = 2$

     27 deaths from 5 to 10 .... $= \frac{27}{9} = 3$

     125 deaths from 10 to 15 .... $= \frac{125}{5} = 25$

I subjoin a table of the average deaths in England and Wales, deduced from observations. From this it will be seen that of 1000 infants born, 174 die the first year: that of 1000 persons living from 25 to 30 years old, 10 die annually, &c. This must not be confounded with a table shewing what becomes of 1000 children born. It is true that of 1000 children born, 174 die the first year, leaving 826 living; but it is not true that of these 826, 64 die the second year. These 64 are the number that die the second year, out of 1000 children living.

Average Number of annual deaths out of 1000 living.*

Of infants under	1 year...............	174
at 1 year and under	2	64
2	3	34
3	4	24
4	5	18

* Registrar General, 5. xii.

at 5	years and under	10	....	9
10	....	15	....	5
15	....	20	....	8
20	....	25	....	9
25	....	30	....	10
30	....	35	....	10
35	....	40	....	13
40	....	45	....	12
45	....	50	....	16
50	....	55	....	17
55	....	60	....	27
60	....	65	....	32
65	....	70	....	54
70	....	75	....	70
75	....	80	....	121
80	....	85	....	167
85	....	90	....	274
90	.. ..	95	....	347
95	....	100	....	430
100 and upwards	....			419
Doubtful ages I set down as	....			40

It will occur to every one that these numbers are irregular
and apparently inconsistent with each other: but it must
be remembered that they are abstracted from actual returns
of many years; and that these returns are made by the
friends of each deceased person, with a very moderate
approach to accuracy. I use the numbers however, in the
present case, for the investigation of other returns, made in
the same way, and probably containing errors in the same
direction, and to about the same extent, with those returns

from which the numbers are deduced. I use them also, altogether for the purposes of comparison, and not as though they were absolutely true.

In order to obtain the real mortality of any place then, I divide the number of deaths at a particular age, by the number set down in the last table against that age. If I find that during the year 1846, in a particular town, 550 infants died under a year old, I divide 550 by 174, which gives me $\frac{550}{174} = 3.16$. I call 3·16 the real mortality of the infants that year. I go through all the deaths at each age in the same way.

By this mode I have computed the real mortality during nine years, of England and Wales, of Cornwall as representing a healthy county, of London, of Liverpool, of Manchester, and of Birmingham. The male and female deaths are returned separately: I have taken the male deaths, as indicating the results of the prevailing occupations as well as of the ordinary sanitary conditions.

I had intended to give eleven years, from 1841 to 1851 inclusive: I have omitted 1843 and 1844, merely because I have not met with the necessary returns in the Registrar's reports. I by no means desire to say that they are not contained in these reports, for it is nearly impossible to affirm with certainty, what is or what is not, in 15 bulky blue books full of facts and figures.

Real Mortality of Males in England and Wales during Nine years.

	1841	1842	1843	1844	1845	1846	1847	1848	1849	1850	1851
Under 1 year	238·18	253·16			250·12	301·08	283·99	278·01	295·50	278·09	305·39
1 and under 2	218·55	230·44			224·44	274·12	260·03	244·78	249·70	224·82	254·18
2	221·06	222·94			208·77	236·94	261·18	266·18	255·09	205·70	238·38
3	209·50	202·16			194·54	199·50	243·75	256·00	242·75	191·66	205·50
4	201·11	190·05			195·78	191·30	228·44	260·83	255·22	200·66	198·39
5 and under 10	1010·33	961·88			905·56	917·33	1084·00	1179·78	1288·00	942·44	1016·12
10	895·60	888·80			850·20	934·80	1017·60	991·40	1223·80	894·00	947·20
15	700·50	681·25			677·00	758·00	825·12	766·12	861·37	674·00	1617·87
20	737·00	720·33			762·74	841·56	913·33	857·67	962·88	716·66	
25	604·50	578·70			597·40	666·20	720·40	681·60	827·00	596·70	1253·10
30	542·20	523·20			542·30	610·00	658·50	622·10	777·40	551·70	
35	414·23	410·85			484·62	459·85	524·31	480·62	595·38	444·07	965·15
40	437·58	440·20			459·67	501·16	571·42	530·67	654·08	490·12	
45	332·62	333·00			355·31	382·12	444·81	410·19	513·69	383·50	770·82
50	333·70	325·82			332·24	352·24	408·24	374·65	458·82	366·41	
55	200·67	205·07			224·22	237·52	281·00	256·11	295·08	236·52	486·97
60	221·56	213·28			210·91	228·56	270·22	247·37	281·22	240·94	
65	127·43	133·78			143·98	150·15	170·30	152·35	167·37	146·85	267·44
70	109·00	111·61			112·01	120·62	141·37	127·96	138·23	123·60	
75	57·78	59·68			62·11	65·83	77·17	68·22	70·28	64·34	96·54
80	32·08	33·20			33·11	34·98	39·75	34·37	35·23	33·79	
85	10·37	10·23			10·70	11·31	12·71	11·04	10·88	10·28	12·35
90 and under 95	2·59	2·63			2·57	2·84	2·90	2·45	2·38	2·34	
95 and upwards	·58	·56			·62	·65	·70	·53	·53	·47	·49
Doubtful	8·50	6·80			5·72	5·95	6·35	5·47	7·10	5·00	8·15
	7867·22	7739·62			7796·64	8484·61	9447·59	9106·47	10468·98	8024·66	8644·04
No. of deaths registered	174198	176594			177529	198325	212426	202265	221801	186491	200500

Real Mortality of Males in CORNWALL during Nine Years.

	1841	1842	1843	1844	1845	1846	1847	1848	1849	1850	1851
Under 1 year	3·72	3·98			3·71	3·55	3·58	4·34	4·19	4·42	5·17
1 and under 2	3·36	4·70			2·98	2·14	2·55	3·50	3·33	3·53	3·92
2	3·79	6·44			2·94	2·78	2·44	2·65	4·03	4·06	4·41
3	3·42	7·96			2·58	2·12	1·50	3·33	4·04	4·00	4·71
4	3·55	7·61			2·44	1·56	1·89	2·67	4·39	3·77	4·33
5 and under 10	18·77	39·33			14·22	11·78	10·11	12·22	21·00	20·33	28·44
10	16·80	29·20			11·00	14·60	11·80	14·40	17·60	17·80	22·20
15	12·50	17·12			16·12	13·62	12·89	13·00	11·50	15·25	33·75
20	17·55	17·11			14·77	20·22	13·44	12·00	16·11	12·22	
25	13·20	11·80			10·40	11·80	9·90	7·50	12·20	9·50	18·20
30	9·80	10·00			8·50	7·70	7·90	7·90	9·70	7·50	
35	8·92	7·61			8·08	7·46	7·15	6·38	6·77	7·54	16·46
40	6·42	8·88			7·08	7·16	6·75	8·25	9·50	8·08	
45	6·56	6·87			6·19	7·31	5·87	7·12	9·06	6·31	16·35
50	6·12	7·18			7·35	7·65	5·82	6·71	8·35	6·23	
55	4·19	4·15			5·19	4·30	4·70	4·78	5·48	4·63	9·77
60	3·69	4·16			4·97	4·59	4·87	4·84	4·41	4·90	
65	2·59	2·72			2·41	2·46	2·74	3·37	3·05	2·92	5·25
70	2·11	2·18			2·13	2·47	2·53	2·56	2·79	1·99	
75	1·31	1·41			1·33	1·49	1·56	1·65	1·34	1·48	2·17
80	·69	·77			·59	·86	·81	·92	·77	·86	
85	·28	·21			·34	·31	·27	·27	·23	·20	·26
90 and under 95	·04	·06			·06	·06	·08	·07	·07	·04	
95 and upwards	·01	·00			·01	·02		·00	·00	·00	·01
Doubtful	·57	·02			·27	·15	·07	·10	·15	·20	·32
	149·46	201·37			135·66	188·16	123·22	130·53	160·06	147·76	175·72
No. of deaths registered	3181	3916			3049	3038	2926	3254	3510	3352	3832

Real Mortality of Males in London during Nine years.

	1841	1842	1843	1844	1845	1846	1847	1848	1849	1850	1851
Under 1 year	28·57	29·93			30·65	34·86	35·88	35·83	38·31	33·11	38·64
1 and under 2	35·56	35·70			40·73	36·48	42·58	42·41	46·58	33·44	42·87
2	35·03	34·47			37·47	32·00	43·32	48·41	47·79	31·26	40·24
3	27·29	29·75			33·33	24·87	37·46	50·08	44·79	25·79	33·08
4	22·83	23·94			26·00	23·22	34·17	48·89	44·17	24·28	27·67
5 and under 10	105·44	103·22			110·00	92·00	135·77	199·89	210·33	105·11	125·56
10	75·20	80·00			78·40	83·40	95·60	111·00	175·80	78·20	91·80
15	64·75	57·37			65·50	75·00	86·12	88·37	110·75	69·25	192·37
20	90·77	76·77			81·88	94·00	107·44	113·44	139·00	87·00	206·80
25	81·50	81·20			87·50	86·50	110·20	100·50	131·80	83·90	
30	89·70	84·70			92·50	101·40	108·60	112·90	146·10	92·50	180·15
35	73·77	75·15			82·38	83·00	93·46	91·69	121·38	88·69	
40	87·00	88·50			86·25	96·75	103·33	99·42	126·25	91·50	140·18
45	62·81	61·44			69·12	71·62	81·94	75·87	100·12	69·06	
50	61·82	53·76			59·29	60·76	70·06	67·06	85·88	66·06	75·10
55	34·22	32·89			35·29	36·44	48·15	41·44	51·26	37·11	
60	36·00	31·78			31·65	34·66	42·50	37·62	46·62	35·72	34·87
65	16·31	17·33			19·81	19·98	24·98	20·41	25·89	19·24	
70	12·91	12·70			13·04	13·57	18·26	13·67	16·83	14·81	8·95
75	5·48	5·41			6·02	6·55	8·54	5·91	7·16	6·12	
80	1·98	2·33			2·53	2·84	3·44	2·50	3·18	2·88	1·00
85	·65	·56			·70	·62	·91	·70	·80	·77	
90 and under 95	·14	·15			·14	·12	·16	·16	·16	·14	·05
95 and upwards	·04	·03			·04	·05	·07	·03	·04	·03	·77
Doubtful	·82	·60			·50	·27	·47	·27	1·00	1·00	
	1050·59	1019·68			1090·72	1110·96	1333·41	1408·45	1721·99	1091·97	1240·10
No. of deaths registered	23094	22905			24525	25122	29697	29413	34167	24634	28140

Real Mortality of Males in LIVERPOOL during Nine years.

	1841	1842	1843	1844	1845	1846	1847	1848	1849	1850	1851
Under 1 year	5·97	6·02			6·16	7·99	8·23	5·03	7·31	5·94	6·92
1 and under 2	8·08	8·50			7·23	11·09	11·73	7·64	10·26	7·77	8·48
2	6·88	7·74			6·21	8·41	11·85	8·41	10·41	6·74	8·12
3	6·92	5·37			5·04	7·12	10·54	7·46	10·33	4·66	7·00
4	7·22	5·33			6·89	5·22	9·78	9·28	10·83	4·50	6·33
5 and under 10	20·44	18·78			22·00	17·00	45·33	32·78	50·00	18·00	30·56
10	13·80	11·00			11·00	14·00	26·80	17·20	34·20	14·80	19·00
15	10·00	10·89			9·12	13·50	25·62	12·00	21·87	11·62	31·25
20	13·55	16·00			16·11	17·33	31·22	15·11	27·77	16·44	
25	12·90	14·20			15·10	17·40	31·40	16·50	28·40	13·30	34·50
30	15·40	15·90			15·50	19·80	31·60	17·90	33·80	16·10	
35	13·46	12·77			11·69	16·08	24·46	14·77	27·23	12·38	31·46
40	12·66	13·25			14·08	17·00	38·08	14·75	28·17	13·58	
45	7·37	7·31			8·74	11·44	23·25	11·37	18·81	9·44	19·82
50	7·41	7·29			5·47	8·53	17·35	7·82	17·18	9·18	
55	3·48	3·67			3·89	4·74	7·81	3·85	7·07	3·96	7·57
60	3·25	3·12			3·19	4·31	7·47	3·78	5·75	4·34	
65	1·66	1·41			1·87	2·41	3·07	1·63	2·87	1·68	2·80
70	·87	·97			·93	1·31	2·09	1·07	1·35	1·09	
75	·40	·59			·45	·64	·90	·45	·62	·45	·56
80	·16	·29			·21	·22	·29	·14	·17	·18	
85	·03	·08			·05	·05	·06	·03	·05	·02	·07
90 and under 95		·01			·01	·01	·03		·01		
95 and upwards											·01
Doubtful	·50	·17			·25	·52	·82	·60	·60	·04	·65
	172·41	170·66			171·19	206·12	364·78	209·57	355·06	176·21	215·10
No. of deaths registered	3852	3897			3816	4894	7022	4135	6457	3878	4551

Real Mortality of Males in MANCHESTER during Nine Years.

	1841	1842	1843	1844	1845	1846	1847	1848	1849	1850	1851
Under 1 year	4·56	5·16			5·12	7·15	6·25	5·66	6·87	5·81	5·87
1 and under 2	5·64	6·68			5·92	8·62	8·12	6·36	6·23	7·16	4·75
2	4·15	6·03			4·38	7·21	8·91	6·38	5·73	5·59	4·29
3	3·33	4·62			3·46	5·17	7·96	5·54	4·00	4·66	3·33
4	4·00	4·06			4·06	4·89	7·56	6·39	6·00	4·66	3·89
5 and under 10	14·22	14·56			16·44	18·11	31·88	28·33	22·44	15·77	18·44
10	11·20	9·20			6·80	15·00	16·60	16·60	14·60	10·40	12·60
15	9·00	7·64			10·12	13·37	15·37	13·75	13·62	8·12	25·00
20	10·00	9·33			12·33	13·56	17·44	12·56	16·00	12·33	26·80
25	10·70	7·60			8·60	11·20	15·80	11·30	14·60	9·80	
30	13·00	8·60			10·50	12·00	18·20	12·10	13·50	11·30	19·92
35	9·46	8·15			10·92	8·77	15·15	8·54	10·38	10·54	
40	9·42	·9·17			9·25	12·42	18·00	11·75	15·58	10·25	16·24
45	6·94	5·94			7·56	7·00	13·50	8·44	11·25	8·50	
50	5·47	6·41			6·24	9·24	11·47	6·65	11·53	9·29	7·50
55	2·63	3·15			3·52	4·11	5·48	4·00	5·93	3·92	
60	3·50	3·09			3·00	3·09	5·25	3·94	4·25	3·72	2·78
65	1·46	1·57			1·41	2·09	2·96	2·17	2·07	1·78	
70	1·06	1·12			1·23	1·19	1·64	1·09	1·51	1·24	·65
75	·41	·54			·32	·60	·78	·59	·71	·47	
80	·19	·14			·15	·24	·31	·20	·23	·21	·06
85	·07	·01			·04	·07	·07	·03	·05	·05	
90 and under 95	·02	·01			·01	·02	·02	·01	·01	·01	
95 and upwards							·05				
Doubtful	·10	·05						·02			·05
	130·53	122·83			131·38	165·12	228·77	172·40	187·09	145·58	152·17
No. of deaths registered	2922	3064			3055	4028	4813	3697	4161	3458	3370

Real Mortality of Males in BIRMINGHAM during Nine Years.

	1841	1842	1843	1844	1845	1846	1847	1848	1849	1850	1851
Under 1 year	2·71	2·87			3·02	4·11	3·74	3·72	3·59	3·71	3·14
1 and under 2	3·94	2·90			2·95	5·34	4·58	3·81	2·81	3·57	4·31
2	3·65	2·50			2·76	3·38	5·06	4·27	2·35	2·56	3·76
3	2·29	2·08			3·00	3·08	5·46	4·00	1·96	2·00	3·29
4	2·28	1·83			2·83	2·50	5·00	4·33	1·50	1·83	2·33
5 and under 10	9·33	9·22			11·66	9·89	18·44	14·67	9·22	8·00	10·89
10	6·80	8·20			6·40	9·00	12·00	10·00	8·80	9·80	11·20
15	7·12	7·25			5·25	8·00	7·50	5·87	6·50	6·37	15·00
20	6·44	7·44			5·66	8·44	9·33	8·11	5·44	5·55	
25	6·90	6·50			6·20	6·70	9·50	5·60	6·90	6·10	16·20
30	5·30	7·20			5·80	6·00	8·70	7·90	6·70	7·40	
35	6·00	4·31			5·31	6·38	6·77	6·77	6·15	6·54	13·15
40	4·75	7·58			6·25	6·00	8·16	7·17	6·25	6·08	
45	4·62	4·37			4·00	4·50	6·50	5·37	5·75	5·57	10·12
50	5·18	3·24			3·65	3·88	6·41	4·24	3·82	3·94	
55	2·07	2·07			3·33	2·93	3·74	3·41	2·70	3·11	5·87
60	2·37	2·00			2·00	2·53	2·59	2·66	2·69	2·97	
65	1·20	·91			1·20	1·20	1·78	1·33	1·37	1·33	2·47
70	·86	·90			·79	·99	·96	1·09	·70	·92	
75	·35	·35			·33	·45	·49	·50	·39	·38	·48
80	·18	·18			·15	·15	·23	·17	·17	·18	
85	·05	·04			·05	·05	·07	·03	·04	·04	·06
90 and under 95		·01			·01	·02	·02	·01	·01	·01	
95 and upwards											
Doubtful									·01	·01	·05
	84·39	83·95			82·60	95·52	127·03	105·03	85·82	87·97	102·32
No. of deaths registered	1943	1829			1909	2381	2758	2405	2009	2127	2489

These tables show the real mortality, during nine years, in the districts to which they refer. It appears, for example, that during 1841, while the deaths in England and Wales were 174198, the real mortality was 7867 : or, the real mortality was to the number of deaths as $\frac{7867}{174198} = \frac{45\cdot2}{1000}$.

ABSTRACT OF TABLES.						
	England and Wales.	Cornwall.	London.	Liverpool.	Manchester.	Birmingham.
1841	$\frac{45\cdot2}{1000}$	$\frac{46\cdot9}{1000}$	$\frac{45\cdot5}{1000}$	$\frac{44\cdot7}{1000}$	$\frac{44\cdot7}{1000}$	$\frac{43\cdot4}{1000}$
1842	$\frac{43\cdot8}{1000}$	$\frac{51\cdot4}{1000}$	$\frac{44\cdot5}{1000}$	$\frac{43\cdot8}{1000}$	$\frac{40\cdot1}{1000}$	$\frac{45\cdot9}{1000}$
1843						
1844						
1845	$\frac{43\cdot9}{1000}$	$\frac{44\cdot5}{1000}$	$\frac{44\cdot5}{1000}$	$\frac{44\cdot9}{1000}$	$\frac{43\cdot0}{1000}$	$\frac{43\cdot3}{1000}$
1846	$\frac{42\cdot8}{1000}$	$\frac{45\cdot5}{1000}$	$\frac{44\cdot2}{1000}$	$\frac{42\cdot1}{1000}$	$\frac{41\cdot0}{1000}$	$\frac{40\cdot1}{1000}$
1847	$\frac{44\cdot5}{1000}$	$\frac{42\cdot1}{1000}$	$\frac{44\cdot9}{1000}$	$\frac{51\cdot9}{1000}$	$\frac{47\cdot5}{1000}$	$\frac{46\cdot0}{1000}$
1848	$\frac{45\cdot0}{1000}$	$\frac{40\cdot1}{1000}$	$\frac{47\cdot9}{1000}$	$\frac{50\cdot7}{1000}$	$\frac{46\cdot6}{1000}$	$\frac{43\cdot7}{1000}$
1849	$\frac{47\cdot2}{1000}$	$\frac{45\cdot6}{1000}$	$\frac{50\cdot4}{1000}$	$\frac{54\cdot9}{1000}$	$\frac{44\cdot9}{1000}$	$\frac{42\cdot7}{1000}$
1850	$\frac{43\cdot0}{1000}$	$\frac{44\cdot1}{1000}$	$\frac{44\cdot3}{1000}$	$\frac{45\cdot4}{1000}$	$\frac{42\cdot0}{1000}$	$\frac{41\cdot4}{1000}$
1851	$\frac{43\cdot1}{1000}$	$\frac{45\cdot9}{1000}$	$\frac{44\cdot1}{1000}$	$\frac{47\cdot3}{1000}$	$\frac{45\cdot2}{1000}$	$\frac{41\cdot1}{1000}$

This abstract gives us an opportunity of making a comparison of times and places. We see for example, that in Manchester, the real mortality in 1841 bore a higher ratio to the numbers of deaths, than was the case in 1842: that is to say, that comparing 1841 and 1842 in Manchester, the registrar's reports overrated the mortality of 1841. But we should be glad to know further, what relation the figures 44·7 in 1841, and 40 1 in 1842 bear to the denominator of 1000. We find the numerator rising to 54·9 for Liverpool in 1849, and falling to 40·1 for Manchester in 1842, as also for Cornwall in 1848. We naturally ask what is the average numerator for the whole kingdom during the nine years given: and if we take all the numerators in the first column, we find the average to be about 44·3. We may say, therefore, that wherever we find a numerator 44·3, we may regard the real mortality in that case as equal to the number of deaths: that wherever we find a numerator less than 44·3, we may regard the real mortality as lower than the number of deaths: and that wherever we find a numerator greater than 44·3, we may regard the real mortality as higher than the number of deaths. Liverpool for example, in 1849, exhibits a numerator of 54·9, nearly one fourth above the standard: and this is explained by the hordes of Irish who were driven across the channel, famine pinched, and stricken with pestilence.

But this mode of reading the table is not altogether satisfactory, because it involves the necessity of remembering that 44·3 is the standard; and it would be far easier to use the table correctly, if some level number were the standard. I therefore give another table in which the 44·3 is changed into 1000, and the other numerators are changed in proportion to this. If any numerator were found so high as twice 44·3, it would appear in the transformed table as 2000: if any numerator were found so low as half 44.3, it would appear as 500. I have formed this table from the first tables of real mortality: I have multiplied the totals in those tables by 22·57. Thus, the total real mortality for London in 1841, is 7867·22: the number of deaths is 174198: ratio is $\frac{7867\cdot22}{174198}$. Multiplying this fraction by 22·57, we got 1020. That is, the real mortality is to the number of deaths as 1020 to 1000: or the real mortality is $\frac{1}{50}$ part greater than the number of deaths. After I had made my calculations, I found that 22·56 would have been a more exact multiplier, but the trifling error thus caused makes little difference for the purposes of comparison, because it applies equally to all the times and places given. I call this a table of specific mortality of the different places; for as specific gravity is the weight of a substance in relation to its size, so we may designate as specific mortality the number of deaths in a district in relation to the ages of the inhabitants who die.

	England and Wales.	Cornwall.	London.	Liverpool.	Manchester.	Birmingham.
1841	1021	1060	1027	1010	1008	980
1842	989	1161	1005	988	905	1036
1843						
1844						
1845	992	1004	1004	1012	970	977
1846	966	1026	998	950	925	905
1847	1005	950	1013	1172	1073	1038
1848	1016	905	1081	1144	1053	987
1849	1066	1029	1137	1241	1015	964
1850	972	995	1000	1026	950	934
1851	973	1035	995	1067	1019	928
Average	1000	1018	1029	1068	991	972

Table of SPECIFIC MORTALITY, that is, of real Mortality in proportion to 1000 Deaths Registered.

The above table is to be read thus. In 1841 the real mortality of England and Wales, was 1021 to every thousand of deaths registered : i.e., the real mortality was about $\frac{1}{50}$th part greater than the numerical mortality. But in 1842, the real mortality of England and Wales was about $\frac{1}{91}$st part less than the numerical mortality. What was the actual mortality in each year shall be given in another page.

We can now however, by means of this table answer the principal question with which this long note is concerned. It has been thought that, possibly, the high rates of mortality charged against great towns, existed only as to numbers, and not as to reality. It has been thought that, possibly, the difference between the ages of a town and a country population, the great number of immigrants into towns and the consequent abundance of young families, might swell the register with deaths of young children, without truly shewing great unhealthiness. By a due interpretation of this last table, we can answer the question whether this conjecture is well founded.

The first column is that of England and Wales. I have made the average of the nine years 1841, &c., equal to 1000 : I assume the real mortality to be the same with the number of deaths.

This assumption is the principle on which the table is framed. But in this first column, comparing one year with another, we find a considerable variation ; the real mortality going as low as 972 in 1850, and as high as 1066 the year before. It is remarkable that the highest rate should be in 1849, the cholera year, when the number of deaths registered was considerably greater than usual. It seems, therefore, that to the miseries of that year must be added the fact, that the persons who died were to an unusual extent, those of robust ages. The number of male deaths in 1849 was about $\frac{1}{15}$th above the average (increase of population considered); i.e. in round numbers, 20,000 in excess: but the real mortality was about $\frac{1}{6}$th above the average; i.e. in round numbers 35,000 in excess. It appears, then, that the mischief of the cholera year was nearly twice as great as appears from the registers.

Comparing the other columns, it is singular that the highest average is that of Liverpool; and that this is true even if we exclude the fatal 1847. It follows that, pre-eminent as Liverpool previously appeared in unhealthiness, it is worse even than was thought. Cornwall too is something more unhealthy than was supposed, though to so trifling an extent as hardly to be worth notice. London suffers by the comparison a little more than Cornwall. Manchester comes off a shade better than mere numbers of deaths indicate: and Birmingham benefits about as much as London is injured. I have already stated that the registered mortality of London for 10 years, is 25 in 1000 inhabitants: that of Birmingham 26: but that taking the whole borough of Birmingham, its numerical mortality is 25, just as that of London. Comparing, however, the real mortality of the two places, and observing that that of London is something more, while that of Birmingham is something less, than the numerical mortality, we must conclude that the borough of Birmingham was really more healthy, during ten years, than the metropolis was. The figures stand thus:—

	No. of Deaths.	Real Mortality.
The Metropolis	25 per 1000	25¾
Birmingham, parish	26 ,,	
,, borough	25 ,,	24⅓

It appears, then, that the Borough of Birmingham was considerably more healthy than the Metropolis. No doubt, the happy absence of cholera from Birmingham in 1849, accounts for a part of this difference.

If we set Liverpool and Manchester together, we see that the comparative real mortality of Liverpool is very high, and that of Manchester rather low, (i.e. only as comparing real with numerical mortality, not absolutely). But the number of deaths registered in Liverpool is out-rageously great; and taking both these facts into account, the actual unhealthiness of Liverpool is put in a striking point of view.

1841—50 in a 1000 living.	No. of Deaths.	Real Mortality.
Manchester	33	32¾
Liverpool, excluding 1847	36	38
Liverpool, *not* excluding ,,	39	41½

Looking then, at the question of excess above the average of the kingdom, it appears that—

That of Manchester is more than 10
That of Liverpool excluding 1847 is 15
That of Liverpool not excluding 1847 is 19

During 10 years therefore, bad as was the sanitary state of Manchester, that of Liverpool was very far worse.

It must be remembered, however, that what is true of Birmingham, is true also of the two great towns above: I mean that the register omits a large portion of the inhabitants, and that the most healthy portion. To make a fair comparison of Liverpool and Manchester, with London, or with the Borough of Birmingham, the better districts of Liverpool and Manchester should be included. In the case of Birmingham, this enlargement of the district only reduces the mortality from 26 to 25: but a similar enlargement would affect Liverpool and Manchester far more, if, as I presume, the better classes are about as healthy there as they are in the environs of Birmingham.

The next table is in substance the same with the last: but it gives the full numbers of deaths registered, and the same numbers modified according to the specific mortality in the last table.

After that, follows a table shewing how many deaths occurred annually out of a thousand *males* living; and giving the same numbers modified according to the specific mortality in the last table but one.

I am aware that this table has no pretensions to accuracy: both because I have assumed the proportion of males living to females living, according to a proportion scarcely justified by the census, and because I have assumed the increase of population to have taken place by increments of equal numbers in each year. For the purpose of comparison, however, I hope the results are accurate enough.

Table of Male Deaths actually Registered, and of the Real Mortality indicated by those Numbers.

	1. ENGLAND AND WALES.		2. LONDON.		3. CORNWALL.		4. LIVERPOOL.		5. MANCHESTER.		6. BIRMINGHAM.	
	No. of Deaths.	Real Mortality.	No. of Deaths.	Real Mortality.	No. of Deaths.	Real Mortality.	No. of Deaths.	Real Mortality.	No. of Deaths.	Real Mortality.	No. of Deaths.	Real Mortality.
1841	174198	177563	23094	23712	3181	3373	3852	3891	2922	2946	1943	1905
1842	176594	174683	22905	23014	3916	4545	3897	3852	3064	2772	1829	1895
1843												
1844												
1845	177529	175970	24525	24618	3049	3062	3816	3863	3055	2965	1909	1864
1846	198325	191498	25122	25074	3038	3118	4894	4652	4028	3727	2381	2156
1847	212426	213232	29697	30095	2926	2781	7022	8233	4813	5163	2758	2867
1848	202265	205533	29413	31788	3254	2946	4135	4730	3697	3891	2405	2371
1849	221801	236285	34167	38865	3510	3613	6457	8014	4161	4223	2009	1937
1850	186491	181117	24634	24634	3352	3335	3878	3977	3458	3286	2127	1985
1851	200500	195096	28140	27989	3832	3966	4551	4855	3370	3434	2489	2309

Table of ANNUAL DEATHS out of 1000 MALES living: with the same Numbers varied according to the Specific Mortality.

	1. England and Wales		2. London		3. Cornwall		4. Liverpool		5. Manchester		6. Birmingham	
	No. of Deaths per 1000.	Real Mortality per 1000.	No. of Deaths per 1000.	Real Mortality per 1000.	No. of Deaths per 1000.	Real Mortality per 1000.	No. of Deaths per 1000.	Real Mortality per 1000.	No. of Deaths per 1000.	Real Mortality per 1000.	No. of Deaths per 1000.	Real Mortality per 1000.
1841	22·35	22·77	24·19	24·84	18·90	20·05	35·25	35·60	30·99	31·25	28·69	28·12
1842	22·36	22·12	23·49	23·60	23·18	26·91	35·11	34·70	31·90	28·86	26·32	27·27
1843												
1844												
1845	21·67	21·48	23·67	23·77	17·85	17·92	32·85	33·25	30·14	29·26	25·54	24·94
1846	23·92	23·10	23·79	23·74	17·71	18·18	41·51	39·46	39·07	36·15	31·13	28·19
1847	25·32	25·42	27·59	27·96	17·00	16·15	58·69	68·82	45·89	49·23	35·25	36·65
1848	23·83	24·21	26·82	28·98	18·83	17·05	34·07	38·98	34·67	36·49	30·07	29·64
1849	25·83	27·52	30·59	34·80	20·24	20·83	52·46	65·11	38·38	38·96	24·58	23·69
1850	21·47	20·85	21·66	21·66	19·25	19·15	31·07	31·86	31·39	29·83	25·48	23·77
1851	22·82	22·12	24·31	24·18	21·93	22·69	35·97	38·37	30·10	30·68	29·20	27·09
Average	23·29	23·29	25·12	25·95	19·43	19·88	39·66	42·91	34·73	34·52	28·47	27·71

In this last table, the places mentioned occupy an order as to comparative healthiness, quite different from that which I have given in an earlier part of this note. But the averages in this page, and in that, are calculated for a different term of years: in this page for 9 years from 1841 to 1851, omitting 1843 and 1844; in that page for 10 years from 1841 to 1850. Besides, this is for males only, roughly estimated. The object of this table is to give the difference between numerical and real mortality, and not to fix with accuracy the actual mortality per thousand of the population.

Since I constructed these tables, I have found that I might have saved myself a large proportion of the calculations I have made. I have already explained how I estimated the real mortality from the number of deaths. For example, if in a place the number of annual deaths of children under a year old, were 1000, I divided the 1000 by 174, (the normal number of such deaths.) The deaths from 1 to 2 years old, I divided by 64, and so on. But a late report * furnishes the means of abridging this process. Instead of taking the children from birth to 1 year, from 1 to 2, from 2 to 3, &c., I find it quite enough to take them from birth to 5 years old, from 5 to 10, &c. And as to later periods of life, instead of taking terms of 5 years, I find it quite enough to take terms of 10 years. The following table shews what divisors to use:—

For children under 5 years   67

5 years and under 10   9

10 .... 15   5

* Registrar General, 14. xvi.

15 years and under	25	....	8
25	35	....	10
35	45	....	13
45	55	....	17
55	65	....	30
65	75	....	64
75	85	....	141
85	95	....	291
95 and upwards			457
Doubtful, I say..........................			40

I tried this schedule for the case of Cornwall in 1850; and the result was that instead of my previous real mortality of 147·76, I arrived at one of 147·30; a difference of little importance for the purpose of comparison. If therefore, I were to enter on this subject afresh, I should calculate the real mortality by this last schedule, a course that would save much trouble, and would proportionately lessen the danger of error.

On the whole, I cannot flatter myself that the result of this note is of very high importance. But other persons may have felt, in the absence of enquiry, the same doubts which occurred to me, as to the accuracy of inferences drawn from the mere number of deaths, without allowance for the ages of the deceased. If the tables I have furnished in this note, are tolerably correct, it follows that comparing the specific mortality of one district and of another, the difference is not so formidable as to vitiate the ordinary reasoning on the subject. We find that, during ten years, the specific mortality of England and Wales being taken at 1000, the highest specific mortality is that of Liverpool, which stands at 1068 ; the lowest being that of Birmingham, which stands at 972. Comparing London, Cornwall, Manchester, and Birmingham, the difference is far less.

I think it right to say that all the calculations have been made by myself, and not having been checked by any one else, contain, no doubt, many inaccuracies.

NOTE ON CHAPTER XIII.

It is much to be regretted that we have no adequate tests of the state of the working classes as to education and morality. With regard to the former we have the report of the acquirements of criminals, and on a wider scale, the return of the number of signatures to the marriage registers. As respects morality, we know how many illegitimate children are born in different places, and we have some registers of the numbers of commitments by magistrates, of summary convictions, of trials at Sessions and Assizes, of convictions and sentences. These returns for 1856 have lately been published under the title of *Judicial Statistics, Part I: England and Wales: Police, Criminal Proceedings, Prisons.* This blue book, of no unmanageable size, contains much important information, but has not yet, as I think, attained to anything approaching perfection in its contents or its arrangement.

In the introductory Report, pp. vii. and viii., we find that " The Commitments for Trial in the last year shew an unprecedented decrease, especially when the decrease in the previous year is considered. This must be largely, but not wholly, attributed to the extended powers of Justices to deal summarily in cases of larceny under the Criminal Justice Act 18 and 19 Vict. c. 126, which has been in operation over the whole of the year." This statement is literally true, but as I imagine, very likely to mislead all readers of it, except those few who are familiar with the subject. Remembering the notorious tendency of statistical returns to lead to fallacious conclusions, I feel that all persons concerned in making them should put them in such a form as to prevent as far as possible, any probable misinterpretation. The paragraph I have quoted would by most persons, I conceive, be understood thus: " The return of last year's Commitments for Trial is of a very gratifying kind, since it shows an unprecedented decrease, especially when the decrease in the previous year is considered. This satisfactory change must be attributed largely, but not wholly, to the extended powers of Justices to deal summarily with cases of larceny," &c. The notion in the mind of the reader would be, that the summary jurisdiction of the Justices had checked crime and diminished the number of offences. He would be surprised to hear that nothing of the kind is meant; but that nearly all that is intended, is, to express that of the number of the offences proved to have been committed, fewer than usual have been sent to Quarter Sessions and Assizes for adjudication, because under the Summary Jurisdiction Act, a large number have been dealt with by the Justices.

This false notion should have been guarded against by a notice that this decrease proves little as to the criminal state of the population, but is a mere result of new judicial arrangements, which have greatly enlarged the powers of magistrates. But instead of this, the mental confusion of the reader is rather increased by being informed in a sentence of the same paragraph, that comparing the commitments for grave offences at the close of this war, with similar commitments at the close of the last, the result is very gratifying. The whole paragraph is read as one intended to convey congratulation. The false impression is confirmed by the subsequent comparison of commitments for twenty years, divided into periods of five years. I do not question the accuracy of the figures, but I doubt the utility of the table; because confessedly, it teaches nothing. What do we learn from the facts that the commitments were fewer in the quinquennial period of 1852—56, than in the quinquennial period of 1847—51? Nothing whatever, because the increase of justices' summary jurisdiction, vitiates the comparison. This table only tends to mislead, unless it is emphatically guarded by a protest against the obvious misinterpretation; and the best protest is, to omit the table.

At page xvii. is another return, which is even more calculated to mislead, and which I have found to have actually misled two most intelligent readers, both of them familiar with the subject. This return is one of the " Relative criminality of different counties:" i.e., of the criminality in proportion to the population. We find from this that—

In Middlesex there is one commitment for every 98 persons

„ Lancashire .... 118 „

„ Surrey .... 118 „

„ Warwick .... 167 „

„ Northumberland .... 170 „

„ Herefordshire, Shropshire, Yorkshire, each

  of them .... 257 „

„ Cumberland .... 469 „

„ Merionethshire, &c. .... 1849 „

The account comprises all the 26 counties of England and Wales, but I have given only the extremes, with a few of the medium examples.

The reader of this table, if he happens to be a native of Middlesex, feels a blush overspread his face; and he asks, can it be really true that Middlesex is preeminent in crime? He remembers that in London, which constitutes a very large part of the county, the number of illegitimate births is far lower than in the metropolis of any other great country, and far lower than in the other parts of England itself: and he remembers also, that education in London is more advanced than in most English towns, as estimated both by the number of children at school, and by the proportion of autographs to the marriage registers. Can it be true that in spite of the prevalence of education and in spite of the comparative chastity, the relative criminality of Middlesex is greatly above that of any other county, and nearly twenty times as high as that of Merionethshire?

To persons long familiar with this subject, it may appear extraordinary that the Middlesex man should feel distressed on reading this table; because it has been proverbial for these thirty or forty years, that the number of commitments bears no exact proportion to the offences committed. In Merionethshire, for instance, there is perhaps no rural police, and a person detecting a thief in the very exercise of his vocation, would rather let him go than incur the trouble and expense of sending him to a distant town, to which the prosecutor himself must afterwards go to prefer the charge, besides having the expense and trouble of the subsequent prosecution. If we constructed a table of the relative commitments in New York, and of those in the most depraved of the remote parts of California, infested by black-legs and absconded thieves, we should probably find New York as predominant over the distant settlement, as Middlesex is over Merionethshire. Where there is virtually no police, there will be actually very few commitments.

The question arises therefore, whether the heading, " Relative Criminality," is an accurate one. The table really shews only the relative commitments: and it is assumed that these commitments bear an exact proportion to the criminality of different places: but if this assumption is a false one, it follows that the heading is utterly incorrect. It is true that in the body of the text, it is said that notwithstanding certain imperfections, " These commitments nevertheless, form a scale of the relative criminality of different counties, *so far as can be shewn by its detection and punishment*." But in the margin no such qualification appears, but the notice is, " Relative criminality of different counties." Now it is the marginal note by which most readers are guided. The heading should rather be " Relative *commitments* in different counties, which, however, prove nothing as to the relative *criminality* of those counties."

It may be thought that however true it may be that this return is deceptive as a means of comparison between Middlesex with Merionethshire, the same objection does not apply to it as a means of comparison between Middlesex with Lancashire, or Warwickshire with Worcestershire, pairs of counties which may be regarded as similarly situated as to police regulations. This conclusion I believe, would be quite incorrect. The table does not appear to me to prove that the population of Middlesex is more criminal than that of Lancashire, nor that the population of Warwickshire is more criminal than that of Worcestershire.

This opinion is not founded on the same grounds with those on which I objected to the comparison of the Metropolitan county with the remote Welsh one. The efficiency of the Liverpool and Manchester police may be equal to that of London: the efficiency of the Worcestershire rural police may be equal to that of Warwickshire.

But it must surely occur to every mind, that no two counties are really similarly situated, so as to make a comparison of the commitments a fair test of relative criminality. I have mentioned town police and rural police. The words suggest at once, that counties in which rural police prevail, will have fewer commitments in proportion to offences, than will be found in counties where town police prevail. If a farmer catch a boy stealing turnips, he thrashes the offender, but a green grocer hands over to the police any one who fingers his baskets. A tramp who makes free with standing corn is perhaps hounded off with the dogs, but the same tramp caught in a town timber yard is sent to the lock up. In any country in which towns are numerous, there will be more commitments than in other counties of equal criminality, in which towns are few. It follows that a comparison of counties by commitments, without allowance for the nature of the population, is quite fallacious. Middlesex, which is almost all town, will of course, be at the head of such an imperfect list.

There is another reason why commitments will be more numerous in towns, I mean the greater opportunities for offences. A ploughman or a hedger and ditcher may be at work day after day, without any great temptation presenting itself. But a man cannot walk along the streets of a town without being solicited at every turn by goods exposed to view, by handkerchiefs dangling from the pocket, by valuable property within reach during working hours. A certain proportion of the commitments are those of men, women, and boys, who generally earn their living by industry, but who in an unguarded moment give way to temptation, and who, encouraged by impunity, repeat the offence until at last they are discovered. But a great part of the criminals, as is well known, make a business of thieving, and as it is only in towns that their shameful avocations can be practised, they largely swell the lists of town commitments. If we could divide urban populations into professional thieves and professionally honest people, the ordinary workman might perhaps be found to be of a higher moral character than the country labourer, as having been more exposed to temptation, and thus strengthened in goodness.

There must of necessity then, be more commitments for trial in towns than in the country, on account of the greater efficiency of the police, of the more frequent opportunities for offending, and of the greater resort of professional criminals to towns. It follows that a comparison of town and country by means of the relative commitments, proves nothing, and only tends to mislead. The table, however, of which I am complaining, is not a comparison of town and country, but of county with county. Yet it is obvious that the same fallacy is involved. Middlesex is nearly all town; Merionethshire is nearly all country: to compare the two is as unsatisfactory as to compare London with a country parish. Carrying on this idea, we see that to compare Middlesex with any other county is open to the same objection; and that to compare one county with

another is altogether fallacious, because the proportion of
town and country varies in all.   Without knowing anything
about the proportionate criminality of one county and
another, we could guess what names stand at the head of
such a list as the one I am discussing.   The small county
of Middlesex, consisting almost entirely of town, would
of course be first: Surrey, with that part of London and
its environs south of the Thames, would not be far off:
Lancashire with its Liverpool, Manchester, Salford, and
other manufacturing towns, would be high on the list:
Warwickshire, containing Birmingham and Coventry would
rival the others.   It has been suggested to me by my friend
Mr. Burt, * that this list will to a considerable extent
coincide with a list arranged according to density of population: not that a dense population is more criminal, but
because it will have more commitments, for the reasons I
have assigned.   Population generally, will be dense, according to the prevalence or absence of towns.   I subjoin a
list of a few of the counties arranged according to commitments, and according to density of population.

Order of counties according to commitments.	Order according to density of population.
Middlesex	Middlesex
Lancaster	Lancaster
Surrey	Surrey
Warwick	Warwick
Northumberland	Stafford
Stafford	Chester
Durham	Durham
Kent	Kent
Chester	Worcester

* The Chaplain of Birmingham Borough Gaol, and formerly of Penton-
ville : author of a valuable work on Prison Discipline.

The first four counties are in the same order in both columns : then comes Northumberland, which has a pre-eminence in commitments not to be explained by the density of its population: Stafford, Durham, and Kent are very near their right places : but Chester makes a better appearance than its density would lead us to expect. It must be observed however, that the difference in the number of commitments is not very considerable from Warwick to Chester. I have also been obliged to omit York from the comparison, because the *Judicial Statistics* confound together all the three Ridings of that large county, blending together the manufacturing and the agricultural parts ; whereas the Census very properly distinguishes them. This comparison of the two lists of commitments and of density will, I suppose, convince most persons that this table in the *Judicial Statistics* proves little or nothing : or if anything, only that a town population has uniformly more commitments than an agricultural population, a fact that requires to be proved by no such elaborate statement of figures.

It would be a great mistake, however, to suppose that all town populations have an equal amount of commitments in proportion to population : that Manchester and Salford with their joint population of 400,000, have the same number of commitments with Liverpool which has about the same 400,000 inhabitants : or that Birmingham with its 230,000 people has something more than half as many commitments as Liverpool. Now, if the compiler of the *Judicial Statistics* would furnish the public with a comparison of the commitments in the different towns, he would perform a valuable service. He might do this as to Liverpool and Manchester, each of which boroughs prints every year a detailed return of the number of persons taken into custody within the borough, and of the numbers discharged, summarily convicted, and committed. In Birmingham the number of commitments could be ascertained by application to the authorities of the Borough Gaol: and I suppose the same return might be obtained elsewhere.

In comparing the great towns I have mentioned, we shall naturally remember that their rate of mortality, as exhibited in a previous note, varies greatly: that while the real mortality of Birmingham does not exceed that of the metropolis, the real mortality of Manchester is far greater, and that of Liverpool outrageously greater. We should rather expect to find that the commitments of the three boroughs bore a direct proportion to the mortality. An unhealthy population may be prophecied to be an immoral one. This appears to be actually the case. I have been informed by the authorities of the Birmingham Gaol, that the commitments from the borough during the year 1855 scarcely exceeded, in proportion to the population of the borough, the average commitments of the whole kingdom: a fact that astonished my friend the Chaplain, who would have anticipated a very large number of offences against property, in consequence of the great number of persons within reach of portable metals, and the facilities existing for making counterfeit coin. I am assured however, that such is the fact. The returns from Manchester are far less favourable. I will not give them in detail because I fear I may stumble among questions of whether the numbers given as commitments, include those prisoners who at once pay fines levied, without the humiliation of actual incarceration, whether they include cases of remand, and of persons admitted to bail. But after making all allowances for possible misapprehensions, it is clear that the relative commitments in Manchester are far more than half as many again as those of Birmingham. And as a comparison of commitments in different *towns* does seem a fair test of the criminality of these towns, we must pronounce that the criminality of Manchester exceeds that of Birmingham by more than one-half.

The comparison between Manchester and Birmingham seems a peculiarly fair one, because both those towns are large manufacturing places. If we go to Liverpool, we have a great seaport with a shifting population, consisting to a considerable extent of sailors, who in the intervals between their voyages are generally expected to run riot; and of a low class of labourers and hangers on to the docks. That is no reason however, why we should not number the actual commitments, and compare them with those of other towns; though it is a good reason why we should not complacently sit down to censure the better classes of the town, as though the excessive criminality were attributable to their neglect and supineness. I forbear in this instance, also, to quote the figures given in the borough return I have alluded to, lest I should fall into the errors I have pointed out in the case of Manchester. I will only say generally that the commitments, in proportion to the population, appear to reach the high rate of double those of Manchester, and therefore of more than three times those of Birmingham: an astounding excess!

An objection may be raised, that a comparison even of town commitments proves little as to relative criminality, because the offences punished may be of a very varying dye. In one place, it may be thought, drunkenness prevails, in

another thefts of a trifling character, in a third highway
robberies and burglaries. With regard to drunkenness I
may observe that offenders against temperance cannot be
included in commitments, because magistrates have power
only to fine drunkards, and not to send them to gaol in
default of payment. There may be some difference in the
gravity of other crimes punished in one town and another,
as it appears that there is an excess of violence in Scotch
crime compared with English. One test would be a
tolerably fair one : the aggregate length of sentences pronounced : and this would be ascertained not very inac-
curately, by a comparison of the daily average of prisoners
in the gaols belonging to each borough. Those committed
to the assizes, or sent away as long sentenced prisoners,
should be added for perfect accuracy. If in a particular
town, the offences committed were few, but of a grave cast,
the long sentences pronounced would swell the daily average
of prisoners in gaol : while a number of trifling offences
punished by short imprisonments in another town, would
add little to the daily average in gaol. It would be very
desirable, therefore, that the *Judicial Statistics* should give
us this daily average of the occupants of gaols for every
borough. At page xxiii. of the volume before us, we have
incidentally a return of the daily average of several places.
We find that—

Manchester and Salford together had

    a daily average of ....   1132 prisoners

Birmingham had 359

But some of the Birmingham pri-

    soners were sent to Wakefield, say   41

    Making a total of ....   —— 400   „

NOTE ON CHAPTER XIII.

The number of inhabitants of Manchester and Salford, was in 1851, to the number in Birmingham, as about 40 to 23. If we reduce the Manchester and Salford prisoners in this proportion, we should have for a population of 230,000, a daily average of prisoners—

In Manchester and Salford 651
In Birmingham 400

and this corresponds pretty well with what I have said as to the greater number of commitments in Manchester as compared with those in Birmingham. I must observe, however, that I am working very much in the dark, and with no pretensions to official accuracy: because I do not know that I have any right to mix up Manchester with Salford; nor do I know what is meant by the Salford *County* House of Correction; nor do I know whether Manchester had prisoners sent to other boroughs, as Birmingham had at Wakefield. All these are facts easily ascertainable by a person acting under the authority of the Home Office.

Another remark and I have done. The table at p. xviii. is calculated on the census of 1851. In the absence of any subsequent enumeration, it may seem inevitable to adopt that of 1851. Yet this course is open to considerable objections, as tending to mislead persons superficially acquainted with the subject, as giving an undue appearance of a steady increase of commitments, and as exaggerating our apparent criminality in comparison with that of other countries. There is also this consideration; that the counties of England grow in numbers very unequally. Thus, from 1801 to 1851, there was an increase of—

Monmouthshire people to the extent of 244 per cent.

Lancashire	201	,,
Durham	160	,,
Surrey	154	,,
Staffordshire	151	,,
Cheshire	137	,,
York (W. Riding)	132	,,
Warwickshire	130	,,
Herefordshire .... only	31	,,
Yorkshire (N. Riding)	35	,,
Wiltshire	38	,,

There would be a greater approach to accuracy, if it were assumed that the population of each county had continued to increase since 1851, at the rate which prevailed during the ten previous years, and if any table of relative criminality were arranged according to this amended estimate of population.

I should be very glad therefore, if hereafter the following alterations should be made in the Judicial Statistics.

1st. It should be distinctly stated that no fair comparison can be drawn as to commitments in former periods and at present, both because of the recent alteration which gives extensive summary jurisdiction to Justices, and also because of a *former alteration* which gave similar jurisdiction as to juvenile offenders.

2nd. The table at page viii. should either be omitted, or should include in the latter periods all cases in which the new summary jurisdiction was exercised.

3rd. The comparison of counties at page xviii. should be omitted, as teaching nothing, or tending to mislead. Under any circumstances the three Ridings should be kept distinct. A comparison of the commitments in towns should be given, including cases under summary jurisdiction. If any comparison of counties is given, it should be a comparison, *density of population considered.*

4th. A comparison of the daily average of prisoners belonging to each borough, wherever confined, should be added, as a test of the gravity of the offences committed.

5th. The population should not be taken from the census of 1851, but should be corrected according to the rate of increase during the previous ten years.

I do not for a moment mean to throw any doubt on the accuracy, or the good faith, of the able men concerned in compiling these tables. The little experience I have had in these matters, has taught me the great difficulties in carrying out any such enquiries as those in question. I have offered the suggestions in this note, because, living in the world, and among the persons and things with which these tables are concerned, I see them from a point of view quite different from that which presents itself to gentlemen concerned in the administration of government.

THE END.